Greek Warfare

GREEK WARFARE

Myths and Realities

Hans van Wees

Bloomsbury Academic
An imprint of Bloomsbury Publishing Plc

B L O O M S B U R Y
LONDON · OXFORD · NEW YORK · NEW DELHI · SYDNEY

Bloomsbury Academic
An imprint of Bloomsbury Publishing Plc

50 Bedford Square	1385 Broadway
London	New York
WC1B 3DP	NY 10018
UK	USA

www.bloomsbury.com

BLOOMSBURY and the Diana logo are trademarks of Bloomsbury Publishing Plc

First published in 2004 by Gerald Duckworth & Co. Ltd.
Reprinted by Bloomsbury Academic 2011 (twice), 2012 (twice),
2013, 2014, 2015

British Library Cataloguing-in-Publication Data
A catalogue record for this book is available from the British Library.

ISBN: PB: 978-0-7156-2967-3

Library of Congress Cataloging-in-Publication Data
A catalog record for this book is available from the Library of Congress.

Typeset by Ray Davies

Contents

Contents

Contents

Illustrations

Plates
(between pages 210 and 211)

I. City under siege. Relief from the Nereid Monument at Xanthus, *c.* 400 BC. British Museum. Photo: Ducrey 1986, pl. 164.

II. Classical hoplite equipment. Attic tombstone, late fifth century BC. Staatliche Museen zu Berlin. Photo: Anderson 1970, pl. 12.

III. Pre-hoplite equipment. Bronze figurine from Akraiphnion (Karditsa) in Boeotia, *c.* 700-650 BC. Athens, National Museum inv. no. 12831. Photo: Deutsches Archäologisches Institut.

IV. Characteristic hoplite stance. Bronze figurine from Dodona, *c.* 510 BC. Staatliche Museen zu Berlin, misc. 7470. Photos: Jutta Tietz-Glagow (*left and centre*) and Ingrid Geske (*right*), Staatliche Museen zu Berlin.

V. Peltast. Attic red-figure cup, *c.* 510 BC. Antikenmuseum der Karl-Marx-Universität, Leipzig, inv. no. T 487. Photo: Ducrey 1986, pl. 90.

VI. Classical cavalry. Panathenaic amphora, *c.* 400-350 BC. British Museum 1903.2-17.1. Photo: Spence 1993, pl. 8.

VII. Archaic cavalry. Middle Corinthian oinochoe, *c.* 600-575 BC. British Museum 1814.7-4.491. Photo: British Museum.

VIII. Attendant and hoplite at departure. Attic red-figure pelike by the Cleophon Painter, *c.* 440-430 BC. Museum of Fine Arts, Boston (Francis Bartlett Collection). Photo: Anderson 1970, pl. 8.

IX. Archaic departure scene. Attic black-figure amphora, *c.* 510 BC. British Museum B 184 (= A 173). Photo: British Museum.

X. Classical departure scene. Attic red-figure amphora from Vulci by Cleophrades Painter, *c.* 500-475 BC. Munich 2305. Photo: R. Lullies & M. Hirmer, *Griechische Vasen* (Munich 1953), pl. 49.

XI. *Sphagia.* Attic red-figure cup from Gela by Chairias Painter, *c.* 490-480 BC. Cleveland Museum of Art, Dudley P. Allen Fund, inv. no. 26.242. Photo: Ducrey 1986, pl. 177.

XII. Ambush. Attic black-figure lekythos by Painter of Vatican G49, *c.* 490 BC. Metropolitan Museum, New York 26.60.76. Photo: Vos 1963, pl. VIII.

Illustrations

Figures

Acknowledgements

This book began as a long draft for a short piece on 'The city at war' which appeared a few years ago in Robin Osborne's *Classical Greece* (Oxford 2000), 81-110. Tom Harrison suggested that I might expand this long draft into a short book and Deborah Blake at Duckworth allowed it to grow into an ever larger and more detailed study, which took several years beyond its original deadline to complete. Without Robin's initiative, Tom's encouragement and Deborah's patience this work would not have seen the light of day.

Some – but by no means all – of the ideas about Greek war and society developed here have been aired before in one or more of the papers I have published over the years, and the reader may occasionally find a phrase, sentence or even a paragraph repeated or adapted from these earlier articles. Part I in particular re-uses some material from a chapter on 'War and peace in ancient Greece' in A. Hartmann and B. Heuser (eds), *War, Peace and World Orders in European History* (London 2001), 33-47. But at least 95% of the text is new.

For the illustrations I am indebted to the Faculty of Social and Historical Sciences at University College London, which generously met the cost of acquiring and publishing most of the photographs in the plate section, and to Ray Davies at Duckworth, who admirably met the challenges posed by the often awkward size, shape and arrangement of the figures.

A hundred or so students have influenced what follows through their excellent contributions to my course on war and society in ancient Greece, and dozens of colleagues have shared their insights and knowledge with me in ways which I cannot even begin to reconstruct, let alone acknowledge as fully as they deserve. Three friends and colleagues have made a particular impact on this book: Steve Hodkinson and Phil de Souza commented very helpfully on substantial parts of the text, while Ted Lendon produced 30 pages of acute and searching comment which inspired important corrections and improvements and transformed the shape of this volume. Any remaining errors, flaws or bad ideas are of course mine alone.

Less tangible yet greater debts are owed to three old friends – André Handgraaf, Ben Kal and Huub van der Vlugt – who died too young and are sadly missed. This book is dedicated to their memory, and, as ever, to my family and to Yoshie, whose love and support mean everything to me.

University College London   Hans van Wees

Conventions and Abbreviations

The most familiar Greek names have been given in their widely used Latinised or Anglicised form (e.g. Homer, Thucydides, Arginusae); for less familiar names the Greek form has been retained (e.g. Makartatos, Aigospotamoi). In transliterated Greek words, the circumflex indicates a long vowel (ê for eta, ô for omega).

The following abbreviations have been used:

CVA = *Corpus Vasorum Antiquorum*
D-K = H. Diels and W. Kranz, *Die Fragmente der Vorsokratiker*, 10th ed.
FGrH = F. Jacoby, *Die Fragmente der Griechischen Historiker*
Fornara = C.W. Fornara, *Archaic Times to the End of the Peloponnesian War*, 2nd ed.
Harding = P. Harding, *From the End of the Peloponnesian War to the Battle of Ipsus*
IG = *Inscriptiones Graecae*
Inschriften von Priene = F. Hiller von Gaertringen, *Die Inschriften von Priene*
K-A = R. Kassel and C. Austin, *Poetae Comici Graeci*
LIMC = *Lexicon Iconographicum Mythologiae Classicae*
L-P = E. Lobel and D.L. Page, *Poetae Melici Graeci*
ML = R. Meiggs and D. Lewis, *A Selection of Greek Historical Inscriptions*, rev. ed.
Parke-Wormell = H.W. Parke and S. Wormell, *The Delphic Oracle*, vol. II
SEG = *Supplementum Epigraphicum Graecum*
SV = H. Bengtson, *Die Staatsverträge des Altertums*, 2nd ed.
Tituli Calymnii = M. Segre, *Tituli Calymnii*
Tod II = M.N. Tod, *A Selection of Greek Historical Inscriptions*, vol. II

Introduction

Just as in war the crossing of even the smallest streams tears apart formations, so every difference seems to create conflict. (Aristotle, *Politics*
1303b12)

This observation is often cited in modern studies of warfare, almost always
for its incidental value as evidence for the vulnerability of Greek infantry
formations rather for what it is: a poignant reflection on the causes of civil
war, and indeed all war. Tactics and strategy, arms and armour, the
minutiae of battles and campaigns have retained their traditional position
as the dominant interests of students of Greek warfare. That is hardly
surprising, for they are fascinating subjects. It *is* surprising, however, that
so little work has been done on the bigger picture, ranging from the causes
and goals of war to the relation between war, society and the state.
Everyone agrees that warfare can be fully understood only when seen in
its entirety and related to its social, economic and political context, yet no
one has offered an integrated account of this kind since Yvon Garlan's
admirable *La guerre dans l'antiquité* (1972), translated as *War in the
Ancient World: A Social History* (1975). One purpose of the present book
is to do for Greek warfare what Garlan did for ancient warfare as a whole,
bearing in mind that virtually all aspects of Greek war have been the
subject of vigorous debate during the period of a generation since his study
was published.

The second purpose of this book is to explode a number of myths
surrounding Greek warfare. Some of these myths – such as the idea that
wars were traditionally fought by propertied citizen-militias alone or that
campaigns and battles were conducted by a set of strict sportsman-like
rules – were propagated by ancient sources. Other myths – such as the
notion that war rather than peace was the natural state of affairs, or that
classical infantry battles were massive pile-ups in which two masses of
soldiers relied on physical shoving to drive the other side off the battlefield
– are the creation of modern scholars. Above all, this book will argue that
current models of the development of Greek warfare are based on an
unduly selective and somewhat naïve reading of the limited and unreliable
ancient evidence.

Two key stages are usually identified in the development of Greek
warfare: first the creation of the heavy-armed infantryman, the hoplite,
and his particular style of waging war and doing battle, sometime between

1

750 and 650 BC; and then the gradual disintegration of hoplite tactics and values at a time variously dated to shortly after the Persian Wars (480-479 BC), during the Peloponnesian War (431-404 BC), or in the course of the fourth century. The problem with this model is that for the period before the Peloponnesian War, and especially before the Persian Wars, our evidence – with the exception of the Homeric epics, which are so controversial that many prefer not to use them at all – is extremely limited. As a result, the model relies on positing change on the basis of claims made by later sources about how things used to be, while in parts also positing continuity and projecting elements of classical Greek warfare back into the archaic age. This is hardly satisfactory. True, the dismal state of the evidence sometimes leaves no other option, but more often than not a careful consideration of literary, iconographic and archaeological evidence does in fact allow us to construct a more reliable picture of archaic Greek warfare, based to a greater extent on contemporary sources.

More generally, the problem with the study of Greek warfare of any period is that so many ancient authors tell us about military ideals, of which they often needed to remind themselves and their audiences, whereas so few of them tell us about the humdrum military realities with which they were only too familiar. If there is one common failing in modern work on the subject, it is that it underestimates how wide the gap between ideal and reality could be.

In what follows, a critical study of both archaic and classical evidence will show why the Greeks fought (Part I), who did the fighting (II), how armies were organised (III), how they conducted campaigns (IV) how they fought battles (V), and how warfare at sea compared with warfare on land (VI). We shall see that attitudes towards war, and the causes and goals of war, remained essentially the same from Homer to Aristotle. The way in which wars were fought, however, changed gradually over the centuries, with a major transformation taking place between 550 and 450 BC as a result of developments in state-formation during that period. Although hoplite armour came into use in the late eighth century, the tactics, rules and rituals which we most closely associate with hoplite warfare took centuries to emerge – and they always went hand-in-hand with the uninhibited and brutally pragmatic forms of warfare which have wrongly come to be associated with the decline of the hoplite tradition.

Part I

War and Peace

'A war-lover', said Xenophon, himself an enthusiastic mercenary in his younger days, is 'someone who likes to spend money on war as if on a boyfriend or some other pleasure'. He is the kind of man who 'chooses to make war, when he could perfectly well live in peace without suffering any shame or harm' (*Anabasis* 2.6.6). On that definition, ancient Greeks did not love war. Most agreed that 'no one is so senseless as to *choose* war over peace'.[1]

> If it really has been fated by the gods that mankind must wage wars, then it is up to us to be as slow as possible to start any, and, if a war does break out, to end it as soon as we possibly can. (Xenophon, *Hellenica* 6.3.6)

Yet it usually did not take much to convince a Greek community that it was right and necessary to make war, however disagreeable, in order to avoid harm or wipe out shame. Especially if there was a chance of making a profit in the process.

Warfare was so pervasive that some intellectuals formulated the idea that all states were by definition at war with one another. One of the speakers in Plato's *Laws* declares that 'what most people call "peace" is nothing but a word, and in fact every city-state is at all times, by nature, in a condition of undeclared war with every other city-state' (626a). The same image is conjured up by Thucydides' account of the Peloponnesian War (431-404 BC): in his vision of the Greek world every state was out to increase its power at the expense of others and unscrupulous politics had reduced all ethical concerns to mere pretence; war was the norm and annihilation the price of defeat.[2]

Such ideas have struck a loud chord with modern readers. Thucydides in particular has been hailed as the founder of 'realism', the school of thought which argues that international relations ultimately boil down to an uninhibited struggle between states for survival and power.[3] The attractions of a 'realist' approach to war and politics are obvious: it reduces the complexities of life to a clear-cut pattern, and appeals to one's critical and cynical instincts by claiming to strip away conventional ideas and fine appearances to reveal an ugly hidden truth. No wonder, then, that this way of thinking has found favour with many intellectuals, especially those who, like Thucydides, personally experienced war at its worst. But a 'realist' approach cannot adequately explain war in the modern world,[4] and it certainly cannot explain fully how and why wars were fought in ancient Greece.

A myth which must be dispelled at once is the notion, long held by the majority of classical scholars, that the Greeks saw war as the *normal* relation between states and peace as a temporary aberration. On the strength of the passage just cited from Plato's *Laws* it is assumed that a Greek state regarded itself as in principle at war with anyone and everyone else, except those few with whom it had formally concluded a peace treaty. By implication, 'every war was justified, unless in waging it one broke a treaty'.[5] This is simply not true. Plato certainly did not say so. He introduced the proposition of an undeclared war of all against all only to knock it down,[6] and he made it perfectly plain that 'Greek politicians, soldiers, and the general public had no idea that such a state of war might even exist. When the notion is introduced, it is followed by a sneer at 'the stupidity of the masses' because 'they *do not realise* that everyone, throughout his life, is always engaged in a continuous war against all the other city-states' (*Laws* 625e). Clearly, the undeclared war of all against all was then, as it is now, a purely *theoretical* human condition posited by 'realist' intellectuals. It was not, and is not, a principle overtly applied in the conduct of international relations.[7]

How a Greek community did see its relations with the outside world is nicely illustrated by the legend of how Greece and Asia became enemies. The first offence was committed when some Phoenician traders abducted a Greek princess. The Greeks, instead of seeking justice by diplomatic means, resorted to tit-for-tat retaliation and abducted a Phoenician princess. The second offence was committed by the Greeks themselves when they kidnapped yet another princess and then refused to settle when her father demanded to be 'given justice'. At this point, it was clear that the Greeks had rejected the possibility of diplomatic relations with Asia, so the Trojans seized Helen, queen of Sparta, and refused to 'give justice' in turn. But it was not until the Greeks raised the stakes by invading Asia *en masse* that the two sides considered themselves at war: 'after that the people of Asia always thought of the Greeks as their enemies'.[8] The story assumes that mankind's normal condition is neither war nor peace, but informal neutrality. Enmity and friendship develop only in the course of relations between two communities. The point of the story is precisely that there is no natural state of war, and that the Greeks are responsible for *creating* wars by always favouring the most violent course of action, rather than settling their differences or tolerating low-level hostilities. For this, they are 'greatly to blame' (Herodotus 1.4).[9]

Many of the conventions, beliefs and ideals which shaped Greek international relations actually inhibited the eruption of armed conflict, and there were long-established, ever more sophisticated, procedures for dealing with clashes of interest. If wars nevertheless kept breaking out,[10] it was not simply because of the aggression and selfishness which are a part – and only a part – of human nature, but because there was much in Greek culture, society, politics and economy which positively encouraged communities to resort to violence.

1

Kinsmen, Friends and Allies

The society of states

When the city of Sybaris was sacked and razed to the ground, the people of Miletus, at the other end of the Mediterranean, shaved their heads and went into deep mourning. Miletus and Sybaris, we are told, 'were more closely bound together by friendship'than any cities we know'. Why they were so close we can only guess;[1] the remarkable fact is that two independent, distant communities enjoyed a friendship far beyond the terms of any formal alliance they may have had. Sybaris' failure to 'repay in kind' when Miletus was sacked in turn was greeted with surprise and disapproval, and it was noted that some of Miletus' other friends did know what was expected of them: the Athenians showed 'extreme grief' in 'all sorts of ways', including a ban on performances of *The Capture of Miletus* and a heavy fine for the play's author for 'recalling misfortunes close to home' (Herodotus 6.21).

Informal relations of kinship and friendship between states were more pervasive in ancient Greece than the 'special relationships' between states which exist in the modern world, and they were no less significant than formal relations created by treaties or membership in international organisations. Indeed, the hundreds of Greek communities in the homeland and scattered around the coasts of the Mediterranean and the Black Sea were bound together by such a variety of relationships that they should be thought of as a *society* of states[2] – an international community with its own hierarchy and internal networks, shared rules and rituals, and, inevitably, tensions and conflicts which sometimes turned violent.

Greeks against the world

For a Greek, everyone who lived beyond the borders of his city or region was a 'stranger' (*xenos*); each community took pride in being different from the others in dialect, script, cults and political institutions. Yet the Greeks also believed that all Hellenes, as they called themselves, shared characteristics which set them apart from others: 'the same blood and the same language and common shrines and sacrifices, as well as similar customs' (Herodotus 8.144). All those who did not speak Greek were dismissed as 'jabberers' (the literal meaning of *barbaroi*, 'barbarians') and excluded from taking part in competitions at the great panhellenic festivals. Boundaries between Greeks and others were only slightly blurred at the edges: the 'barbarian' Macedonians were excluded from the games, but an exception was made for their kings, who claimed that they were of distant Greek descent.[3]

Some sense of a distinctive Greek identity emerges already in the earliest surviving poetry, and it grew ever more pronounced. Homer's *Iliad*, composed *c.* 700 BC, presents the Trojan War as a conflict between the united forces of all the Greeks (the 'Panhellenes', or their legendary equivalent, the 'Panachaeans') and a loose coalition of eastern nations who were divided by their different languages and were inferior to the Greeks in military matters.[4] Success in war against the Persian empire during the fifth century fed into this kind of thinking, and inspired a popular theory of ethnic superiority which asserted that Greeks were innately superior and born to rule. Barbarians were born to live as slaves or subjects. The corollary was that in war one should spare Greeks but could legitimately massacre or enslave the 'alien and foreign' (Plato, *Republic* 470c). Xenophon in his historical memoirs approves when the Spartan admiral Lysander punishes the Athenians for their violent treatment of fellow-Greeks, and in the same chapter defends Lysander when he in turn enslaves the people of Cedreae, because 'they were half-barbarian' (*Hellenica* 2.1.15, 31-2).[5] In the fourth century BC, politicians and intellectuals alike urged the Greeks not to wage war against one another at all, but to direct their united aggression outwards against non-Greeks. Aristotle declared that waging war against barbarians with a view to enslaving them was 'righteous by nature', a legitimate form of violence much like hunting animals.[6]

Within the Greek world, all states were notionally equal insofar as they were meant to enjoy political independence (*autonomia*) without undue interference by others. Some were inevitably more equal than others, since the smallest of these communities had territories of only a few square kilometres inhabited by perhaps a thousand people, while the largest covered several thousand square kilometres and had up to a quarter of a million inhabitants, including slaves or serfs.[7] Superior resources could be translated into a recognised but informal position of *hêgemonia*, 'hegemony', also called *archê*, a term conventionally translated as 'empire' ('hegemony's evil twin') but really just another word for 'leadership'.[8]

A position of leadership might extend only to immediate neighbours or allies, or ultimately embrace all Greeks. The Spartans were the first to achieve the position of 'leader of the Greeks' around 550 BC. They presented themselves as legitimate successors to the legendary ruler of all Greece, Agamemnon, by creating a relic cult around the miraculously rediscovered skeleton of his son, Orestes. 'How loudly Agamemnon would wail if he heard that the leadership had been taken away from the

Spartans!', they would say in defence of their dominance.[9] Sparta's leadership was challenged in the fifth century by Athens, and in the fourth century by many another contender, but the idea that *someone* needed to be the leader of the Greeks became deeply ingrained. Unless one state was in charge, the world seemed in 'disorder'.[10] The leader's role was ideally to act as 'champion' (*prostatês*) of the other Greeks. 'Since everyone treats them with the greatest respect, leaders must look out for the common interest, as much as cultivate their own interests' (Thucydides 1.120.1). The Spartans were asked more than once to liberate fellow-Greeks from the Persian empire on the grounds that this was a champion's rightful duty.[11]

Reality fell short of these ideals. Powerful cities infringed, to a greater or lesser degree, the autonomy of nearby towns or more distant allies, and were often accused of relying on coercion, like 'tyrants', rather than on their authority as 'champions'. In war, fellow-Greeks were certainly not always spared: some two dozen small cities were annihilated in the classical period alone. Nevertheless, the ideals of the Greek community were not an irrelevance in international politics. The autonomy of the city-states was taken seriously enough to win enthusiastic support for the greater powers when they announced that their goal in war was the 'liberation' of the weaker, while the taboo on enslaving other Greeks was strong enough to cause an outcry whenever it was broken.[12]

'The same blood and common shrines'

Blood relations were almost as important between Greek states as they were between individuals. The Greeks saw themselves as a single large family, descended from Hellen, son of Deucalion, and the four main dialect groups – Dorians, Ionians, Aeolians and Achaeans – were regarded as kin groups as well, each with a son or grandson of Hellen as common ancestor. Particularly close ties of kinship (*syngeneia*) existed where one city had, or claimed to have, founded another by providing settlers or at least an official founder for it. These affiliations were important enough to be specified for almost every entry in Herodotus' catalogue of Greek forces at the Battle of Salamis ('the Aeginetans are Dorians from Epidaurus', 'the Naxians are Ionians from Athens', and so on; 8.43-8) and to be cited repeatedly in his *Histories* as a motivation in international relations. Whereas Sparta got involved with the affairs of eastern Greek cities in their capacity as 'leader of the Greeks', the Athenians did so on the basis of kinship with 'their colonists'.[13]

In an extraordinary extension of the concept, some non-Greeks claimed kinship with the Greeks. A king of Persia is said to have argued that it was appropriate for the Persians to form an alliance with the city of Argos since they were descended from Perses, son of Perseus, a legendary Argive hero: 'We are your descendants, and it is not proper for us to campaign against our ancestors, or for you to support others and become our adversaries' (Herodotus 7.150). The story is unlikely to be true, but it expresses clearly the Greek notion that kinship between communities should be a major consideration in interstate relations.[14]

Thucydides, by contrast, went out of his way to argue that kinship was only a nominal factor in international politics, or, more precisely, in international politics as conducted by the Athenians. He insisted that 'the truest reason' for the Athenians' interventions in Sicily – officially in defence of kindred cities – was their desire for strategic advantages and, later, for the conquest of the whole island (3.86.4; 6.6.1). At the culmination of Athens' Sicilian expedition, he presented a catalogue of the assembled forces, specifying, in an echo of Herodotus, their kinship affiliations; his purpose, however, was to show that 'they took sides *not* primarily in accordance with justice or *kinship*, but according to either expedience or coercion, as the circumstances dictated in each case' (7.57.1). He noted, therefore, all instances of kinsmen fighting one another (along the lines of 'these Aeolians fought under compulsion against Aeolians, their founders', or 'the Argives, ... for their private gain, as Dorians followed the Ionian Athenians against Dorians', 7.57.5, 9). Because there is no parallel for kinship between states in the modern world, we too may feel sceptical about it as a motive in war, and we may even be tempted to deny kinship any real role at all. But we would be wrong. Thucydides did not categorically dismiss kinship, but freely admitted that some communities supported one another 'on the basis of their kinship'.[15] His claim that the Athenians dismissed such considerations was not a statement of the obvious, but a controversially 'realist' view of their behaviour, argued in opposition to the likes of Herodotus who clearly felt that kinship was a major concern even for Athens.[16]

Blood relations involved shared religious rites. Just as all Greeks took part in panhellenic games and cults, so their ethnic subdivisions and 'family' clusters each had common festivals and rituals. Even at the height of their power and at their most 'tyrannical', the Athenians went to much trouble to forge religious bonds, most spectacularly through their repeated ritual purifications of the sanctuary of Apollo on Delos, a common cult centre for all Ionians. They exhumed and relocated all burials on the island, revived and enhanced the traditional local Ionian festival, and finally purified Delos yet more thoroughly by temporarily removing all its, supposedly polluted, living inhabitants as well. Thucydides, for all his cynicism, accepts that this was done from genuinely religious motives. Athens also obliged its allies and colonists to attend the major Athenian festivals, bringing 'a cow and a panoply' to the Great Panathenaea and a large image of a phallus to the Dionysia.[17]

Some groups of states formed 'amphictyonies', cult-associations responsible for the protection of a sanctuary. Historically the most important of these was the Delphic amphictyony, a league of mainly central and north-

9

ern Greek communities which met at a sanctuary near Thermopylae and, crucially, was also in charge of the Delphic oracle. Further south, we hear of Calaurian and Argive amphictyonies, while the Greek cities in the east divided along kinship lines, with Aeolians, Ionians, and Dorians each maintaining a common sanctuary from which other ethnic groups were banned.[18]

An amphictyony provided a forum for political co-operation and tried to regulate the conduct of its members. The Delphic oath included a promise 'not to destroy any city of the amphictyony nor to cut it off from running water, whether in war or in peace, but, if anyone broke these oaths, to send an army against him and destroy his cities' (Aeschines 2.115). The destruction of the town of Melia by the other members of the Ionian league, perhaps *c.* 700 BC, as a punishment for aggression, may show a similar rule being enforced, but otherwise we know only of attempts to fine aggressors. In 494 BC, the Argive amphictyony tried to impose a fine of 500 talents of silver each on two member states which had helped an outsider, Sparta, invade Argos itself, while after the battle of Leuctra in 371 BC, the Delphic amphictyony tried to impose the same 500-talent penalty on Sparta for their unjustifiable occupation of the citadel of Thebes. These attempts were ineffective, but they do tell us that the Greeks felt strongly enough about religious ties to try, at least, to contain conflict between fellow-worshippers. Those who 'shared the most solemn rituals and sacrifices and the most beautiful festivals' certainly *ought* not to fight one another.[19]

Friendship and reciprocity

Communities had sworn friends as well as family in the Greek world. Around 550 BC, two north-western cities recorded the following:

> THE AGREEMENT OF THE ANAITOI AND THE METAPIOI
> Friendship for fifty years. If anyone from either side is not steadfast, the representatives and the seers may drag him from the altar. If they break the oath, the priests at Olympia must be informed.

At about the same time, some Greek cities in southern Italy became even better friends:

> The Sybarites and their allies and the Serdaioi united in friendship, faithful and without deceit, *forever*. Guarantors: Zeus, Apollo and the other gods, and the city Posidonia.

Sworn friendship (*philia*) was not the same as a military alliance. Sybaris made a clear distinction between its new 'friends' and its old 'allies' (*symmachoi*); many other archaic and classical treaties promised both 'friendship *and* alliance'.[20] This was not an empty formula: the contractual obligations of an alliance differed from the commitments of friendship, which were broader, more open-ended – and more emotionally charged, if the laments of the Milesians for the Sybarites (p. 6) are anything to go by. Even the Trojan War nearly ended with Greeks and Trojans becoming sworn friends, according to the *Iliad*: in a doomed attempt to stop the fighting they 'swore faithful oaths and friendship' (*philotês*) in a ritual which involved the sacrifice of sheep, libations of wine and solemn hand-shakes.[21]

The exchange of favours was central to Greek personal friendship, and so it was in friendships between states. The negotiations which set in motion the Peloponnesian War relied heavily on appeals to this sort of reciprocity. In asking for Athenian military aid the Corcyraeans admitted that Athens did not owe them anything 'on account of either a great good deed or an alliance'; they promised to show 'unshakeable gratitude' for this 'favour' (*charis*; Thucydides 1.32.1, 33.1-2). The Corinthians tried to win back Athens by calling in the favours which they were owed: apart from voting down Spartan action against Athens seven years ago, they said, 'let the younger men be informed by their elders' that some sixty years earlier Corinth had given the Athenians twenty warships, almost free of charge. It was now time for 'some gratitude in return', and a 'timely favour' from Athens would cancel out both the debt and some serious grievances.[22] The appeal to oral tradition about an act of generosity two generations old may seem strained, but the story was seriously discussed in Athens at the time. Herodotus heard it told as proof that the Corinthians had indeed shown themselves 'the best of friends' to Athens on that occasion (6.89). Folk memory was long: the Samians could claim that Sparta had 'returned a favour' by sending military aid in 525 BC, because Samos had done the same for Sparta a *century* earlier.[23]

Athenians liked to think that generosity was part of their national character. 'We win friends by doing rather than receiving favours ... and we are unique in fearlessly helping others, motivated less by calculations of expediency than by faith in generosity', Pericles was supposed to have said in his funeral oration for the war-dead (Thucydides 2.40.4-5). This attitude extended to international relations as well. When the Athenians accepted an alliance with the Boeotians in 395 BC, they were keen to point out that in doing so they were 'returning a greater favour than they had received' eight years earlier when the Boeotians had refused to march against Athens (Xenophon, *Hellenica* 3.5.8, 16). They were particularly fond of citing their crucial role in repelling two Persian invasions at great cost to themselves, not so much as evidence of their bravery, but as proof of their willingness to sacrifice everything for the benefit of others. Usually, such reminders that all Greeks were obligated to Athens served to justify Athenian international leadership: 'having single-handedly destroyed the barbarian, it is proper that we should be in charge'.[24]

Diplomats and politicians who invoked past acts of generosity did not confine themselves to the last few years or even the last few generations, but cited, in all seriousness, examples from legend. A striking example is the envoy to Sparta in 371 BC who argued that, since the Spartans had once upon a time received a gift of seed-grain from an Athenian hero, 'it would be right for us never to bear arms against one another' (Xenophon, *Hellenica* 6.3.6). The Athenians' penchant for advertising past favours as the basis of their hegemony was also evident in their choice of relic cult: whereas the Spartans picked Orestes to hint at a hereditary position of leadership, the Athenians dug up and worshipped the bones of their mythical king Theseus, a selfless protector and benefactor of the vulnerable.[25]

Thucydides felt that Athens cynically exploited such appeals to the past, but the persistence and constant repetition of the themes of friendship, reciprocity and generosity shows that many Greek communities did keep a tally of favours done and received.[26] Obligations to friends were not, of course, the only consideration, and perhaps not often the decisive consideration, in making foreign policy, but they did count. Sparta sent 'an ox as a gift of friendship' to a loyal ally (Xenophon, *Hellenica* 7.2.3). Athens treated exceptional loyalty in its allies as a 'favour' or 'benefaction', and rewarded it with special honours, including Athenian citizenship.[27] Most dramatically, in the *Odyssey* the king of Sparta declares that he should like to reward the Ithacans for their services at Troy by clearing an entire city nearby for them to live in (4.168-80). This might seem an extravagant epic fantasy, were it not that the Spartans in 431 BC actually let the people of Aegina resettle in a city within Spartan territory, because these Aeginetans had been 'their benefactors' in a war some thirty years earlier.[28]

An offer of 'great mutual friendship and closeness', as well as 'peace and alliance' (Thucydides 4.19.1), thus implied a willingness to form ties broader than those of a military alliance alone. Indeed, communities could be friends, or 'close' (*oikeios*), or 'in harmony' (*arthmios*) without making a formal alliance at all. Such relations of reciprocity were taken seriously: even in early Greece, when states and international relations were at their least developed, a raid on a community 'in harmony' with one's own was deemed such an outrage that the raider on his return home could expect to be met by a lynch mob.[29]

Military aid and alliances

In early Greece, communities at war relied on friends and kinsmen to come to the rescue more or less spontaneously. As the *Iliad* pictures it, a city under attack would light fire-beacons 'to be seen by its neighbours, in the hope that these might come to protect them from war' (18.207-13). The poet imagined that kinsmen living abroad came to the aid of Troy of their own accord as soon as they 'heard the news' of the Greek invasion. Others were asked to send troops as 'helpers' (*epikouroi*), and these expected to be rewarded with generous gifts.[30] The invading army was assembled on a similar basis: its commander travelled round Greece asking friends and others to follow him as a favour, in return for a share of the booty. Their 'agreements' (*synthêsiai*) were sealed with oaths, libations and handshakes, but remained short-term, not extending beyond a single campaign.[31]

At the very end of the seventh century BC, we first hear of a long-term military alliance, or 'symmachy' (*symmachia*), concluded between Miletus and the king of Lydia. At about the same time, the Sybarites and the Spartans each started making bilateral military alliances with their neighbours; by 550 BC both had established far-flung networks of allies in southern Italy and in the Peloponnese, respectively.[32] The earliest treaty of alliance of which we know the terms, dating to 550-500 BC, was defined in remarkably broad terms (Fig. 1):

THE AGREEMENT OF THE ELEANS AND THE HERAEANS
Let there be an alliance for a hundred years, starting this year. If there is any need, whether for words or for deeds, let them join together in everything, especially in war. If they do not join together, those who have destroyed the agreement shall give in compensation a talent of silver to be used in the service of Zeus of Olympia.[33]

The relationship between the parties outlined in this treaty was so wide-ranging that it almost amounted to one of general friendship. What makes it different is the effort made to stress the need for mutual military aid ('especially in war') and to enforce the agreement by fining those who did not comply. A moral, reciprocal obligation was made more binding by turning it into a contractual and quasi-legal duty.

Fig. 1. The treaty between the Eleans and the Heraeans, inscribed on a bronze plaque and set up at Olympia, *c.* 550-500 BC.

Not many alliances were so broadly defined. The only Spartan treaty of which the text has survived, in a fragmentary state and of uncertain date, is an alliance with the Erxadieis in Aetolia, which probably represents the standard form imposed by Sparta:

AGREEMENT WITH THE AETOLIANS
On these terms there will be friendship and peace and alliance with the Aetolians ... They must follow wherever the Spartans may lead, by land and by sea, and have the same friend and enemy as the Spartans, and they must not put an end to war without the Spartans, and not slacken in fighting the same opponent as the Spartans do.
   They must not shelter refugees who have shared [...?]
   If anyone marches against the land of the Erxadieis to make war, the Spartans must come to their defence with all the force within their power; if anyone marches against the land of the Spartans to make war, the Erxadieis must come to their defence ....[34]

The promise to 'have the same friend and enemy' featured in many Greek treaties of alliance and meant that one would support *all* the ally's campaigns, both defensive and offensive.[35] Here, the Aetolians alone make this promise: the Spartans do not reciprocate, but instead hammer home their superiority by demanding that their ally must always and everywhere 'follow' them. Sparta takes upon itself only *defensive* duties, in the last clause of the treaty, which constitutes a mutual agreement to send help against enemy invasion, another common element of Greek alliances. It was by imposing such unequal terms upon defeated enemies that Sparta created the set of 'hegemonic' alliances known as the Peloponnesian League.[36]

Other states powerful enough to impose unequal terms on their allies adopted similar terms.[37] Full offensive and defensive alliances in which *both* sides swore to 'have the same friends and enemies' as the other were conceivable, but very few are known.[38] Between equals, the normal treaty of alliance was purely defensive: a mutual promise to send help 'in the most vigorous manner possible' to protect the ally against aggression.[39] In the fourth century, attempts to establish a 'common peace' in Greece (p. 18) involved defensive alliances only, since all participating states were asumed to be equal and willing partners.

The great exception was the so-called Delian League, established by Athens in 478/7 BC. It was founded on a basis of equality, since its members originally joined voluntarily rather than under duress, yet the allies went beyond a promise of defensive assistance and all swore to have the same friends and enemies. That Athens, as the leading power, should have been prepared to commit itself to this extent was a measure of its fierce enthusiasm for a war of revenge against the King of Persia, explicitly named as the enemy in the treaty. Athens was indeed keener to fight than most of its allies, who soon began to resent their leader's habit of campaigning year in, year out, rather than intermittently, as Sparta did.[40]

Modern studies often say that the normal form of *symmachia* was an offensive-and-defensive alliance, and that purely defensive alliances were a late fifth-century invention, a sign that the Greeks' enthusiasm for war was on the wane.[41] This is misleading. Only the defeated, the weak, and the exceptionally driven would accept an offensive military alliance. From the sixth century onwards, most states, given half a chance, would happily impose offensive obligations on *others* but willingly commit *themselves* only to defensive alliances.

Treaties often narrowed down still further the precise rights and duties of each party. Who was to provide overall leadership in a coalition of equals was a sensitive issue which had to be thrashed out before any alliance could made to work.[42] The matter of allocating the cost and the profits of joint expeditions also needed to be dealt with. The Athenians, not content with vague promises of 'vigorous' help, stipulated the exact number of ships or amount of silver which each ally was required to contribute to joint expeditions of the Delian League. In an alliance of 420 BC, they stipulated that any party requiring the presence of allied troops in its territory for more than 30 days should pay a fixed sum per man per day to cover the cost of provisions. An alliance between Cretan cities, notorious raiders, characteristically concentrated on the division of spoils: one of the parties was entitled to half of all booty taken at sea, but only a third of what was taken on land.[43] Many treaties remained vague by modern standards, but they tended to become more like legal contracts and less like the broad reciprocal agreements of old.

The success and durability of an alliance depended on shared interests and genuine goodwill on both sides, as amusingly illustrated by Aristophanes' parody of a politician speaking in support of an allied ruler: 'He really is a huge admirer of Athens. He is your one true lover. So much so, in fact, that he covers walls with graffiti saying ATHENIANS ARE BEAUTIFUL' (*Acharnians* 141-4). When interests changed or good intentions evaporated, an alliance was liable to be abandoned quite quickly, since few states were both able and willing to keep reluctant allies in line by force. Those who tried, like the Athenians, were resented as 'tyrants'. In principle, however, alliances were designed to be durable. All were confirmed by 'the most binding' oaths, sworn by representatives of both sides, in some cases renewed every year, and no alliance, so far as we know, was meant to last less than 50 years. Not coincidentally, the shortest alliances were those between Sparta and its chief rivals, Athens and Argos. The next shortest were concluded for a full century, and most known treaties of alliance either specified no limit in time or explicitly announced that they were made 'for ever'. The members of the Delian League theatrically sank lumps of metal into the sea and swore to keep the alliance until iron floated.[44]

Keeping the peace

When Odysseus was a lad, the elders of Ithaca sent him abroad to demand compensation for 300 sheep rustled by Messenian raiders (*Odyssey* 21.16-21). This may not have been our hero's most exciting adventure, but it is important evidence that the Greeks' first reaction to an international incident was negotiation, not war. The Trojan War itself, we are told, began only when the Trojans refused to negotiate and threatened to kill the Greek ambassadors.[45] A community might admit to public wrongdoing, or distance itself from private offences committed by its members, and pacify the victims by offering some form of compensation, acting as 'a giver of justice'. In international relations as in civic life, it was regarded as the normal and preferable alternative to retaliation and the use of force.[46]

There was no shortage of channels through which negotiation could be conducted. Private contacts abroad were numerous: to have a network of 'foreign friends' (*xeinoi*) with whom one exchanged gifts and favours was for upper-class Greeks as much a part of the good life as having children, horses and hunting dogs (Solon F 23 West). Throughout the archaic and classical periods such contacts were exploited for public purposes. A crucial instance was the personal friendship between Lysander of Sparta and Cyrus, a Persian prince, on the strength of which Sparta gained the Persian financial support which enabled it to win the Peloponnesian War.[47] In addition, from the late seventh century BC onwards, states publicly appointed formal 'foreign representatives' (*proxenoi*), natives of other cities charged with looking after the appointing state's interests in their home towns.[48] When relations became fraught, ambassadors (*presbeis*, literally 'elders') travelled back and forth to conduct negotiations, and sacrosanct heralds (*kerykes*), who could travel safely at all times, ensured that one channel of communication was kept open even when war broke out. In an act of extreme hostility the Spartans and Athenians once killed heralds from Persia, and this was thought such an outrage that two generations later Herodotus was still searching for evidence that the gods had exacted punishment for this crime.[49]

Homer suggests that the people of a community might have enough of a sense of justice to offer compensation and spontaneously punish the wrongdoers among them by stoning.[50] As one would expect, however, the parties to a dispute often could not agree on what was fair. In such situations, they could appeal to a third party to arbitrate. The earliest stories about arbitration are set around 600 BC, when Athens referred its disputes over Sigeum and Salamis to, respectively, the ruler of Corinth and a committee of distinguished Spartans. These arbitrators were evidently chosen for their ability to back up the judgement by military force, if necessary.[51] The appeal to the priests at Olympia in the treaty between the Anaitoi and Metapioi (p. 10), by contrast, relied on their religious authority. Referring the matter to the oracle of Apollo at Delphi was also

16

an option.[52] It was deemed 'not legitimate to initiate action against one who offers justice' (Thucydides 1.85.2) and states which declined to submit their disputes to judgement did so with a guilty conscience. Thucydides, despite playing down the role of religion at large, accepted that Sparta suffered from poor morale throughout the first ten years of the Peloponnesian War because they had refused the arbitration offered by Athens and consequently lived in fear of divine punishment (7.18.2).

In the classical period communities increasingly often concluded a type of treaty, the *symbola*, which regulated private dealings between their respective citizens and defined legal procedures for solving problems which might arise from any cross-border contacts, thereby minimising the scope for conflict and reducing the risk of war breaking out.[53]

Finally, classical Greek states regularly concluded non-aggression pacts called *spondai* ('libations', i.e. 'pledges') in which they swore not to take up arms against one another but to 'give justice' in disputes. In the fifth century BC these pacts were bilateral and of limited duration. For many scholars this is proof that the Greeks saw war as the norm in international relations and could only conceive of peace as a temporary, localised interruption of a universal state of conflict. This might have been the right conclusion to draw if *spondai* had been the *only* type of interstate relation, other than war, known to the Greeks. But they were not. The timeless ties of kinship and common worship which bound together Greek communities were fundamentally incompatible with the idea of eternal war of all against all. The terms of some of the earliest treaties of friendship and military alliance, designed to last 'forever', tell even more explicitly against any such notion. Non-aggression pacts were merely one element of an array of interstate relations, some of which were temporary and some of which were not.[54]

The short-term nature of *spondai* is explained by their origin in armistices and truces, ranging from a few days to recover the bodies of the dead after battle to perhaps a year's cessation of hostilities in which to conduct negotiations.[55] In the early fifth century, we first hear of states extending such truces to many years' duration, to become in effect treaties of peace (*eirênê*) – which is what they were called colloquially, even if in official language they were strictly *spondai*.[56] Truces of five, ten, and thirty years were concluded between states with a long history of mutual enmity who wanted to end or prevent hostilities for the time being without committing themselves to friendship, alliance or permanent peace. Still longer truces, for fifty and a hundred years, accompanied and reinforced defensive alliances of the same duration, making doubly sure that the allies would not fall out.[57] The limited duration of these alliances themselves is hardly surprising: a state would in many cases be wary of binding itself to another indefinitely, since, as someone once put it, 'an alliance does not mean peace, but a change of war' (Xenophon, *Hellenica* 7.4.10).

In the fourth century, a series of efforts was made to put a stop to war among Greek states altogether. Most of these attempts to create a 'common peace' *(koinê eirênê)* were dictated by an external power: repeatedly by the king of Persia from 386 BC onwards, and by the king of Macedon after his defeat of the Greeks in 338 BC. These peace treaties were made 'for all time' and laid down that any state infringing the autonomy of another would be punished collectively by all Greeks, with the support of the king.[58] This new way of organising interstate relations was a remarkable further stage on the road to a less conflict-ridden international society, even if it was not quite as revolutionary as it has seemed to those who believe that universal war had been the norm only decades earlier. Many common peaces were short-lived, but they confirm that for the Greeks, as for us, peace was not only more desirable but more normal than war. Indeed, proverbial wisdom declared peace, not war, part of the natural order: 'in war, the sleeping are woken by trumpets; in peace, by the birds' and, more poignantly, 'in peace, sons bury their fathers; in war, fathers bury their sons'.[59]

The Greek international community presented itself in its ideal form – close-knit and in perfect harmony – at panhellenic festivals such as the Olympic Games:

> After concluding truces with one another and putting an end to any current hostilities, we come together in one place. Then, with shared prayers and sacrifices, we remember the kinship which exists between us and behave with greater goodwill towards fellow-Greeks ever after. We renew old friendships and create new ones. (Isocrates 4.43)

Alongside a show of unity, however, these festivals also offered more than a hint of what drove Greek cities to war: the intense competitiveness of individuals and cities.

2

Justice, Honour and Profit

Causes and goals of wars

A cut of sacrificial meat was once a cause of war between Corinth and its colony Corcyra. The Corinthians 'hated' the Corcyraeans because they 'did not give them the conventional privileges at common religious festivals and did not serve the first portion of sacrificed animals to a Corinthian, as other colonies did'.[1] Such petty causes may seem to belong to the world of legend, where Troy was sacked for the sake of a woman and Calydon nearly destroyed 'on account of a boar's head and hairy hide' (*Iliad* 9.529-49). Yet the war between Corinth and Corcyra in 433 BC was firmly historical, and it was Thucydides, the doyen of realism, who vouched that the Corinthians were provoked above all by their colonists' failure to show them the proper 'respect' in ritual matters (1.25.3-26.1, 38.2-3).

Before dismissing such stories as silly,[2] we should remember the power of symbols to provoke violent emotions. In Northern Ireland, parliament was recalled from its Easter recess in 2001 for an emergency debate about a display of lilies in the assembly building. Horrified Unionists demanded that the displays be removed, on account of the lilies' association with the commemoration of IRA dead. While outsiders and indeed many assembly members mocked the 'lunacy' of this political crisis over 'a bunch of flowers', those most closely involved felt that the issue was of historic significance: 'For the first time in the history of the United Kingdom a government building will be used to display the symbols which honour IRA terrorists'.[3] In studying the causes of Greek wars we find ourselves in the position of outsiders, often bemused or amused, but we must try to see these conflicts through the eyes of the outraged parties to the dispute. What Aristotle said about civil wars applies to all wars: 'they are not about small matters; they may arise *from* small things, but they are waged *about* great things' (*Politics* 1303b17).

Greek states, not surprisingly, tended to cite highly moral and altruistic reasons for fighting, but most Greek authors accepted that 'the three greatest things' motivating war were self-defence, the pursuit of honour, and the pursuit of profit.[4]

19

I. War and Peace

Crusades: piety, justice and freedom

Just before the outbreak of the Peloponnesian War, Sparta sent three embassies to Athens to register complaints, 'so that they might have the greatest possible reason to wage war' (Thucydides 1.126.1). Between them, these missions covered the full range of justifications, other than self-defence, available to a belligerent city-state: the defence of a god or gods treated with impiety, the protection of a friend or ally treated with injustice, and the liberation of fellow-Greeks from 'slavery'.

The first embassy claimed that Sparta wished to 'avenge the gods' (Thucydides 1.127.1) and insisted that Athens should 'drive out the curse of the goddess'. This meant that the Athenians would have to exile their leading politician, Pericles, and all his relatives on his mother's side, on the grounds that their ancestors had committed an act of sacrilege two centuries earlier (126.2-127.3). As a cause for war, this was quite far-fetched, but the fact that the demand was made shows just how important it was for a Greek state to manoeuvre itself into a position where it could claim to be fighting in a religious cause. The Athenian response – a demand that Sparta should expiate *two* curses, both incurred much more recently as a result of similar acts of sacrilege (128.1-135.1) – may sound like a mocking echo of the Spartan claim, but was a serious attempt to trump the enemy in the piety stakes.

Religious justification might take the form of accusing an opponent of encroaching on 'sacred' land belonging to a local sanctuary,[5] or failing to offer due sacrifices. During a lull in the Peloponnesian War, Argos invaded Epidaurus on the official grounds that the Epidaurians had not paid pasture fees to Apollo at his temple at Asine, 'mainly controlled' by the Argives (Thucydides 5.53). The long-running feud between Athens and Aegina was traced back to the Aeginetans' refusal, once upon a time, to make the annual sacrifices which they owed to Erechtheus and Athena Polias at Athens (Herodotus 5.82-7). Sanctuaries which enjoyed the protection of an amphictyonic league (see pp. 9-10) might become the object of a 'sacred war'. 'If anyone plundered what belonged to the god or conspired or plotted in any way against the sacred places,' the Delphic amphictyony swore 'to punish him with hand and foot and voice and all their might'.[6] In the mid-fourth century, Phocis was fined and threatened with a curse for trespassing on Delphi's sacred land, and the amphictyons were forced into a long war when the Phocians failed to comply. Most devastating, if the stories are true, was the First Sacred War of around 600 BC, in which the population of Cirrha was annihilated and their territory reduced to a desolate 'sheep-walk'.[7]

The most sustained appeal to religious justification came in campaigns against the Persian empire. The Athenians, in particular, never ceased to advertise their determination to avenge the Persian destruction of Greek sanctuaries, leaving their own temples in ruins for a generation as a

20

reminder of the need for revenge.[8] In their very first attack on a Persian-held city, they made a gruesome show of punishing its governor for desecrating a hero-shrine: he was crucified while his son was stoned to death before his eyes (Herodotus 9.120.4).

The second Spartan embassy complained about Athens' unjust treatment of three cities (Thucydides 1.139.1). In an international dispute, whether about the forcible seizure of property, a territorial claim, or the imposition of political control by one city over another, a state would normally be expected to demand justice (*dikê*) for itself, but on this occasion the Spartans presented themselves as defending not so much their own interest as the interests of their allies, and indeed of 'anyone who claimed to have been treated unjustly by the Athenians' (1.67.3). In championing the cause of international justice, Sparta made itself the policeman of the Greek world. Few other cities had the power to play this role, but in the years after the Persian War, Sparta was joined by Athens in a campaign to punish so-called 'medizers', communities which had collaborated with the Persians. In the fourth century, Sparta, Athens and Thebes put themselves in charge of upholding one or more of the common peace treaties which forbade any armed aggression between states.

These self-appointed defenders of justice clearly did not always, and probably not often, act from strictly altruistic motives, but they were not always merely cynical either. The medizers of Thebes were fatally mistaken to imagine that their enemies were really only after money: the Spartan regent insisted on their surrender and had them executed without trial (Herodotus 9.87-8).[9] More than a century later, the Athenians declared war on Thebes primarily because of its unjust treatment of other states: a request for help from the 'most blatantly wronged' Corinthians was greeted with spontaneous cheering in the popular assembly. That, at any rate, was how the episode was reported by Xenophon (*Hellenica* 6.5.37), who often stressed his fellow-Athenians' concern with justice, and who in his pamphlet *Ways and Means* urged them to ensure peace and harmony in all of Greece strictly through diplomacy, without recourse to violence or any form of 'injustice'.[10]

Even states which lacked such lofty ambitions accepted that it was a matter of 'justice' to help friends and allies who fell victim to aggression. The Thebans are said to have exploited this imperative and deliberately provoked war with Sparta in 395 BC by staging a minor border dispute between their ally Locris and Sparta's ally Phocis: the need to help their friends gave both sides the legitimate cause without which they felt unable to start hostilities.[11] Political exiles and factions might also qualify as friends in need of help, and a state might go to war in support of such groups in their struggle for power against *internal* enemies. We first hear of such interventions in the sixth century BC, and by the time of the Peloponnesian War civil conflict was everywhere escalating out of control as the great powers constantly intervened on one side or the other. An intervening state might justify its actions as not only those of a loyal friend, but also those of a crusader in a political cause: Sparta made much of its supposed hostility to unconstitutional monarchs, 'tyrants', while classical Athens presented itself as a champion of democratic regimes.[12]

The third Spartan embassy to Athens on the eve of the Peloponnesian War raised a different issue again. It asked the Athenians to 'let the Greeks have autonomy' (Thucydides 1.139.3). The accusation of infringing the independence of others could usually be thrown right back at the accuser, and the Athenians duly replied that they would comply if Sparta would do the same for its own allies (1.144.2). Nevertheless, the claim to be fighting for the freedom of Greek states was in this case, as in others, quite effective. When war broke out, Thucydides claims, 'people felt much goodwill towards the Spartans, especially since they said that they were liberating Greece' (2.8.4), and at the end the walls of Athens were pulled down 'to the music of pipers', as if in celebration, 'since they thought that this day was the beginning of freedom for Greece' (Xenophon, *Hellenica* 2.2.23). All campaigns against Persia were advertised as wars of liberation of the Greeks in Asia.[13] It did not escape the Greeks that the champions of autonomy were the very states which posed the greatest threat to it – including Persia and Macedon, which, as parties to 'common peace' treaties, were supposed to help enforce the freedom of all Greeks.[14] Yet the irony detracted little from the feeling that liberation, like the defence of justice and the gods, was a noble cause for war.

Honour: rivalry and revenge

The love of honour was, in Xenophon's opinion, the defining characteristic of human beings as opposed to dumb animals and of real men as opposed to mere human beings. 'Honour is a great thing', he added, 'for the sake of which people will make every conceivable effort and face every conceivable danger' (*Hiero* 7.1-3). A Greek's 'honour' (*timê*) was both his social status and the respect for his status shown by others.[15] Communities no less than individuals had a place in a ranking-order of honour and demanded the appropriate level of deference from other. 'So long as people stand their ground before equals, are well-behaved towards superiors, and behave with moderation towards inferiors, they will act most correctly', ran one summary of international etiquette (Thucydides 5.111.4). States thus fought to demonstrate the 'excellence' (*aretê*) that entitled them to a place at the top of the tree, and at the same time they fought to stop inferiors from acting like equals, equals from acting like superiors, and superiors from demanding more deference than they deserved.

The pathetic pride which the people of undistinguished Aegium took in their capture of a single small warship from a rival across the Gulf of Corinth best illustrates the importance of status to a Greek city. They immediately sent off to Delphi to ask the oracle: 'Who are the greatest of the Greeks?' The god told them exactly which parts of Greece had the best land, the best horses, the best women, the best men and the second-best men, before witheringly concluding: 'You, Aegians, are not third or fourth; you are not even twelfth.'[16]

A community's status might rest on a number of things,[17] but military success was the main criterion. When Tegea and Athens asked Sparta to settle which of them came second after the Spartans in the Greek rank-ing-order, each reeled off a list of victories stretching back to legendary times, including, on the part of the Tegeans, many wars 'against you, men of Sparta' (Herodotus 9.26-7). Athens' list included three triumphs – their defeat of the Amazons, their role in the Trojan War, and the battle of Marathon – immortalised in large-scale paintings on permanent display in the centre of the city, among many other victory monuments. The Greek cities set up countless memorials and 'treasuries' around the temple of Apollo at Delphi as a record of their struggle for status.[18] Oral tradition even claimed that the men of Sparta wore long hair, and the women of Argos and Aegina wore long dress pins in commemoration of famous victories.[19]

Whatever else might a war might be about, honour was almost by definition at stake as well. Around 600 BC, the Athenians fought hard to conquer Salamis for the sake of prestige as much as for the sake of the land, as we know from a song composed by their leader, Solon, warning that Athens would rank below even the tiniest Cycladic islands if they failed:

> Then I would rather be a Pholegandrian or Sikinite than an Athenian. I would trade-in my fatherland. For instantly this would be the word among people: 'That man is from Attica; he is one of those Salamis-losers' ... Let us go to Salamis, fight for that lovely island, rid ourselves of the burden of shame. (Solon FF 2-3 West)

In many wars, prestige was the main driving force, and material gain a secondary issue at best. After a victory, Sparta often demanded only an acknowledgement of its superiority in the form of an alliance in which the defeated enemy promised to 'follow wherever the Spartans might lead' (see p. 14). This position of 'leadership' (*hêgemonia, archê*), of course, helped to enhance Sparta's military potential and could in principle be exploited to make material gains, but in itself brought only intangible benefits, such as the right to provide supreme commanders and pick the most prestigious battle stations. These privileges were so highly valued that, faced with a Persian invasion, the Spartans would rather lose two major allies than share the leadership: Syracuse's demands were rejected out of hand; Argos pulled out when it was offered only one-third of the command (Herodotus 7.148-9, 157-62). The Athenians demanded a place of honour on the wing at Plataea in 479 BC, and a century later were so sensitive to matters of prestige that they refused to command the allied navy while Sparta led the allied army, because this gave Athens authority only over low-status naval personnel, while Sparta was in charge of high-status infantry. Such episodes give substance to the Athenian claim that they had built up their own leading position first in self-defence, 'then for the sake of honour, and *later* for the sake of profit'.[20]

The honour of a community was always vulnerable. Any hint of disrespect from other cities was seen as a serious challenge. When Sparta declared war on Elis, officially to liberate Elis' subjects, its real motivation, by all accounts, was to retaliate for the disrespect with which it had been treated by Elis over the last 20 years. In 420 BC, the Eleans had banned Spartans from competing in the Olympic Games, and publicly whipped a prominent Spartan citizen who had surreptitiously entered a team for the chariot race. Some years later they had refused to let the Spartan king Agis perform a sacrifice at the altar of Zeus. The two states engaged in many other diplomatic and military skirmishes, but when war eventually broke out, in 402 BC or a little later, its main cause was the memory of these old insults. King Agis expressed Spartan feelings on the matter by sacrificing at the altar of Zeus to let it be known that 'this time no one tried to stop him'.[21]

A string of insults, rather than injuries, were again the fundamental cause of war a few years later when Sparta declared war on Thebes, officially to help its ally Phocis. The Thebans had over the previous decade dared raise questions about Sparta's handling of the booty of the Peloponnesian War, refused to support a military intervention in Athens, and finally disrupted an important sacrifice made by the Spartan king Agesilaus at Aulis, a symbolic act of defiance which was still cited as grounds for Spartan hostility thirty years later.[22] All our sources agree on the chief causes of both wars, and we must accept that Greeks genuinely believed that disrespect – especially repeated disrespect – from equals or inferiors was a threat to the international standing of their community. Not coincidentally, the main complaints of Sparta (and of Corinth against Corcyra, p. 19) concerned snubs and challenges at international religious festivals or large gatherings of allies, which would have been witnessed by representatives of many Greek states.

If the fundamental cause of the Peloponnesian War was Sparta's 'fear' of Athens' growing power, as Thucydides keeps telling us,[23] what the Spartans feared for was their status rather than their freedom or survival. 'You must strive to keep your leadership over the Peloponnese as great as it was when your fathers entrusted it to you', they were told (Thucydides 1.71.7), and they fought to hold on to their allies and thereby to their power and prestige. Athens in turn felt obliged to accept war 'whether for a great or a small reason' because even the slightest concession to Sparta would be an admission of inferiority, given the rule that equals should not 'yield' to equals (1.140-1). The many wars fought for hegemony over neighbours, an entire region, or the whole of Greece, can fairly be described as power struggles, and they often entailed competition for resources as well, but the Greeks themselves clearly saw these conflicts *primarily* as contests for 'honour'.

This is why the communities with the greatest power were the most inclined to wage war. If power and security had been goals in themselves, the dominant states might have felt safe enough to allow weaker states the odd gesture of disrespect. As it was, the greater honour a state claimed, the less defiance it could tolerate. At the peak of its power, in 382 BC, Sparta needed no provocation to declare war on Olynthos, far away in the northern Aegean, other than the simple fact that this city was expanding and had access to resources which might one day make it a serious rival (Xenophon, *Hellenica* 5.2.12-20). Similarly, in 416 BC, Athens, at the height of its naval power, felt that it would be a 'sign of weakness' to allow the island of Melos to be independent and neutral: its population was therefore wiped out.[24]

In this competitive climate a community almost always suspected its rivals of acting in *hybris*, a peculiarly Greek concept meaning unprovoked aggression not motivated by a desire for material gain but by a wish to humiliate the victim and deprive him of honour.[25] The habit of thinking not merely in terms of international clashes of interest, but in terms of rival states deliberately, gratuitously, inflicting dishonour, much increased the likelihood of violence. There was a saying: 'When treated with injustice, reach a settlement. When treated with *hybris*, take revenge' (Stobaeus 3.1.172). 'Friendly' rivalry was even rarer in international relations than it was in civilian life: anger, resentment, enmity, envy, shame and 'vehement hatred' motivated belligerents as they sought revenge.[26] It is an indication of how high emotions could run that Xenophon made a point of warning against losing control:

> I say that ... people should learn above all that one should not even punish a slave in anger. Even masters who become angry often suffer more harm than they inflict, and to proceed against enemies in anger but without good sense is an utter mistake. For anger has no foresight, but good sense sees to it no less that one is safe from harm than that the enemy is hurt. (*Hellenica* 5.3.7)

Quite a few rivalries lasted so long that the communities involved came to think of one another as inveterate enemies, in a relationship nothing short of a feud. Corinth's touchiness where Corcyra was concerned seems still less silly when one considers that 'they have been at odds with each other ever since Corinth founded Corcyra'.[27] Their bad blood spilled over into relations with other states: in 525 BC the Corinthians 'enthusiastically' attacked Samos for having offered Corcyra some help a generation or more earlier. As Herodotus explains, they would not normally have borne such a violent grudge over a minor intervention, but their hatred for Corcyra drove them to extremes (3.48-9). All the fiercest feuds were traced back over several centuries: the hatred of Phocis for Thessaly had allegedly begun as soon as the Thessalians moved into the plains north of Phocis; the 'ancient enmity' between Athens and Aegina went back to the time when Aegina first became an independent power.[28]

The Greeks liked to emphasise their dedication to honour, and fondly imagined barbarians marvelling: 'What manner of men are these, who contend not for money but for excellence?' (Herodotus 8.26). In reality, however, honour often conveniently coincided with profit – in the form of spoils won by predatory seizures of people, animals and other movable wealth, or in the form of territory and tribute, won by conquest and domination.

Spoils of war

Predatory profits from spoils were usually small. By the time an army crossed into enemy territory, most of the countryside would have been evacuated already. Only when the enemy was taken by surprise was an army likely to capture enough livestock and slaves to produce a useful profit. Sparta's invasion of Elis, for instance, was so successful that it became 'a provisioning expedition for the Peloponnese, so to speak'.[29] The stakes were raised when the enemy came out to fight: there were spoils of arms and armour to be taken in battle, prisoners of war to be ransomed or sold into slavery. These practices are attested throughout Greek history: the captured Trojan prince in Homer's *Iliad* who was traded for valuables 'worth a hundred oxen' and later ransomed by a friend for 'three times as much' has an exact parallel in the fourth-century Athenian Nikostratos, captured, sold as a slave in Aegina, and then ransomed by his brother for 2,600 drachmas.[30] Around 500 BC a ransom of 200 drachmas was accepted as standard in most of Greece; by 400 BC the standard rate had fallen to 100 drachmas, a level which seems to have been arrived at because it was just marginally more than a prisoner was likely to fetch as a slave.[31]

Some cities might be intimidated into buying off attackers rather than facing a siege and possible sack. Around 700 BC it was a familiar procedure for a community to collect up its movable property under a solemn oath not to hold anything back, and to present half of it to the besiegers as the price of peace (*Iliad* 18.509-13, 23.111-28). Down to the time of the Persian Wars, sums of up to 100 talents (600,000 drachmas), probably not much less than half of most cities' movable wealth, were regularly demanded by besieging armies. The Athenian force which descended on Paros in 489 BC, for example, stipulated this amount, notionally as a fine for the Parians' collaboration with the Persians, but really – as Herodotus saw it – because Athens saw a chance to extort money from a seemingly defenceless victim:

> Miltiades asked the Athenians for seventy ships and an army and money, *without telling them which place he intended to attack,* but saying only that he would make them rich if they followed him since he would lead them against the kind of place from which they could easily bring back gold in abundance. With these words he asked for the ships, and the Athenians liked his plan and let him have them.[32]

The sacking of towns and temples produced the greatest booty of all. The conqueror's right to seize all property and sell the entire population into slavery was upheld in principle as a 'universal and eternal custom' about which there could hardly be any debate.[33] In practice, the exercise of this absolute right was more often than not inhibited by a variety of pragmatic and ethical restraints, including qualms about the morality of enslaving fellow Greeks,[34] but when the victors exploited their success to the full, the sale of plunder and slaves could bring in hundreds of talents. Alexander the Great earned himself 440 talents from the sale of 30,000 Thebans. Indeed, a decade of spectacular successes brought the Spartans thousands of talents in booty, including the sackfuls of silver sent back by Lysander from the campaign that won the Peloponnesian War in 405/4, and the proceeds of Agesilaus' three years of campaigning in Asia – 1,000 talents and some proudly paraded camels.[35]

The sacking of temples was strictly taboo, but the vast wealth in dedications accumulated in certain sanctuaries sometimes proved too tempting. Dionysius I of Syracuse once plundered 1,000 talents from a single Etruscan temple, twice as much as he made from his campaign against the nearby city. The undoubted piety of the Greeks had its limits, and in a crisis most would probably have echoed the sentiments of an Athenian dispatch to the general Iphicrates who was unsure whether he should intercept a valuable dedication in transit to Delphi: 'No need for theological inquiries; just make sure you feed your soldiers.'[36]

Yet we should not overestimate the importance of predatory gains as a cause and goal of war. The large sums cited above are on record because they were notable windfalls for the attackers; revenues will usually have been much smaller. Moreover, the income from war was balanced by its cost; even the vast amounts realised from sacking cities probably barely made up for the great expense of lengthy sieges.[37] Finally, since most warring communities were pretty evenly matched, one year's gains were as likely as not to be wiped out by next year's losses. Only where the odds were clearly in favour of the attacker are predatory motives likely to have played a decisive part in causing war. Athens and Sparta in their heyday enjoyed a military superiority which enabled them in principle to make sustained profits from predatory warfare. The Arcadians, according to Xenophon, rode on Sparta's coat-tails, joining Spartan campaigns only when they promised easy booty – which was all they wanted, he claims, until they belatedly developed leadership ambitions of their own.[38] For most states, most of the time, however, booty, ransom, extortion and enslavement were a useful means of meeting the cost of warfare rather than a primary goal of war.

Border land and other territories

Wherever there were boundaries between states, land was a cause and goal of war. Almost as soon as Samos and Priene had destroyed their neighbour Melia around 700 BC and divided up its territory, they began fighting over the newly established border between them, at first 'with moderation' but by the early sixth century in ferocious pitched battles that left thousands dead. The conflict rumbled on for another four centuries, despite attempts at arbitration every 50 years or so.[39] So, too, within a generation of becoming an independent state Messenia challenged Spàrta for control of borderland around the temple of Artemis of the Lake: the award of the land to Messenia by Philip of Macedon initiated another four-century struggle which involved arbitrations by Julius Caesar and the emperor Tiberius, among others.[40] Spartan expansion towards the east in the sixth century BC led to a dispute with Argos over the region of Cynouria, which lasted until the Romans stepped in.[41]

Some border regions were of vital economic importance, whether for their farmland, pasture (the source of endless dispute between Locris and Phocis over grazing rights on Mt Parnassos) or other natural resources.[42] Yet it is not at all clear that in these wars economic interests were usually dominant. The main area disputed between Samos and Priene was called Batinetis, 'The Brambles', which hardly suggests rich natural resources, and while Cynouria may have been a more fertile district, the Spartans had so little actual need of it that they gave it away to their allies. There is some truth in the ancient claim that Greek cities fought over 'little bits of not particularly good land and tiny boundaries' (Herodotus 5.49). In quite a few border conflicts the material value of the land seems to have mattered less than the opportunity to prove one's superiority in a trial of military strength with one's neighbours: the chief goal of war here was status rather than wealth.[43]

It was rare for a city to go beyond occupying disputed border land and seize the enemy's entire territory. The conqueror's right to the territory of the defeated was unquestioned. The Athenians could even justify their occupation of Sigeum in the Troad on the grounds that their legendary role in the Trojan War entitled them to a share of the land that had once belonged to Troy (Herodotus 5.94.2). Yet even when the inhabitants of a city were massacred or sold into slavery, or indeed when they were spared but ordered to leave town with literally nothing but the clothes on their backs,[44] the enemy did not always occupy the vacated land. After the sack of Sybaris, the site was flooded to make it uninhabitable; it was not reoccupied until two generations later.[45] The Spartans, having massacred the last remaining defenders of Plataea in 427 BC, found themselves in such a quandary about what to do with the site that, as a stop-gap solution, they handed it over to some refugees for one year. By the end of that period they had hit upon the imaginative expedient of razing the place to the ground, converting the rubble into a temple of Hera with an adjoining large circular two-storey hotel for visitors; the land was leased to farmers from nearby Thebes.[46]

The Athenians were unusual in sending out groups of between a few hundred and a few thousand settlers, so-called 'allotment-holders' (*klêrouchoi*), to occupy the sites of at least a dozen sacked cities and other annexed territories.[47] However, there were clear limits to even the Athenians' interest in land. In their re-conquest of the whole of Euboea in 446, for example, they left most cities alone and took only the territory of Hestiaea and part of the territory of Chalcis. Again, in a campaign which later became a byword for Athenian aggression, they first sacked Mende but made a point of sparing the population and restoring the city to them, then sacked Torone where they enslaved the women and children but spared the men, who were taken prisoner and later allowed to return to their city, and finally sacked Scione where they enslaved the women and children and killed the men, but did not occupy the territory, which they gave away to the survivors of the Spartan sack of Plataea.[48]

Since communities were sometimes annihilated even when the conqueror did not need or want their land, contemporaries were right to attribute such acts of brutality not to greed but to 'anger'. The clearest illustration may be the Athenian sack of Thyrea, the new home in Cynouria of the Aeginetans who had been expelled from their homeland by Athens seven years earlier. All captured Aeginetans were transported back to Athens and there executed 'on account of the enmity which had always existed between them' (Thucydides 4.57.3-4). The destruction of Thyrea brought no territorial gains and little material profit of any kind, and the massacre in cold blood of its inhabitants can only be understood as Thucydides explained it: as an expression of deep-seated hatred.[49]

A city which did seek new land for its citizens most commonly acquired it, not by conquest at the expense of fellow-Greeks, but by establishing new settlements overseas. Greek settlers sailed abroad to found 'colonies' (*apoikia*) all around the Mediterranean and the Black Sea. Once established, some of these new communities invited additional settlers from all over Greece to join in a massive land-grab at the expense of the natives. In the mid-seventh century, 'the scum of all Greece flocked to Thasos' to fight Thracian tribes for the gold mines on the island and the mainland opposite.[50] A century later, a rush to settle in Libya was supported by a startlingly unambiguous Delphic oracle: 'I say unto you: whoever comes to lovely Libya late, when the land has been divided up, he will regret it afterwards.'[51] Some of these ventures were state-organised; others, especially among the earlier expeditions, were private ventures which only later came to be regarded as colonies of a particular mother-city. Either way, the new settlement was always essentially independent. The founding state was owed respect and ritual recognition, as we saw in the case of the Corinthians and Corcyraeans, but it did not exercise direct imperial control over its 'colony'.[52]

Tribute: archaic and classical imperialism

Conquerors sometimes reduced entire defeated populations to a status 'between free men and slaves' (Pollux 3.83) in the archaic period, forcing them to surrender heavy tributes of agricultural produce and submit to a variety of other humiliating duties. The Spartans exploited the Messenians as their labourers and servants, 'helots' (*heilôtai*), after the conquest of Messenia in the seventh century. At least two of the other mainland Greek cities known to have subjected neighbouring communities during the archaic period also employed semi-slave labour forces, and it is likely that there was a connection. Argos exploited a group called 'the naked ones' (*gymnêtes*), who may well have been the inhabitants of the surrounding territories (including Cynouria), conquered c. 700-550 BC, while the so-called 'sheepskin-coat-wearers' (*katônakophoroi*) of Sicyon were probably the inhabitants of nearby Pellene and Donoussa, enslaved c. 600-550 BC.[53] The origins of other comparable groups such as the Laconian helots, the Thessalian *penestai*, and the various dependants found in Crete are obscure, but it is probable that they too were created in the course of piecemeal conquests lasting into the archaic age.[54] Greeks settling abroad reduced native populations to such semi-slavery in at least three places ('probably only a few tips of a large number of nasty icebergs'[55]): at Syracuse in the late eighth century, at Byzantium in the mid-seventh, and at Heraclea-on-the-Black-Sea in the mid-sixth.

Lighter tributes and less humiliating duties were sometimes imposed on another group of subordinate communities known simply as *perioikoi*, 'neighbours'. Sparta had some eighty perioikic communities; Elis and the main cities of Thessaly and Crete each had a smaller but sizeable number of their own. Most *perioikoi* were subjected by conquest, though not all: Elis won Lepreon by offering protection against aggressive neighbours and Epeion by making its previous rulers an offer they could not refuse.[56] The sole figure for tribute cited in classical sources is that of one talent paid annually by Lepreon to Elis, but hellenistic Cretan treaties indicate the other sorts of arrangement that might have existed: Praisos demanded first 10%, later 5%, of the revenues from harbour dues, fisheries and purple production in Stalai, while Gortyn claimed 10% of all Kaudos' annual harvests (vegetables excepted), plus fixed quantities of salt and juniper berries. In addition to paying tribute, *perioikoi*, like serfs, were generally obliged to perform military service for their masters.[57]

From the middle of the sixth century, Sparta and other states usually made of their defeated enemies neither serfs nor *perioikoi*, but subordinate allies, obliged in principle only to provide troops or warships, not tribute. The leading city could, however, impose a special levy to help meet the cost of war, and might allow allies to contribute sums of money *in lieu* of sending men and ships. Special levies did not leave much of a surplus, judging by Sparta's mixed bag of modest contributions from communities and private individuals, paid in silver, wheat and raisins. Substitution payments, on the other hand, were a major source of income for Athens as leader of the Delian League. As the alliance took the field every season and more and more allies chose, or were forced, to contribute money rather than manpower, the payments became in effect an annual tribute (or 'contribution', *phoros*, as it was called). Starting at 460 talents, growing steadily, and raised to about 1,500 talents in 425 BC, this tribute brought in more than sacking a large city every year.[58]

Finally, from the early fifth century onwards, we hear of a few conquering cities which did not impose any form of subjection on their enemies but integrated them as equals into the community. The first known example is the expansion of Syracuse from 484 BC onwards: the entire population of Camarina, half the population of Gela, and the 'fat people' (i.e. the upper classes) of Megara Hyblaea, Naxos and Catana were all made citizens of Syracuse; the lower classes of the last three cities were sold into slavery as being 'most unattractive to live with'.[59] Not much later, Argos began a similar process of 'dissolving Tiryns, Hysiae, Orneae, Mycenae, Mideia and any other little settlement in the Argolid not worth mentioning' and extending citizen rights to those of their inhabitants who did not choose to go into exile.[60] For a while in the early fourth century, Olynthus also, by persuasion, intimidation and force, united many cities in the northern Aegean in a much enlarged state with Olynthian citizenship for all (Xenophon, *Hellenica* 5.2.12-19).

The variety of ways in which Greek communities sought to extend their control over natural resources and manpower produced a bewildering range of systems of domination, from the enduring control over subject populations enjoyed by Sparta and others, to the less long-lived rule over a far-flung alliance exercised by Athens, to the countless 'micro-empires' of Greek cities clinging to power over a few neighbouring towns and villages.[61] Our knowledge of the nature and development of the vast majority of these larger and smaller empires is too patchy to generalise with much confidence, but it does seem as if there was a shift from a heavily hierarchical archaic model of conquest, in which enemies were reduced to serfs or *perioikoi*, to a more egalitarian late archaic and classical model, in which enemies were reduced only to subordinate allies or even incorporated into the citizen body.

The trend was thus towards forms of domination which brought *fewer* economic rewards. The example of Athens, however, shows that it was perfectly possible to extract large amounts of wealth even from subordinate and even notionally equal allies, and the profit derived from long-term control over more manpower and greater natural resources was clearly important enough to rank on a par with honour as a major cause and goal of war.

*

Honour, it must be said, was always the more respectable of the two goals. Even the most blatantly imperialist actions, such as Sparta's conquest of Messenia and Athens' conquest of Lemnos, were defended as acts of revenge for the ultimate insult to collective honour: the Messenians had raped Spartan girls celebrating a festival at the temple of Artemis of the Lake; the Lemnians had raped Athenian girls fetching water from the well *and* abducted Athenian women worshipping at the temple of Artemis at Brauron. Needless to say, the Lemnians and Messenians denied any guilt and blamed their enemies' pure greed for land.[62]

At times honour and profit pulled in opposite directions. This tension was a central concern in the *Iliad* and *Odyssey*: the heroes had to decide at every turn whether to accept rich gifts in ransom and compensation or reject such offers and fully restore honour by killing their enemies and prisoners. In the idealised world of these epics, men always choose reputable honour above less reputable profit.[63] In the real world, the choice was harder. The best illustration is Thucydides' account of the Athenian debate about how to deal with a rebellious ally, Mytilene. The first speaker, Cleon, saw the rebellion as an act of *hybris*, a gratuitous insult, and thus a matter of honour (3.39.4-6). The Mytileneans had begun their revolt by accusing Athens of 'enslaving the Greeks' at that very public occasion, the Olympic Games (3.8, 10.3). Cleon argued that *hybris* required instant retaliation, before one's anger became 'blunted'; if there was a delay, the victims had to remind themselves how strongly they had once felt (3.38.1, 40.4-7). The other speaker, Diodotus, countered that an angry response would indeed be 'just', but a less emotional response, tempered with 'good sense', would be less costly in material terms (3.42.1, 44.1-4, 46.4, 47.5). Instead of taking the issue as a matter of honour and massacring the Mytileneans, he presented it as a matter of weighing costs and benefits and executing only the politicians most directly responsible. Cleon won the first vote; then there was a change of mood and a second assembly produced 'an almost equal show of hands – but Diodotus won' (3.49.1). This time, honour lost out, but only by the narrowest of margins.

Some modern studies argue that profit and honour were merely two aspects of the real ultimate objective of competition, power.[64] It is certainly, and obviously, true that power was a goal of war. 'We believe that it is the way of the gods, and we know for certain that it is universally the way of human beings, by natural compulsion, to rule whatever one can', Athenian representatives are supposed to have said once (Thucydides

32

5.105.2; cf. 1.76.2). They were merely repeating in a more philosophical vein what they had sworn as young men on first joining the citizen militia: 'I shall not hand on the fatherland [to the next generation] in a reduced state, but *larger and stronger*'.[65] Yet to the Greeks power was not an end in itself, but only the means to a further end, which was precisely to win respect and wealth.[66] We should not invert the Greek hierarchy of values, nor gloss over the tension between prestige and profit, by subordinating both to a supposed ultimate goal of power.

Ancient authors often accounted for wars by listing causes, without distinguishing between more and less important factors, and even those who did make such distinctions, like Thucydides, only went so far as to single out 'the truest reason' among a range of causes which were all true to a degree.[67] Modern historians are more inclined to impose a hierarchy on causes, separating mere pretexts from genuine reasons, immediate from profound origins.[68] Still, we can accept the essentials of the ancient view: concerns about piety, justice and the freedom of the Greeks were a significant factor, at least insofar as they provided a legitimate *casus belli* without which it was morally impossible to declare war. The two truest reasons were the love of honour and the love of profit, which varied in relative importance from one case to another, but on balance carried equal weight as causes of war.

3

Pleonexia

Structural causes of war

Only a city of pigs could live in peace with its neighbours, Plato observed (*Republic* 372d). Grazing contentedly on acorns and myrtleberries, the swine would have no need to fight for more land. Human beings, however, need 'couches, tables and other furniture, and fine foods, of course, and perfumes and incense, courtesans and cakes, all kinds of everything' (373a), and as they 'give themselves over to the unlimited acquisition of wealth', they will inevitably seek to expand at the expense of their neighbours. Plato closed his discussion with a triumphant 'We have discovered the origin of war' (373de; cf. *Phaedo* 66c).

Setting aside his reckless oversimplification in reducing all war to conflict over material resources, Plato made a striking point: conflict sprang not from a want of necessities but from greed for luxuries. Aristotle made the same observation in a more balanced fashion, noting that the root of civil war, and by implication all war, was 'greed for more' (*pleonexia*), 'whether for property or honour or both'. 'People commit the greatest acts of injustice for the sake of superiority, not for the sake of necessity', he added.[1]

Great wealth and high status were not only goals of war, but were commonly regarded also as causes of war: a sense of superiority encouraged aggression. 'Surfeit breeds *hybris*' was a proverbial saying repeated by archaic poets,[2] and expanded by Thucydides into 'abundance inspires greed for more through *hybris* and ambition' (3.45.4). In other words, a community which enjoyed prosperity would develop a sense of ambition (*phronēma*) and a feeling of aggressive contempt towards others (*hybris*) which would combine to inspire greed for more and lead to war. This was Herodotus' explanation for the aggression of sixth-century Spartans and Aeginetans, and Thucydides' for the behaviour of fifth-century Corcyreans and Mytilenaeans. Xenophon reported in the same terms on fourth-century Olynthians and Arcadians, remarking that 'god has ordained that people's ambitions grow in direct proportion to their power'.[3] A closer look at some key features of Greek society and culture will show that all these authors were right to believe that their wars were not driven by a struggle for survival, but by open-ended rivalry, always escalating because success only bred a desire for greater success.

A culture of leisure and greed

From the couches and tables to the courtesans and cakes, all the things listed by Plato as required for a civilised life were paraphernalia of the *symposion*, the drinking party, central to an upper-class life style. The Greek ideal was for a man to live his life as a gentleman of leisure, avoid 'money-making' work of any kind, and devote himself to war and politics. When people spoke of 'the poor' (*penêtes*), they did not mean those who lacked the means to survive, but those who worked for a living, as opposed to those who lived a life of leisure. In Aristophanes' comedy *Wealth*, Poverty personified tells the audience that she is not the same as Beggary, and actually represents a healthy and admirable state of being: 'the life of a poor man is an existence of thrift and application to work; he has no surplus, but he does not lack anything either' (552-4). She is booed off stage by the heroes of the play. 'For me, it is better to be rich. You can go and crack your own head open.' 'God, yes! And I want to wallow in my wealth ... and fart on manual workers and their poverty' (611-18). Even when these enemies of poverty were 'poor' themselves, they owned slaves: it was understood that anyone who could afford it would buy slaves to relieve him of as much of his work as possible.[4] In all seriousness, the sixth-century poet Theognis denounced the 'poverty' of a working life as a fate worse than death.[5]

These sentiments were not confined to a narrow elite. The lower classes in Athens, at any rate, aspired to a leisured lifestyle as well, and engaged, as often as they could manage it, in the kind of drinking and sporting pastimes that characterised the upper classes.[6] The state catered for this by subsidising public *gymnasia* and festivals for all. Xenophon proposed to take the next logical step: to do away with poverty altogether by 'creating for every Athenian a suitable livelihood at public expense', a sum of three obols a day. Throughout his long career, Isocrates advocated an even more ambitious programme: a united campaign of conquest which would reduce all barbarians to helots and turn all Greeks into leisured serf-owners.[7]

A society which believes that productive work is undignified, that any self-respecting man should aim to live off the labour of others, inevitably puts a strain on its resources. When Aristotle said that it would require a territory the size of Babylonia to sustain a mere 5,000 families 'in idleness', he was exaggerating,[8] but he had a point: few Greek states had the means to maintain more than a small non-productive upper class.

The strain would have been bad enough if the ambitions of most men had gone no further than a life of simple leisure, but everyone from Solon to Aristotle regarded it as human nature always to want more. 'No clear limit to wealth is set for men: those of us who now have the greatest livelihood double their efforts', said Solon (F 13.71-3 West), expressing the common belief that an abundance of wealth satisfied no one, but only aroused *pleonexia*, greed for still more wealth. This attitude drove the rich and powerful to acts of greed and aggression within their communities. Many usurped ownership of public and private land, turned debtors into bondsmen or sold them as slaves, exploited free labour to the hilt, and generally treated the lower classes with *hybris*. Poets and political thinkers all identified such behaviour as a major threat to the political stability of a city-state, and advocated a culture of 'moderation' as the main solution. Greece's long history of civil wars, often ignited by popular demands for the redistribution of land or cancellation of debt, bears out their analysis of the problem, but shows that their solution was only rarely adopted.[9]

The pursuit of a leisured existence and the competitive, aggressive acquisition of wealth meant that the economic resources of a Greek city, no matter how prosperous, by definition fell short. The relative scarcity created in this way was a key factor driving the Greeks to war. When the limits of exploitation of the internal labour force had been reached, the resources of others were made to take the strain, through raiding, conquest and imperialism. The only time in archaic or classical history that calls for a redistribution of land were heard in Sparta and Athens, in the late seventh century, the ruling classes resorted to wars of conquest to solve the problem. The Spartans embarked on the (re)conquest Messenia, while the Athenians occupied Salamis and Sigeum.[10] Such campaigns not only alleviated economic pressure on the poor, but also helped to reassert the legitimacy of the ruling elite by demonstrating its military leadership qualities. These and subsequent conquests contributed much to the comparative social and political stability which Sparta and Athens enjoyed throughout most of their history.

Absolute scarcity of resources and overpopulation have been cited by some modern scholars as a fundamental cause of war in ancient Greece, and no doubt these factors played a part at times.[11] It is not at all clear, however, that population levels exceeded their absolute limits in most parts of Greece for most of our period. Archaeological evidence suggests, for instance, that by the late seventh century Athenian territory was by no means fully under cultivation: settlement was still spreading as late as the fourth century.[12] Insofar as pressure on economic resources brought about warfare – and of course this was not the primary cause of all wars – absolute shortages were in all likelihood a less pervasive and persistent problem than the relative scarcity created by an essentially parasitical and exploitative set of values.

Xenophon's pamphlet *Ways and Means* proposed a radical scheme to liberate the Athenians from the need to work without resorting to imperialism (1.1), but this still relied on tens of thousands of public slaves being put to work in the silver mines, and the ultimate source of slaves was of course warfare or raiding. Others, like Isocrates, simply accepted that a life of leisure for more than a few could be secured only by means of violence against outsiders.

36

The warrior ideal

Built-in pressures to increase the wealth and enhance the honour of the community made warfare almost inevitable, and martial valour was therefore a vital part of Greek masculinity. Soldiers rallied to a simple cry of 'Be men, my friends!'[13]

The leisured classes in particular were expected to devote themselves to war. For almost a thousand years, since the days of the mythical lawgivers Sesostris in Egypt and Minos in Crete, Aristotle claimed, it had been a fundamental principle of social organisation that 'the community must be separated into classes, a warrior class and a farming class' (*Politics* 1329a40-b35). Greek political thinkers from Hippodamus of Miletus in the early fifth century to Aristotle himself supported a separation between cultivators and soldiers (1267b31-4). Indeed, Aristotle dismissed as unoriginal the scheme for an ideal city proposed by his teacher Plato in the *Republic*, since it amounted to little more than a law that 'the Guardians', the warrior class, 'should not engage in farming – a practice which the Spartans are trying to uphold even now' (1264a9-10). There was no disputing 'that a community which is to have a fine political system must enjoy leisure from the works of necessity', he concluded; the only question was how best to create a docile farming population.[14]

> The cultivators should ideally – in a perfect world – be slaves who are neither all of the same origin nor of spirited character, so that they will be useful in their work and safe insofar as they will not rebel. Second best are barbarian 'neighbours' who are similar in nature to the above (1330a26-9).

Such schemes were close to reality in Sparta, Crete and Thessaly, where citizens did devote themselves to war, politics and leisure pursuits, while serfs cultivated their estates. Spartiates were positively forbidden to work as craftsmen, while in Thessaly farmers and craftsmen were banned from the *agora* where citizens spent their leisure. The ideal of the warrior living at the expense of his serfs was vividly expressed in an archaic Cretan drinking song:

> I have great wealth: a spear, a sword, and the fine leather shield which protects one's skin. For with this I plough, with this I harvest, with this I trample the sweet wine from the vines, with this I am called master of the serfs. Those who dare not hold a spear, a sword, or the fine leather shield which protects one's skin, all cower at my knee and prostrate themselves, calling me 'Master' and 'Great King'.[15]

In most Greek states, including Athens, no sharp separation of soldiers and cultivators existed, but the greatest moral and legal military obliga-

Fig. 2. 'Civilians' wearing swords, on an Attic Late Geometric I kantharos, *c.* 760-735 BC (Athens EPK 630, *left*) and a Boeotian Geometric oinochoe, *c.* 750-735 BC (Athens NM 236).

tions did rest on the leisured classes, even if the warrior ideal also applied to ordinary farmers, craftsmen and labourers.[16]

In early Greece, men were expected to be ready to fight not just on the battlefield but in the streets, to defend their reputations, families and homes. A man did not go anywhere without a sword in the Homeric world: he put it on first thing in the morning and wore it at home and outdoors, at feasts, funerals, games and dances. When he attended a public meeting, he carried a pair of spears as well, and weapons were prominently displayed in his house: seventeen shields and helmets hung on the walls of Odysseus' dining hall, twenty spears stood in a rack by the door.[17] Contemporary vase-paintings show that Greek men routinely wore swords until *c.* 650 BC, and carried spears in public until the late sixth century (Figs 2, 3). Dining rooms continued to be hung with arms and armour, initially on a scale to match Odysseus' display – walls glittering with the shine of bronze and 'the entire ceiling decorated with gleaming helmets' (Alcaeus F 140 West) – but later in a more modest manner, as other forms of decoration took precedence.[18] The gradual disappearance of weapons from civilian life in the course of the archaic period marked a growing central control over the means of violence: rivalries were conducted in less violent ways and conflicts increasingly resolved through courts. This left fewer and fewer legitimate arenas for the display of courage, making the demonstration of prowess in battle a more and more vital proof of masculinity.

By the late seventh century, Tyrtaeus was already proclaiming that no physical or intellectual qualities were of any account by comparison with the courage 'to look upon the bloody slaughter, stand face-to-face with the enemy, and reach out to kill' (F 12.1-2 West). In classical Greece, the word 'manliness' (*andreia*) simply meant courage, and the standard euphemistic phrase for dying on the battlefield was 'becoming a good man'.[19] Speakers in law suits and politicians often tried to influence their audiences by reciting their own military record and disparaging their opponents'. Aeschines went so far as to cite the records of his brother, brother-in-law, and 94-year-old father, as well as his own, while implying

Fig. 3. 'Civilians' carrying spears, on a Siana cup by the Heidelberg Painter, *c.* 550-540 BC (Taranto IG 4408).

that even his mother had more courage than his adversary Demosthenes, 'you who claim to be a man, though I would not dare say that you are a man, since you were charged with desertion'.[20]

As courage in war became an ever more important ingredient of manhood, it was more emphatically denied to women. 'War is men's business', of course, as Hector told his wife in the *Iliad* (6.492), but Homer still presented women as relatively closely involved. They watch the fighting from the walls and the gates, and although they worry for 'their sons, brothers, townsmen and husbands' (6.237-40), they remain composed enough to offer informed comment and advice (3.146-244; 6.431-41). An image on the shield of Achilles shows women actually defending the walls alongside the old men and boys when the men march out against the enemy (18.514-15). The sixth-century poem *The Shield of Heracles*, by contrast, has a different picture of women in war: only the old men stand at the gates, praying; the women are confined to the safety of the walls and have entirely lost their composure: 'the women uttered sharp cries on the well-built towers and lacerated their cheeks' (238-48). This image recurs in classical art (Plate I), but classical sources give the impression that women were generally banned even from the city walls. Aeschylus portrays the female population of a city under attack as running around in a panic, 'screaming and howling' with fear at the mere sound of the enemy. They are warned that women in these circumstances should stay at home, where, instead of undermining the courage of their own men by shouting wildly, they should encourage them by uttering the ritual cry *ololugê*, a kind of high-pitched whooping, from the roofs of their houses.[21]

In practice, women occasionally played a more active role during sieges. The priestess Telesilla's leading role in defending the walls of Argos when the men had been massacred in battle at Sepeia has parallels in other periods of history, and so does the dressing of women as soldiers at Sinope to frighten off the enemy.[22] Whether the role of women in sieges really changed significantly is hard to say, and it certainly seems unlikely that women became more fearful over the centuries, but the important point is that classical Greek men no longer believed women capable of the kind of fortitude which Homer had attributed to them, and therefore proclaimed that a woman's place during a siege was on the roof of her house, at best making encouraging noises or pelting the enemy with rooftiles if he entered town. At worst, women were thought incapable of even this much. Aristotle argued with perfect symmetry that the women of Sparta, whose husbands were superior to other Greeks in war, were inferior to other Greek women, 'no use at all', in the face of an enemy invasion.[23]

The widening of the gender gap made it more imperative than ever that a man should play his part in war, or risk being ridiculed as a passive homosexual (*kinaidos*) or a 'woman'.[24] This in itself constituted another pressure for war. At the start of the Peloponnesian War 'there were many young men in the Peloponnese and many in Athens who, with their lack of experience, were far from unwilling to engage in war' (Thucydides 2.8.1): from time to time, Greek men wanted war because they needed an opportunity to prove themselves.

An army of wanderers: mercenaries, exiles, adventurers

The same factors which drove Greek communities to war also drove individuals to go abroad as mercenaries, raiders and settlers. In a striking juxtaposition of high ideals and grubby realities, Herodotus tells us that the Persians heard about the Greeks competing at Olympia 'not for money but for excellence' from, of all people, 'a few deserters from Arcadia, who lacked the means to live and were looking for employment' (8.26; see p. 26). Like these Arcadians, the majority of those who tried their luck abroad were no doubt poverty-stricken. By 600 BC many Athenians had left the country 'to escape their debts, and no longer spoke the Attic tongue because they had wandered so far and wide' (Solon F 36.10-12). In the fourth century, Isocrates keeps telling us, many Greeks were 'forced to serve as mercenaries because they lack what they need to survive from one day to the next'.[25]

Yet Xenophon claimed that many of his fellow-mercenaries were not poor at all:

> some had come leading their own men, and others were spending their own money; some among them had run away from their fathers and mothers, and others left behind their children in the hope of coming back when they had made money for them, because they had heard that the other Greeks with Cyrus were doing a lot of good business (*Anabasis* 6.4.8).

He was probably optimistic in claiming that 'most' of his comrades were like him in fighting to enrich their already respectable estates, rather than to earn a 'meagre living', but people in that category were certainly not uncommon. One example is Astyphilos, who spent his entire life commanding a band of mercenaries ('whenever he heard that an army was being assembled somewhere, he went abroad to all these places') and after his death in battle was buried by 'his friends and fellow-soldiers', despite owning a sizeable estate in Athens over which his half-brother and cousin proceeded to fight (Isaeus 9.3, 14). Or take the two young Acharnians who, on inheriting their father's estate, married off their two sisters with a dowry of 2,000 drachmas each and then took mercenary service in Thrace. 'When we had made ourselves a name as men who were worth something, and made a bit of money, we sailed back here' (Isaeus 2.6). Insofar as they needed money, it was clearly not because they were poor, but because they had spent so generously to make good matches for their sisters.[26]

As the brothers were eager to point out, their time abroad was not just about making money, it was also an opportunity to make their name, 'since we were of a suitable age'. This suitable age will have been the period between becoming a legal adult at 18 and starting a family of their own, which a man was supposed to do at about 30 years of age. For those whose fathers were still alive, the first dozen years of adulthood were awkward, since they found themselves living at home under paternal authority in a society which greatly valued male independence. In households which employed slaves, moreover, adult sons had no useful economic role to play. The tensions inherent in this situation explain why many of Xenophon's comrades were young men who had 'run away' from their parents: going abroad was a way to make themselves economically independent and stake their claim to manhood in the process.[27]

Yet another contingent of travellers were those who lost out in rivalry for honour and power. Political rivalry and civil war often led to entire families and factions going into exile, and many embarked on a violent career abroad. The poet Alcaeus' brother Antimenidas, during one of the family's several periods of exile, travelled 'to the ends of the earth' and performed heroic deeds as an 'ally' of the Babylonians (F 350 L-P). Many exiles turned to a career of raiding and piracy instead. Even members of Spartan royal families might leave the country in frustration at having to take second place. Dorieus thought it so 'terrible' that his older half-brother ruled over him that he tried to create a new kingdom for himself by leading a group of settlers first to Libya, where the natives drove them out, and then to Sicily, where most of them died fighting. Such was the scale of mobility driven by political conflict that more than 20,000 people were believed to be in exile across Greece in 324 BC: the figure must be a guess, but is not at all implausible.[28]

Oddly enough, modern scholars have often argued that high levels of geographical mobility were peculiar to the fourth century: the Peloponnesian War supposedly caused widespread impoverishment and political instability, triggering a 'mercenary explosion' as vast numbers of men were left with no option but to offer their services as hired soldiers.[29] In fact, the only area which suffered sustained devastation during the Peloponnesian War was Athens, which did not produce many mercenaries, while the vast majority of mercenaries came from Arcadia and Achaea, two regions barely touched by the war at all.[30] More importantly, there is no reason to assume that there were more Greek mercenaries at large in the fourth century than at any earlier time. The kingdoms of Egypt and the Near East had hired soldiers for their expeditionary forces, garrison troops, and rebel armies since the Late Bronze Age, and they had employed Greeks at least since the seventh century. We can only guess at their numbers, but they must have run into the thousands at least. The 10,000 or so soldiers from all over Greece employed by Gelon of Syracuse just before the Persian Wars, at any rate, match the more than 10,000 Greek mercenaries hired by Cyrus soon after the Peloponnesian War.[31]

The most important objection to the myth of the fourth-century mercenary explosion is that we cannot measure poverty and political dislocation by the number of mercenaries alone. We need to consider also the number of men making a living from piracy and raiding, and the number of those migrating to start a new life abroad, or indeed to found a new settlement. These were not fundamentally different categories of people, but part of the same spectrum, shading into one another. Ionians sailed to Egypt as raiders, found themselves hired as mercenaries, and ended up settling there. Mercenaries often turned colonist, and sometimes colonists turned mercenary: Dorieus and his followers, on their way to settling in Sicily, were said by some to have got side-tracked into fighting as 'helpers' in a war in Southern Italy.[32] Whether they were private or public enterprises, new settlements attracted the poor and greedy from across the Greek world – it was, after all, 'the scum of all Greece' who seized Thasos and its mines from the Thracians, and men from all over the Peloponnese and the Cyclades who joined the land-grab in Libya (p. 29) – and thus drew on a large pool of people who might otherwise have turned to mercenary service or piracy.[33]

Clearly, poverty and mobility were nothing new in the fourth century, but constant features of the Greek world. If the proportion of Greeks making a living as mercenaries was higher after the Peloponnesian War, it was not because rising poverty created a greater supply but, as we shall see (pp. 71-5), because the services of mercenaries were in greater demand.

*

The abundance of men, citizens and itinerants, who were prepared – indeed keen – to fight for personal prestige and wealth reinforced the willingness of Greek cities to wage war for the honour and profit of the community. Competition for collective honour and profit was in any case always liable to escalate, as the Greeks themselves saw when they noted that success only bred a desire for still greater success. A military victory which brought new resources and made a city economically significantly stronger than its rivals might make it possible to break out of a cycle of small-scale tit-for-tat warfare which profited neither side in the long run, and to aim for further permanent material gains at the enemy's expense. A military victory which brought great prestige meant that a city in future had a position of greater honour to defend, so that it could tolerate fewer insults or acts of defiance, and was bound to go to war more quickly. All these pressures pointed towards conflict, and if the city-states did not fight even more often than they did, it was not least because they were inhibited by obligations of kinship, friendship, treaty and alliance which, despite the scepticism of ancient and modern Realists, prevented Greek international relations from degenerating into a free-for-all.

Part II

Citizens and Soldiers

When a long-haired man with a distinctive cloak and staff entered Syracuse in 414 BC, people knew that the long-awaited Spartan reinforcements had arrived. His name was Gylippus and, to the amusement of the enemy, he was in fact the *only* Spartan in the entire relieving force. The rest consisted of about 400 helots and ex-helots (*neodamôdeis*) and an array of allies. When further reinforcements arrived next year, they again included a single solitary Spartan citizen, accompanied by 600 helots and ex-helots.[1] In fact, all Sparta's overseas expeditions in the late fifth and fourth centuries involved at most a few dozen Spartiate citizens as commanding officers and advisors, while the fighting was done by mercenaries, allies, ex-helots and the inhabitants of subordinate communities within the territory of Lacedaemon, 'the neighbours' (*perioikoi*), as the Spartans called them.[2]

This extreme reliance on soldiers who did not have full political rights (*perioikoi* and *neodamôdeis*) or no political rights at all (helots, mercenaries and allies) has rightly been called 'a serious breach in the principle of the citizen militia' (Cartledge 1987, 40). Not only in Sparta but everywhere in Greece the ideal was for a city to field armies of citizens only, and, conversely, for all men who played a significant military role to enjoy citizen rights. Specifically, it was felt that a city's most important weapon was generally its heavy-armed infantry, the hoplites, and that this force above all should therefore consist of citizens with equal political rights. If the ideal ought to have been upheld anywhere it was in Sparta, where political, social, economic and cultural life were all geared towards warfare to a degree which seemed extreme even to their mostly admiring fellow-Greeks. Yet the Spartans blatantly ignored their own principles, and they were not alone in doing so.

The general levy for an Athenian incursion into Boeotia in 424 BC, for instance, involved citizens of all classes, resident foreigners, slaves, and any members of allied states who happened to be in the city – in short, just about all available manpower.[3] The entire Athenian cavalry of 1,000 horsemen was present, along with about 7,000 heavy infantry, which meant every single heavy infantry soldier who could be spared from guard-duty on the city walls, and 'many times more' than 10,000 light-armed men, which must have meant the vast majority of the rest of the male population.[4] They were accompanied by 'a great number' of baggage-carriers, slaves serving as the soldiers' personal attendants.[5] There can hardly have been an able-bodied male who on this occasion was not either manning the fortifications or marching in the invasion army. Not every act of war involved quite such a high proportion of men – overseas expeditions, in particular, were necessarily smaller – but mobilisation 'by general levy' (*pandemêi* or *panstratiai*) was common in warfare between neighbouring cities. There was a period when the Athenians invaded next-door Megara twice a year, seven years running, often committing all available man-power.[6]

Greek armies may have been small in absolute terms – numbering in the thousands or tens of thousands, compared to the hundreds of thousands of soldiers in the forces of modern European states, and the millions in the armies of the superpowers – but their relative size was often enormous. The active service of almost every adult male resident during a general levy stands in stark contrast to the proportion of one percent, or less, of the population which typically serves in the regular army of a modern nation-state. Even the infamously high rate of participation reached in the First World War – when in Britain and France the cumulative totals of those who saw active service amounted to almost 50% and 80% of men aged 15-49, respectively – was frequently surpassed in Greek warfare.[7]

Moreover, men were liable to military service for an extraordinarily long time: from the ages of 18 to 60. Contrast, for example, the upper age-limits of 36 and 40 for service in the militias of eighteenth-century Spain and France, or the call to arms of the *levée en masse* of the French Revolution, which extended to 18-25 year-olds only.[8] Early Greek poetry gives us stiff-legged elderly warriors like the 'grizzled' hero Idomeneus, or a Spartan 'with white hair and grey beard', and this is no poetic licence. In a general levy of 418 BC, all Sparta's citizens and their serfs marched to the border, at which point the oldest and youngest were left behind as a home guard, while those aged 20-54 carried on and ended up fighting the Battle of Mantineia.[9] Athens, in the classical period, had vast fortifications to defend and probably committed most men over the age of 40 to service in the home guard.[10] Even so we know of quite a few citizens, including Socrates and Demosthenes, who saw service abroad in and after their forties. According to oral tradition, the most fortunate man who ever lived was an Athenian who died on the battlefield when he was already a grandfather.[11]

Greek city-states thus advocated the use of militias of politically equal citizens while at the same time demanding an exceptionally high rate of military participation by men of very different political, social and legal statuses. Ideal and practice were sharply at odds.

4

Men of Bronze

The myth of the middle-class hoplite

Easily the most prestigious branch of the militia was the heavy infantry. The heavy-armed soldier or hoplite (*hoplitês*), armed for hand-to-hand combat, protected by body armour and a large shield, was an iconic figure in Greek culture, who dominated in art, literature, political discourse and historical writing. His courage in close combat was extolled in the battle songs of Tyrtaeus as the only true form of bravery, indeed the only true form of excellence. His discipline in standing by his comrades in battle was regarded as a characteristically Greek virtue of which Persians and other barbarians were incapable. Even his armour, it was fondly imagined, was so uniquely Greek that foreigners could mistake him for a 'man of bronze'.[1]

Modern scholars usually say that the bulk of the hoplites belonged to a 'middle class'.[2] Up to a point, this must be true: the poorest citizens were excluded from hoplite service because they could not afford the equipment, while the richest citizens were under-represented in the hoplite ranks because many served instead as cavalrymen or as captains of warships, costly duties which only they could perform. But the gap between the *very* rich and the *very* poor was wide, and merely falling between the extremes did not make the majority of hoplites a group of social and economic peers, or a 'middle class' in any meaningful sense. The Greeks thought of their communities as polarised between the rich (*plousioi*) who could afford to live a life of leisure, and the poor (*penêtes*) who needed to work for a living (see above, pp. 35-6). A concept of 'middling' citizens (*mesoi*) did exist, but even Aristotle, in whose theories it played an important part, believed that in reality there were few such people. 'Since in the city-states the middle class is often small, either the propertied classes or the common people are always dominant' (*Politics* 1295a23-6). The hoplite militia, too, far from being a solid middle-class body, was polarised between leisure-class and working-class soldiers.[3]

The development of hoplite arms and armour

The distinction made by the Greeks between hoplites and others was even sharper than our distinction between heavy- and light-armed: it was a contrast between those who were 'equipped' – the literal meaning of *hoplitês*[4] – and those who were not, the 'unequipped' (*aoploi*), 'naked' (*gymnêtes*), or 'light' (*psiloi*). The only piece of equipment carried by the average classical hoplite that was truly 'heavy' was his large round wooden shield, sometimes covered with a sheet of bronze or bronze attachments. Its average diameter of 3 ft (90 cm) and weight of some 15 lbs (7 kg) made it too heavy to be carried with one hand. Instead, the weight was distributed over the entire left arm and shoulder: the bearer thrust his lower arm through an armband (*porpax*) in the centre, grasped a handle (*antilabê*) at the rim, and put his shoulder under the upper edge of the bowl-shaped shield (see Fig. 4). His primary weapon was a six-to-eight-foot spear, its iron or bronze head balanced at the other end by a bronze spike colloquially known as 'the lizarder'.[5] A shield and spear were all that one strictly needed to be able to count as a hoplite, and when in the late fourth century the Athenian state began to issue military equipment to its citizens, a shield and spear were all it provided (*The Athenian Constitution* 42.4). Most soldiers in addition carried a short sword, and in the classical period wore a simple conical helmet, the *pilos*, of either felt or bronze, covering only the top of the head, and a loose tunic, tied with a belt around the waist (see Plate II).

Some soldiers adopted more elaborate body-armour. A range of helmets was available which provided more extensive cover, with neck-guards and cheek-pieces. Bronze greaves could be clipped on to the shins and calves, which might also be protected by a 'shield curtain', a length of cloth suspended from the bottom of the shield. Only a few wore a bronze cuirass, or a corslet of leather or padded linen, over their tunics. Even mercenaries did not usually wear corslets – barely a few dozen could be scraped together among Xenophon's Ten Thousand and in the lavishly equipped Syracusan mercenary army of 399 BC only one in ten men wore a cuirass. There was clearly no standard equipment, beyond shield and spear, and much variation in just how heavily armoured 'heavy' infantry was.[6]

As scholars have traditionally reconstructed the history of hoplite equipment, it follows a perfect arc. Beginning in the late eighth century, we witness the gradual introduction of hoplite armour culminating in the universal adoption of the full hoplite panoply by the middle of the seventh century. Then, from the middle of the sixth century onwards, parts of the panoply begin to be discarded until, by the end of the fifth century, we reach the rather lightly equipped hoplite already described.[7] This tidy picture needs some modification.

In the early Iron Age, before the introduction of hoplite equipment, Greek warriors had been very lightly armoured (see Plate III). They used a variety of lightweight leather or wicker shields, carried by a central handle and a strap around the shoulders; most were either round or of the so-called Dipylon type, which is also round or oval but with scallops taken out of the sides. Crested helmets were worn, probably made of perishable

Fig. 4. Hoplite equipment, as illustrated in a scene of heroic combat (Menelaus and Hector fight over the dead body of Euphorbus). Prominently featured is the hoplite shield with central armband and handle at the rim. The decoration on the inside of the shields is unusual and may not be realistic. As is common in archaic vase-painting, torso, arms and shield are shown from the front or back, while head and legs are shown in profile; for more naturalistic representations, which show the shield leaning against the right shoulder, see e.g. Figs 14 and 15 and Plate IV. All three warriors wear a short tunic, crested helmet, greaves, and the characteristic archaic 'bell-corslet', consisting of a front- and back-plate fitted together with hinges and straps, decorated with incised outlines of chest and stomach muscles.

materials rather than bronze. The only piece of metal armour we come across is a broad belt, the *zôster*, which makes quite a few appearances in the *Iliad*, both as a piece of military equipment and as a precious gift. Otherwise, warriors seem to have worn only tunics, or indeed gone naked. Their weapons were a large sword and either a bow and arrows or a pair of javelins. Some rode to battle on horseback or in chariots, but all fought on foot.[8] Distinctions between heavy-armed, light-armed and cavalry had no meaning yet.

Onto this stage, metal body armour and the heavy hoplite shield made a dramatic entry. Around 720 BC, a man was buried in Argos with a bronze helmet and cuirass, the earliest known in Greece since the beginning of the Iron Age. Bronze greaves, as recent studies have shown, came into use at about the same time, although it used to be thought that they did not appear until two generations later. The last addition was the hoplite shield, by about 700 BC. The hoplite panoply was thus created quite quickly, in the span of a generation.[9]

The availability of body armour did not mean, however, that it was immediately and universally adopted. In some areas, there was no sign of cuirasses or greaves until the middle of the seventh century, while older types of helmets and the metal belt remained in use. More importantly, even those who did make use of the new armour did not necessarily adopt all of it. It is true that in archaic Greek art the great majority of hoplites is fitted out with the entire panoply, but actual finds of armour show that art presented a highly selective image of life. Judging by the hundreds of pieces of equipment dedicated at Olympia, in the archaic period about one in three soldiers wore greaves and one in ten a metal cuirass.[10] In other words, the picture is pretty much the same for the archaic and the classical period, with a minority adopting the full panoply and the majority using only the basics. There was no gradual shedding of armour, merely a change in what artists chose to depict: archaic painters and sculptors preferred glamorous fighters in top-of-the-range armour, whereas their classical successors liked to represent the less elaborate outfits as well.

The development of armour did not stand still, but changes were minor. The most notable development of the sixth century was the introduction of rare additional pieces of armour, upper and lower arm-guards, thigh-guards, ankle-guards, and in Crete also abdominal guards. Such extra pieces were last seen in the early decades of the fifth century, a period which also saw the last of the archaic type of cuirass, which was short and 'bell'-shaped, curving outwards at the waist. It was first modified by adding 'wings' (*pteryges*), leather flaps which provided cover below the waist, and then replaced by a type which not only had the flaps, but was longer and more closely modelled around the waist and abdomen. At the same time, the linen or leather corslet began to appear in art much more commonly than it had done. The long-established 'Corinthian' helmet, which provided the most extensive cover but also restricted sight and hearing, became far less common than the more open models.[11] None of this amounted to a fundamental change in equipment, but it did mean that classical hoplites *looked* rather different from hoplites before the Persian Wars.

The most significant point overlooked in the traditional history of hoplite equipment is that its most basic components, the shield and the single thrusting-spear, were not universally adopted until shortly after the Persian Wars. Until that time, artists regularly represent warriors who carry pairs of light spears, suitable for use as both missiles and hand-weapons (p. 177), or light, so-called 'Boeotian', shields, which are much like the old Dipylon shield, except that they have the hoplite double grip instead of a single central handle (Fig. 5).

These pieces of equipment have been almost unanimously dismissed as an 'extraordinarily persistent' artistic convention without any basis in reality, because it is believed that neither missiles nor light shields were compatible with the hoplite style of fighting. We shall see, when we come to the history of Greek pitched battle (Chapter 12), that there are no grounds for this belief. The objections of some scholars to the shape of the Boeotian shield, and the way in which it is carried, have been convincingly countered by Sir John Boardman.[12] There is thus no reason why the Boeotian shield and the pair of spears could not have been used. Artists do and did have their conventions, but it is one thing to argue that they were selective in what they represented and quite another to say that they continued to represent pieces of equipment that had gone out of existence centuries earlier, especially when these appear, as they often do, in scenes that are otherwise highly innovative and meticulous in showing contemporary detail (see Plate IV and Fig. 5). Moreover, if the Boeotian shield and

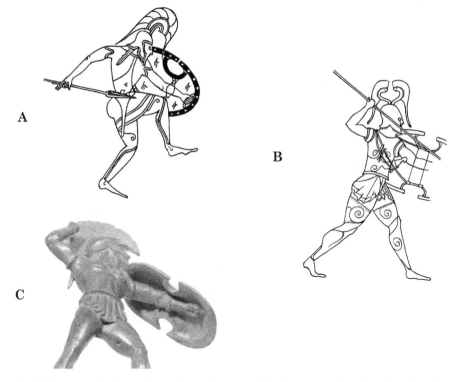

A

B

C

Fig. 5. Boeotian shields, carried with stretched arm. (A) also carries a javelin with a throwing loop. The shield of (B) is suspended from a shoulder strap and has a central grip made of strings rather than metal, which indicates that it is much lighter than the standard hoplite shield. (A) and (B) are stylised representations (see the caption to Fig. 4 above) which show the inside of the shield facing the viewer, as if it were held beside the body and the 'scalloped' edges were at the top and bottom. (C), another view of the statuette shown in Plate IV, presents a realistic profile view in which the shield makes a quarter-turn towards the viewer, along the axis of the stretched arm, and the scalloped edges are at the sides.

the pair of spears had existed only in the minds of artists as symbols marking an image as 'heroic', why did these artists stop applying this age-old custom to heroic scenes in the early fifth century? The evidence makes much more sense if, long after the widespread adoption of the heavy shield and single spear, a minority of hoplites continued to use modified versions of the lighter equipment which had been the norm before the late eighth century.

Archaic hoplites thus ranged from men covered head-to-heels in bronze and armed strictly for close combat to men who were barely more than light-armed infantry. After the Persian Wars both extremes disappeared, but even the classical hoplite was never a uniform creature.

Dress to impress: display and protection

On the eve of Athens' expedition to Sicily, says Thucydides, 'the infantry engaged in very intense rivalry with one another in the matter of equipment and dress' (6.31.3). No doubt Athenian hoplites made a special effort as they set out to fight this new, ambitious war, but their competitiveness was not unusual. Greek states did not, as a rule, issue equipment to their citizens, but each man bought himself the best arms and armour he could afford. The result was a range of outfits as different as the social statuses they represented.

Demand was high enough, especially in a large city such as Athens, to create something of an arms industry – small-scale and primitive by modern standards, but at a level of economic sophistication rarely seen in the ancient Greek world. Military equipment was produced in bulk by large workshops: Lysias' father ran a shield-factory with 120 workers, and 700 shields in stock at the time it was confiscated; Demosthenes' father owned a sword-factory which had more than 30 slave labourers. Indeed, demand in Athens was so high that it could sustain specialist retail traders who sold arms and armour only.[13] In the markets, shops, and bazaars of other cities, too, one could find for sale a 'mass' of weapons, 'piles of shields and boxes full of daggers' (Aeneas Tacticus 30.1-2). Even in tightly organised Sparta, swords were freely sold in the market square, in the ironware section, alongside spits and sickles (Xenophon, *Hellenica* 3.3.7).

The shield and spear which a citizen needed to fight as a hoplite would, at classical prices, set him back about 25-30 drachmas, the equivalent of a month's wages for a skilled worker or soldier.[14] The *pilos* and the leather or linen corslet were relatively inexpensive additions, but the cost of a full classical bronze panoply has been estimated at 75-100 drachmas, the equivalent of about three months' wages.[15] The expense meant that a set of hoplite armour was not just an item of practical use but also a status symbol. In fact, one of the reasons for adopting bronze armour was precisely that it was not cheap. Most pieces were hammered from sheets of bronze less than 1 millimetre thick, so thin that bronze cuirasses did not actually afford better protection than the less costly and less uncomfortable leather and linen alternatives. The bronze sheets fitted onto shields likewise added very little to the strength of the wood.[16] If the Greeks nevertheless preferred bronze, it was because the material lent itself so well to display. Xenophon's explanation of the advantages of a bronze-plated shield was simply that bronze was most easily polished to a high shine (*Spartan Constitution* 11.3).

Conspicuous consumption on the battlefield went far beyond the cost of a basic hoplite outfit. The rich bought ornate and gilded armour, and there were show-offs who decorated their helmets with three crests *and* a pair of ostrich feathers, or boasted about the exotic dye used for their military tunics. Comedy might mock such figures ('if he ever needs to fight in that tunic, it will soon be dyed brown'), but even Xenophon, who set great store by the effectiveness of arms and armour, felt that military equipment should reflect the owner's social status. He himself set out on his mercenary career 'equipped for war in the finest way possible ... since he deemed himself worthy of the most beautiful things'. A preference for the precious to the practical can be traced all the way back to Homer, for whom the material value of armour was so important that he gave some of his heroes expensive, but soft, heavy and quite unsuitable shields of solid gold and greaves of tin.[17]

Armour was meant not only to protect the wearer and display his wealth, but also to intimidate the enemy by projecting a terrifying image. Most types of helmet, though not the *pilos*, had horsehair crests – some early types of crestholder were particularly tall – and their intended effect is clear from the reaction of Hector's infant son to the sight of his father's crest 'nodding frighteningly from the top of the helmet': 'the child shrank back into the bosom of his nurse, screaming' (*Iliad* 6.467-70). What the sight of a polished panoply is meant to do to the enemy is hinted at in mythological fantasies of divine armour too frightening to look at.[18] The effect was enhanced by the modelling, which always emphasised the body's musculature, in stylised outline on archaic armour and in impressively moulded sets of pecs and abs on the 'muscle'-cuirass of the classical age. Decorative elements such as snake patterns on cuirasses, ram's heads on cheekpieces, and Gorgon's heads protecting the kneecaps, all added to the image. The soldier's tunic was often dyed dark red, the colour of blood, a 'manly' shade which 'had least in common with female dress and was most warlike', both because its psychological effect on the wearer would be to make him 'inured to sight of blood flowing', and because it would make his opponent take fright.[19]

Shield blazons, painted, chased in bronze, or even moulded in relief, more often than not sent further threatening messages. Some bore fearsome frontal images of Gorgons staring out at the enemy, fangs bared. Most common, judging by representations in art, were images of animals signalling the soldier's fighting prowess – lion, bull, boar, ram – and deadliness – snake, scorpion, bird of prey. Less directly intimidating emblems emphasised other qualities: a hare, speed; an anchor, steadfastness in action; a fighting-cock, courage; a tripod (the ancient equivalent of a gold medal), ambition. Also common were pictures of a human eye, a symbol thought to ward off danger. A man could choose a blazon to suit his own taste and personality, which produced devices ranging from the wittily understated – a tiny, actual-size image of a fly, playing on the notion that the fly is the bravest of animals because it keeps coming back however often it is brushed aside by a man many times its size – to the outrageously flamboyant – the thunderbolt-wielding Eros on a golden shield ('not a traditional emblem', we are helpfully informed) which advertised Alcibiades' fabled sexual prowess.[20]

Alcibiades' choice of emblem caused a scandal, because it was felt to express aggressive arrogance (*hybris*). Classical accounts of the war of the Seven against Thebes also make much of the elaborate blazons of the enemy leaders betraying boastfulness and aggression, in contrast to both the 'modest' undecorated shield of the wise man, and the simple white-painted shields of the common soldier.[21] The average hoplite was probably expected to adopt a simple and unspectacular blazon, or run the risk of ridicule. As the ordinary hoplite came to the fore in art after the Persian Wars, the trend was accordingly to show 'tame and dull' emblems compared to the 'splendid or terrifying' blazons of the elite hoplites prevalent in archaic representations. One option, first attested on Athenian vases from *c.* 500 BC, was to use a national icon – the trident of Poseidon for Mantineia, the club of Heracles for Thebes – or the initial letter of one's city's name, instead of a personal blazon. One of the earliest images shows a scene from the sack of Troy in which an Athenian hero carries a shield inscribed AΘE, i.e. Athe(ns). It is tempting to see this clumsily added inscription as a sign of a new democratic spirit, claiming the hero as just an ordinary Athenian citizen.[22]

Most hoplite armies must have presented a motley appearance, ranging as they did from soldiers who could afford no more than the cheapest mass-produced spears and shields with simple emblems to the likes of Xenophon and Alcibiades in their ornate, custom-made, highly individualised panoplies. The exception was the Spartan army. In classical Sparta red tunics – not cloaks, as is often claimed – and bronze-faced shields were regulation battle dress, compulsory for all soldiers, including commanders and kings.[23] The shields bore the national symbol of 'glinting *lambdas*', i.e. the letter Λ for Lacedaemon picked out in the bronze (Eupolis F 394 K-A). Military uniformity was part of a general Spartan policy of minimising all forms of display which would show up social and economic inequalities amongst its citizens. Other Greeks admired the principle, but never put it into practice.

4. Men of Bronze

Leisure-class and working-class hoplites

As a warning to rich men so obsessed with making money that they no longer exercise their minds and bodies, Plato vividly sketched two types of hoplite in action (*Republic* 556cd):

> When the ruling class and their subjects find themselves thrown together ... as fellow-soldiers, even in the face of danger they will be watching one another. There, the poor will not in the least be regarded with contempt by the rich; by contrast, a poor man, wiry and sunburnt, stationed in battle beside a rich man who lives his life in the shade and carries lots of superfluous flesh, will often see him breathless and clueless.

Side-by-side with the pampered man of leisure, who will grow fat and enervated unless he makes an effort to keep in shape, we have the working man whose hard physical labour keeps him lean and fit for war. Farmers and shepherds were thought to make particularly good soldiers on account of their healthy outdoor work.[24]

The typical working-class hoplite was probably a small but independent farmer who owned about 10-15 acres of land (4-6 ha), worth 2,000 to 3,000 drachmas, and who could just about afford a hoplite panoply.[25] Craftsmen at a similar economic level also fought as hoplites, although it was alleged that they were 'effeminate' fighters as a result of working indoors, sitting down ('some even spend the whole day in front of a fire').[26] Poorer men would get themselves a shield and spear if they had the chance. Socrates, who had no regular income and whose house and furniture were worth no more than 500 drachmas, nevertheless fought as a hoplite in the large force which laid siege to Potidaea in 432-429 BC and in the general levy which invaded Boeotia in 424 BC. Men in his position, keen to serve but probably unable to afford it from their own means, might be helped out by better-off neighbours and friends.[27]

Despite some sense of respect for the toughness of farmers and shepherds, however, the model hoplite was not the working man whose fitness for war derived from hard labour, but the man of leisure who owed his fitness to dedicated physical and mental training. Those who theorised about the ideal state agreed that soldiers should not cultivate land, or do any productive work, but live off the labour of others and devote themselves to war and politics, and this type of soldier was no figment of political theory, but an idealised version of the leisure-class hoplites who formed a large part of the militia everywhere in Greece (pp. 35, 37).

Military duties, and political rights, were intimately connected with wealth in Greek city-states. Men who met a certain property qualification were legally liable to hoplite service and entitled to full citizen rights, while those who fell below the threshold were exempt from the obligation and denied the rights. In Athens, from 594 BC onwards, the line was drawn at an annual income of 200 measures of farm produce. Above this threshold, the Athenians recognised three property classes, called, in ascending order, *zeugitai* ('yoked men'), *hippeis* ('horsemen'), and *pentakosiomedimnoi* ('500-bushel-men'). These were allowed to hold political office and required to serve as hoplites. Below them was a single large class, labelled *thêtes* ('labourers'), which enjoyed voting rights but was not allowed to hold office, and not under an obligation to fight.[28] Almost every modern study has assumed that the threshold must have been set at a level which included everyone who could afford hoplite equipment, down to the working owner of a ten-acre farm. Reasonable as this assumption may seem, calculations show that it is wrong. Legal liability for hoplite service was actually confined to a much more exclusive social and economic group.

The minimum qualification of 200 dry or liquid measures of produce represents 8 metric tonnes of wheat, or almost 6.5 metric tonnes of barley, or just under 175 gallons (8 hl) of wine or olive oil. A harvest of that size was enough to sustain at least 10 to 15 people, so that a *zeugitês* could easily feed his family as well as several slaves and still retain a sizeable surplus. On average, it would have taken a farm of at least 22 acres (9 ha) to produce this much, an estate which at classical land prices would have been worth some 6,000 drachmas or one talent. This was two or three times as much as the working hoplite farmer owned, and just enough to lift its owner into the ranks of those who could afford to live a rentier's life of leisure.[29] As Aristotle put it, the three top property classes in Athens included only the 'rich' and 'notables' (*Politics* 1274a16-22, 1303a8-10).

Only the Athenian leisured classes, who had the time and means to exercise and go on campaign, were thus under a formal obligation to be available for hoplite service. For the Athenian working class, the *thêtes*, service was optional: it was up to them whether or not they bought hoplite equipment. Given the prestige of serving in the heavy infantry, most will have chosen to buy the necessary arms and armour if they could afford to. Such working-class hoplites would join in general levies and could volunteer their services when an expedition was mounted; in particular it was normally from among these men that Athens recruited the hoplites who fought as marines on board warships.[30]

What proportion of hoplites in the general levy belonged to each class is hard to say, but it is clear that there were thousands of leisure-class hoplites, since forces of up to 3,000 men at a time were levied 'from the list' of those liable to service, and it is equally obvious that there must have been many thousands of working-class men among the *c.* 24,000 citizen hoplites which Athens could muster at the start of the Peloponnesian War. It seems likely that working-class hoplites made up more than half of Athens' heavy infantry.[31]

As Athens became increasingly democratic, political distinctions between the property classes began to be ignored, although they were never officially abolished. Military class distinctions, on the other hand, were maintained throughout until a year or two after the Greeks had been defeated by the Macedonian army in 338 BC. Only then did the Athenian state begin to provide all its citizens with weapons and training at public expense, making it possible for the first time to impose compulsory service also on the working class.[32]

Spartan citizen hoplites were subject to roughly the same property qualification as leisure-class hoplites in Athens. In order to qualify as a full citizen, as one of the 'peers' (*homoioi*), a Spartan was obliged to contribute to the communal messes large amounts of food and drink – enough to feed at least three men – and the annual income required to sustain these contributions seems to have amounted to just over 200 measures of produce.[33] The life of leisure which in Athens was merely possible for those above this threshold was dictated by law in Sparta, where full citizens were forbidden from engaging in any productive work. The political and military position of men who fell below the threshold or otherwise did not qualify as 'peers' is obscure, but we do know that they were called 'inferiors' (*hypomeiones*) and that some resented their lot badly enough to have become ringleaders of an attempted revolt (Xenophon, *Hellenica* 3.3.4-11).

Other oligarchic states also linked political rights and military duties to a high property census. As a rule, service was compulsory for the politically enfranchised rich, who could be fined for not owning arms and armour or for not training, but optional for the excluded poor, who were 'allowed not to possess any equipment' and came under no pressure to take exercise.[34] Aristotle felt that one could strike a perfect balance between oligarchy and democracy by extending political rights and military duties to just over half – the richer half – of the population; he expected that the disenfranchised poor would still happily volunteer for war 'if someone gave them rations'.[35] Through all these variations, the principle is the same: a large section of the working class was capable of serving in the heavy infantry and made a major, voluntary, contribution to the strength of the hoplite militia, but ultimately 'the hoplite force belongs more to the rich than to the poor' (Aristotle, *Politics* 1321a13-14), insofar as only men of the leisure class were legally bound to arm and train and fight.

Hoplite elites: mounted infantry and crack battalions

Not content to distinguish himself with a panoply of 'finest' armour, Xenophon rode a horse worth fifty gold *dareikoi*, more than 1,000 drachmas, when he joined the mercenaries of Proxenos. He fought on foot, but travelled on horseback wherever possible. Even when the troops stood ready in formation before the Battle of Cunaxa, he remained mounted and rode out alone in front of the army to greet their supreme commander. Xenophon was at the time a private soldier, and his dramatic gesture had no point other than to make him conspicuous as one of the few mounted hoplites in the army. Being conspicuous in this way exposed him to some resentment from his comrades, which, by his own account, he was quick to diffuse. When a footsoldier complained about his travelling on horseback, Xenophon immediately traded places and did not mount his horse again until the other soldiers *made* him do so.[36]

Horse ownership set the very rich apart from the rest of the leisure class. The economic gap was not wide, but it was significant: the minimum annual income of the Athenian property class of 'horsemen' was 300 measures of produce, one-and-a-half times as much as that of the regular leisure-class hoplite. A horse cost at least four or five times as much as a full set of armour: 500 drachmas is a common price in surviving classical records, and a horse costing 300 drachmas, a skilled worker's annual income, was embarrassingly cheap. The cost of maintenance was equally prohibitive, since a single horse ate as much barley as six adult men.[37] A four-horse chariot, for obvious reasons, was the ultimate status symbol. In the game of rivalry in the display of costly arms and armour, very rich hoplites like Xenophon could play a trump card by bringing their horses on campaign.

In the archaic period, horse-owners in most states served as mounted infantry, i.e. they fought on foot and used their horses merely to travel to war and back. Among the heroes of the *Iliad*, some are so worried about the risk to their precious horses that they refuse to take them into a war zone (5.192-203), while others are so driven by the desire to advertise their social status and be 'made resplendent by chariot and horses' that they remain mounted even in the thick of the action (12.110-15), but most compromise. They advance to battle in their chariot, but then leave their horses in the care of the charioteer just outside missile range, while they themselves dismount to fight on foot. Archaic art similarly shows heavily armoured men fighting on foot, while at some distance behind them a charioteer stands waiting in his chariot, or, more often, a young attendant on horseback keeps a second horse ready for his master (see Plate XX). This arrangement must be what the sixth-century poet Theognis of Megara had in mind when he greeted the news of war by telling his young friend Kyrnos to 'get the horses ready' (549-53). An indication of the numbers of mounted hoplites in archaic Greece is that Eretria, ruled by an oligarchy called 'The Horsemen', held an armed parade featuring 60 chariots and 600 horsemen as well as 3,000 infantry.[38]

In the classical period, by contrast, most states began to employ horse-owners primarily as cavalrymen, i.e. as soldiers actually fighting from horseback rather than dismounting for combat (see pp. 65-8). This sharply reduced the numbers of horse-owners among those serving as hoplites and perhaps discouraged the remaining few from bringing their horses along, especially in the more democratic and egalitarian city-states. Classical art and literature accordingly barely mention mounted infantry, but most armies probably continued to include at least a few eminent hoplites travelling on horseback, as is evident not only from Xenophon's example, but from the fact that the Athenian expedition to Sicily, which had no cavalry, nevertheless included a transport ship carrying thirty horses (Thucydides 6.43).

First attested at the time of the Persian Wars is another kind of hoplite elite: specially selected and trained regiments of 300 men in Sparta, Boeotia, and Athens. In Sparta, this unit was known as the *Hippeis*, 'Horsemen', and it first appear in the historical record in 479 BC, providing an escort for Themistocles as he travelled home in 'the most beautiful chariot in Sparta'.[39] We first hear of them in combat during the Peloponnesian War, when they fought – on foot – 'before the king'. Selection for service in this special force was so fiercely contested that those who failed to make the grade could not contain their resentment and often provoked successful candidates to fist-fights in the street.[40]

If they had not been fighting on the 'wrong' side, we might know more about the '300 foremost and best' of the Thebans who fought to the death at Plataea (Herodotus 9.67) or about the 300 so-called *Heniochoi kai Parabatai*, 'Charioteers and Chariot-fighters', who formed the front rank of the Boeotian hoplite formation at Delium (Diodorus 12.70.1).[41] The Charioteers' more famous fourth-century successors, the 300 hoplites of Thebes' *Hieros Lochos*, 'Sacred Band', were organised in pairs of 'lover' and 'beloved', fighting side by side, and initially also stationed in the front rank, though later deployed as a separate unit. Like its predecessor, the Sacred Band was unique in Thebes as the only military unit to be kept permanently under arms and in training at public expense.[42]

Athens' elite band of three hundred was well-known in antiquity, but is quite obscure to us. Herodotus introduced 'the 300 picked men' and 'the archers', who together scored a notable victory against Persian cavalry at Plataea, as if they needed no introduction (9.21-22), and they are mentioned in this context by several other sources, but never heard of again.[43] They clearly no longer existed by the time of the Peloponnesian War. Athens was unusual in no longer maintaining an elite unit by then, since, Sparta and Boeotia aside, we know of picked bands also in Syracuse and Elis, and there were no doubt others. For a while, Argos had the most impressive elite corps of all: The Thousand, a body recruited among the richest citizens, which, like the Sacred Band, was kept permanently in training at public expense.[44]

Since they fought on foot, it is curious that the Spartan and Theban crack troops were called 'horsemen' and 'charioteers', and the most obvious explanation is that they originated as units of mounted infantry. The Theban troop may originally have travelled to war in chariots, or else they may have ridden horses, but received their grandiose title in order to distinguish them from the other 'horsemen', the regular cavalry, which the Boeotian cities employed long before it existed in Sparta and elsewhere. One late source also describes Athens' 300 as 'horsemen', and although this is not very reliable information, it is neither implausible nor contra-dicted by any other evidence.[45] If these units did begin life as mounted infantry, they must have been recruited amongst the rich, as was later certainly the case with the picked troops of Argos and Elis: elite forces in every sense.[46]

Archaic art shows mounted hoplites mingling with ordinary hoplites, reflecting a loose military organisation in which rich horsemen fought alongside their less well-off personal friends and dependants, rather than operating in separate units. Elite bands were probably established only in the late sixth century, when army organisation began to be much more centralised (see pp. 233-5). A couple of fourth-century political speeches claimed that Athens had first 'established 300 horsemen and bought 300 Scythian archers' sometime in the first half of the fifth century, which may well refer to the creation of the bands of picked men and archers men-tioned by Herodotus.[47] It is likely that during the Persian Wars, the Spartan, Theban and Athenian bands still operated as mounted hoplites, if they had indeed been established no more than a generation earlier. Classical sources, however, never mention their horses, so the picked men must have become pure footsoldiers not long afterwards.

*

Such is the evidence for a deeply divided hoplite militia which spanned a wide range of social and economic statuses, privately advertised by the soldiers' equipment and publicly recognised by city-states which made legal and political distinctions between 'rich' and 'poor' hoplites, and set apart the very richest citizens by organising them in special infantry units. Against this, the evidence for a solidly middle-class militia amounts to little more than a passage in Aristotle's *Politics* which suggests that hoplites were in general 'middling men' (1297b16-28). That notion is inconsistent with the view, repeatedly expressed by Aristotle elsewhere (and repeatedly cited above), that it is primarily 'the rich' who served as hoplites, and the claim is in any case meaningless in the mouth of a philosopher who was prepared to stretch his definition of 'middling citizen' to include a Spartan regent and member of the royal dynasty 'because he was not a king' (1296a20). The middle-class hoplite army is, in short, a modern myth based on an isolated and ill-founded ancient generalisation.[48]

5

The Other Warriors

Light infantry, cavalry, body-servants
and mercenaries

Herodotus described in loving detail how three hundred Spartan hoplites made their last stand at Thermopylae, sacrificing their lives in the noblest way imaginable. He mentions their serf attendants only to say that one of them pointed his blinded master in the direction of battle, then shamefully ran away (7.229). Yet in the aftermath of battle passing reference is made to helot corpses lying on the battlefield (8.25), from which it seems a fair inference that many had fought alongside the citizen hoplites as light-armed. At Plataea, in the following year, the story more or less repeats itself. This time, to his credit, Herodotus did stress that the Spartan forces included 35,000 light-armed helots and only 5,000 heavy-armed citizens (9.28-9), but in his account of the battle he again entirely ignored this horde of light-armed, right up to the moment when the fallen helots are buried in a mass grave, separately from the citizens (9.85). On neither occasion is there any hint that the serfs might deserve some share in the immortal glory gained by their hoplite masters.[1]

The light infantry of other states suffered a similar neglect, despite consisting of free men. When historians gave detailed information about armed forces, they rarely acknowledged, let alone counted, the mass of ordinary light-armed citizens. Thucydides knew the precise number of Athenian heavy infantry invading Megara, but waved away the light-armed as 'a not inconsiderable crowd' (2.31.2). Xenophon, trying to impress upon the reader the military potential of Thessaly, noted that the region could field 6,000 horsemen and 10,000 hoplites, but would say no more than that its light infantry was 'large enough to take on the whole of mankind' (*Hellenica* 6.1.8, 19). Most battle narratives ignored the light-armed altogether.

Admiration for the bravery of citizen hoplites may have led Greek historians to develop something of a blind spot for other kinds of troops, but we know enough to say that great numbers of poor light-armed citizens almost always fought alongside the heavy infantry, and that in various ways cavalry, personal attendants, mercenaries and other 'helpers' all played a vital military role in ensuring the success of a campaign, and indeed victory in battle.

The role and status of light infantry

A man who could not afford a hoplite shield and spear might still want to equip himself with weapons in case he was called upon to join a general levy, or served as a rower in the fleet. A bow and quiverful of arrows would set him back two or three weeks' wages, only half as much as a basic hoplite outfit. A javelin cost about three drachmas, the equivalent of three days' wages for a soldier or skilled worker.[2] If that was still too much, he could simply pick up stones to hurl or sling at the enemy: numerous references to stone-throwers show that this was common practice.[3] In northern Greece, a type of light infantry existed which differed from the ordinary light-armed citizen in carrying a shield, the crescent-shaped wicker or leather *pelta*, after which they were named 'peltasts', *peltastai* (see Plate V).[4]

Thucydides' allusions to light-armed make it clear that they would turn out in large numbers for general levies in classical Greece, and the appearance of light-armed in the heroic armies of Homer and the early Spartan army of Tyrtaeus' day shows that they had played the same role at least since the seventh century BC.[5] Far fewer light-armed poor probably went out on overseas expeditions in the archaic period, when warships were small and their commanders presumably tried to fill them as far as possible with hoplite soldiers. In the classical period, however, warships were much larger and were rowed by precisely the same classes of poor men and serfs or slaves who also served as light-armed in general levies. When such ships made landings in enemy territory, not only their contingents of hoplites but apparently also most of their rowers disembarked to fight – although the role of rowers as light-armed is almost entirely obscured in the evidence, and unnoticed or even denied by modern scholars.[6]

The classical historians rarely tell us about the role of rowers in combat, except on special occasions. Athenian commanders might convert their rowers into peltasts by providing them with wicker shields, scraped together on campaign (Thucydides 4.9.1) or procured in advance at home (Xenophon, *Hellenica* 1.2.2). A Spartan commander once equipped his rowers as hoplites (Thucydides 8.15, 17.1). But the very fact that it only took a shield to turn a rower into a peltast implies that rowers could be counted on to bring their own weapons as a matter of course. This is confirmed by the Athenian assault on Sphacteria in which the rowers took an active part, 'each equipped as he was' (Thucydides 4.32.2), and the Spartan defence of Aegina in the 380s, during which 'many' of the free men among the ships' crews fought, 'each with whatever weapon he could' (Xenophon, *Hellenica* 5.1.11). It would not have been normal practice for rowers to arm themselves unless it was also their normal practice to disembark and fight as light-armed alongside the hoplites.

Indeed, unless rowers took some part in fighting on land, naval expeditions would not have been viable. The classical warship carried only ten hoplites and four archers, but up to 170 rowers. When the Athenians sent out an expedition of 30 ships to conduct raids on the Peloponnese, as they did in 426 BC (Thucydides 3.91.1), they were employing more than 5,000 rowers in order to transport a mere 300 heavy-armed. Larger expeditions might include an additional 1,000 hoplites or more, sent along in troop transports, but even then the rowers outnumbered the soldiers by far. A fleet needed supplies on a massive scale, and the only way to obtain these in enemy territory was by force. The hoplites would not have been capable of gathering enough for the entire fleet, so the oarsmen would have had to do their own plundering, just as in friendly territory they did their own provisioning. In a letter home, the general Nicias commented on the casualties suffered when his rowers were attacked by the enemy cavalry while out 'gathering wood, pillaging, and fetching water' (Thucydides 7.13.2). Oarsmen were therefore bound to arm themselves to the best of their ability, with knives, swords, slings, bows or javelins.

In these circumstances, it would have been an extreme waste of light-armed manpower if they had not been deployed also in skirmishes, pitched battles, and sieges. Casualties in light-armed combat were low, and the loss of a few oarsmen did not cripple a ship. With little to lose and much to gain by mobilising the rowers, it is unlikely that they would have been kept sitting on the beach in their thousands while a few hoplites did what little damage they could.

What happened in the Athenian assault on Sphacteria – when the top two tiers of rowers, just over a hundred men, from each ship joined the fighting, 'each equipped as he was', while the rest stayed by the ships – cannot have been the exceptional tactic it is usually supposed to be, but must have been common practice in naval expeditions. On the rare occasions when rowers were formally equipped to fight, it was at a rate of a hundred men per ship, presumably the same top two tiers of rowers.[7] If the episodes at Sphacteria and on Aegina *appear* exceptional this is because the combat role of the oarsmen, explicitly mentioned here, was elsewhere taken for granted. The Athenian light-armed who appear out of the blue in the course of naval expeditions against Spartolus, Cythera and Syracuse, for example, surely included the rowers, whose role as light infantry Thucydides could take as read.[8]

The most remarkable failure to acknowledge the presence of light-armed rowers occurs in Thucydides' account of how a horde of Aetolian javelin-throwers slaughtered an Athenian invasion force. He described the Athenian force as consisting of the 300 hoplite marines who served in the fleet of thirty ships, accompanied by an unspecified, but clearly not large, number of allies from Zacynthus, Cephallenia and Naupactus (3.95.2).

One gets the impression that the 5,000-odd rowers of this fleet took no part in the invasion at all. But it is inconceivable that the Athenians would have committed a mere 300 hoplites to the conquest of Aetolia, dispensing with the services of thousands of light-armed when they knew that their weakness was precisely in not having enough trained light-armed (3.97.2). And a tiny force of hoplites only could not have offered prolonged resistance when set upon by javelin-throwers from all over Aetolia (3.97.3). Thucydides' initial description certainly did not give a full picture of the invasion army, since he later attributes a key role to Athens' archers, who had not previously been mentioned (3.98.1). The Athenian force must have included thousands of rowers, and their contribution as light-armed must have been considerable. Thucydides' neglect of these men, in contrast to his praise for the hoplite casualties 'as the best men to be killed during this war' (3.98.4), is on a par with Herodotus' treatment of the helots at Thermopylae as a stark illustration of just how selective ancient historiography could be.

Many of these light-armed citizens did little more than throw stones, and all were left to fight as best they could, without formal leadership or indeed any form of organisation. They clearly did not form the most efficient of forces. Yet a hail of stones and other missiles could make serious dents in the morale and armour of heavy-armed soldiers, especially since hoplites found it almost impossible to counterattack against light-armed. They might try to run after the light-armed as they retreated, but even the youngest and fittest men, weighed down by their shields, could rarely run quite fast enough to catch up. In a direct confrontation with heavy infantry light infantry could inflict particularly severe damage when attacking from the rear or on the right flank. More generally, the mobility and range of light-armed made them better able to operate in rough terrain, and more effective raiders, than hoplites.

For a long time, certainly until the late seventh century and probably throughout the archaic period, hoplites, horsemen and light-armed troops all mingled on the battlefield, fighting in a single, mixed, formation (see Chapter 12). When light infantry eventually began to operate as a separate force, stationed in front of or beside the heavy infantry, it usually found itself pitted against its counterpart in the opposing army rather than against enemy hoplites, which made it easy to dismiss their contribution as a mere side-show to the clash of the heavy-armed. Missile combat between highly mobile crowds rarely saw a decisive result, so that Thucydides, in his narrative of a battle between Athenians and Syracusans in 415 BC, could dismiss the light-armed in a sentence: they skirmished with fluctuating fortunes 'as is usual with these troops' (6.69). But such a dismissive attitude was only possible for those who had light-armed of their own to neutralise the serious threat to hoplites posed by a direct assault by a mob of thousands of stone- and javelin-throwers, slingers and archers.

Hoplite forces suffered famous defeats at the hands of light-armed: the massacre of a small Athenian army by native javelin-throwers in Aetolia in 426 BC; the unprecedented surrender of Spartans to a mass of light infantry, mostly rowers armed *ad hoc*, at Sphacteria in the following year; and the defeat of Athens' hoplites by a barely organised and poorly armed crowd of poor citizens in the civil war of 403 BC. Aristotle was moved to say that light-armed actually found it 'easy' to defeat hoplites (*Politics* 1321a14-26), and even better proof of their potential effectiveness is that many states took the trouble of hiring light-armed mercenaries, especially peltasts. In the Corinthian War, Athens' mercenary peltasts were feared 'as little children fear the bogey-man' by all except the Spartans, and ultimately shook even the Spartans' confidence by slaughtering a regiment of citizen hoplites.[9]

In each case, the victorious light-armed far outnumbered the defeated hoplites, and there was no doubt strength in their numbers even more than in their tactics. Herodotus' figures for the Greek army at Plataea assume that the Greek city-states, many of them fighting quite a long way from home, fielded about as many light- as heavy armed (9.29-30), with Sparta exceptional in mobilising, as we have seen, seven helots for every hoplite. In fighting close to home a larger proportion of the poor was able to serve: at the battle of Delium, at any rate, the 7,000 hoplites on each side were easily outnumbered by the 'more than 10,000' citizen light-armed among the Boeotians, and 'many times more' than this among the Athenians (Thucydides 4.93.3-94.1). Population figures suggest that in Athens those with enough property to serve as hoplites were outnumbered 2:3 by the light-armed poor.[10]

Despite being deployed in large numbers and to some effect, citizen light-armed received little attention or credit from our sources partly because they were not organised, so that it was hard obtain information about them, partly because they were of lower-class status, so that the elite had little interest in finding out about them, and partly because their hit-and-run style of fighting was in direct opposition to the classical hoplite ideal of standing one's ground in battle at any price. Missiles were regarded as effeminate – arrows were like spindles, mere women's tools – and un-Greek.[11] In the concept of 'flight without shame', cited by Plato, we may catch a glimpse of a counter-ideal advocated by the light-armed themselves, but typically it was cited only to be denounced as an outrageous inversion of decent values (*Laws* 706c).

The role and status of cavalry

A cavalryman could equip himself as he wished. Xenophon's *Horsemanship* recommended a pair of javelins and a short slashing sword (12.11-12), but many a rider chose to carry the same sort of spear and sword as hoplites did. The same treatise urged cavalrymen to wear a Boeotian helmet, a specially adapted cuirass, 'the so-called arm' (a left-arm guard substituting for a shield, apparently a recent invention at the time) and leather boots; the horses were to be protected by 'head-, chest-, and thigh-pieces' (12.1-10). However, only helmet and cuirass are regularly represented in art, and even these are not common: most horsemen wear nothing but a tunic, cloak and broad-brimmed hat (*petasos*); most horses have saddlecloths at best (Plate VI). Pressure to be 'beautifully equipped', as cavalrymen could afford to be, must have been offset by a desire to dispense with armour for the sake of greater mobility.[12]

Cavalry tactics relied heavily on throwing missiles during quick, repeated charges and retreats, much like light-infantry combat. Where the hoplite was exhorted to meet his enemy face-to-face, the cavalryman was told: 'we recommend throwing the javelin from the longest possible distance' (*Horsemanship* 12.13). In some forces, the regular cavalry were assisted by mounted archers or *hamippoi*, light-armed soldiers who ran with the horses, holding them by the tail. In pitched battle, horsemen could play much the same role as light infantry, launching missiles against the enemy's vulnerable flanks while protecting their own heavy infantry from attack by opposing horsemen. Above all, cavalry could be devastating in pursuit of fleeing infantry. As Xenophon put it somewhat overenthusiastically, if hoplites did not have the protection and support of their own cavalry in flight and pursuit, 'it was perfectly clear that they would not be able to kill even a single man if they were victorious, and that none of them would survive if they were defeated'.[13]

Its speed and long-range weapons also made cavalry an effective raiding force. The Athenians on occasion sent cavalry to invade neighbouring territory by itself, and took horsemen along even on overseas raids (Thucydides 2.31.3, 56.2; 4.42.1). Equally useful was the ability of cavalry to contain the invading forces of others. By harrying stragglers, horsemen could force an enemy army to stay close together, severely limiting their opportunities to plunder and destroy. The success of the Athenian cavalry in containing the damage done by Spartan invasions during the Peloponnesian War inspired the belief that, without the help of allied cavalry to counter the Athenian threat, the Spartans would not have bothered to invade at all (Thucydides 4.95.2).

On the other hand, there were some practical limitations to what cavalry could do. Much terrain was unsuitable for horses, especially since horseshoes were not used and hardening hooves was a laborious business (*Horsemanship* 4.4-5). The ground might have to be 'made suitable' before horses could be deployed. Also, the lack of saddle and stirrups made it harder to achieve the steady seat needed to fight from horseback. Finally, the cost of keeping horses meant that most cavalry troops were small, outnumbered ten (or more) to one by the hoplites.[14]

The history of cavalry in Greece is rather chequered, varying not only from place to place according to the suitability of the terrain to cavalry combat and the proportion of the population which owned horses, but also over time. Literary and iconographic evidence suggests that most horse-owners dismounted for combat and fought on foot throughout the archaic period. From the early sixth century BC onwards, however, Corinthian and Athenian art featured images of cavalrymen and scenes of fighting on horseback as well (Plate VII and Fig. 21A). At about the same time, or perhaps even earlier, Athens seems to have organised its cavalry to the extent that each of the administrative districts of Attica could be required to provide two horsemen, adding up to a modest force of 96, later 100, cavalry.[15] Cavalry forces are also attested in sixth-century Thessaly and early fifth-century Boeotia and Sicily.[16] Unlike mounted hoplites, who simply joined the regular hoplites in battle, and unlike the light-armed, who mingled with the hoplites in the archaic period (see Chapter 12), cavalrymen required so much room for manoeuvre that they necessarily fought apart from the footsoldiers.

In most of the places mentioned, cavalry forces continued to exist throughout the classical period. Athens invested substantial resources in expanding its cavalry, which from about the middle of the fifth century onwards counted 1,000 horsemen, plus 200 mounted archers.[17] Corinth, however, apparently lost its cavalry in the fifth century. Indeed, there was no cavalry anywhere in the fifth-century Peloponnese until it was adopted 'against custom' by Sparta in 425 BC, because it was the only effective way of countering Athenian raids. Afterwards, it gradually spread until by 370 BC just about every Peloponnesian city-state had its own force.[18] Perhaps cavalry had not existed at all in the Peloponnese before this time, but the case of Corinth suggests another possibility: that cavalry had been used in the archaic period, but was subsequently abandoned for a few generations before being reintroduced.

The main reason for a Greek community to dispense with cavalry was that its mobile, long-range combat tactics, similar to those of the light-armed, gave it a bad name as safe and undemanding in comparison with service as a hoplite. Even where cavalry was prominent, as in Athens, a man who served in the cavalry when he should have been serving in the infantry could be prosecuted for cowardice, while a man who chose to join the hoplites when he could have joined the cavalry could cite this as evidence of his bravery.[19] In Sparta, no self-respecting citizen could be asked to fight on horseback, so when the Spartans were eventually forced to create a cavalry, they adopted a curious system whereby horses were provided by rich citizens, but riders were selected among the 'physically weakest' who were 'least concerned with honour' (Xenophon, *Hellenica* 6.4.11).[20] If Corinth and other Peloponnesian states did indeed disband their cavalry forces at the end of the archaic period, it may have been because hoplite ideals were gaining a new prominence at the time, as we shall see (Chapter 13). Alternatively, the development of cavalry may always have been inhibited by strong hoplite ideals. In any case, the spread of cavalry in the Peloponnese from the late fifth century onwards suggests that in the end these ideals lost out against the evident practical advantages of cavalry which Athens, Thebes, Syracuse and other major Greek powers had long enjoyed.

Shield-bearers and other servants

During a fierce attack by Kurds 'the shield-bearer deserted Xenophon, taking the shield with him' (*Anabasis* 4.2.20). Many months into his mercenary expedition, this is Xenophon's first and last mention of his servant. That rich soldiers employed personal attendants whose existence they barely acknowledged is perhaps not surprising. But it is remarkable that, whereas in modern armies only a privileged few have servants, in classical Greek militias thousands of private soldiers had their own 'shield-bearers' (*hypaspistai*), 'baggage-carriers' (*skeuophoroi*), 'retainers' (*akolouthoi*) and 'attendants' who not only carried arms, armour and provisions, but pitched tents, fetched water, cooked, and even fought.[21]

Every Spartan citizen hoplite had his own attendant, as is clearest from an incident in which a Spartan regiment came under fire and, we are told, the dead and wounded were carried to safety by 'their shield-bearers' (Xenophon, *Hellenica* 4.5.14). Among Athenian soldiers the use of personal attendants was so widespread that each of the 3,000 hoplites besieging Potidaea at the start of the Peloponnesian War received a daily wage of 'one drachma for himself, and one drachma for his servant' (Thucydides 3.17.4). Only after suffering catastrophic reverses in Sicily did Athenian hoplites and horsemen 'themselves carry their own provisions, contrary to normal practice, some because they had no retainers, other because they did not trust them' (Thucydides 7.75.5). It does not follow that *every* Athenian hoplite had a servant: the soldiers serving on these distant expeditions against Potidaea and Syracuse were levied from the leisured classes who were legally liable to military service. Such men could easily afford to bring along an attendant, and no doubt felt that they should. Working-class hoplites, on the other hand, surely could not often afford to keep personal servants.[22]

A Spartan citizen would have a helot serving as his attendant, while an Athenian would normally be attended by a chattel slave, his 'boy' (*pais*). In vase-painting, attendants are usually shown wearing a short cloak, fastened at the right shoulder; boots with bindings much like puttees, reaching halfway up the calves; and either a conical cap (*pilos*) or a broad-brimmed hat (*petasos*; Plate VIII). This was quite a smart outfit – something very similar was worn for travel and riding by wealthy young men – and clearly hoplites pursued their rivalry in conspicuous consumption also through their servants. One impoverished but free young man, already humiliated by being forced to serve his mother's cousin 'in place of an attendant' during the Corinthian War, suffered the further indignity of being accused of looking too shabby when he turned up in 'a cheap cloak and slippers'.[23]

The nice outfit, of course, was not the servant's own and his pay was handed over to his master. An army servant had to be content with whatever rations were allocated to him. The Spartans besieged on Sphacteria negotiated twice as large a food allowance for themselves as for their helot attendants (Thucydides 4.16.1), and when Xenophon's mercenaries got their hands on an abundant supply of dates they selected the best ones for themselves before giving the rest to their slaves (*Anabasis* 2.3.15). There was much worse. The sons of Conon 'emptied their chamberpots and bladders' over other hoplites' servants for producing too much smoke when cooking (Demosthenes 54.4). Even if such treatment was untypical, it is no wonder that during the Sicilian expedition many slaves ran away, and the loyalty of the rest was suspect. The Spartans distrusted their own servants so much that, while on campaign, they never went anywhere without their spears, and stayed near their arms and armour even 'when answering the call of nature' (Xenophon, *The Spartan Constitution* 12.4).

Nevertheless, attendants in art are sometimes shown fighting beside their masters and regularly carry a spear or a couple of javelins. Modern scholars find this hard to believe, mainly because in their picture of the classical hoplite phalanx there is no room in the ranks for light-armed.[24] Yet the formation was probably more open than is usually assumed (see Chapters 12 and 13) and at least a few men in the front line must have kept their servants at their sides, or else the dying question of the Theban general Epaminondas would not have been whether his shield had been rescued from the battlefield by his 'boy' (Diodorus 15.88.6). Not all shield-bearers stayed at the front, but only '*some* of the baggage-carriers' returned to camp after carrying their masters' arms and armour to the battlefield (Xenophon, *Hellenica* 6.4.9). The rest apparently stayed close behind the lines. Hence an army which broke right through enemy ranks, as for example the Thebans did at Coronea, found themselves among the crowd of the hoplites' personal attendants (ibid. 4.3.18). It is a fair assumption that, at the back of the heavy infantry formation, servants and citizen light-armed mingled and threw stones and even javelins at the enemy, over the heads of the hoplites. Like the light-armed, these attendants are bound to have made some impact on battle, but were lucky to get so much as a mention among the casualties. Thucydides' figures for the men who died in the battle of Delium are as good as it gets: 'Athenians: just under a thousand, including the general Hippocrates. Light-armed and baggage-carriers: a large number' (4.101.2).

We may find it hard to imagine that masters would trust their slaves or serfs with weapons and indeed with their lives, but during the American Civil War many soldiers in Confederate armies employed their slaves in exactly the same way, even as they were fighting against the abolition of slavery. American slaves were motivated by a sense of loyalty to their masters and their country as well as the prospect of booty. One black body-servant wrote home:

> If I kin kill a Yankee and git a gold watch, and a pair of boots, my trip will be made. How other niggers do to stay at home, while we soldiers are havin' such a good time is more than I can tell. (Rollins 1994, 8-9)

The helot attendants who allegedly swiped some of the spoils from the battlefield at Plataea and sold them cheaply to Aeginetan traders (Herodotus 9.80) may have felt pretty much the same. In Greece, moreover, slaves fought in the knowledge that deserting to the enemy would not mean freedom but merely a new master.[25] All things considered, unless the odds in war turned overwhelmingly against them, hoplites could by and large rely on the loyalty of their servants, if only because loyalty was a slave's best bet.

Slave attendants had not always been as prevalent as they were in the classical period. There is no sign of them in Homer's epics. A leading Homeric hero was always surrounded by men prepared to help him arm and disarm, relieve him of his shield 'whenever he was overcome by exhaustion and sweat' (*Iliad* 13.709-11), take charge of his spoils and captives, and, in camp, 'to light a fire, chop wood, carve and roast meat, and pour wine – the kinds of thing that inferiors do for their betters' (*Odyssey* 15.322-4). These attendants, however, were not slaves but free men, often men of high status, potential leaders in their own right, and they were not light-armed but 'close-fighting' soldiers.[26] In Homer's armies, personal services were a way of expressing a hierarchy of status and power among the warriors.

The attendants who appear in archaic art, looking after the horses of mounted hoplites, are invariably beardless youths. One famous Spartan vase shows such youths carrying the corpses of bearded hoplites. The pairing of a bearded man and beardless youth in Greek art suggested an older 'lover', who was also a mentor in social and political life, and his pupil and 'beloved', a type of relationship highly prominent in Greek culture. A model of such an erotic and educational relationship was sketched in the poems of Theognis, addressed to his protégé Cyrnus. Theognis did indeed expect his beloved to serve as his attendant in war (549-53). The use of upper-class retainers thus continued in the archaic period, but changed in character: instead of expressing a hierarchy of power and status, the relationship now expressed a hierarchy of age, between experienced warrior and new recruit, which allowed a sexual dimension to develop.[27]

To what extent slave attendants also played a part in war alongside young elite retainers in the archaic period, and when they became the normal type of body-servant, we cannot say. It is likely, however, that the use of slaves as attendants in the army was encouraged by two related developments. One was growing state control over military organisation, which meant that an individual's obligation to serve the state as a soldier came to override any obligation he might have to serve another citizen as a personal attendant. The other development was a growing emphasis on the equality of all citizens, which militated against master-servant relationships between free men.[28] By the classical period, only slaves or serfs were thus available and deemed suitable for service as attendants, and employing a personal servant had become primarily yet another form of conspicuous consumption, a means of advertising the master's status as a gentleman of leisure.

Epikouroi: mercenaries and other outsiders

The Trojan War would have been over very quickly, Agamemnon reckoned, if the Trojans had tried to fight the Greeks by themselves, outnumbered as they were by more than ten to one.

> But they have *epikouroi* ('helpers') from many cities, spear-wielding men who greatly frustrate my efforts and will not let me do what I want to do: sack Troy. (*Iliad* 2.123-33)

The word *epikouroi* was used from Homer to the fifth century for various kinds of foreign soldiers brought in to help fight a war. It included both allies (*symmachoi*), i.e. troops sent publicly by another state, and private forces which did not represent a state and were called volunteers (*ethelontai*) or, if they served for an agreed wage, mercenaries (*misthophoroi*). If one looks at mercenaries alone, as scholars usually do, the historical picture shows sporadic employment in Greece until the late fifth century and then an explosive increase in the fourth, which gives the impression of a fundamental change in attitudes towards the use of outsiders in war. The bigger picture, however, shows that Greek states had relied on foreign 'helpers' of various kinds since the days of Homer and that the rising use of mercenaries corresponded to a declining use of allies and volunteers – not to a decline of citizen militias, despite the alarmist claims made by some fourth-century politicians.

At Troy, the 'far-famed *epikouroi*' are clearly distinguished from the home nation: they belong to different ethnic groups, speak different languages, and are repeatedly said to fight far from home against an enemy who poses no threat to their own homes and families.[29] They do so because they have been 'widely summoned' by the Trojans (*Iliad* 4.438, 10.420), who are paying heavily for their services: 'I gathered all of you here from your cities', says Hector, and 'I exhaust my own people to raise gifts and food, while I build up the spirit of each one of you' (17.222-6). The fabulous riches of pre-war Troy have dwindled, since 'many of our possessions have been sold and have gone to Phrygia and Maeonia' (18.288-92; 9.401-3). The line between allies, volunteers and mercenaries is hard to draw here.

Some of the leaders of *epikouroi* are certainly native rulers and might be acting in a public capacity, but at the same time they are serving as personal guest-friends (*xeinoi*) of Trojan princes (13.660-1; 17.150), just as most of the mercenary commanders who led the Ten Thousand under Cyrus served him because they were his guest-friends. The *epikouroi* clearly expect significant material rewards as well, and a man like Othryneus of Kabesos, 'who had recently arrived after hearing of the war' and offered his services at a high price, comes as close as anyone could in the seventh century to being a mercenary. Even the form of his reward – marriage to a Trojan princess (13.363-82) – is not a fairy-tale motif, but paralleled by a series of marriages between classical Greek mercenary commanders and the daughters of the Thracian chiefs who employed them.[30]

Early Greeks did recognise a distinction between public allies and private supporters, which became even clearer when formal military alliances, *symmachiai*, began to feature in Greek international relations in the sixth century.[31] In practice, however, bands of leaders and personal followers remained a prominent feature even of public armies until at least the late sixth century, and when a community sent aid to an ally it must have relied on one or more of such bands to volunteer their services.[32] The formalisation of military alliances shows Greek states keen to move beyond relying on *ad hoc* support and to secure a long-term, regular supply of external military manpower, but when such help was not available they happily employed the services of private volunteers. A thousand men from Argos, led by a distinguished athlete and champion duellist, came to the aid of Aegina in 491 BC when their government had turned down a request for public military support (Herodotus 6.92.2). Among the East Greek cities and Aegean islands, employing the services of 'barbarian' soldiers was apparently already common practice by the early seventh century, when the stereotypical *epikouros* was a Carian. 'The Carian runs your risks' was a popular expression among the Greeks, who even believed that the hoplite shield had been a Carian, not a Greek, invention.[33]

Mercenaries were not clearly distinct from volunteers in archaic Greece. The line drawn in the classical period between soldiers 'persuaded by pay' and soldiers acting from other, higher, motives[34] was not meaningful at a time when relations between employers, leaders and followers were seen in terms of friendship and reciprocity, rather than reduced to monetary transactions. The story of the first Greeks to serve in Egypt tells how the future pharaoh Psammetichus gained their support because he 'performed acts of friendship' for them and promised future rewards which included allotments of land for everyone (Herodotus 2.152.5, 154.1). A certain Pedon set up an Egyptian statue back home in Priene inscribed with the boast that the king had given him 'a golden bracelet and a city as prizes for his excellence'.[35] The employer's friendship extended primarily to leading men, no doubt, but these in turn were followed by their own friends and personal dependants. The proverbial line 'an *epikouros* is a friend for as long as he fights' (Archilochus F 15 West) sums it up well: the foreign soldier was sought out and rewarded for a specific task, but he was still a friend, not merely a hired man.

The first soldiers explicitly called 'hired men' or 'hired *epikouroï*' by classical and later authors are those employed by archaic 'tyrants', rulers who came to power by *coups d'état*. There is reason to suspect, however, that in describing such troops as mercenaries the sources are guilty of both anachronism and anti-tyrannical bias.[36] A thousand Argives among the supporters of Peisistratos of Athens, for instance, were called 'hired men' by Herodotus (1.61.4) but described elsewhere as volunteers raised by virtue of Peisistratos' marriage ties to a prominent Argive family.[37] Gelon of Syracuse rewarded his leading *epikouroi* so well that several were able to commission victory odes and statues at Olympia to celebrate their sporting triumphs and other glories, and he rewarded even their followers with land and citizenship rather than simply pay.[38] These forces must have been much like the private army brought to Athens in 508 BC by the Spartan king Cleomenes himself in support of his personal friend Isagoras:[39] based on relations of friendship and reciprocity rather than on a mercenary contract.

Whatever their exact status, private foreign forces were employed in large numbers. Modern scholars routinely claim that their use was confined to a few hundred guards for the tyrants' personal protection, except in Sicily where they fought in their thousands in campaigns of conquest.[40] Yet in the mid-sixth century Peisistratos not only had his thousand Argives but volunteers from Naxos and probably also from Eretria and elsewhere as well, adding up to a force large enough for him to defeat a general levy of the Athenian army, 'firmly root his tyranny with many *epikouroï*', and go on to capture Naxos and Sigeum. At the same time, Polycrates of Samos and his successors established their power with 'a great mass of hired *epikouroi* as well as native archers', who fought off a Spartan invasion before being defeated by the Persians.[41] Standing forces of 'spear-bearers' were clearly only the most remarkable aspect of a much wider use of private foreign troops by tyrants and archaic city-states.

In the fifth century, the major wars were fought by the Spartans and Athenians, who at the time could draw on wide networks of allies able to provide a great deal of manpower and a range of specialist military skills. If they rarely hired mercenary soldiers – Athens did of course employ thousands of mercenary rowers – it was simply because they could almost always raise the necessary numbers and kinds of troops from their own resources or those of their allies. Sparta could raise vast numbers of soldiers across the Peloponnese and used mercenaries only for expeditions far outside this range, as we have seen.[42] Athens had an even more far-flung and varied range of allies, and accordingly even less need for hired help. When Athens wanted specialist peltasts, for instance, they could usually be raised from within the alliance: allied Locrian peltasts were meant to counter the Acarnanian light infantry which ultimately defeated the general Demosthenes, and it was allied peltasts and archers who soon afterwards helped Demosthenes win his famous victory over the Spartans on Sphacteria. Mercenaries were hired only when Athens could not count on its usual sources of support, such as in the campaigns in northern Greece of 423-422 BC, when many local allies had deserted, or in its expedition against Sicily, far outside Athens' usual sphere of operations, where local allies were few. Significantly, a mercenary force which arrived too late to join the expedition was sent away on the grounds that it was not worth paying them to fight a campaign closer to home.[43]

Less powerful states did not have the luxury of being able to call on allies almost at will, and if their wars became more ambitious and demanding, they might be forced to turn to mercenaries, as Corinth did when it sent hired troops to defend remote Potidaea in 432 BC (Thucydides 1.60.1). The near disappearance of mercenaries from the fifth-century record is an optical illusion, created by our very detailed knowledge of the wars fought by two states which were exceptional in rarely needing mercenaries, and our almost complete lack of information about the wars of states whose reliance on mercenaries was more extensive and more typical. The slaughter of a mercenary army at Pharsalus at the end of the century illustrates just how skewed our record is: we would be completely unaware of this event if its sheer scale had not so affected the wildlife that it rated a passing mention in Aristotle's *History of Animals* (618b).

By the time of the Peloponnesian War, the foreign troops which were hired did deserve the label mercenaries. The decline of archaic war-bands changed the organisation of private forces serving abroad, just as it had transformed citizen militias: personal obligations were reduced to the point where almost the only tie holding private troops together was a contractual exchange of services for money.[44] Xenophon protested that he and his friends in the army of Cyrus were not in it for the money, and personal relations inevitably did continue to play some part, but his fellow-mercenaries forced Cyrus to renegotiate wages and were available for employment by anyone who offered them a good deal, regardless of previous connections or status. A certain Coeratidas of Thebes briefly became their leader purely on the strength of his ability to provide them with food and lead them to plunder – and they abandoned him at once when his supplies of grain, wine, olives, garlic and onions ran out on the very first day.[45]

The Athenians lost all their allies at their defeat in 404 BC, so when they next needed specialist troops, they resorted to hiring mercenaries on a grand scale, establishing a unit of up to 4,000 peltasts which proved highly successful during the Corinthian War. The Spartans did remain at the head of a large coalition, but their imperialist ambitions outstripped their resources. Sparta's allies became more and more reluctant to provide troops, and were sometimes allowed to substitute money, with which Sparta hired mercenaries.[46] The rival alliances which emerged were comparatively small and formed for defensive purposes only (see pp. 14-15); a state which wanted to raise a large force for an offensive campaign had no choice but to hire soldiers. The length and range of campaigns, and more professional standards of soldiering may all have contributed to the growing prominence of mercenaries in the fourth century, but its main cause was the shrinking and attenuation of networks of alliances.

After the collapse of Spartan hegemony in 371 BC, Greece became so fragmented that committed allies were next to impossible to find, and from then on mercenaries featured in almost every Greek war.[47] By the mid-fourth century there were dire warnings that 'larger and stronger armies are now formed from these wanderers than from people who live in their own cities' and that mercenaries were becoming 'a common terror and a growing danger to us all', on account of the damage they could do when large numbers suddenly found themselves unemployed or fell into the hands of an ambitious general.[48] Anxieties about employing mercenaries, however, were offset by the need for extra manpower as well as an appreciation of the superior fighting skills of professional soldiers. Xenophon even dared argue that the quality of citizen troops improved in the presence of mercenaries who set a high standard of excellence to emulate.[49]

*

The same voices which warned of the mercenary menace complained that professional soldiers were in the process of replacing citizen militias altogether:

> We want to rule everyone, yet we do not want to go out and fight. We start wars against nearly the whole of mankind, yet we do not train ourselves for this purpose, but leave it to stateless exiles, runaways and other drifting miscreants – people who, if anyone were to give them higher pay would follow *them* against us (Isocrates 8.44).

Demosthenes claimed that mercenaries nowadays were waging war 'by themselves' (4.24), and expressed outrage at citizens 'sitting idle, enjoying their leisure and being helpless, while they listen to reports about the mercenaries of General X winning a battle' (3.35). But such claims were made for rhetorical effect, to shame Athenian citizens into taking military action. There was never a genuine danger that citizen-militias would disappear. Demosthenes' comments, for instance, prompted the Athenians to send 2,000 citizen hoplites into a war at Olynthus to which they had previously already committed 6,000 hired peltasts. This was a very large number of citizen hoplites: even during the Peloponnesian War only two comparably remote expeditions, to Potidaea and to Sicily, involved more than 2,000 citizens. What is more, Demosthenes' expeditionary force was sent into action although another citizen levy had already fought a war in Euboea earlier that year.[50] Again, when the Greeks joined forces against Macedonian domination, it was still citizen hoplites and cavalry, no doubt supported by great masses of light infantry and personal servants, which made a stand at Thermopylae, and it was citizen levies which fought the crucial battles in Boeotia, in the same way – if ultimately with less success – as they had once done in the face of the Persian invasion.[51]

If on some occasions mercenaries far outnumbered citizen troops, it was not because the number of citizens seeing active service was small, but because the number of mercenaries was so large. The ideal of the citizen-soldier remained strong enough, to the end of the classical age and beyond, to ensure that citizens felt obliged to take an active part in the wars of their cities, but it was never so strong that it prevented any Greek city from deploying in war every form of manpower which they were able to tap, regardless of whether or not these additional forces enjoyed full, or indeed any, political rights as citizens.

6

Politics and the Battlefield

Ideology in Greek warfare

From the commander-in-chief to the humblest slave attendant, so many different kinds of people contributed in so many different ways to the success of a military campaign that there was plenty of room for disagreement on who played the most vital, decisive role and who therefore deserved to be rewarded with the greatest power and privileges. A character in Euripides' *Andromache* goes so far as to argue that no single man, not even the general, makes a greater contribution than any other, and that military leadership constitutes no claim to political power:

> Oh, what a bad custom we have in Greece! When an army puts up trophies over its enemies, people do not regard this as the achievement of those who did all the work. No, the credit goes to the general, who is just one man wielding his spear among ten thousand others – who does no more than any one man, yet enjoys greater fame. Arrogant men sit in office in the city, thinking that they are better than the common people, when in fact they are nobodies. (693-700)

This was a rare point of view, perhaps confined to the radically democratic climate of Athens in the 420s. More typical were the many Greeks who, throughout the archaic and classical periods, insisted that there ought to be a link between military merit and political power.

Over the centuries, decisive roles in war and politics were claimed for a variety of troop types, and modern scholars have often concluded that military developments drove political change: as new types of forces gained a dominant role in war, new social groups came to power. Our sources, however, betray blatant political bias in discussing the relative merits of hoplites, light-armed, cavalry and navy. Regardless of changes in warfare, everyone was prepared to claim a decisive role in battle for whichever social group they wanted to see in power, and to deny that any other social group played a military role of any significance. This pattern of inventing partisan military justifications for political preferences is already prominent in Homer's epics and finds its most elaborate and influential expression in Aristotle's *Politics*.

77

Aristotle and the citizen-soldier

'The political community must consist *only* of those who possess hoplite arms and armour.' Aristotle could not have put it more clearly (*Politics* 1297b1-2),[1] and he left no doubt either about why his took this view: in good political systems, rulers 'govern to the benefit of the community', but most people have little to offer their community other than martial valour, so 'in this political system those who defend it are the highest power' (1279a26-30, a40-b4). Aristotle was developing an idea which had been widely current in Greece, but which it is surprising to find him reasserting as late as the 320s BC, when it had become quite hard to argue that citizen hoplites were the city-states' main defenders. The navy, light infantry and cavalry had all come to be recognised as indispensable to military success, and for about a generation people had claimed that citizen hoplites were about to be replaced by mercenaries.

Aristotle gave the navy and light infantry short shrift. Granted that every state needed a fleet to defend itself, he said bluntly, the 'naval mob' of rowers and sailors should simply be excluded from political rights – 'there is no need for these people to be part of the *polis*' – and a share in power should be granted only to the few hoplites who served on board warships as marines, 'free men and members of the infantry, who are in charge and control of the ship's crew' (*Politics* 1327a40-b11). He identified naval personnel and citizen light infantry as 'purely democratic' elements, dangerous because of their military superiority: 'being light-armed, they can easily compete with cavalry and hoplites'. His advice was to neutralise the threat by forming upper-class youths into a counter-force of elite light-armed (1321a14-26). It is painfully obvious that Aristotle was not interested in making sure that military roles were fairly rewarded with political power. His chosen criterion for full political rights was a high property qualification,[2] and he merely attributed a decisive military role to those who met it, while refusing to acknowledge the claims of the less well-off.

The only group other than the hoplites which Aristotle was prepared to give some credit was the cavalry, provided by the rich. In some places, 'where the territory is suitable for horses, conditions are naturally suited to setting up a strong oligarchy, for the security of the inhabitants depends on this type of force' (1321a8-12). In the distant past, he added, all Greek communities had depended on their horsemen in war, because hoplites did not yet operate in regular formations and were therefore 'useless', so there had been oligarchies everywhere.[3] This last argument is demonstrably incorrect. Aristotle assumed that in early Greece horsemen fought as cavalry, as they did in his own day; in fact, as we have seen, most rode to battle but fought on foot, so that they were as 'useless' or useful as ordinary hoplites were. Reluctant as he was to acknowledge the role of the poor in

78

war, Aristotle was apparently quite happy to invent a spurious military justification for the power of the rich.[4]

His reputation as a great thinker, model researcher, and man of sound common sense has unfortunately tended to blind historians to the bias in Aristotle's political writings. Modern scholars have often taken his observations on hoplites and cavalry at face value and made them the basis for their own interpretations of Greek military and political history. They have argued that the rise of the hoplite phalanx did indeed give the 'middling' classes the right and confidence to demand political power and led to the creation of the earliest forms of democracy and indeed the city-state itself.[5] Along the same lines, many have thought that the experience of serving in the fleet stimulated the growing political consciousness and organisation among the lower-classes which made possible the rise of radical democracy in fifth-century Athens.[6] Some have taken this line of argument to its logical conclusion and claimed that the spread of mercenaries in the fourth century spelled the end of the city-state: the link between military and political roles was broken, and the *polis* defended by its citizens was soon to be superseded by large territorial monarchies maintained by professional armies.[7]

This is a neat and superficially attractive account of Greek history, but it is little more than a myth, a story of what *ought* to have happened if Greek communities had consistently put into practice the ideal that military duties and political privileges should go hand-in-hand.

War and politics in Greek history

Power in Homer's world lay firmly in the hands of aristocratic 'chiefs' (*basileis*) who mounted debates and made decisions while the common people gathered round and cheered, or walked away in mute disapproval. The chiefs also received gifts of food and drink, and shares of booty from their people. Their powers and privileges were primarily based on hereditary status and wealth,[8] but they were expected to prove themselves worthy of them by upholding justice and excelling on the battlefield,

> ... so that some heavy-armoured Lycian may speak thus: 'They are certainly not without their fame, our chiefs who rule over Lycia and eat fat sheep and drink choice sweet wine; no, their prowess is great when they fight in the Lycian front lines.' (*Iliad* 12.317-21)

Homer's battle narratives suggest that the aristocracy fully lived up to expectations: they were kept in the spotlight throughout and credited with such superhuman strength and divinely inspired courage that they could defend their communities single-handedly, without help from the mass of common soldiers. The poet Callinus projected the same image when he praised a great warrior as a 'bulwark' to his community and 'the equal of the demi-gods', 'because by himself he matches the deeds of many' (F 1.18-21 West). Conversely, commoners were at one point in the *Iliad* denied any military significance: they were beaten into silence and told: 'You are no warrior; you have no strength; you are of no account in war or counsel' (2.198-202).

Yet Homer also offered glimpses of a different perspective. A few chiefs were accused of enjoying their privileges but failing to meet their military obligations: they were 'devourers of the community', 'robbers of sheep and goats among their own people' (*Iliad* 1.231, 24.262). Moreover, Sarpedon, the Lycian chief who made the speech about his duty to fight in the front line, shortly afterwards conceded that he could not win battles by himself:

'Why do you not engage in the rush of battle, Lycians? Strong as I am, it is hard for me to break through by myself ... Follow me! More men do better work.' (*Iliad* 12.409-12)

None other than the great Achilles appealed to the mass of Greek soldiers in the same vein (20.353-7), and one of Aias' many exhortations to the crowd was addressed explicitly to 'everyone', including 'you who are average and you who are rather bad' (12.265-72). The multitude of commoners, despite being kept out of the limelight, can nevertheless be seen to play an active part in Homeric battles, and the poet occasionally acknowledged that the tide of battle could be turned by collective effort as well as by individual heroics. A poem by Archilochus also came down on the side of the ordinary soldier in preferring a commander with the plain looks of a commoner to one with the well-groomed appearance of an aristocrat.[9]

The relative merits of mass and elite in warfare were clearly a matter of debate in the early seventh century. Champions of the hereditary aristocracy stressed the outstanding prowess of the chiefs, while challengers cast doubt on their effectiveness and claimed that the common man played at least an equal part in war. The sceptical view was surely right: battles fought by thousands of men could never have been dominated by a few dozen aristocrats – try as they might to stand out from the crowd in action and in appearance, with their horses and splendid armour. But that did not stop the elite claiming a decisive military role, just as the realities of late classical warfare did not stop Aristotle making the same claim for the hoplites.

By the end of the seventh century, hereditary status was giving way to wealth as the main basis of prestige and power, and political rights were being tied to property qualifications. As before, those who enjoyed political rights were expected to earn them by fighting for their country. From Solon's reforms in 594 BC onwards, everyone in Athens with an annual income of at least 200 *medimnoi* of agricultural produce was entitled to hold office and legally obliged to provide himself with hoplite arms and armour. Similar arrangements existed in Sparta and elsewhere. As we have seen, property qualifications were set at a high level: an estate which produced 200 *medimnoi* could sustain 10-15 people and allowed its owner to live a life of leisure. In other words, political rights and military duties were extended to the leisured class, but not to working-class hoplites, perhaps half or more of the total number of citizens capable in principle of serving as heavy infantry.[10] Nor did the leisured classes share power equally: the highest offices were only opened to all in 457/6 BC, a new privilege which probably came with a new military duty attached: hoplite service abroad in overseas expeditions.[11]

Selective, rather than full, enfranchisement of hoplites was much-favoured by the Athenian upper classes. The oligarchs who briefly ruled Athens in 411 BC proposed to confine political rights to about 5,000 hoplites, on the grounds that these men 'brought the greatest benefit to the city by means of their possessions and persons' (Thucydides 8.65.3). Although the 5,000 are later equated with '*all* those citizens who also provide arms and armour' (8.97.1), Athens probably had more than 12,000 citizen hoplites at the time, and accordingly no fewer than 9,000 men actually turned up to register as members of the 5,000.[12] The reference to serving the community 'by means of their possessions' shows that the oligarchs intended to enfranchise only the wealthiest hoplites. These made up only about half or less of the citizen hoplites available, and so corresponded to all the citizens who met the traditional property qualification and were legally obliged to provide arms and armour. The oligarchs thus turned back the clock and disenfranchised the social classes which over the past generation had informally gained access to political office, working-class hoplites and non-hoplites alike. This earnt them lavish praise from Thucydides (8.97.2) and the author of *The Athenian Constitution* (33.2).[13]

Aristotle similarly thought that the political rights extended to hoplites should not necessarily be extended to all hoplites. His ideal property qualification was set at a level high enough to ensure that the enfranchised only just outnumbered the disenfranchised, whom he expected to continue serving as hoplites happily enough even without political rights, so long as they were decently treated and provided with rations on campaign (*Politics* 1297b2-13).[14]

Being a hoplite was not enough in itself to qualify a man for political rights – neither in Aristotle's hoplite-friendly philosophy nor in democratic Athens.[15] It cannot have been the rise of the hoplite phalanx, therefore, which brought about the emergence of more democratic political systems, as many scholars have thought. In any case, the rise of the phalanx was a far less dramatic development than has traditionally been assumed, since mass participation was a feature of warfare already under the aristocratic regimes portrayed by Homer – and the specific close-order tactics of the classical phalanx did not finally take shape until the fifth century.[16] Instead, structural social and economic change produced timocratic political systems, which were legitimated in the traditional manner by an appeal to military roles: fighting for one's community became a legal as well as moral duty and this duty was extended from a small elite of birth to a broader elite of wealth.

If the military contribution of working-class hoplites could be ignored, so could the role of the rowers. Aristotle's suggestion that among the 'naval mob' only the hoplite marines deserved a share in citizen-rights was foreshadowed in the earliest account of the great naval battle of Salamis, Aeschylus' *Persians*. In a scene-setting dialogue, the Persian queen asks her council of elders what makes Athens such a formidable opponent: 'Do they have such a multitude of men in their army?' The elders answer: 'Indeed, an army of such quality that it has inflicted great damage on the Persians already', and they go on to explain that it consists of hoplite infantry (235-8). This emphasis on the army has so surprised scholars that some have suspected that a reference to the navy must have gone missing from the text somewhere.[17] Yet the same emphasis occurs when Aeschylus recounts how immediately after the sea-battle the marines disembarked on the small island of Psyttaleia and massacred Persian troops stationed there: he describes this hoplite engagement as 'weighing twice as much in the balance' as the entire naval battle (435-71). Later sources cut the events at Psyttaleia drastically down to size,[18] and the fact that Aeschylus could offer his extraordinary assessment in front of an Athenian audience a few years after the battle shows just how easy it was to be selective in awarding credit for military achievements.

The author of *The Athenian Constitution* went so far as to claim that the Areopagus council, composed of ex-officeholders from the highest property-classes, had been responsible for victory at Salamis because they had paid the rowers, and accordingly gained in power (23.1-2). The citizen-rowers at Salamis thus received little recognition at the time and indeed witnessed a retreat from democracy, with the temporary dominance of the Areopagus council.[19]

It was only when Athens moved towards a more and more democratic regime from the late 460s BC onwards that the vital role of rowers began to be acknowledged. The rowers of Salamis featured in Aristophanes' plays as part of an idealised earlier generation, 'our forefathers', 'the soldiers of Marathon', who were credited indiscriminately with naval and infantry victories over Persia. He alluded to 'the men of the top rowing-bench, saviours of the city' (*Acharnians* 162-3) and had a chorus of elderly citizens argue that people who have 'never picked up an oar, spear or blister in defence of our land' should not receive fees for jury-service (*Wasps* 1117-21).[20] The so-called Old Oligarch, who played devil's advocate in putting the rowers' claims to power, offered more a specific acknowledgement:

> This is why the poor and the common people there rightly have more than
> the noble and rich: because it is the common people who row the ships and

who add to the power of the city ... much more than the hoplites and the noble men and good men.[21]

An openly hostile version of the same idea was expressed, inevitably, in Aristotle's *Politics*:

> When the naval mob was responsible for the victory at Salamis and thereby for the hegemony of Athens, which was based on its sea-power, they made the democracy stronger (1304a22-4). They began to have big ideas and took worthless leaders in political opposition to the decent people. (1274a13-15)[22]

All these views were formulated at a time when the oarsmen should, if anything, have been easier to ignore than they had been after Salamis, because the fleet was manned largely by metics, foreigners and slaves. Only a minority of oarsmen were citizens.[23] What had happened in the meantime, however, was a democratisation of politics made possible by the growth of the Athenian empire, which did much to improve the material circumstances of the lower classes. As ever, this development was retrospectively justified by an appeal to their military function – which is why the importance of citizen-rowers was accepted by friend and foe alike when they played a minor role, while it had been studiously ignored when their role was major.

The citizens and soldiers of Sparta

So we return to the 'serious breach in the principle of the citizen militia' committed by Sparta in sending out army after army composed of helots, ex-helots, *perioikoi*, allies and mercenaries all fighting as hoplites, with only a single citizen in charge (p. 45). The Spartans' reliance on men of inferior and non-citizen status is usually explained as a reluctant response to a manpower crisis. The number of Spartan citizens was in steady decline in the classical period, so it is tempting to assume that sheer demographic pressure forced Sparta to abandon its cherished ideals and draw its military manpower increasingly from social groups which were politically underprivileged or indeed disenfranchised.[24]

Yet the *perioikoi*, at any rate, were an integral part of the Spartan army already during the Persian Wars, before manpower shortage became an issue. At Thermopylae, 700 'neighbours' fought and died alongside the 300 Spartans. Herodotus concentrated so hard on immortalising the heroics of the Spartans that he completely neglected to mention these *perioikoi*, just as he almost forgot about the helots. But other sources, no less concerned to glorify Sparta, say clearly that the 300 Spartans were part of a larger group of 'a thousand picked Lacedaemonians', all of whom fell at Thermopylae. Indeed, Herodotus' own totals for the troops stationed here do not to add up unless one adds the 700 forgotten *perioikoi*.[25] Next year, at

Plataea, 5,000 Spartiates and 5,000 *perioikoi* stood side by side, and although they were apparently brigaded in separate units, they stayed together throughout the troop movements before and during the battle, and formed in effect a single contingent of 'ten thousand Lacedaemonians'.[26] Whether the Spartan levy was large or small, then, units of 'neighbours' were an integral part of it by 480 BC at the latest.

At some point between the Persian and Peloponnesian Wars, probably as part of a broad reform of military organisation, the *perioikoi* were even more fully integrated into the Spartan army, and began to serve in the same units as citizens, rather than in separate companies.[27] But this reform merely reinforced the established practice of mobilising non-citizens to fight as hoplites alongside citizens. It marked no fundamental break with the past. It did not even affect the proportion of non-citizens included in the Spartan army in any clear-cut way. At Thermopylae, *perioikoi* accounted for 70% of Lacedaemonian hoplites. At Plataea, it was 50%, but according to Herodotus the *perioikoi* contributed only 'picked' troops, so they were perhaps underrepresented by comparison with Sparta which raised a normal levy.[28] In the fully integrated Lacedaemonian force at Sphacteria in 425 BC *perioikoi* accounted for 50 or 60% of the soldiers, and at Leuctra in 371 BC they once again constituted 70%.[29] The 'neighbours', then, made up half or more of the Spartan army throughout the classical period – despite the fact that they had no political rights in Sparta and no share in the public messes, the educational system, or indeed any part of Sparta's social and cultural life.

This situation clearly cannot be explained as a response to a demographic crisis. It was simply the case that the Spartans structurally relied on large numbers of hoplites who did not enjoy full citizen-rights, in flagrant disregard of the ideals of the citizen militia. 'They allocate them man-for-man to a station alongside themselves, and they even put some in front', fulminated Isocrates in anti-Spartan mode (12.180), adding that they also sent the *perioikoi* out to fight on their own 'when the Spartans themselves are afraid of the trouble, danger, or the length of time of involved', all the while treating them as little better than slaves. This was no doubt an exaggeration, as was the claim that the *perioikoi* were among the many inferior groups ready 'to eat the Spartans raw', but it was true that they were unhappy enough with their fate for some of them to revolt at times.[30]

The mobilisation of helots and ex-helots and the hiring of mercenaries for hoplite service was thus not quite as radical a step as it may seem. Thucydides certainly did not suggest that it was anything new or shocking when he first mentioned the practice in 424 BC, by which time a colony of 1,000 ex-helot hoplites was apparently already established at Lepreon,[31] and another 2,000 helots 'who had been the best men in their service in the wars' had been promised their freedom but were treacherously killed (4.80.3-4).[32] These helot, ex-helot, and mercenary hoplites feature mainly on remote expeditions, as opposed to campaigns within the Peloponnese and central Greece, so even their employment was not driven purely by manpower shortages: the Spartans simply did not like fighting distant wars in person, and happily mobilised groups whose civic status, if any, was still lower than that of *perioikoi*.[33]

*

The pure citizen militia which was the Spartan and Greek ideal did not exist in classical Sparta, and it would be naïve to assume that once upon a time – during the archaic age, for which we have no relevant evidence – it was any closer to being realised.[34] The ideal of the citizen-soldier was always prominent but never became more than a small part of reality. Wars fought exclusively by full citizens, political systems in which power and status were a direct and fair reflection of one's role in war – these things dominated the pages of Plato and Aristotle and the imaginations of countless Greeks, but in the real world the relation between war, state and society was far less neat and simple. All social groups played a part in war at all times, whether as horsemen and ship's captains, as heavy infantry and marines, or as light-armed and oarsmen, and it was not the needs of warfare but the prevailing political and social order which determined who counted for something and who was dismissed as marginal.

Part III

Amateur Armies

The comic potential of an amateur militia trying to measure up to professional standards of soldiering was not lost on Xenophon. In his historical novel *The Education of Cyrus*, a group of aristocratic Persians amuse one another with stories about the clumsiness of commoners newly drafted into the army. Having exhausted the subject of boorish table manners, they move on to the recruits' inability to understand, let alone perform, basic formation drill:

> I put their commander in front, a young lad behind him, and the rest of them where I thought they should go. Then I stood facing the unit and at the appropriate moment gave the order 'Forward march!' And, what do you know, that young lad marched forward right past his commander.
> 'What are you doing, man?' I said.
> 'Going forward, as you told me to,' he said.
> 'I gave the order not just to you, but to everyone!' I said.
> Then he turned round to the men in his unit and said: 'Can't you hear the man ranting? He wants *everyone* to march forward.' So all the men came towards me, straight past their commander. When the commander called them back, they were furious and said: 'Who are we supposed to obey? One tells us to go forward and the other won't let us!'

The squad eventually grasp that they must always 'follow the man in front', but the punchline is that they apply this rule too literally and thereafter tail their commander at all times, trotting after him as he goes about private business (*Education of Cyrus* 2.2.6-9).

This bit of slapstick comedy served to make a serious point which Xenophon never tired of repeating. Although ostensibly about Persia, the story was meant to poke fun at ineffective citizen militias everywhere, including Greece. 'Only the Spartans are true experts in warfare, while the other Greeks in military matters make things up as they go along', he remarked in his treatise on *The Spartan Constitution* (13.5). In his historical work, he stressed that militiamen did not stand a chance against well-trained mercenaries because 'the armies of the city-states contain some soldiers who are already past their prime and some who are not yet fully grown, and of course very few men in any given city take physical exercise' (*Hellenica* 6.1.5). The same theme cropped up in his collection of anecdotes about Socrates, who was supposedly asked by a newly elected general: 'When will the Athenians take physical exercise, like the Spartans? Not only do they neglect their own fitness, but they make fun of people who look after themselves .... In military affairs, where self-discipline, orderliness, and obedience are most vital, they devote themselves to none of these things' (*Memorabilia* 3.5.15, 21).

If in the eyes of a dedicated soldier like Xenophon Greek militias outside Sparta rarely rose above the level of bumbling amateurs, it was not only because of a lack of training, but because of a lack of specialisation and professionalism in all aspects of military organisation. Hierarchy and discipline were usually minimal, combat units unwieldy and loosely structured, mechanisms of mobilisation laborious, and logistics improvised. The superiority of Sparta in all these respects reflected a level of state control over military affairs unmatched in other Greek communities, where military organisation was highly decentralised and left largely to the initiative of private citizens. An important long-term trend in Greek history was the growing power of the state, a process which made an early and dramatic impact in Sparta. Other Greek cities gradually caught up, but by modern standards the power of their governments remained weak and their institutions simple even at the end of the classical period. This low level of state-formation accounts for many of the peculiarities and limitations of the Greek way of war.

7

Bodies of Men

Training and organisation of the militia

Hand-to-hand combat with spear or sword was regarded as 'a manner of fighting which requires enthusiasm rather than skill' even by the most ardent advocate of military exercise (Xenophon, *Education of Cyrus* 2.3.11). Pericles is said to have gone so far as to praise the Athenians for being 'relaxed' in their preparation for war, putting their trust in 'our own native courage', rather than devoting themselves to hard exercise, as their Spartan rivals did (Thucydides 2.39.1, 4). Modern studies, if they do not skip the subject entirely, tend to complain about the lack of evidence for hoplite training.[1] This is because we tend to look in the wrong places, searching for evidence of collective training in weapons- and formation-drill, perhaps even battle exercises, of which there is not a whisper until well into the fourth century. The hoplites' normal training regime was fundamentally different from that of the modern soldier, and as such is hard to recognise although it is well-attested: they took mainly informal, private exercise, most of it aimed at general physical fitness rather than specialist combat skills.

Military organisation was equally undeveloped. 'Almost the entire Spartan army consists of officers above officers', marvelled Thucydides (5.66.4), but his admiration for the Spartans' hierarchy said less about their sophistication than about the organisational simplicity of the other Greeks. Citizen light-armed did not muster in units, and slave attendants did not form a regular 'baggage-train': they simply gathered in crowds. The heavy infantry and cavalry did gradually develop a formal structure, but it remained at a rudimentary level – not only by modern, but also by Macedonian, Hellenistic and Roman standards.

Gymnasium and battlefield

The secret of Sparta's success, wrote Aristotle in the late fourth century, had been that until recently none of the other Greeks had trained for war at all.

So long as the Spartans attended to their laborious forms of exercise, they were superior to others, yet now they are left behind by the rest both in athletic and military contests, for their superiority was not due to their manner of exercising young men, but strictly to the fact that they trained when others did not .... Now they have rivals in their system of education, which they did not have in the past. (*Politics* 1338b25-39)

A generation earlier, Plato had expected his audience to find laughable and 'silly' his view that 'everyone must train for war, not when war has broken out, but when they are living in peace' (*Laws* 829ab, 830b, d). He recommended fixing one day a month, 'whatever the weather', for collective exercises, including sham battles, but noted that 'no such group training and competition is currently to be found in any state at all, except maybe on a very small scale' (829bc, 830d-831b). The Spartan army and small elite units excepted, citizen hoplites did not receive regular centrally organised training until the second half of the fourth century BC.[2]

In the absence of collective training, there was no opportunity to practise any kind of formation-drill – until war broke out and an army actually took the field. Even on campaign drill exercises were not standard practice. They were not unknown, as is evident from both Plato's comments and Xenophon's story of the awkward Persian recruits (p. 87), but they do not seem to have been routine either. If they had been, Xenophon would not have singled out for praise commanders who made their units fight sham battles and rehearse simple movements from column to line and back (*Education of Cyrus* 2.3.17-22), nor would he have felt bound to explain at length how Spartan units and armies executed their manoeuvres (*Spartan Constitution* 11.5-10). Thucydides' explanation of the practical use of pipe music in keeping the Spartan army in orderly formation would have been redundant if his readers had been trained to march in step. Even that basic skill was apparently unfamiliar: most Greeks assumed that the pipers played 'for some religious reason' (5.70).

Weapons-drill could be practised in private and was therefore better established than formation-drill. By the late fifth century one could hire specialist weapons instructors, *hoplomachoi*, who advertised their services by giving exhibitions of their skills, some using gimmicky weapons of their own design.[3] Yet by no means everyone was persuaded of the need to practice the handling of shield, spear and sword. Plato's *Laches* features a lively dispute between two distinguished generals, Nicias and Laches, about the merits of weapons training. Nicias argues that young men should be trained to handle weapons, because it is a healthy and proper form of physical exercise, which makes a man a better fighter, more ambitious, more confident and more frightening to the enemy (179e, 181e-182d). Laches, however, launches into a blistering attack on the instructors as cowards and incompetents, and their art as worthless. His main objection is that there is simply not much of use to be learnt about handling weapons, and he adds that anyone claiming to be a trained fighter will be regarded as a boaster and expose himself to ridicule at the slightest slip-up (182e-184c).

Laches' final rejection of training as pretentious was certainly not shared by either Plato or Xenophon, though his appeal to the general ridicule awaiting the self-proclaimed expert suggests that popular ideology favoured a form of extreme amateurism, hostile to any form of specialised military training. Laches' main, more moderate objection, on the other hand, would have found some sympathy even among those who, like Plato himself, were in favour of military training. In the *Education of Cyrus*, the common men whom Xenophon had portrayed as unable to execute formation-drill are immediately at ease when first encouraged to fight with hand-weapons. Close combat, says one of them, is

> a manner of fighting which, I can see, all human beings know by nature, just as other creatures purely by instinct are good at fighting in their own peculiar way – the bull with its horns, the horse with its hooves, the dog with its teeth, and the boar with its tusks.
>
> Let me tell you, when I was a little boy I would grab a sword as soon as I saw one, and I knew instinctively, without having learnt from anyone, how to hold it. In fact, I used to do that even when they tried to stop me ... and, by Zeus, with my sword I slashed everything I could get away with ... because I thought that it was fun as well as a natural thing to do. (2.3.9-10)

Hoplite hand-to-hand fighting skills were thus supposed to come naturally, and not to require much training. In other words, boys learned to handle weapons so gradually and informally that it seemed as if they had never really had to learn at all.

Most Greek hoplites until the late fourth century came no nearer to being formally trained in the use of weapons than when they practised the war-dance, *pyrrichê*, which mimicked combat movements with shield and spear, performed to high-pitched pipe music.[4] Spears and swords were also used in hunting boars, stags and other large game, and the hunt was praised as a fine way of preparing young men for war. It is worth remembering, however, that in the classical Athenian countryside, at any rate, large game was rare. The most popular pursuit was the deeply unwarlike hare-coursing, in which hares were chased by dogs, caught in nets, and clubbed to death.[5] If such limited and informal training was deemed adequate for hoplites, the general level of competence must have been quite low. It is no coincidence that skill with weapons played little part in Homeric stories of battle. Other epic traditions may dwell on feats of swordsmanship, but in the *Iliad* more often than not a single blow was fatal, and combat was strictly a matter of courage and brute strength.[6]

A well-known story about the Spartan king Agesilaus' tactics in trying to get his troops in top condition speaks volumes about the nature of most hoplite training. The king offered prizes for the best javelin-thrower, the best archer and the best horseman, but among the hoplites the prize was destined for the man 'who had the best body' (Xenophon, *Hellenica* 3.4.16). It is telling that training was encouraged through competition, rather than imposed as a matter of discipline. Even more significant is the fact that hoplites were judged not by their ability as spear- or swordsmen, but by the general fitness, strength, and agility which produced 'the best body'. All-round athletic exercise in the gymnasium – running and jumping, wrestling and boxing, throwing the javelin and discus – was far more prominent than either formation- or weapons-drill. The obligation to possess hoplite equipment was regularly linked with an obligation to take regular exercise in the gymnasium: according to Aristotle, oligarchic states imposed both requirements on the rich, while in Crete slaves were set apart from free citizens precisely by being forbidden both ownership of weapons and access to the gymnasium (*Politics* 1297a29-32, 1264a20-3). Wealthy men exercised in their own and their friends' private sports-grounds; the young and enthusiastic did so on a daily basis. The less well-off paid at least occasional visits to public gymnasia.[7]

In Sparta training was more regimented. All male citizens exercised regularly in organised groups, boys from the age of seven in so-called 'herds' (*boua*), and adult men probably in their mess-groups.[8] On campaign, soldiers exercised twice a day, before breakfast and before the evening meal (*Spartan Constitution* 12.5-6). The Spartans' comparative proficiency in battlefield manoeuvres means that their training must have included some formation-drill, but even in the field athletic exercises were the norm in the Spartan army, as in others. Each regiment had its own running track in camp. A commander killed in the field while 'competing in prowess in the Spartan manner' with a friend was in fact caught by the enemy while throwing the discus.[9] Not much appears to have changed in this respect since the days of Homer, whose heroes 'amused themselves with the discus and the bow and throwing the javelin' when they were not fighting the Trojans (*Iliad* 2.773-5). In keeping with the emphasis on athletic ability, any Spartan victor in the Olympic or other crown games automatically qualified for the elite unit of *Horsemen* (Plutarch, *Lycurgus* 22.4).

In the absence of more specialist training, it is not surprising that ancient authors tried to argue that athletic exercise was a suitable preparation for war, but it will be obvious that the long jump and discus were hardly disciplines tailored to military needs, that running and javelin-throwing were skills which the classical hoplite, who was meant to stand his ground and fight hand-to-hand, was not really supposed to rely on, and that wrestling and boxing were at best of indirect value. Already in archaic poetry there was a strand of thinking which dismissed athletic prowess as next to useless. Athletic exercise was primarily a leisure pursuit for the wealthy, and if it long remained the main form of military training, this is testimony to the strength of the Greek ideal of the hoplite as a leisured gentleman.[10]

As the range of prizes awarded by Agesilaus shows, the light-armed and the cavalry were judged by their skill rather than their general physical fitness. Citizen light-armed were by definition too poor to devote time to specialist training, but many will have picked up shooting and throwing skills while herding animals or complementing their farm work with hunting. Cavalrymen, on the other hand, had plenty of leisure in which to learn the three basic skills listed in Xenophon's manual *The Cavalry Commander*: vaulting onto the horse's back, riding and maintaining a steady seat on all terrains, and throwing the javelin from horseback. Characteristically, riders were largely left to acquire these skills for themselves. The commander's role in weapons training was merely to set a good example by being himself a proficient javelin-thrower, and his role in training riding skills extended only to encouraging his men to practise by taking their horses off-road when riding to and around their farms, 'for that has roughly the same beneficial effect as taking them out on exercises, but is much less trouble'. Simulated battle manoeuvres were occasionally practised, but were a matter of much less interest than the organisation of cavalry parades. Even so, Xenophon suspects, many will find his recommendations 'a lot of work' (1.5-6, 17-26; 8.5). The spirit of amateurism clearly ruled among the cavalry as it did among the hoplites.

Becoming a soldier

A man might train enthusiastically to improve his strength and stamina, pick up basic weapons skills and absorb the Greek military ethos, but none of this could really prepare him for the terror of battle or the deprivations of campaigning. In order to help young men adjust to the experience of war, they were often gradually inducted into military life. In the Homeric world, youths who were regarded as too young to take part in pitched battle might be allowed to gain experience by going out raiding, a slightly less dangerous and traumatic pursuit.[11] Several myths and rituals suggest that it may have been common in archaic Greece for boys from the elite to go through a period of segregation from normal life, by way of a rite of passage into adulthood, which may often have included an element of preparation for war.[12] In classical Crete, an upper-class boy would be subjected to a staged abduction by an older 'lover' with whom he would live in isolation for two months, spending much time hunting, to be awarded the trappings of adulthood, including armour, at the end of the period. In a peculiar twist on such customs, selected Spartan boys took part in the so-called *krypteia*, 'time of hiding', during which eighteen- or nineteen-year-olds were sent out into the countryside within a minimum of clothing and supplies to live rough and survive in hiding for a year or more. Armed with daggers, they would stalk the roads at night trying to catch and kill helots – combining something of a headhunters' coming-of-age ritual with the functions of a secret police.[13]

III. Amateur Armies

The classical Athenian way of preparing adolescents for war was less dramatic, less violent, and more likely to reflect a practice commonly adopted elsewhere. In the fifth century, 'the youngest men', as Thucydides referred to them (1.105.4; 2.13.6-7), presumably the eighteen- and nineteen-year-olds, were assigned guard-duty on the city-walls and in forts on the Athenian border, rather than drafted into field armies. Guarding the city-walls was probably not a regular or full-time occupation unless these were under direct attack, but those stationed in border posts and in Piraeus, Athens' port, the so-called 'patrols' (*peripoloi*), were inevitably taken away from their daily lives for a considerable period of time, during which they might gain some experience of combat in dealing with raiders. One cohort of 'patrols' was used as an ambushing force in a surprise attack on Megara (Thucydides 4.67.2, 5; cf. 8.92.2, 5). They were not, however, subjected to any regular programme of training: in an anecdote set in the late fifth century, when he himself was growing up, Xenophon has Socrates say to an unfit young man: 'just because *the city offers no public military training* is absolutely no reason why you should neglect it in private, too' (*Memorabilia* 3.12.5).

In the fourth century, the institution of the 'patrols' underwent a remarkable development. For a long time, whether or not 'to become a patrol of the territory for two years' must have been a matter of choice, since for the orator Aeschines it was later a point of pride that he had joined as soon as he was old enough, in the late 370s (2.167). In the late 350s, however, Xenophon's pamphlet *Ways and Means* alluded to 'those *instructed to train*' alongside 'those who guard the forts and those who serve as peltasts and patrols of the territory' (4.52). The introduction at some point in the fourth century of a regular military training programme for this age group – the 'ephebes' (*epheboi*, 'young adults') – was one important move away from pure amateurism; the introduction of *compulsory* training and patrol service, apparently around 360 BC, was another. Such training and service could have been compulsory only for members of the leisure class, however, because the ephebes served at their own expense.

Ways and Means proposes that in future ephebes should instead be maintained at public expense, so as to inspire greater dedication to their duties and make the whole city 'better in warfare' (4.51-2). Some fifteen years later, probably in 336 BC, a reform implemented this suggestion. The system of training which resulted entailed eighteen-year-olds being organised in ten 'tribal' groups, stationed in two forts in the Piraeus, and assigned a range of specialist trainers to instruct them for a year not only in *hoplomachia*, but in archery and javelin-throwing, and even in the use of the catapult, the latest technology in siege-warfare. Their second year was spent, as before, manning the forts and patrolling the border. Throughout, the state now paid their living expenses, to the tune of four obols per man per day. What is more, the state provided each ephebe with a basic hoplite outfit, a shield and spear, on completion of his first year of training (Aristotle, *Athenian Constitution* 42.2-5). In principle, everyone could now train and serve as a hoplite, no matter how poor. Surviving rosters show that 500 or 600 ephebes a year signed up, a clear majority of the population.[14]

This reform was almost certainly a reaction to Athens' catastrophic defeat by the Macedonians at Chaeronea in 338 BC. As an attempt to catch up with this far larger and more professional military power, and its successors in the Hellenistic kingdoms, it failed. But its importance as a stage in the historical development of citizen militias cannot be overestimated. It drew a line under the ideology of amateurism which had so long been dominant in Greece, except perhaps in Sparta, but had gradually been losing ground in the fourth century. More dramatically still, in creating an egalitarian militia which in principle embraced all citizens, trained and equipped identically, Athens broke with the tradition of elitism which everywhere in Greece, including Sparta, had until then privileged leisured-class hoplites at the expense of working-class hoplites, cavalry, and the light-armed poor.

War bands and the early state

Just as military training long remained non-specialist and was left to private initiative, so military organisation for a long time consisted of little more than groups of relatives, friends and neighbours joining forces and merging into large combat units under a handful of officers.

The battles of the *Iliad* were fought by bands consisting of a leader and his personal retinue of 'attendants' (*therapontes*) and 'companions' (*hetairoi*). Leading men competed among themselves for followers, and those who agreed to serve under them did so on the basis of kinship or friendship, or as a favour, or because they were afraid to say no. Refusal was taken very personally and could start a violent feud. A Cretan who wanted to be a leader in his own right and refused to serve directly under his king 'as a favour' became the target of revenge attacks on his property, retaliated by assassinating the king's son, and finally left the country to save his life (*Odyssey* 13.256-75). By the same token, one could escape service by making a personal gift to the leaders: one rich Sicyonian gave Agamemnon a racehorse 'so that he would not have to follow him to windy Troy, but could stay at home and enjoy himself' (*Iliad* 23.296-9). Some warriors were close 'feasting-companions' or 'age-mates' but commensality and age were merely two of a wide variety of ties which bound Homer's warriors together.[15]

Epic armies consisted of many war bands, which might temporarily merge with one another or split into smaller groups. Insofar as there was a hierarchy among these units, it was determined by a combination of the leaders' hereditary privileges, the number of their followers, and their

95

personal reputations. The position of a Homeric leader in relation to other leaders and to his followers was much like the position of 'chieftain' known in many pre-state societies. Occasionally a paramount leader gathered the assembled warrior bands into five short-lived *ad hoc* attack columns, but otherwise the organisation was informal and fluid.[16]

War bands were not purely private armies, however, but subject to a degree of community control. Public opinion had a major impact on the choice of leaders and men for an expedition. The two men who commanded the Cretan army at Troy were 'told' to do so by their fellow-countrymen: 'there was no way we could refuse; the harsh talk of the people forced us' (*Odyssey* 14.237-9). When leaders recruited the rest of their armies, they had the authority of the community behind them. Any man who refused to serve might suffer 'the severe penalty of the Greeks' (*Iliad* 13.669), evidently a collectively imposed punishment. And anyone who left the army without permission 'must collect all his property and give it to the people for public consumption' (*Iliad* 18.300-2); in other words, deserters were liable to the confiscation and public sale of their possessions.[17]

There is even a hint, near the beginning of the *Iliad*, of a formal organisation superimposed upon the informal structure of war bands: the old king Nestor suggests that the troops should be arranged 'by tribes and phratries' (2.362-3). His advice is highly praised (369-74) and apparently implemented (437-46), but nothing more is heard of the arrangement. Greek communities divided their people into three or four 'tribes' (*phylai*), often subdivided into 'phratries' (*phratriai*, literally 'brotherhoods'), which were notionally kinship groups with a common ancestor, and the use of such tribes as military units is attested from the late seventh century BC onwards (see below). Nestor's advice may reflect a recent development, not fully integrated into the epic tradition, at the time when the poem was composed.

Formal and centralised military structures emerged in the archaic period, but informal warrior bands could still play a role within the new organisation. The archaic Athenian army was led by the *polemarchos*, 'war leader', an elected annual magistrate, who was supported, according to an oral tradition recorded by Herodotus, by the 'chiefs' (*prytaneis*) charged with mobilising troops and ships in the 48 'ship-districts' (*naukrariai*) of archaic Attica, as early as 630 BC (5.71). This claim was challenged by Thucydides (1.126.7-8) and scholars have been sceptical of it ever since, but an inscribed potsherd of the 480s BC which alludes to these 'accursed chiefs' shows that Herodotus was drawing on a genuine local tradition. The district militias probably merged into four 'tribal' regiments.[18] Liability for hoplite service was formally defined by property census in 594 BC if not earlier. Those who qualified were obliged to equip themselves with hoplite armour; otherwise, they were probably obliged only to join general levies of the militia; smaller overseas expeditions relied on volunteers.[19]

At the same time, networks of friendship, patronage and dependence continued to characterise Athenian society and also penetrated military organisation. A favourite theme in archaic art is the 'departure scene', featuring a mounted hoplite and charioteer, their horses surrounded by half a dozen or so hoplites and light-armed troops (Plate IX). These often represent scenes from legend, but are likely to reflect contemporary war bands consisting of a mounted hoplite, his young squire, and a handful of friends or dependants. In the Persian Wars, a few rich men served on their own private warships with crews of 200, and might have been capable of mobilising similar numbers for campaigns on land. The very rich Cimon fielded a large group of personal friends as late as the middle of the fifth century.[20] Private, informal war bands were slowly on their way out, however. Relations of dependence in Athens were gradually undermined by political, social and economic reform in the course of the sixth century. Departure scenes from the end of the century onwards increasingly show, not a group of warriors, but a single hoplite, sometimes accompanied by a single light-armed man, saying goodbye to his family (Plate X).[21] They imply a new perception of soldiers as individuals fulfilling a duty owed directly to the state, rather than as a members of groups whose military obligations are as much to their relatives, friends and patrons as they are to their communities.

Developments in Sparta initially followed the same pattern. By the late seventh century, the Spartan army, under the supreme command of the kings, fought in three units based on tribes,[22] which in the sixth century may have been replaced by five units based on area of residence.[23] Informal war bands probably continued to play their part within these structures. When the Spartans further formalised and centralised their military organisation, however, military changes were more radical than anywhere else in Greece, with the possible exception of Crete. The reform was later attributed to an ancient lawgiver, the legendary Lycurgus. Yet one key institution, the public mess-groups, was in fact established some time after the middle of the sixth century BC, and it seems likely that the whole system was a creation of the late archaic or early classical period and did not precede developments at Athens by much.[24]

The armies of classical Sparta and Athens

The three military institutions created by Lycurgus, according to Herodotus, were the 'sworn bands' (*enômotiai*), the 'thirties' (*triakades*), and the 'messes' (*syssitia*; 1.65.5). The 'thirties' are otherwise unknown, but the bands and messes were quintessentially Spartan forms of military and social organisation throughout the classical period. Every adult male citizen belonged to a group which met every day in a public mess-hall to share meals in an atmosphere of equality and austerity. It is not at all clear whether these dining-groups formed military units, but they were evidently designed to foster solidarity in the ranks.[25] Every citizen also belonged to a 'sworn band' of some 40 men, about the size of a modern platoon, which was the basic unit of the Spartan army.[26] Their oath probably ran as follows:

> I shall not desert my *taxiarchos* or the leader of my *enômotia*, whether he is alive or dead, and I shall not leave the battlefield unless our commanders lead us away.[27]

Sworn loyalty to state-appointed officers thus took precedence over personal obligations.

Within each *enômotia* there were six designated file leaders, each effectively in charge of an average five men (Xenophon, *Spartan Constitution* 11.4-6). Since rank-and-file formations were the norm in classical Greek hoplite armies, one might have thought that the file would have been a recognised unit everywhere. However, Xenophon took such pains to explain the principle of designating file leaders (not as 'convoluted' as most Greeks thought, 11.5) and its advantages in making possible manoeuvres which even specialists found 'very hard' (11.8), that we must conclude that the practice was not widely known. In other Greek militias, files must have been arranged *ad hoc*, without a recognised leader or any established order.[28]

The hierarchy of units above the level of sworn bands is uncertain, because no two sources say the same thing and their terminology is often vague: the most common terms, *lochos* ('band') and *taxis* ('formation'), are applied to units of widely differing sizes, at different levels of the command structure.[29] The Spartan army of the Persian Wars had an unknown number of *taxiarchoi* ('*taxis*-commanders'); the only one named commanded the '*lochos* of Pitana', one of Sparta's main settlements (Herodotus 9.53.2).[30] In the Peloponnesian War, the Spartan army had nine or more *lochoi* of just over 600 men led by a *polemarchos* ('war-commander'); each of these units was subdivided into four *pentekostyes* ('fifties') and sixteen sworn bands.[31] Xenophon's account of the Corinthian War implies a similar structure: he called the largest unit *mora*, not *lochos* – presumably using the official Spartan name rather than the generic Greek term –, but this unit still consisted of more than 600 men led by a *polemarchos* and subdivided into fifties and sworn bands. Unfortunately the numbers of units are not specified.[32] By the time of the battle of Leuctra in 371 BC, however, there were only six *morai*, each subdivided, according to Xenophon's *Spartan Constitution*, into four *lochoi*, eight fifties and sixteen sworn bands. After 371, Xenophon speaks exclusively of 'the twelve *lochoi*' of Sparta.[33]

One way to explain all this is to posit a series of organisational changes. The army of the Persian Wars had only two tiers: *lochoi* or *taxeis*, subdivided into sworn bands. A change around the middle of the fifth century created the three-tier army of the Peloponnesian and Corinthian Wars, with its *lochoi* or *morai*, 'fifties', and sworn bands. A further reform in the 380 or 370s added a fourth tier: *morai*, then *lochoi*, then 'fifties', then sworn bands. We have evidence for other military changes in the mid-fifth century and in the 370s, as we shall see (pp. 195-7), so it would not be surprising if organisational structures became more complex at these times. The disastrous losses suffered in the battle of Leuctra, however, made it necessary to halve the number of units and shrink the command hierarchy, leaving Sparta with twelve *lochoi*.[34] A military system transformed three times within a century may not fit the ancient myth that Sparta's institutions were age-old and unchanging, but such experimentation and adaptability do fit the ancient and modern picture of Sparta as a state devoted above all else to success in war while grappling with a growing manpower shortage.[35]

In any case, there were several constant features which made the classical Spartan army unique among the amateur militias of its day and a model for mercenary forces and other, later, more professional armies: no operative units larger than about 600 men,[36] subdivisions down to the small platoon-sized sworn band, and files with their own internal structure.

The Athenian militia was always at least one step behind the Spartans, but does seem to have gone through a similar pattern of development in the classical period. In the last decade of the sixth century, the reforms of Cleisthenes transferred most of the political and military functions of the old tribes and *naukrariai* to ten newly created tribes and about 140 so-called 'demes' (city neighbourhoods, villages and rural districts). Troops were now mobilised by deme (see p. 103) and local levies combined to form ten tribal units, each commanded by a *taxiarchos*, elected on an annual basis. In 501 BC, the *polemarchos* was first joined in supreme command, and later superseded, by an annually elected committee of ten *strategoi* ('generals'). The practice of assigning not only political office but military command to elected officers, and indeed to committees, is a striking feature of Athenian democracy.[37]

By the time of the Peloponnesian War, when the assembly decided to send a hoplite force on an expedition, the board of generals and the *taxiarchoi* personally selected every single soldier, up to the number allocated. The men picked were under an absolute obligation to serve: draft-dodging (*astrateia*) and desertion (*lipotaxia*) counted as criminal offences, tried by the army, rather than a regular court of law. The statutory penalty was loss of citizen rights – which meant not only exclusion from politics, but also from public religious ceremonies and from the town square – without loss of property. The court could in addition impose a fine or even resort to confiscation of possessions.[38] Hoplites were now liable to serve not only in general levies but on select, remote, lengthy expeditions, entirely at the discretion of the state.

Perhaps this system was put into place by Cleisthenes, at a time when soldiers were already beginning to be seen as directly obliged to their community rather than to their comrades in informal war bands (above, pp. 96-7), but there are signs that it was a more recent innovation. As late as 457 BC, Cimon – not coincidentally a famously generous patron – was able to form a hundred of his friends into an informal unit which fought as part of a general levy of the Athenian militia in the battle of Tanagra, when he himself was unable to take part:

> They took his panoply and placed it in the midst of their band – and as they stood their ground side by side with a passion, all hundred fell (Plutarch, *Cimon* 17.3-5).

In 456 BC, Tolmides, having been authorised to mobilise 1,000 men for a raiding expedition around the Peloponnese, instead managed to raise a force of 4,000 by telling people that they would be drafted unless they volunteered first, which would look better (Diodorus 11.84.4). Later Athenian expeditions occasionally relied on voluntary service,[39] but we know of no other instance in which the threat of conscription was used a means of raising 'volunteers', and the story makes most sense if at this point compulsory service in expeditionary forces had only recently been introduced. The rules which governed hoplite service by the time of the Peloponnesian War may thus have been introduced only in the early 450s. Military pay was introduced around this time, and in the very year of Tolmides' campaign, 457/6 BC, the right to hold the highest political offices in Athens was extended to all citizens who met the hoplite property qualification – perhaps to compensate for their newly extended military duties.[40]

A second tier of units, subdivisions of the tribal regiments, may have been instituted at about the same time. We have no information about their number or size; all we know is that they were called *lochoi*, and that their commanders were appointed by the *taxiarchoi*, not elected.[41] This is as complex as Athenian military organisation ever became: the *taxeis* and *lochoi* formed the entire hierarchy of divisions. The tribal *taxis* was roughly the size of a modern British regiment or American battalion: in the field army at Delium, for instance, it consisted of an average 700 men. The *lochos* presumably consisted of at least 100 soldiers. In modern terms, it is as if there were no units smaller than the company, and no officers below the rank of captain: no platoons or sections, no lieutenants, sergeants or corporals.[42]

The military hierarchy was not only simpler in Athens than in Sparta, but also less powerful. Whereas the Spartans swore loyalty to their officers, the Athenians, if they took an oath at all, swore loyalty to their fellow-soldiers.[43] Punishments for desertion, although severe, were not systematically enforced. In the absence of a public prosecutor, it was up to private individuals to take one another to court, and they would rarely do so unless they were motivated by personal hostility. Demosthenes was once charged with desertion by a group of his enemies, but the case never came to court. One of his prosecutors had allegedly been bought off, and was later found dead – brutally murdered and mutilated by a madman who, by some strange coincidence, had once been a friend of Demosthenes'.[44]

8

The Bare Necessities

Mobilisation and maintenance of armies

The process of mobilising the militia for a military expedition in classical Athens, as mockingly described by Aristophanes, left a great deal to chance and to private initiative:

> The expedition leaves tomorrow, but here is a man who has not yet bought his provisions, because he has no idea that he is going. Then he looks at the call-up list posted at the statue of Pandion – and sees his own name. He runs off in a helpless panic, with a face as sour as fig-juice at the thought of his bad luck. (*Peace* 1181-4)[1]

Raising, feeding and controlling an army is never a simple matter. In Greece, where soldiers and commanders were not only amateurs but more or less one another's equals, and where each man was expected to provide not only his own equipment but his own provisions and supplies, mobilising and managing an army from the militia was quite a challenge. Most citizens could not afford to spend much time away from their families, properties and other business; in particular, farmers were available for military service only during the slack agricultural period between the grain harvest in May and the vintage in September, or the ploughing in November at the latest. Adequate supplies could not usually be found for more than a few weeks at a time. Discipline – never strong – weakened as conditions deteriorated and provisions ran out. For all these reasons, there were serious limitations to what Greek armies could do in war.

Calling out the troops

At dinner time, one autumn evening in 339 BC, the presiding committee of the Athenian council received word that Philip II of Macedon was on the warpath, only a few days' march from Athens. Some councillors immediately cleared the town square of traders and street vendors and made a bonfire out of the wicker market stalls. Others 'sent for the generals and called the trumpeter'. Alerted by the conflagration and all-night trumpet-calls, the Athenian people met in assembly at the crack of dawn, then marched out to the border.[2] The raising of general levies everywhere followed this same simple pattern for centuries. Fire- and trumpet-signals, attested as far back as the *Iliad*, alerted the citizens in an emergency, while in less urgent situations messengers went round shouting instructions to muster under arms, in the town square (once cleared of traders and stalls), an open-air theatre, gymnasium or sacred precinct.[3] Groups of men mobilised in villages, country-towns and city neighbourhoods, then made their way to the designated place.[4] Some citizens took their time to get ready and caught up with others only just before – or indeed after – battle.[5]

The mechanisms for raising smaller expeditionary forces, by contrast, were varied and changed significantly over time. A combination of personal and public obligations played a part from the *Iliad* and *Odyssey* onwards, but over the centuries these obligations became increasingly formal and impersonal (see above, pp. 96-7). In late fifth-century Athens, the commanders of the ten tribal regiments collaborated with the board of ten generals in hand-picking the men who were to serve in each unit in any particular expedition. Their selection was announced by posting call-up lists (*katalogoi*) on whitewashed boards in the town square, at the foot of the statues of the heroes after whom the tribes were named. (Notices of charges of draft-evasion and desertion were also posted here.) The officers aimed to pick the best men and get 'useful lists' (Thucydides 6.31.3), but had to take an oath 'to enrol those who had not served', that is, to distribute the burden evenly and not always select the same citizens (Lysias 9.15). Despite the evident attempt to ensure that the process was fair and open, there were complaints during the Peloponnesian and Corinthian Wars that the selection was influenced by the officers' personal friendships and enmities and that the rosters were continually tampered with: 'they put some of us on the list, while erasing the names of others, here, there and everywhere, two or three times'.[6]

Such problems were eliminated when Athens increasingly began to rely on two different and entirely impersonal forms of partial mobilisation: 'by sections' and 'by eponymous heroes'. Every year, the cohort of young men who had reached the age of 18 were registered as belonging to a year-class, which was named after a legendary hero. The authorities could therefore mobilise a limited number of soldiers by simply selecting a number of year-classes for service. Alternatively, they could designate any 'section' (*meros*) of the army, whether one or more of the tribal regiments or some other group, and thereby mobilise the men, of all age-groups, who were liable to serve in those particular units. Or they could combine the two modes, as they did in the Lamian War of 323 BC in raising a field army from all those between the ages of 20 and 40 who belonged to any of the seven selected tribes (Diodorus 18.10.2). There was no sudden transition from one system to the other: there was at least informal differentiation by age even at the start of the Peloponnesian War, and occasional missions undertaken by selected tribal regiments went back further still. But by 370 at the latest, mobilisation by year-class or section or both had become the norm, and the practice of 'listing' individuals is no longer heard of after about 350 BC.[7]

Mobilisation by unit and age-group had by this time long been the norm in Sparta. Its forces at the fateful battle of Leuctra in 371 BC consisted of 35 age-classes (20-54) drawn from four of the six regiments; mobilising two-thirds of the units, with or without further age-restrictions, was 'what they usually did' already in the early years of the Peloponnesian War.[8] Since these forms of mobilisation were obviously more efficient and inherently less controversial than individually selecting hundreds or thousands of men, it is remarkable that Athens for so long stuck with the mechanism of 'listing'. The explanation may be that, unlike in Sparta, the quality of Athenian citizen-soldiers' training and equipment was so uneven that the laborious business of hand-picking troops repaid the effort – until a gradually evolving system of military training brought most citizens up to roughly the same basic standard (see pp. 94-5) and made the selection process redundant.

'Unless someone carries a spare': Greek logistics

The first panic-stricken thought of a citizen who belatedly discovered that he was due to leave for war next morning was that he had some emergency shopping to do. 'Come with provisions for three days' was a standard clause in Athenian mobilisation-orders during the Peloponnesian War. Each hoplite carried, or had his servant carry, a bag of flour, jars of wine and water, a drinking cup, cooking pot, and a basket of 'sharp, pungent, and salty' snacks (*opsa*) such as cheese, onions, or salted fish wrapped in fig-leaves. The smell of war was not gunpowder or napalm, but the whiff of the soldier's provision basket.[9]

In addition to food and drink, and of course arms and armour, soldiers carried sleeping-mats (*strômata*), spare clothing, medicines and bandages, and hand-mills for grinding grain. Those who wanted to be prepared for all eventualities might also carry a repair kit: a file and rasp for repairing spears, a supply of leather straps for all other purposes. 'For most things used by people and horses are fixed with straps and when these wear thin and snap, everything grinds to a halt – unless someone carries a spare', as Xenophon explained with the air of a man who has learned from bitter experience (*Education of Cyrus* 6.2.30-2).

Some men brought along donkeys or mules or even ox-carts to carry tents, as well as shovels, hoes, axes, sickles – used in war as the instruments of agricultural devastation – and any booty which came their way. A wealthy soldier might be accompanied by several pack animals and drivers, while a group of poor men might share a single mule between them and take turns at driving the animal themselves.[10] The soldiers' own

servants, animals, carts, food, drink and other supplies normally constituted the whole of the baggage train: the Greek states – apart from Sparta
– did not send centrally organised supply trains along with their armies,
except in very unusual circumstances, and then only in a supplementary
role.[11]

The Spartan army did have the benefit of a regular baggage train which
had its own officers, senior enough to be part of the kings' war council. The
train included craftsmen, levied just like soldiers, as well as a convoy of
donkeys, mules and carts carrying essential supplies provided by the
state. On the rare occasions when an enemy broke through the Spartan
ranks, he ran into a regular wagon camp guarded by hoplite sentries,
rather than into the usual swarm of personal servants and pack animals.[12]

When their initial supplies ran out, the troops had to find new provisions locally, and to that end they carried some goods to barter and as
much 'travel money' (*ephodion*) as they could afford, or could borrow. We
hear of two Athenian soldiers who felt able to join the levy only after a
wealthy neighbour gave them each 30 drachmas in travel money, which
was probably enough to buy food for a month or two, a large amount for an
expedition going only just across the border into Boeotia.[13] The size of
these sums shows that soldiers were, understandably, reluctant to rely on
irregular income from plunder or even on state pay, which began to be
provided in the mid-fifth century but was often badly in arrears (see pp.
236-9). It is no surprise that Athenian troops stocked up so heavily for the
long and distant Sicilian expedition that at its disastrous conclusion two
years later they still carried enough change between them to fill four large
shields (Thucydides 6.31.5, 7.82.3).

A major source of new provisions was the 'market mob', the irregular
crowd of travelling merchants and pedlars which always tagged along on
campaign, happy to sell the troops what they needed, frequently at exor-
bitant prices since demand was high and supply limited.[14] The practice is
attested as early as the *Iliad*, in which the Greek soldiers barter their
booty for wine brought to their camp by traders from Lemnos and Thrace
(7.467-75; 9.71-2). Although we cannot put a figure on the numbers of
merchants involved or the scale of their trade, both Homer and classical
sources give the impression that private, unorganised trade made a vital
contribution to keeping armies in supplies.[15] Alternatively, friendly or
frightened locals might give an army access to the local market-place or
set up a special market outside town. Allies would be under a moral or
even contractual obligation to do so, but neutral communities might not
co-operate, since to them a passing army presented a potential threat as
well as a golden economic opportunity. Few would be as helpful as Tarsus,
where, at the approach of an army, the city was abandoned by the entire
population 'except the shopkeepers' (Xenophon, *Anabasis* 1.2.24).

In enemy territory, armies tried to subsist on plunder. Their best
chance lay in surprising a village or town and capturing it before the

inhabitants could evacuate the place and rescue their stored supplies. But this did not often happen, and more usually invaders would have to live directly off the land, which was easier said than done.[16] An expedition had to catch the precise moment when the grain was ripe enough to eat but had not yet been harvested, and even the Spartans did not always manage to get the timing quite right: on one occasion they invaded Attica 'too early, when the grain was still green' and as a result ran out of food so fast that they returned home after a mere fifteen days (Thucydides 4.6.1-2). A supply of wine, almost as vital as grain, could of course never be secured in this way. A few lucky soldiers might stumble across a deserted country house or village well-stocked with jars of vintage wine, but vineyards were simply trampled by passing armies. Xenophon went so far as to suggest that troops might be trained to do without wine, and drink water only. No one followed his advice.[17] Moreover, armies had to scatter in order to forage, which made them highly vulnerable to counter-attack, especially by enemy cavalry, which in turn restricted their plundering range.[18] However well-timed, therefore, no invasion could last long if the army lived mainly off the land. The longest campaign by a Spartan army in Attica ended after only forty days (Thucydides 2.57.2).

A large share of the grain was eaten by the beasts of burden, which also needed great quantities of fodder. Troops could therefore only go where there was pasture, and it was half-jokingly observed that armies followed where their donkeys led.[19] Xenophon set an example followed by many later generals in improving the mobility of his mercenaries by first getting rid of their ox-carts, and later reducing the number of pack animals as well.[20]

The most urgent requirement for man and beast was water, and no ancient soldier would have made the mistake of many modern scholars in taking its availability for granted: 'only those without water really appreciate how many are its uses'.[21] The Spartans told how one of their legendary kings safeguarded the city's conquests through his ability to do without water even in the most extreme circumstances (Plutarch, *Moralia* 232a), and admirers of the Spartans' military professionalism pointed to their characteristic drinking cup (*kôthôn*), which made drinking from rivers less unpleasant, since its lip filtered out impurities and its dark colour disguised the muddiness of the water.[22] In practice, however, the Spartans made sure that they were first in the queue for a good water supply. Moving against the Persians at Plataea, they stationed themselves next to a spring, but left their allies to drink from the river Asopus (Herodotus 9.25, 49). Later allegations that the Spartans subsequently alienated their allies by insisting on first access to water – and fodder, and straw for bedding (Plutarch, *Aristides* 23) – seem only too plausible. As with food and fodder, soldiers relied very heavily on local resources. When local springs and streams were fouled, or ran dry in summer, or were insufficient to begin with, the army was forced to move on or go home.

8. The Bare Necessities

The provision of shelter was no better organised than any other aspect of logistics. Indeed, shelter was a general's lowest logistical priority. As soon as Xenophon was put in charge of the mercenaries, he made them burn their tents, as being 'useless for fighting or provisioning purposes' (*Anabasis* 3.2.27), and for the rest of the expedition the men slept in the open air unless they found villages where they could safely scatter and sleep in the houses. Xenophon's belief that a good general should make provisions an absolute logistical priority is evident also in his historical novel, where the model commander orders the troops to carry extra food even if it means leaving behind their sleeping-mats. 'Don't worry that you may not sleep comfortably without your mats – and if you can't, blame me!', he adds, unreassuringly (*Education of Cyrus* 6.2.30).

A Greek army camp was accordingly a ramshackle affair, a mixture of tents, improvised bivouacs, and groups sleeping in the open air. Despite a tradition of mocking the luxurious tents of Oriental rulers (Herodotus 9.82), large and well-furnished tents were no less of a status symbol for travelling Greeks (Plutarch, *Themistocles* 5.4) and presumably did duty on campaign as well. In the *Iliad*, most of the Greek army lives in 'huts' (*klisiai*), evidently built from materials found on the spot. Many classical Greek soldiers cut down trees and gathered other materials to construct what must have been similar semi-permanent shelters.[23] Others still appear to have used animal hides as very basic one-man bivouacs (Xenophon, *Anabasis* 1.5.10) or simply slept around their campfires, as some Greeks and Trojans did in Homer. Apart from a central open space for assemblies and sometimes a defensive trench and palisade – again improvised from locally available materials, not built from ready-made stakes such as Roman legionaries carried with them – camps showed no sign of central organisation.[24] In an Athenian camp, at any rate, soldiers formed groups of 'tent-fellows' (*suskênoi*) or 'mess-mates' (*syssitoi*) of their own choosing, which did not necessarily correspond to military units: Alcibiades and Socrates, who belonged to different tribes, had their meals together at Potidaea. Those who owned tents no doubt put up their friends and relatives, while the rest of the men made their own arrangements.[25]

All this is a world away from the fictional encampment described in the *Education of Cyrus*, where each unit of soldiers eats and sleeps together in a single large tent, provided by the king (2.1.25), 'everyone knows the size and the location of his own space' so that 'all take their position at an undisputed spot', and the tents of the officers are identified by banners so that they may be easily located (8.5.3, 6, 13). Obvious and elementary as these things seem to us, the fact that Xenophon felt the need to explain the advantages of such arrangements at length (2.1.25-7, 8.5.3-14) shows that they were not the norm. Greek soldiers evidently not only formed their own mess-groups, but pitched their tents wherever they chose, with all the attendant quarrels over who got the best spots and uncertainty about where exactly the commanders might be found on any particular day.

The Spartans, as ever, and perhaps the Cretans, formed at least partial exceptions. Here, the mess-groups which were elsewhere constituted informally for the duration of a campaign were a permanent feature of social life: all adult male citizens were obliged to have their daily meals in these messes. Presumably their basic organisation remained in place on campaign, although we do not know how they related to fighting units.[26] A Spartan camp, moreover, was usually of a regular circular shape, within which each regimênt had its own space. But, like other Greek camps, it often lacked fortifications – and it always lacked any form of sanitation, beyond a rule that soldiers should relieve themselves at a spot sufficiently remote 'so as not to cause one another distress' (*Spartan Constitution* 12.1, 4-5).

Logistical support was thus very limited. The Greeks were well aware that armies were more effective when better supplied: Thucydides, for one, argued that the Trojan War would not have lasted ten years if the Greek heroes had brought more provisions (1.11). Even so, low levels of state organisation and limited central control of resources meant that most cities, most of the time, were forced to rely on rudimentary, largely private and informal, supply systems which seriously constrained their armies' striking power.

Keeping order: discipline among citizens

The very first battle narrative in Greek literature opens with a repeated contrast between good order among the Greeks, who advance in silence, obeying their leaders' commands, and chaos among their Trojan enemies, whose confused shouts are likened to the noise of a flight of cranes or a flock of sheep (*Iliad* 3.1-9, 4.427-38). Centuries later, the contrast reappears when the quiet cohesion of Greek troops is opposed to the noisy indiscipline of Macedonians and Illyrians who engage in 'fully autonomous combat' (*autokratôr machê*) and accept no orders at all (Thucydides 4.126.5). At the other extreme are the subjects of the Persian empire, who allegedly need to be literally whipped into action by their officers and will fight only 'under the lash', unlike the Greeks, who fight without any coercion (Herodotus 7.103-4, 222-3). Greeks liked to think that they were unique in attaining perfect discipline: a nice balance between willingness to fight and respect for authority.[27]

Reality was less simple, of course – Xenophon was not too surprised to see Persians marching in silence and obeying orders with model alacrity (*Anabasis* 1.5.8, 1.8.11) – but Greek national pride was not entirely unfounded. Their armies did rely heavily on self-imposed discipline rather than coercion, since not only did they have few officers, but these few officers had little power to enforce orders.[28]

In the *Iliad*, commanders occasionally threaten that they will personally kill anyone who disobeys orders, but their bark is worse than their bite. In practice, no one suffers anything worse than a beating with a staff, and even this applies only to the rank and file. Aristocrats are usually admonished 'with gentle words' alone.[29] In Homer's world, a man must always assert his ability to uphold his authority by violent means, if necessary, which explains why a leader might rhetorically threaten his followers with death. His scope for actually using force, however, was restricted, because any act of violence would be seen by his followers as a personal insult rather than as a legitimate exercise of authority. They would feel obliged to retaliate, or at least to withdraw their services. Only those lowest down the social scale could be more aggressively disciplined without fear of repercussions. In all but the most extreme situations, leadership was therefore not so much a matter of enforcing orders, or even merely giving orders, but of inspiring the men by exhortation and example.[30]

As army organisation grew more centralised, commanders began to owe their authority to election or appointment, rather than to personal ties with the soldiers, yet their powers remained limited. Generals did have the power to execute any soldier on a charge of treason, but for most disciplinary offences punishments were either light or hard to enforce. Athenian generals had the right 'to bind, bar, or fine any disorderly soldier'. 'But', adds Aristotle's *Athenian Constitution* (61.2), 'they usually do not impose fines.'[31] Commanders were evidently reluctant to use the full range of their powers, and we know of incidents which suggest that they regularly let their men get away with serious indiscipline.

In 394 BC, a certain Simon failed to report in time for an Athenian general levy sent off to Corinth. Then, when he belatedly reached the army camp, he became embroiled in a violent quarrel which culminated in his beating up a superior officer, the tribal commander. Simon's punishment was to be 'barred' from further military service, the only Athenian in the entire levy to be so excluded (Lysias 3.45). It was deeply shameful to be debarred from serving as a soldier – Plato saw it as the nearest thing to being 'turned from a man into a woman' (*Laws* 944de) – but shame does seem a comparatively mild penalty for such extreme insubordination. What is even more remarkable is that the generals used their disciplinary powers against only one single man among their many thousands of hoplites.

Short of imposing formal punishment, an officer might, at his own peril, try to enforce discipline by punching a soldier, beating him with a staff, or even stabbing him with a spear. Xenophon admits to having in his time punched a few men who left their stations, or showed signs of cowardice or laziness. As a result, he found himself accused of gratuitously and arrogantly assaulting his soldiers; he was forced to defend himself twice, first in a court martial and later in his written account of the expedition (*Anabasis* 5.7.34, 8.10-18). Using a stick or spear to punish soldiers was the mark of a strict disciplinarian. The Spartan Clearchus, an effective but unpopular commander – described in his obituary as 'harsh and savage' and ferocious in administering punishment – carried 'a spear in his left hand and a stick in his right' and hit disobedient or slacking soldiers with whichever of the two was 'appropriate' (*Anabasis* 2.3.11, 2.6.9-12). This two-handed system of punishment was not unusual: the Spartan Mnasippus also hit one insubordinate officer with the butt of his spear and another with his stick (*Hellenica* 6.2.18-19). A cut with a spear was presumably seen as the more severe penalty, appropriate to the more serious offence. Soldiers often responded violently to such treatment. At the mere threat of a beating, the victim's comrades were liable to start pelting the commanding officer with anything that came to hand. Some generals were killed by stoning; others, including Clearchus, who had an axe thrown at him, narrowly escaped with their lives. Towards the end of his own expedition, Xenophon feared that all the authority of the elected commanders would crumble in the face of ubiquitous 'self-appointed generals' starting another stoning with a shout of 'Throw! Throw!'[32]

An officer might well think that trying to discipline his men was more trouble than it was worth, and decide to turn a blind eye to some offences. The general in charge of a garrison on the Athenian border took no action against a small group of his men who spent most of their time getting drunk and making a nuisance of themselves in camp. When a neighbouring mess-group lodged a complaint, he merely issued a verbal reprimand. That very night, the offenders burst into their neighbours' tent and physically assaulted them: the general and other officers came out to separate the brawlers – and left it at that.[33]

This episode offers a glimpse, not only of indiscipline going unpunished, but of the unregimented nature of life in an Athenian garrison post or army camp, which featured none of the routines and rituals associated with the modern military. Soldiers seem to have risen, eaten, and gone to bed pretty much when they pleased, and to have spent the rest of their time as they liked. Even with the enemy close at hand, some cavalrymen might still be asleep in their beds while their comrades were already taking up their stations and the grooms were up and about currying the horses (Xenophon, *Hellenica* 2.4.6). Some men might still be having their morning meal when others had long finished and were passing the time playing dice – or were asleep again, having gone straight back to bed (Herodotus 1.63). Spartan soldiers, as one would expect, found their time more regimented, with heralds announcing the time for morning and evening meals (both preceded by compulsory training sessions) and probably also the times to rise and retire. But in a Spartan camp, as elsewhere, soldiers were free to spend the rest of the day in 'amusements and siestas' as they saw fit.[34]

Clearchus is reported to have punished on the principle that soldiers must be more frightened of their commanders than of the enemy, while Xenophon defended his own and Clearchus' use of physical force as analogous to the punishments meted out by parents to their children or by schoolmasters to boys (*Anabasis* 2.6.10, 12; 5.8.18). The fact that the legitimacy of punishment needed to be defended in this way points to the same conclusion as the fact that many a strict commander was set upon by a lynch-mob: soldiers generally did not think that their officers had any right, or reason, to inflict corporal punishment.

Most known instances of mutiny or resentment sparked off by threats or beatings involve Spartan officers in charge of non-Spartan troops. This is surely no coincidence, but the result of a clash between Sparta's comparatively hierarchical system of command and the egalitarian conventions of other Greek militias. The Spartan army had not only more officers (pp. 98-101), but officers with greater disciplinary powers. The threatening use of a stick to enforce authority appears to have been quite common in Sparta in other contexts as well, and beating subordinates may have been more acceptable among Spartans than elsewhere. Moreover, Sparta had a distinctive shaming penalty for indiscipline (*ataxia*): the culprit was made to stand for a long time holding his heavy shield.[35]

The Greeks, then, were right to claim that the discipline of their hoplites relied on coercion only to a very small degree. Generally, the formal powers bestowed on classical Greek officers amounted to little more than the personal authority enjoyed by Homeric leaders, because soldiers refused to regard even the highest-ranking commanders, including Spartan kings, as anything more than fellow-citizens and peers. Ordinary soldiers in the ranks felt free to shout out tactical advice to their generals, who might actually do as they suggested.[36] As a mercenary commander, Xenophon let it be known that any soldier should feel free to approach him at any time, even if it meant interrupting his meals or waking him (*Anabasis* 4.3.10). In this egalitarian atmosphere, extensive disciplinary powers could find no place.

Instead, an effort was made to strengthen discipline by punishing cowardice (*deilia*), which was considered a profound moral failure for all men alike, without any imputation of subject status in a hierarchy. Two Spartan polemarchs who disobeyed a direct order from their king were accordingly prosecuted, not for insubordination, but for cowardice (Thucydides 5.72.1). Acts of cowardice, specifically throwing away one's shield, as one would when running away, were not dealt with in the field but referred to courts back home to be judged by the whole community rather than by an individual officer. Cowardice was in this respect on a par with draft evasion and desertion, and clearly treated as a more serious matter than mere indiscipline. The penalty, in Sparta as in Athens, was loss of all or some citizen rights (*atimia*). Great shame attached to being a convicted coward. The Athenian politician Cleonymus, for instance, as a known 'shield-flinger', suffered at least ten years' worth of jokes and scathing comment in comic plays. In Sparta, convicted 'tremblers' (*tresantes*) became socially marginal figures, with whom no one wanted to eat or wrestle or play ball-games, let alone form marriage ties. They had to give way in the street and give up their seats to full citizens. In a theatrical gesture, these 'tremblers' were also forbidden personal grooming – a serious stigma in a community where carefully dressed long hair, in particular, was a status symbol – and were humiliatingly forced to shave off half their beards so as to advertise their status as half-men.[37]

True to form, the Spartans seem to have made a point of systematically investigating and penalising any alleged acts of cowardice.[38] In Athens, however, also true to form, prosecutions for cowardice were left to private initiative, so that many cowards might never be charged at all. Those who were charged could always try to counter-sue: a false claim that another man had thrown away his shield carried a stiff penalty of 500 drachmas. A certain Theomnestus, accused of throwing away his shield, responded in just this way, suing his prosecutor for defamation and suing one of the witnesses for perjury. He was himself sued again by a second witness for slander (Lysias 10.1, 12, 24-5). In such circumstances, convictions must have been few and haphazard, and not even the threat of prosecution under the laws against cowardice can have done much to reinforce discipline.

If Greek armies nevertheless maintained better order than most, this was due to a discipline which soldiers by and large imposed upon themselves and upon their comrades. Every soldier needed to contribute actively to the maintenance of discipline, as Xenophon put it, for success required 'ten thousand Clearchuses, instead of one' (*Anabasis* 3.2.30-1). Mutual exhortations and appeals to feel shame before one's fellow-soldiers are prominent from early Greek poetry onwards (see below, pp. 163-4). But it is important not to follow the Greeks themselves in idealising this kind of discipline, and to note its limitations. It sufficed to keep soldiers together in combat, but it did not give a commander much control.

Battlefield manoeuvres were next to impossible to execute not only because soldiers did not practise formation drill, but also because officers had so little power over their men. The insubordination of two Spartan polemarchs, already mentioned, ruined a risky manoeuvre and cost many lives at Mantinea. Broader tactical decisions could also be difficult to enforce: a junior officer's blunt refusal to follow an order to move camp in search of a better water supply exposed the Spartans at Plataea to an attack which could have been fatal. Typically, the supreme commander in this case, rather than relieve a subordinate of his rank, spent all night trying to reason with him and in the end simply left him and his unit behind (Herodotus 9.50-7). Above all, it was extremely difficult to keep soldiers under control when provisions, spoils or their personal property were at stake. Many soldiers deserted the Athenian army in Sicily in order to chase after their runaway slave attendants (Thucydides 7.13.2); many of Xenophon's rearguard in Kurdistan left their stations during a crucial action in order to check on the safety of their luggage (*Anabasis* 4.3.30).

Individuals and entire units going out provisioning or pillaging against express orders were a constant problem, which divided armies and made them more vulnerable to retaliation.[39]

*

Archaic and classical Greek armies, in short, had their limitations. They were not always easy to raise. Once raised, they could usually not be kept together, or stay in the same place, for long. The 'war season' lauded by Demosthenes (p. 115) was a product of practical constraints: quite apart from the need of many soldiers to return to their farms, winter warfare was made almost impossible by primitive logistics. Soldiers could only fight when there was food to be found in the fields; when their movements were not too restricted by swollen rivers, floods, snow and stormy seas; when the weather simply was not too cold and wet to allow camping in the open. Even the hardiest farmer was advised to stay indoors in winter and wrap up warm 'to keep your ears from getting wet' (Hesiod, *Works and Days* 493-558). Finally, when an army had been assembled and its logistical needs met to the best of a general's ability, there was only so much that soldiers could be expected or made to do. If, as we shall see, campaigns were often short, and fought in what seems a restrained manner, it was to a large extent because the Greeks were not *capable* of doing more than wage limited wars.

Part IV

Agonal and Total Warfare

Nostalgia is a source of many myths, and even war can inspire nostalgia. 'Nothing nowadays is as it used to be,' said the orator Demosthenes in the summer of 341 BC, 'and nothing, I believe, has changed and spread more than warfare' (9.47).

> I hear that in the old days the Spartans and all the others invaded and ravaged enemy territory with hoplite citizen armies for four or five months – the war season – and then returned home. They were so old-fashioned, or rather civic-spirited, that they did not bribe anyone to do anything, but fought wars according to rules and openly. (9.48)

These thoughts were provoked by the arrival of a new enemy, the Macedonians under Philip II, who allegedly relied on treachery rather than pitched battles, employed mercenaries as well as citizens, fielded light infantry and cavalry as well as hoplites, attacked cities with siege engines, and waged war all year round, ignoring the limits of the war season (9.49-51). It is tempting to imagine that Demosthenes was alluding to the distant past, and that hoplite warfare in its original, archaic form was indeed so hemmed in by rules and restrictions that it was almost a ritual, or at least a game.[1] However, the good old days of which Demosthenes spoke were not centuries ago, but at most two generations. By 'the old days' he meant the second half of the Peloponnesian War (413-404 BC) at the earliest.[2] Warfare at that time had in reality been nothing like a ritual or game: pitched battles were not often fought and, as we have seen, never by hoplites alone; many towns were besieged and captured by treason; entire populations were destroyed. Demosthenes was peddling a nostalgic myth.

Two centuries later, the 'misbehaviour' in war of another king of Macedon, Philip V, provoked the same sort of reaction. 'These days, people say that it is the mark of a poor general to execute a military operation openly', sighed Polybius. It had not always been so:

> The ancients ... felt that no victory was glorious or secure unless they had crushed the spirit of their opponents in an open battle. Therefore they even agreed among themselves not make use of covert missiles or long-range projectiles against one another. They felt that only a hand-to-hand, close-

range battle could truly settle matters, so they would give one another advance notice of wars and battles ... and of the places where they intended to go and take their battle stations (13.3.1-8).

From Polybius' *Histories* we might expect greater historical accuracy than from a political speech by Demosthenes, yet even these comments were not based on reliable knowledge of early Greek warfare. Polybius later reports a speech in which Philip V's destruction of cities is contrasted, not with archaic practices, but with the 'noble' way of war of previous Macedonian kings, who until the reign of Pyrrhus – a mere three generations earlier – had supposedly never harmed cities, but fought pitched battles 'in the open country' (18.3.2-8). This claim is wholly false. Philip V's predecessors had conducted sieges on an unprecedented scale. His great-grandfather was actually nicknamed 'The Besieger', and a more distant predecessor was none other than Philip II, accused by Demosthenes of breaking all the rules – and of razing to the ground more than thirty cities in Thrace alone (9.26).

It is in the nature of nostalgia to project ideals onto the past, to make believe that the highest standards and noblest achievements used to be everyday realities. For Demosthenes and Polybius, pitched infantry battle clearly was such an ideal: a form of combat more prestigious than any other. So it was for others. From Homer onwards, we occasionally hear warriors express their disdain for ambushes, surprise attacks, or any form of 'unfair' advantage. 'A brave man thinks it unworthy to kill his enemy by stealth; he meets him face to face ... Do not praise the clever spear of one who *steals* victory' (Euripides, *Rhesus* 510-11, 709).[3] Some denounced the use of fortifications and siege engines as cowardly. The Spartans were particularly proud of managing for centuries without city walls, and one of their kings is said to have lamented the invention of the siege catapult as heralding 'the end of bravery in men' (Plutarch, *Moralia* 191e).[4] Herodotus went so far as to suggest that the concept of an open and fair battle was typically Greek and difficult to grasp for a barbarian: the Persian commander Mardonius is made to ridicule the ideal, scoffing at the 'stupidity and clumsiness' of the Greeks in not trying to catch the enemy at a disadvantage but staging battles 'on the finest, flattest terrain they can find', so that even the winners suffer many casualties and the losers are wiped out (7.9b).

Pitched infantry battle was always important to the Greeks, both as a military ideal and as a military practice, but precisely *because* it was an important ideal we cannot trust Demosthenes or Polybius when they nostalgically claim that it was once the *only* significant form of warfare in Greece. And even Mardonius' colleagues realised that his 'silly stories' were a mere caricature of the Greek way of war (Herodotus 7.10η). These unreliable ancient claims have nevertheless led many modern scholars to believe that pitched battle dominated warfare in the archaic period but began to decline in importance at the time of the Persian Wars, or later, during the Peloponnesian War. Yet throughout the history of Greek warfare, agricultural devastation, assaults on settlements, ambushes, and surprise attacks were at least as common as pitched battles, and far more common than pitched battles of the most ritualised kind. Greek war always had two faces. Ideally, it was 'agonal', that is, fought by a set of restrictive rules which made it seem like a game. In reality, a ferocious pursuit of profit and honour constantly strained against any such restrictions and frequently drove the Greeks to the most uninhibited, destructive kind of 'total' warfare.

9

Rituals, Rules and Strategies

The structure of campaigns

In the summer of 419 BC, the Argive army twice invaded Epidaurus and laid waste to its territory without meeting any resistance. The first invasion took place only three days before the start of a sacred period during which war was banned, but the Argives bought themselves extra time by intercalating extra days into their calendar. Thus they could legitimately carry on fighting while Epidaurus' allies, who observed the sacred period at the normal time, were unable to respond (Thucydides 5.54.2-4). During the second invasion, the Spartans mobilised in aid of their allies in Epidaurus, but turned back at the border when the omens proved unfavourable for a frontier-crossing. The Argives 'cut down about a third of the territory' and went home unmolested (55.2-4).

After a winter of sporadic fighting – 'there was no pitched battle, only ambushes and raids in which a few men on each side were killed' – Argos raised the stakes. In spring 418 BC, its troops 'went to Epidaurus with ladders', but failed to storm the city (Thucydides 5.56.4-5). A few months later, Sparta and its allies came to Epidaurus' rescue with 'the finest Greek army ever yet assembled' (60.3), yet both sides were reluctant to engage and made a truce for four months (59.5-60.1). During this truce, the Argive army marched out to fight a new war in Arcadia, at which point the Epidaurians saw their chance to retaliate and invaded 'in full force', killing many of Argos' home guard (75.4). This in turn provoked the Argives and their allies to march on Epidaurus again and besiege the city until the beginning of winter, when everyone except a small garrison went home (75.5-6). A peace settlement was agreed soon afterwards (77).

Short and not particularly eventful, as wars go, this conflict between Argos and Epidaurus was typical of most Greek warfare. The drastic scaling down of military activity in winter, the observance and manipulation of religious rules, the objectives of destroying farmland and capturing cities, and the resort to ambushes and raids as well as great showdowns in pitched battle, all featured prominently in archaic and classical Greek wars.

9. Rituals, Rules and Strategies

The constraints of religion

Juggling with the religious calendar in time of war became something of a habit in Argos. Thirty years after the Epidaurian War a Spartan army was met at the Argive border by two priests who warned them not to invade, because Argos was observing a sacred month. The Spartan commander, king Agesipolis, had anticipated this move. He trumped it by citing two oracles which had ruled that sacred periods could be ignored if they were proclaimed too late and in bad faith. Agesipolis went on to interpret away an earthquake and ignore a lightning-strike before further bad omens forced him to retreat. If religion was not cynically exploited, its flexible rules were certainly stretched close to breaking-point.[1]

The Argives were unusual in tabooing war for a whole month (Carneios, in August-September), but all Greek states tried to avoid fighting during major religious festivals.[2] In summer, the Spartans celebrated the Hyacinthia, Gymnopaidiai and Carneia, each lasting several days. It was the Carneia which not only prevented them from helping Epidaurus but from sending more than a tiny advance guard to face the Persians at Thermopylae in 480 BC. The Hyacinthia was one of the reasons for the delay in sending troops in 479 BC, and custom required that all inhabitants of the Spartan town of Amyclae should be released from active duty even in the middle of a war so that they could celebrate the festival at home. On the other hand, the Spartans did at least once postpone the Gymnopaidiai in order to fight a war.[3] Sacred truces were proclaimed all over Greece for the celebration of the festivals at Delphi, Nemea and the Isthmus every other year, and at Olympia every four years.[4] The Greek summer was thus punctuated with periods when fighting was inhibited.

Keener sky-watchers than most Greeks, the Spartans had a custom of never starting a military campaign in the first half of any lunar month, so that they sat at home waiting for the full moon while the Athenians fought the battle of Marathon without their promised help. The custom gave rise to the expression 'Laconian moons', meaning unreliable agreements. The suggestion that the moon was merely a poor excuse to wriggle out of an onerous commitment may be a little harsh, but it is true that we know of no other occasion on which this rule affected a Spartan campaign. Nor were the Athenians' war efforts much impeded by their custom that campaigns should not start during the first six days of any month.[5]

War was banned from sacred places as well as during sacred periods: armies were meant to steer clear of temple precincts and estates. Once, the Thebans were so outraged by their enemies' use of a sanctuary as a basis of operations that they took the extreme and highly unusual step of refusing them permission to retrieve their dead from the battlefield.[6]

Omens and oracles guided Greek warfare at all times. The Homeric world already knew specialist diviners (*manteis*) and the practice of reading omens from sacrifices, but out on the battlefield Homer's heroes observed only spontaneous signs – the flight of birds, thunder and lighting, unusual events – and did not call on the services of a designated *mantis*. Anyone who thought he knew the meaning of a sign might say so. The corollary was that commanders had little hesitation in silencing would-be diviners among their followers with threats of violence when their prophecies were unwelcome.[7]

Classical armies, by contrast, employed highly paid and sought-after specialists to consult the gods every step of the way, both by means of animal sacrifice and by the observation of spontaneous omens. The way in which a victim collapsed, the flow of its blood, the swirling and intensity of the flames and smoke as its fat and bones lay burning on the altar, and especially the animal's liver and other entrails, all held clues to the future. An army could not move from home or camp, cross a river or engage in combat until the *manteis* declared that the signs were favourable.[8] Stories were told about armies which ignored the omens and duly came to a sticky end, as well as about armies which waited for good omens even under the most desperate circumstances – troops dying under Persian fire rather than fighting without divine support, mercenaries staying put and starving for three days rather than moving out in search of new supplies while the signs were unfavourable – and won.[9]

The growing role of divination reflected a general trend towards a more formal military organisation: the reading of omens was institutionalised as part of a process in which convention and personal authority gave way to regular units, appointed officers and fixed procedures. But the main reason why divination became more important probably lay in the changing nature of combat. The open-order skirmishing of early Greece was indecisive and undemanding compared with classical infantry battle (see below, pp. 166-83), and one can understand the need of classical Greek hoplites for constant reassurance of divine support in order to cope with increased physical and emotional strain and the uncertainty of risking all in a single battle. Tellingly, the final blood-sacrifice took place, not when the light-armed began battle with their skirmishes, but only when the hoplites moved into action (Plate XI).[10]

How much influence *manteis* and their rituals really had on the conduct of war is hard to assess. When in 419 BC the Spartans went home because the omens did not allow them to cross the Argive border, their decision was probably inspired as much by a lack of enthusiasm for this war as by respect for the gods. After all, they mobilised three times in two years but never actually struck a single blow (p. 118). Where there was a will, there was usually a way around omens: in exactly the same situation, 75 years earlier, the Spartan king Cleomenes had accepted that the sacrifices were unfavourable for crossing the Argive border, but instead of giving up he put his troops on ships and launched an assault from the sea (Herodotus 6.76). Agesipolis' unorthodox insistence that the tremor which hit his camp was a form of divine encouragement rather than a warning (p. 119) is another illustration of how a determined general might save his campaign.[11] The authority of the *mantis* must have been great enough to justify the efforts made to contract the most talented diviners, but he was always subordinate to the commander, who was expected to know enough about entrail-reading and related practices to be able to form his own opinion on the omens. Ultimately, in classical Greece as in the Homeric world, the general could override religious concerns with an appeal to patriotism, glory or necessity.[12]

No one imposed greater religious constraints upon themselves in war than the Spartans, who were unique not only in observing the phases of the moon, but also in consulting omens at border-crossings. They would pay almost any price to get the best diviners, and their armies were accompanied by notoriously large herds of sheep and goats for sacrifice.[13] That the state most governed by concern for the supernatural was also the dominant military power in Greece shows how effectively the Greeks combined piety and expediency in war.

Devastation of town and country

Once across the border, troops invariably began 'slashing and burning' (*koptein kai kaiein*), trampling, cutting down, and setting fire to crops and trees, smashing agricultural machinery such as olive presses, and destroying farm houses. At the same time, they engaged in 'driving and carrying' (*agein kai pherein*), driving off animals and captives as booty and carrying off any movable property. A war might pass without a pitched battle or siege, but never without a rampage through enemy countryside. 'Destroying the crops' and 'rustling cattle and horses' were archetypal acts of war already to Homer (*Iliad* 1.154-6), and the Delian League against Persia was formed simply 'to avenge what they had suffered by ravaging the land of the King' (Thucydides 1.96.1). To harm and humiliate the enemy by means of agricultural devastation was arguably the essence of Greek warfare.[14]

Plunder was vital insofar as invaders needed local resources to supplement their provisions and were always keen to make a profit from war (pp. 26-8, 105-6), but destruction was an even more prominent element of ravaging. Light-armed troops, with some support from hoplites and cavalry, would descend on farms and villages to find them deserted and stripped of anything edible or valuable that could be moved, including 'everything with which their houses were furnished, even the woodwork of the houses themselves' (Thucydides 2.14.1). Farmers moved to the city or other fortified places whenever an incursion was expected; livestock was driven to the city, if space and the water supply allowed, or else to the safety of remote peninsulas and mountain regions. Before the Peloponnesian War, the Athenians mounted what must have been a massive operation to ferry their animals across to Euboea. Most of the crops had often already been harvested, since only after gathering their own harvest could most communities spare the manpower to attack their neighbours. The emphasis in the sources on damaging 'the trees' shows that there was usually little left except olives, figs and vines. Invaders were thus largely reduced to vandalising immovable property, rather than taking booty.[15]

The anger and anguish of a family watching from the city wall as the enemy wrecked their farm will have been hard to bear, and their short-term losses substantial, but we should not overestimate the long-term damage to any individual farm, let alone to a community's economy as a whole. Without the aid of explosives, chainsaws or tractors, it was extremely hard to uproot trees and vines, and very time-consuming to cut them down; just how much damage it is possible to do by trampling a vineyard with 'great fat feet' remains a matter of some dispute. The main weapon of destruction was fire, but this did not work on green vines, and did little structural damage to olive trees, or indeed to stone and brick buildings and installations from which the woodwork had been removed. Field crops were only combustible during a few weeks before harvest, and not all crops or all fields reached this point at the same time. Families returning to their farms would have their work cut out, but it was salvaging and rebuilding work; they did not need to start again from scratch.[16]

Whatever the suffering of unfortunate individuals, the damage done by agricultural devastation did not normally affect the whole community. An army could not cover much ground while slashing and burning, even when it met no resistance. Often, cavalry came out to harass the invaders as they scattered, slowing down progress even further. Since logistical limitations dictated that an invasion could last only two to six weeks (p. 106), there was rarely enough time to ravage 'the whole territory systematically and without missing a bit' (Xenophon, *Hellenica* 4.6.2-6), so most farms would be spared.[17]

Serious economic damage could be inflicted when a large army invaded a small territory, as in the Argive invasion of Epidaurus which left one-third of the country destroyed (p. 118), when the enemy was taken by surprise, as in Agesipolis' invasion of Argos during a sacred month (p. 119), and when the invasion began early enough and lasted long enough to prevent the harvesting of the year's crop or the sowing of the next crop. Agesilaos' expeditions against Acarnania in 389 and 388 BC are a case in point: the first meticulously destroyed crops and included a surprise raid into the mountains where the Acarnanians kept their cattle; the second was timed so early that the Acarnanians would have lost their entire harvest, a prospect which led to their immediate surrender (Xenophon, *Hellenica* 4.6.1-7.1).

Unless these conditions applied, a city would not find it difficult to survive an incursion. Athens coped with devastation by a vast Persian army two years running, and later was little troubled by a series of annual

Spartan incursions. In order to do real long-term harm, the enemy needed to establish a permanent presence within the territory, a fortified position manned by a garrison which could mount raids all year round and encourage the desertion of slaves or serfs. This tactic, known as *epiteichismos*, was a major force during and after the Peloponnesian War, when the Athenians raided Sparta from Pylos and Cythera, while the Spartans terrorised Attica from their base at Decelea, and later Corinth from Lechaion.[18]

Agricultural devastation thus played different roles in different circumstances. It could serve as a form of economic warfare, when the damage was severe enough to force the enemy to surrender. It might serve as a challenge, designed to lure the enemy into an open confrontation, even if only token damage was inflicted; the Spartans in 431 BC did not try to destroy as much of Attica as possible but subtly targeted their ravaging for maximum provocative effect.[19] Perhaps most often agricultural devastation was not so much a means to an end as a military objective in itself. If the Spartans continued to ravage Attica every year, and the Athenians ravaged Megara twice every year, without any real hope of provoking their opponents to come out and fight or subjecting them by economic coercion, it was not because they were stuck in tradition and could not think of a more effective strategy. They kept laying waste to enemy territory because each unopposed campaign was a victory in its own right, a means of gaining honour for oneself and shaming one's enemies through an act of conspicuous destruction.[20]

A small invasion force might not wait for the defenders to respond, but withdraw with its spoils after a hit-and-run raid. The epic prototype was Nestor's cattle-raid in retaliation for the injuries and insults suffered by his people at the hands of their more powerful neighbour, Elis. His band of young men crossed the border at night, rounded up vast herds of livestock, and drove their booty home before daybreak (*Iliad* 11.670-761). Historical analogies include raids on Athens by its weaker neighbours: Aegina always relied on coastal raids rather than full-scale invasion in its wars, Thebes often sent raiding parties across the mountains, and Megara in the early sixth century tried to seize Athenian women in raids on sanctuaries.[21] At some religious festivals women assembled in large groups separate from the men and on such occasions there was always fear of 'raiders coming for the women'.[22] Athens itself resorted to raiding tactics on a larger scale when waging war against the Peloponnesian League: its fleet would make landings in enemy territory but usually retreat before the victims could strike back.[23] Like the first winter of the war between Epidaurus and Argos, long phases of many a conflict were spent exchanging 'ambushes and raids'.

A large invading army, by contrast, would expect to face the defenders in battle. The purposes of a pitched battle, from the aggressor's point of view, were as varied as those of agricultural devastation. At a minimum, a victory would be another point scored in the competition for prestige, adding to the damage already done to the fields. Classical Greeks in particular came to regard success in battle as a goal in its own right, emphatically marked and commemorated (see pp. 136-8). But battle was often only a means to yet a further end: high casualties might force the defenders, if not to admit defeat immediately, to relinquish control of the countryside and leave the town itself open to attack.

There never was a time when all wars were fought out in the plain and did not touch the towns, as fondly imagined by Demosthenes and Polybius.[24] Cities first emerged in Greece in the eighth century BC, and before the century was out cities were being attacked and destroyed by their neighbours. The first known victim was Asine, its population expelled and buildings razed to the ground by Argos.[25] Melia, Arisbe and Nauplia were annihilated in the seventh century. Cirrha, Pellene and Donoussa, all on the Gulf of Corinth, were razed early in the sixth century. Another three cities, Camarina, Siris and Sybaris, all in the western Mediterranean, were wiped out between c. 550 and 510 BC.[26] In absolute terms, the destruction of ten cities – out of several hundred – in the course of two centuries may not sound like much, but we must remember that our extremely limited evidence for the archaic period records only a fraction of what happened, and that the number of cities known to have been sacked is larger than the handful of pitched infantry battles – no doubt also out of several hundred – which we know to have been fought during these centuries.

For every city destroyed, many more must have been captured, and more still unsuccessfully besieged. The scrappy sources mention only a few – the captures of Smyrna, Leuconia, Chios and Sigeum, all before the end of the seventh century, and the failed siege of Samos by Sparta around 525 BC [27] – but it is telling that in archaic poetry the typical city at war was a city under siege: 'one side fought to protect their parents and their city, while the other was intent on destroying it'.[28] The *Iliad* assumes that the goal of almost all legendary wars was the destruction of a city, and devotes an entire book to an assault on the fortifications around the Greek camp. Homer not only constantly evoked the future destruction of the Troy but cited a standard scenario for 'all the grief suffered by the people of a captured city: the men killed, the city burnt to the ground, the children and women led away by strangers'.[29] At least three archaic poets picked up where the *Iliad* left off and told the story of the sack of Troy in full. Its grisliest episodes – the battering to death of a baby boy, Astyanax, the killing of old Priam, and the rape of Cassandra – decorated many an archaic vase and shield-ornament (Figs 6 and 21A).[30]

Throughout the archaic period, Greek settlers overseas also attacked native settlements. An early seventh-century poem described an assault on a Thracian town, and Aristagoras of Miletus met his death while besieging another Thracian town in the early fifth century.[31]

Fig. 6. Scenes from the sack of Troy. *Top right & bottom left*: panels 14 and 16 of the so-called Mykonos pithos, a large storage vessel of *c.* 670 BC, decorated with 20 relief scenes from the sack of Troy, 17 of which show men attacking and killing women and children (published in *Archaiologikon Deltion* 18.1 (1963), 37-75). *Top left & bottom right*: drawings of panels from the bronze band decorating the inside of shields found at Olympia, showing a hoplite (Neoptolemos) attacking an old man (Priam) who has taken refuge at an altar (*c.* 570-560 BC) and another hoplite (Aias son of Oileus) seizing a naked young woman (Cassandra), who has taken refuge at the cult statue of Athena (*c.* 590-580 BC).

As soon as our sources become more detailed, the number of known attacks on towns multiplies exponentially. In the first two decades of the fifth century alone, Athens captured Myrine on Lemnos and laid siege to Aegina and Paros; in Sicily, Gela captured four neighbouring cities and unsuccessfully besieged Syracuse, while Syracuse not only captured but destroyed three of its neighbours; in Sparta, king Cleomenes was put on trial for failing to sack Argos when he had a chance.[32] Immediately after repelling the Persian invasion, the Greek alliance went on to besiege and capture Thebes and Sestos, while the very first action of the Delian League was an attack on Eion in Thrace. Polygnotus' monumental wall-paintings of the sack of Troy (Pausanias 10.25-7) were in tune with the times. The next century-and-a-half saw another two dozen cities destroyed and countless towns besieged.[33]

The capture of a city put an end to war, allowing the conqueror to impose any terms he wished. The startling regularity with which, from the eighth century onwards, the victor insisted on the complete elimination of the defeated community, massacring all adult men, enslaving their dependants, and annihilating the town – the ultimate act of conspicuous destruction – highlights again a key goal of Greek offensive strategy: the display of power, whether in *hybris*, revenge or punishment, by inflicting maximum damage.[34]

Defence of town and country

The sort of strategic debate that might take place in a community under attack was vividly dramatised in Euripides' *The Phoenician Women*. The warlike first response would be to want to march out and face the enemy in the open (712-20). After contemplating the odds against them, however, the defenders might want to consider other options. 'What if we assault them from an ambush at night?' That would be possible, but risky (724-7). 'How about if we attack while they are having dinner?' That would certainly cause a panic, but might still not be enough to ensure victory (728-31). 'Could we harass them with cavalry?' Not if the enemy can fight back with cavalry of his own (732-3). The final decision might well be that the best chance lies in defending the city from behind the walls (737-50).

The Phoenician Women was produced in 409 BC, not long before the end of the Peloponnesian War, and some would argue that it was very much a product of its time, when the traditional 'agonal' ideals of the Greeks had been undermined by the Peloponnesian War, or perhaps already by the Persian Wars. Earlier generations, it is said, had had no choice but to march out and offer battle. Hiding behind fortifications or exploiting the element of surprise, or indeed intercepting invaders at the border and keeping them out of the territory in the first place, had been regarded as unacceptable strategies.[35] There is plenty of evidence, however, from Homer to Euripides and beyond, to show that Greek ideals were always tempered by pragmatism, especially in war, and that Greek armies were always prepared to employ almost any defensive strategy which seemed feasible.

The moral pressure to come out and fight rather than hide behind fortifications was certainly strong, and indeed there is no sign that it was ever undermined at all. At the end of the classical period it was as strong as it had ever been. In 330 BC, the orator Lycurgus praised the forces which had marched out to fight at Chaeronea: 'they regarded their own bravery as a safer defence than a circuit-wall of stone, and they were quite rightly ashamed to watch the devastation of the land which reared them' (*Against Leocrates* 47). In the same year, Aeschines mocked that his rival Demosthenes' involvement in the construction of new fortifications at Athens did not deserve public recognition but criminal charges (3.236). Demosthenes apologetically replied that he had not protected the city alone with 'stone and brick' but defended 'the whole country' with infantry, cavalry and ships (18.299-300). Years earlier, he had urged the Athenians not to let the enemy devastate their territory, both because of the economic cost and because 'the *hybris* and the shame of the situation – the greatest loss of all for right-thinking people' (1.27). Plato found fortifications 'unhealthy' and took the extreme view that cities ought to have no walls at all (*Laws* 778d-779a).

Piety also encouraged defenders to fight back, since evacuation of the countryside meant abandoning many sanctuaries and ancestral graves.[36] The sheer discomfort of living with the entire population squashed together within the city walls was another factor. It was of course worst for the farmers and villagers, many of whom were forced to live in makeshift shelters, but the townsmen, especially upper classes, were also unhappy: 'May we never again see the charcoal-burners and their wagons come into the city from the hills, with their sheep and their cattle and the little woman in tow'.[37] In the *Iliad*, Hector gives as his reason for marching out to fight the enemy that he is 'fed up' with being stuck inside (18.287).

Shame, piety and concern about the quality of life all drove defenders to meet the enemy in the field, regardless of the level of economic damage done by devastation. Nevertheless, many Greeks from Homer onwards saw city-walls as a precondition for any form of settled and civilised life, and fortifications developed spectacularly in the fifth and fourth centuries.[38] This was because the power of shame had its limits: as Hector's wiser friend Polydamas pointed out, it is preferable to face the invader in the plain *only* so long as the odds are roughly equal (*Iliad* 18.253-311). Honour and risk were still balanced in the same way by Aristotle: faced with equal or slightly greater numbers, the militia should offer battle; faced with a clearly superior enemy, they should rely on fortifications (*Politics* 1330b33-1331a24).

The Epidaurians were not being particularly cowardly or radically innovative when they sat tight while a third of their territory was ravaged by the Argives in 419 BC. Nor were the Athenians or Megarians or any of the other communities which refused battle during or after the Peloponnesian War. In the late seventh century, the Milesians suffered eleven annual invasions by Lydian forces, but came out to fight only twice. Attacked by the Persians in 500 BC, the Naxians hid behind their walls for four months until the invaders went away. In the same situation ten years later, the Eretrians 'concentrated their efforts above all on defending their walls; they made no plans to come out and fight'.[39] All these cities were simply following the principle, accepted from Homer to Aristotle, that honour did not require a community to fight against the odds. When the odds where overwhelming even running away was acceptable: entire communities took to the mountains, sought refuge in nearby cities, or started a new life overseas. In Herodotus' opinion, the Ionians who submitted to Persian conquest in 546 BC ought to have emigrated to Sardinia instead.[40]

The Athenians were always divided on the proper response to invasion by such dangerous enemies as the Persians, Spartans and Macedonians. Some felt that Athens owed it to its status as a leading power to send out the militia. Others favoured staying within the walls, or evacuating the city, or migrating *en masse* to Southern Italy. Miltiades barely managed to tilt the balance towards facing the Persians at Marathon in 490; Themistocles persuaded most, but not all, Athenians to evacuate in 480; Pericles with difficulty imposed his strategy of never meeting the superior Spartan infantry in battle, however many Athenian farms went up in smoke, in 431 BC.[41] The strategies of Pericles and Themistocles, often treated as if they made radical and controversial breaks with Greek military tradition, were in fact well within the range of conventional responses to invasion. The only matter of controversy was whether these were the right strategies for the occasion, whether they struck the right balance between shame and safety in the circumstances. Their proposals met with no more and no less resistance than Miltiades' proposal to go out and fight, opposed by five out of ten generals on the grounds that 'they were too few', and that the risks of fighting were greater than Athens' status as 'the first city of Greece' was worth (Herodotus 6.109.1, 6).[42]

Between all-out battle and a city-bound defence lay the range of strategic options suggested in Euripides' play, relying on surprise rather than sheer force of weapons and numbers. These too were considered legitimate from Homer onwards, and existed alongside yet other strategies which sought to restrict and regulate combat (see Chapter 10).

The possibility of intercepting invasion armies at the border before they had a chance to damage any farms or villages was considered very seriously. In the fourth century, and later, throughout the hellenistic period, every self-respecting town protected its territory with substantial border forts and signalling stations, the remains of which are still visible today.[43] Not even the most vocal opponent of relying on fortifications, Plato, saw anything wrong with this defensive strategy. On the contrary, he devised an elaborate system of border defence for his own ideal city (*Laws* 760b-761a), similar to the contemporary Athenian system of manning the forts with ephebes in their second year of training (pp. 94-5). While fourth-century states invested greater resources than ever before in creating more, stronger, better-organised forts, border defence as such was by no means a new strategy.

By the beginning of the Peloponnesian War a number of garrisoned forts already existed in Attica, as did a regular body of 'border-patrols' (*peri-poloi*). Garrison commanders could deal with minor incursions and had the power of summary execution of any raiders caught. When larger-scale incursions threatened, a section of the militia might be called up to reinforce the garrison.[44] We know of such low-level military activity only from passing references in the ample sources available for this period, and the lack of evidence for it in the much more limited sources for earlier periods does not mean that this sort of border defence was not already in place decades or even centuries before the Peloponnesian War. Certainly when the Athenians did decide to fight invaders, they met the enemy as close to the border as possible. When the Spartans landed at Phaleron in 512 BC and the Persians at Marathon in 490 BC, Athenian forces marched out to fight them at disembarkation point, 'at the border', rather than let them advance any further into Attica. A Spartan invasion by land was met at Eleusis, just beyond the Athenian border with Megara, in 506 BC. When the Athenians temporarily gained control of Megara in 457 BC, they drew the line of defence even further from home by blocking the Megarian mountain passes.[45]

Some borders were completely sealed off with walls rather than merely guarded by forts. The so-called Dema wall built by Athens in the fourth century had illustrious archaic predecessors, including the wall built by the Phocians across the pass at Thermopylae to keep out the Thessalians and the four-mile long wall built in the mid-sixth century across the isthmus of the Chersonnese by Miltiades the Elder. The Spartans' pride in keeping their city without fortifications did not stop them from restoring the Phocian wall and using it as a defence against the Persians, or indeed from constructing from scratch a wall across the entire isthmus of Corinth to keep the Persians out of the Peloponnese.[46]

Whenever possible communities tackled invaders at the border, wher-ever possible with the aid of natural or man-made defences. The improved organisation and grander scale of border defences in the fourth century reflects the growing material resources and growing central power of Greek states, rather than a fundamental change in attitude.[47] If armies often fought in the plains rather than near the frontier, it was because very few territories were so inaccessible that they could be effectively defended by a simple wall or fort. Everywhere else, border garrisons could do no more than intercept small raiding parties and give early warning of enemy movements. Greek city-states were not the Roman empire and had nothing like the resources needed to protect their frontiers with enough troops to fight off full-scale invasions. It would not take very long for the militia to mobilise and march to the border, but it would usually still be too long to prevent invaders from entering the territory, and the battle, if any, would end up taking place on 'the finest, flattest terrain'.

Ambush, Battle and Siege

Changing forms of combat

At Hyampolis, the pass which led from Thessaly into Phocis was the scene of the most ferocious border warfare in Greek history. It began when Thessalian mounted raiders fell into an ambush: as they galloped across the pass the ground collapsed beneath them and they crashed into pitfalls which broke the horses' legs. Phocian ambushers finished off the riders. The Thessalian general levy then prepared to invade in full force, wiping out a band of 300 Phocian night-raiders attempting to enter their camp. In response, the Phocians staged a last-ditch defence, vowing to fight to the death, immolate their women and children, and destroy their own property rather than surrender. Against the odds, they won the battle. A later Thessalian attempt to force the pass was foiled by what appeared to be a ghostly army. A raiding party of 600 Phocian fighters, bodies and armour covered in whitewash, descended on the camp at night and in the terror and confusion killed 4,000 men.[1]

The Thessalians' revenge was grim. Their alliance with the Persians in 480 BC put them in a position to demand 50 talents of silver in compensation for their sufferings, and when the Phocians refused to comply, the Thessalians led their new allies across the border.

> The barbarians overran the entire land of Phocis, for this is how the Thessalians guided the army: wherever they directed them, they slashed and burned everything and set fire to the cities and even the sanctuaries ... They killed some Phocians whom they caught taking to the mountains, and gang-raped some women to death. (Herodotus 8.29-33)

These Thessalian-inspired atrocities are as unusual in the Greek record as the Phocians' stratagems; emotions clearly ran high in this war. 'Phocian desperation' became proverbial and no doubt helps explain their methods of fighting. These tactics were, however, only a more spectacular version of the ambushes, night-raids and attacks on camps widely encountered in Greek warfare. An appreciation of cunning was as much a constant factor as admiration for fair and open combat. These two elements combined to produce a wide variety of forms of combat which changed significantly over time but always ranged from the game-like and restrained to the uninhibited and highly destructive.

'Thefts of war': the element of surprise

Ambushes were regarded by Homer as the best test of a man's courage: only the bravest could bear the nervous tension of waiting in hiding for the right moment. The rest will turn pale and fidget, their hearts pounding, teeth chattering and legs trembling; it will be all they can do not to burst into tears.[2] At Troy, the Greeks frequently send out ambushing parties at night to lay in wait near the city and catch anyone who dares venture out first thing in the morning. A counter-ambush in which the defenders set upon the invaders at a watering-hole for their livestock is imagined as a typical incident of war.[3] The practice continued uninterrupted from Homer to the classical period. Athenian oral tradition told how Athens had ambushed and wiped out Megarian forces, while the Aeginetans told how they had ambushed and wiped out an Athenian army, all in the early sixth century. Miltiades the Elder was ambushed and captured during his attack on Lampsacus around 550 BC.[4] Archaic vase-paintings often represented both ambushes from legend and generic scenes of groups of soldiers squatting behind trees or in undergrowth, ready to pounce on an unsuspecting enemy (see Plate XII).[5] The same tactics were applied with much success by the general Demosthenes during the Peloponnesian War,[6] and were still envisaged as typical in Aeneas Tacticus' manual *How To Survive Under Siege* (15.7-16.13; 23). Spartan boys were accordingly taught ambushing skills from an early age.[7]

Few tactics could be more deadly than a surprise attack on an enemy camp. Diomedes and Odysseus entered the Trojan camp at night and butchered thirteen men in their sleep (*Iliad* 10.469-97). Fighting at night was rare, since it was almost as dangerous to the attacker as to the victim given the difficulty of distinguishing friend from foe in the dark (hence the Phocians' use of whitewash). Attacking a camp at dawn or during mealtimes, on the other hand, was a well-established tactic. The so-called battles of Pallene, *c.* 546 BC, and Sepeia, *c.* 494 BC, were in fact assaults on camps where the enemy was still having breakfast and unable to put up any resistance (Herodotus 1.63; 6.77-8); the attack at Sepeia is said to have left 6,000 dead (7.148). In Demosthenes' dawn attack on the camp of the Ambraciots in 426 BC so many were killed that Thucydides counted it among the greatest blows suffered by any city during this war (3.112-13), and we know of at least half a dozen later examples of this tactic, including a naval variation at the battle of Aigospotamoi, which to all intents and purposes decided the Peloponnesian War.[8]

Ambushes, surprise attacks and other deceptions were almost a necessity to those who faced a superior enemy, but the strong were no less happy to exploit such tactics as a means of inflicting maximum damage at minimum risk. Their importance was a constant theme in Xenophon's work. Among the qualities he admired in his hero Agesilaus was superior skill at deception 'once war had been declared and in consequence deceit had become legitimate and right' (*Agesilaus* 1.17). He urged unequivocally that every commander should 'himself devise a ruse for every occasion, since in war nothing is more profitable than deceit .... Think about successes in war, and you will find that most of the greatest have been achieved by means of deceit' (*Cavalry Commander* 5.9-11). The record for archaic and classical Greece bears him out. Victims of surprise attacks and other stratagems might complain that such tactics fell short of the ideal of open and fair confrontation, but the victors were no less proud of successes achieved by cunning than of their victories in pitched battle.[9]

Champion and restricted combat

At the less destructive end of the spectrum we encounter the strikingly game-like institution of single combat, fought as a side-show to battle and put on purely for the personal glory of the duellists. In the *Iliad*, Hector challenged all comers to a duel in which nothing was at stake but spoils for the winner, a conspicuous grave for the loser (7.37-312). A few historical figures are known to have followed his example. The Athenian commander and former Olympic champion Phrynon during a war around 600 BC over territory near Troy challenged 'whoever wished' to a duel, only to be killed by the enemy's general Pittacus.[10] Eurybates, a top pentathlete and leader of a band of volunteers helping to defend Aegina during a siege by Athens in 491 BC, challenged a series of opponents to single combat and killed three before being killed by the fourth man, Sophanes of Decelea (Herodotus 6.92, 9.75). Competitive sportsmen evidently liked to display their physical prowess on the battlefield, too. Single combat for display is widely attested, from Papua New Guinea to Republican Rome, and may well have been common in archaic Greece, although the practice was abandoned later.[11]

More significant forms of restricted combat are attested occasionally. Sparta and Argos selected 300 soldiers each to settle the dispute over Cynouria in the Battle of Champions of *c.* 550 BC. Sadly, they failed to agree on who had won and went on to commit their full forces to war. 'Many fell on both sides', after all. The right to contest Cynouria under similarly restricted conditions was written into a draft treaty of alliance at Argos' insistence in 421 BC, yet at the next available opportunity, six years later, the Argives abandoned all thought of champion combat and instead mounted a raid on Cynouria which 'took much plunder from the Spartans'.[12] Samos and Priene in their interminable rivalry over the plain of Anaia (p. 28) at first 'suffered and inflicted damage with moderation', which suggests some form of restricted combat. Yet when the Prieneans saw their chance they did not hesitate to kill 1,000 Samians in a single battle. The Samians in turn brought in a powerful ally and massacred the Prieneans in the so-called Battle at the Oak; the episode lived on in local tradition as 'the darkness at the oak' (Plutarch, *Moralia* 296ab). The protracted war between Chalcis and Eretria over the Lelantine plain was famous for two things: on the one hand, the warring parties had at some point agreed 'not to use long-range missiles'; on the other, both sides had brought in numerous allies, more than in any other archaic war. If the ban on bows and slings suggests the spirit of agonal warfare, the mobilisation of allies points in the opposite direction, to the escalation of conflict and the spirit of total warfare.[13]

The restrictions on manpower or weapons observed in these wars covered in each case only a brief phase of a long-running conflict which was at other times fought in a far from restrained manner.[14] Agonal rules of this kind were not regular archaic Greek practice, but occasional, local, and usually unsuccessful, attempts to contain an escalation of violence when the warring parties agreed that this was to their mutual advantage. At any other time, such restrictions would either not be considered at all or rejected by whichever side felt that its interests would be better served by mobilising all available military resources. Sparta simply ignored a Persian challenge to champion combat, and dismissed Argos' eagerness for a Battle of the Champions re-match as 'idiotic'.[15] A few isolated episodes of restraint in war, however, were enough to catch the nostalgic eye of later writers such as Polybius: a single famous ban on slings and arrows was all the evidence they needed for sweeping generalisations about 'the ancients' and their rejection of 'covert missiles' (p. 115).

Protocols of battle

Full-scale pitched battles knew some 'agonal' restraints, especially in the classical period, but they were never the formal engagements of Polybius' imagination, fought by arrangement at a stipulated time and place (13.3.8). Battles were often fought *as if* they had been arranged, because there was rarely much room for surprise when a general levy marched out to meet invaders in the plain where they had been destroying farms. Before engaging, the forces might remain encamped opposite one another for a few days, or even a week. They might try to sting the enemy into action by sending out cavalry to taunt them: 'Women!' (Herodotus 9.20) 'Are you planning to *settle* here?' (Thucydides 6.63.3). Conditions thus superficially resembled those of a duel. But delays were due to neither side wanting to make itself vulnerable by being the first, say, to cross a river or ravine, and the challenges were attempts to provoke the enemy into making the first move. There is not a shred of evidence that the delays were spent negotiating the time and place of battle, or even merely that armies waited until the other side was ready to fight.[16]

The signal for battle was simply the sight of the enemy, up to a mile away across the plain, beginning to advance. Where hilly or wooded terrain obscured the view, one might be unpleasantly surprised and forced to get ready in a hurry when the enemy suddenly emerged nearby. One Athenian general found himself cut short in mid-harangue by the unexpected speed of the enemy advance. Conversely, more than one Spartan commander found himself advancing against an opponent who refused to fight back: Agis, for one, came within a stone's throw of the enemy before retreating because the other side did not stir from its advantageous position. The agonal spirit was strong enough to inspire 'shame' at a failure to fight when the enemy offered battle, but not so strong that it made armies accept battle under any circumstances. Some generals resorted to outright deception to secure a favourable position for their forces, and a very few even managed to set ambushes and attack the enemy in the rear or flank during battle.[17]

The end of battle was no more regulated than its beginning. It might continue without decision until dusk, when darkness would force both sides to pull back, as was usually the case in Homeric battles, or it might end with a decisive breakthrough when one side turned to run and was unable to re-group, as generally happened in classical battles. Whenever the enemy was routed, the victors gave chase as fast and far as they could, killing and capturing as many as possible. Restrictions on pursuit were tactical, not moral, in nature: the danger of losing cohesion or moving too far from one's base and facing a sudden rally by the enemy meant that dense classical hoplite formations, in particular, could do only limited damage in pursuit, unlike the slaughter wrought by the more loosely ordered armies of Homeric heroes. But given a chance, even classical hoplites would pursue the enemy right up to, and through, the city gates. If the unfortunate routed army was unable to make its escape, it would be massacred to a man. Thousands of Argives in 494 BC and thousands of Corinthians in 460 BC ran for refuge only to reach a dead end: the Argives were burned alive when the Spartans set fire to the wood where they were hiding; the trapped Corinthians were surrounded by Athenian light-armed and stoned to death. In one of the battles of the Corinthian War, the Argives found themselves literally with their backs against the wall; those who were not trampled in the crush were slaughtered by their relentless attackers. 'They had no shortage of people to kill, since God granted them a success beyond their wildest prayers.'[18]

Pitched battle was not entirely without its rules. The practice of making a blood-sacrifice before battle and the custom of singing a hymn, the *paian*, during the advance were strictly speaking religious rituals rather than agonal conventions, although they did have the effect of limiting the speed and surprise of an attack.[19] Expressly restrictive rules, however, governed the treatment of the fallen and the marking of victory in the aftermath of a hoplite battle.

Mutilation of the dead was condemned in classical sources as 'the most unholy' of actions, 'more suitable for barbarians than Greeks'; it was seen as an excessive form of revenge which would invite divine punishment.[20] The victors were supposed to confine themselves to stripping the bodies of weapons, armour, clothing and any other possessions, leaving them naked – it was a show of special consideration to leave the dead wearing their tunics (Xenophon, *Hellenica* 2.4.19). Modern soldiers all too often mutilate enemy dead in defiance of strict moral and legal rules, and there are hints that classical Greek soldiers were also known to offend,[21] but the principle at least was clear. By contrast, no such prohibition was known to Homer, for whom mutilation of the dead was a perfectly acceptable form of revenge: in the *Iliad*, decapitation is common, the cutting off of limbs is mentioned, and the Greek leaders take turns at stabbing the dead body of Hector.[22] An image in later poetry of an old warrior lying dead on the battlefield, stripped naked and 'holding his bloodied genitals in his hands', may also refer to mutilation. Perhaps disfiguring the dead did not become universally taboo in Greece until after the Persian Wars, when some leading figures still thought it acceptable to decapitate the fallen Persian commander, and an admittedly idiosyncratic vase-painter could still depict hoplites carrying severed heads (Fig. 7).[23]

The most clear-cut agonal element in classical Greek warfare was the formal procedure for establishing the winner of a battle. By the time of the Peloponnesian War, the universally accepted criterion of victory was having control of the dead bodies strewn across the battlefield: whichever side asked the enemy permission to retrieve the stripped corpses of their men admitted defeat. The victors asserted control of the battlefield by attaching a set of captured arms and armour to a stake or tree as a *tropaion*, 'trophy' (literally 'turning-point marker'), at the spot where the enemy had been routed (Plate XIII). The rules were firm: the winner should always grant a truce for the recovery of the dead when requested, and the loser should always leave the enemy's trophy intact until it collapsed of its own accord, even if this meant tolerating a constant painful reminder of defeat just outside the city walls. The Thebans tried to bend these rules by attaching conditions to the truces they granted and by setting up a permanent rather than a perishable trophy to immortalise their victory at Leuctra; their actions were met with widespread condemnation.[24]

Armies took great risks and much trouble to ensure that their victories were formally recognised. After a drawn battle against Athenian forces in 460 BC, the Corinthian soldiers withdrew immediately, while the enemy stayed to put up a *tropaion*. Almost two weeks of continuous verbal abuse by their elders eventually shamed the Corinthians into marching out again for the sole purpose of setting up a trophy of their own. It was this attempt which led to a renewed Athenian attack and the massacre already mentioned.[25] On a much later occasion, when the Corinthians had killed some of the Theban Sacred Band in a skirmish, they 'dragged' the dead

Fig. 7. Mutilation of the dead. *Above*: three soldiers carrying severed heads on an Athenian lekythos decorated by the Beldam Painter, *c.* 490-480 BC (British Museum B 658). *Below*: a woman holding the severed head of a man on a fragment of a Chian vase decorated by the Naucratis Painter, *c.* 575-550 BC (British Museum GR 1886.6-1.510). Mythological interpretations of this scene have been offered (see A. Lemos, *Archaic Pottery of Chios*, vol. I (Oxford 1991), 108), but it may well represent a woman who has been presented with the head of an enemy in revenge for the death of a husband, brother or son; cf. *Iliad* 17.33-40.

over a distance of about half a mile from the battlefield to the city to make sure that no one could get at the bodies without asking permission and thereby admitting defeat. Conversely, the losers might be so determined to avoid formally conceding victory that they would try to retrieve the dead by force rather than ask for their return.[26]

All these efforts to gain control of the battlefield and the dead show that for the Greeks victory in battle was not only a means to an end, but also an end in itself. They might fight with extreme violence to strike a devastating blow which would bring them as close as possible to whatever ultimate goal they were pursuing in war, but when the battle had been won, their first preoccupation was to confirm and commemorate their victory. Unlike the Thebans, who tried to exploit victories by using the dead as a bargaining counter, demanding political and military concessions in exchange for the bodies, most classical Greeks sought control of the battlefield for the sake of symbolic gain – the recognition of superiority.

By the late fifth century, these conventions were described as 'ancestral custom' (Thucydides 4.98.5), but they were not in fact very old. In Homer, armies simply separate and go home at the end of a battle. No trophies are raised. Truces for the recovery of the dead are concluded only occasionally, by mutual agreement and without any implication of victory or defeat (*Iliad* 7.394-432; 24.656-67). This is not surprising, given that in Homer many days of battle may pass without either side scoring a decisive victory as troops gather, scatter, rally and scatter again in a series of clashes of greater or lesser importance. It was only when battle began to take its classical form of a single decisive clash that it became possible to determine the winners, and meaningful to mark gaining control of the battlefield as an achievement in itself. The Homeric war-dead, moreover, are largely dealt with *during* battle: many are carried to safety behind the lines by personal followers and friends; others are seized by vengeful personal enemies and deliberately left exposed to scavengers and the elements. It was not until military organisation became less personal and battle formation less open that it became the business of central command to deal with the dead after battle.[27]

Archaic poets assumed that many corpses would remain on the battlefield, lying exposed until they rotted away, and, according to tradition, the Battle of the Champions failed precisely because in the mid-sixth century there were still no agreed rules for determining the winner: the Spartans judged victory by possession of the field, the Argives by the number of casualties.[28] There is no evidence for regular burial truces or battlefield trophies in any war up to and including the Persian invasions. About a decade after the Persian Wars, however, the *tropaion* is mentioned as a familiar object and not much later it begins to be represented in art.[29] Some of the most distinctive and widely observed rules of Greek warfare thus apparently came into general use only at the very beginning of the classical period – primarily as a result of significant developments in combat, but in part perhaps also in response to the trauma of the Persian invasions which may have heightened sensitivity to the significance of 'turning back' the enemy and made it a duty to ensure burial for all those who had fought so heroically.[30]

Cities under fire

Methods of attacking fortified places changed fundamentally, if slowly, over the centuries, but here too deceit was a constant factor. Trojan Horse-style stratagems might work from time to time, but more, perhaps most, cities and forts were taken as a result of treason. We have evidence for treachery from the moment we have detailed evidence for sieges,[31] and rivalry between political factions was always so intense that in earlier centuries, too, patriotism will often have taken second place to partisan interests, as some faction or other opened the gates to a foreign army in exchange for support against opponents at home. The spectre of the enemy within haunted Aeneas Tacticus, who devoted more space to the prevention of treason than to fighting off an enemy assault, and obsessively listed the many ways of tampering with the locks on the city gates (*How To Survive Under Siege* 18-20). During a siege, he urged, private gatherings should be prohibited and letters censored, while black-outs should be imposed to prevent signalling to the enemy with lamps or torches (10).

The storming of city-walls took more casualties than any other type of combat. There was no element of surprise, unless one mounted a dawn raid on an utterly unsuspecting town, as one general did in order to find employment for 1,300 redundant mercenaries (Thucydides 7.29). One might try to rush the city after battle, while its gates were still open to receive the routed army, but defenders would be quite prepared to shut the gates early, leaving their own men huddled below the battlements 'like bats' (Xenophon, *Hellenica* 4.7.6). Normally, the only option was an open assault in which the odds were heavily in favour of the defenders en-sconced behind their fortifications.

In the *Iliad*, the Trojans attack the wall of the Greek camp, a monumental fortification to rival the wall of Troy itself (7.446-53), by concentrating their forces in five groups and assaulting several sections of the wall at once. They launch a barrage of stones to dislodge the defenders, who respond in kind with stones – stockpiled on the walls – and other missiles. The attackers clamber up the wall without the aid of ladders, use boulders to smash their way through the wooden gates, and apparently use no tools other than simple stakes serving as levers: 'they tugged at the layers of the wall, pulled down the battlements, levered out the protruding foundation stones' (12.258-60).[32] This epic picture is not mere heroic fantasy – identical storm tactics were practised by the Gauls (Caesar, *Gallic War* 2.6.2) – but reflects the simplicity of Greek siege warfare around 700 BC, in sharp contrast to sophisticated siege techniques already in use among Greece's eastern neighbours, especially the Assyrians.

The introduction of new weapons of assault and new means of defence was gradual at first, but eventually picked up pace and developed into a veritable arms race between defence and assault technology. Early fortifications were mostly rather flimsy structures of sun-dried brick on stone foundations; a wall of this kind still surrounded Mantinea in 385 BC and proved its undoing when flooding so weakened the bricks that the structure collapsed. In the course of the fourth century, however, cities began to construct ever more massive walls and towers with all-stone inner and outer faces, bonded by a rubble fill. The fortifications incorporated increasingly elaborate gate buildings, bastions, and other defensive structures, including artillery positions and moats (see Fig. 8).[33]

Assault techniques kept pace with these developments. For as long as walls remained vulnerable, attempts continued to be made to topple them with levers and spades under cover of missile fire (Euripides, *Phoenician Women* 1132, 1155). Scaling ladders were known in Athens by the 460s at the latest, and their use may be one of the reasons why the Athenians had by that time acquired a reputation for skill at taking fortifications.[34] As fortifications grew stronger, the first 'devices' (*mêchanaí*), as siege-engines were called, made their appearance. The Athenians are said to have been

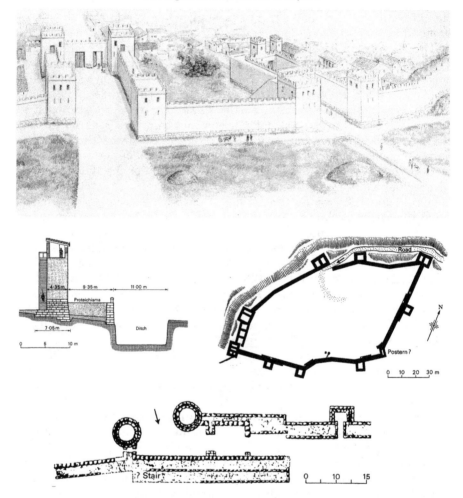

Fig. 8. Fortifications. *Top*: reconstruction by Peter Connolly of a section of Athens' fifth-century fortifications, showing two of the main city gates, the Dipylon Gate (*left*) and the Sacred Gate (*right*). *Centre left*: section of Athens' fourth-century city wall, with covered battlements, a lower 'advance wall' (*proteichisma*) and a moat. *Centre right*: plan of circuit wall of Aeolic Larisa, with a single main gate, a probable postern gate, and regularly spaced towers, *c.* 500 BC. *Bottom*: plan of a gate in the city wall of Mantineia, built in 371 BC.

among the first to experiment with these, during their siege of Samos in 440 BC, and Thucydides' accounts of the sieges of Plataea and Delium in the 420s give every impression that assault techniques were still in the process of being invented with great ingenuity. Mechanical battering rams, consisting of large beams with reinforced ends, suspended for greater leverage, and operated from within mobile shelters ('tortoises') for greater safety, were widely adopted. The Spartans constructed a sophisti-

Fig. 9. Siege engines. *Top*: covered battering ram, as first used in the siege of Samos, 440 BC. *Centre*: a flame-thrower as used in the siege of Delium, 424 BC. A cauldron full of highly flammable material is suspended from the end of a long pipe through which a bellows attached to the other end sends a powerful jet of air to project the flames. *Bottom*: artist's impression of scaling ladders, a siege tower with built-in battering ram, and a mining tunnel deployed against a city-wall.

141

cated siege ramp at Plataea; the Plataeans are the first Greeks known to have dug a mine; and the Thebans devised an effective flamethrower (Fig. 9).[35]

Apart from building stronger walls, defenders found ways of actively countering these threats. Rams were snagged and lifted with chains or rope, smashed by dropping great weights on them from the wall, or incinerated by pouring down pitch and then dropping a torch. Mines were located by tapping the ground with a bronze shield, which would ring when it hit the hollow of a tunnel, and counter-mines were dug from which to attack the sappers or smoke them out. Walls were fireproofed with bird-lime, vinegar, or felt and raw hide coverings; sails were suspended behind the walls to catch incendiary missiles.[36] Aeneas Tacticus' siege manual suggested such refinements as releasing bees and wasps into enemy mines and cushioning the blows of a battering ram with airbags (32.3-6; 33.1; 37.4-7).

Two key innovations attributed to the engineers of Dionysius I of Syracuse, used in his early fourth-century campaigns against the Carthaginians and adopted everywhere within a generation, were heavy artillery and mobile siege towers. Heavy artillery, generically called 'cata-pults' (*katapaltai*) and first mentioned in 399 BC, was the most significant invention. Initially probably little more than large, mechanical versions of bows and slings, by the time of Philip II at the latest a range of different 'catapults' had been developed which, using twisted sinew or rope, ex-ploited the principle of torsion to propel massive arrows and stones over great distances (see Fig. 10).[37] Siege towers, first mentioned in Greek use in 397 BC but apparently copied from Carthaginian models, were multi-storey structures designed to carry troops and artillery in relative safety close to the city wall; their crews could then fire missiles from an elevated position or even lower gangplanks to gain access to the walls or the roofs of houses. These towers became ever larger, and by 340 BC Philip II of Macedon was using one 120 feet tall. Apart from setting fire to such machines, or raising the city-wall with stones and sandbags to match their height, defenders mined the approaches to the city so that siege towers being wheeled up would sink into the ground.[38]

The most powerful weapon of all against a city under siege was hunger, but archaic armies apparently did not try to starve their opponents into surrender. In the *Iliad*, the Greek army mostly remains in camp, and makes no attempt to blockade the city. In the real world of archaic Greece, attackers similarly concentrated on storm and deceit rather than block-ade, judging by the very short duration of early sieges: the Spartans lasted only 40 days against Samos, the Athenians 26 days against Paros (Hero-dotus 3.56, 6.135.1). In the classical period, by contrast, the blockade became a major siege tactic. Besiegers surrounded the city with fortifica-tions – anything from a palisade to a double brick wall – while the besieged tried to keep their supply lines open by the construction of cross-cutting counter-walls, sallies against the siege works, and covert provisioning

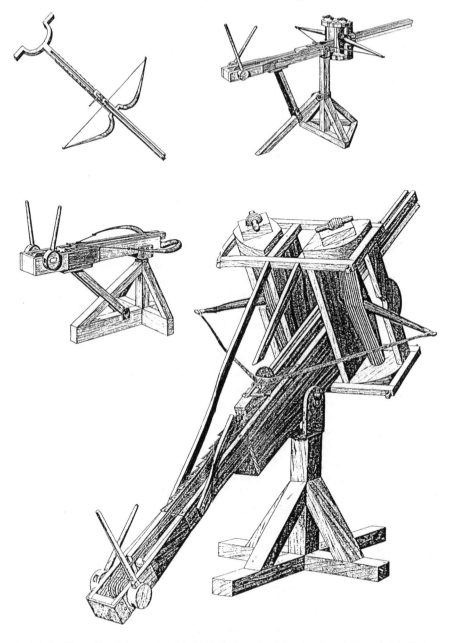

Fig. 10. Artillery. *Top left*: the hand-held 'belly-launcher' (*gastraphetes*) invented in 399 BC. *Bottom left*: an early fourth-century 'bolt-shooter' (*oxybeles*). *Top right*: a mid-fourth-century *oxybeles*, relying on torsion, with a range of *c.* 400 m. *Bottom right*: a late fourth-century 'stone-thrower' (*lithobolos*), capable of launching stones of up to 80 kg a distance of almost 200 m.

143

expeditions.[39] Even if supplies were cut off, it would take a long time before stocks ran out. Once the harvest had been brought in, a town with a largely agricultural population would have food for a year, and stores could be made to last longer still by an early evacuation of all those unfit for service. So long as it had access to water, a city might hold out for over two years, as did Thasos in the 460s, Potidaea in 431-428 and Plataea in 429-427 BC. Die-hard defenders survived on boiled leather, or ate the grass which grew just outside the city wall (if the enemy had not sent out cattle to graze it bare). Some, like the Potidaeans, allegedly resorted to cannibalism.[40]

Sieges were the most demanding form of warfare known to the Greeks. Both attackers and defenders needed to be continually on guard, working in shifts for months or years on end, under harsh, and always worsening, conditions. The besieged were forced to call on the services of the old and young who were normally excused military duties, and we are told that in a siege of Sinope even women were made to stand guard on the walls with makeshift armour so that from a distance they would look like hoplites, under strict orders not throw missiles, because they would give the game away by throwing like girls (Aeneas Tacticus 40.4). Capture by treason or assault often involved house-to-house fighting within the walls, during which both sides would suffer heavy casualties. Among the defenders no one would be exempt any longer, as the women climbed onto the roofs of their houses to encourage the men with their ritual cry of *ololygê*, and hurl heavy rooftiles at the enemy.[41]

Since archaic Greeks were no less interested in capturing and destroying cities than classical Greeks were, the persistence of primitive assault tactics and the absence of blockading until the classical period require some explanation. Ambivalence about relying on walls and 'devices' rather than physical prowess may have done something to inhibit the development of fortifications and siege warfare. Scruples about cutting off food and water supplies may also have played their part.[42] But these inhibitions existed throughout the classical as well as the archaic period, yet clearly did little to stop the rapid growth of siege technology in the fourth century. The slow rate of earlier developments therefore cannot be attributed to agonal attitudes and moral scruples alone. The answer is, rather, that most communities in the archaic period lacked the material resources and political organisation to do more than make an occasional, brief attempt to capture a rival town by simple storm.

Although in an emergency quite substantial fortifications could be put up by a communal effort – if 'men, women and children' all pitched in and were prepare to rob their own houses and grave monuments for building materials (Thucydides 1.90.3, 93.1-2) – normally it required a great deal of money and organisation to fortify a city. Siege engines, unlike the ordinary weapons which everyone owned, needed to be constructed at the order of a central authority with access to sufficient funds and specialists. To keep an army in the same place, let alone to keep it operating effectively, for more than a few weeks required much more logistical support than was normally available: at the very least soldiers would need to be supplied with food or pay. It is surely no coincidence that the Spartans' siege of Samos lasted exactly as long as their longest invasion of Attica: 40 days.[43] The frequency but short duration of other early sieges confirms that it was not the will which was lacking in the archaic period, merely the means. Only when Greek states developed to the point where they controlled sizeable resources of money and manpower (pp. 233-40) were they able to pursue their old ambition to capture and destroy cities with ever more devastating efficiency.

Aftermath: war-heroes, prisoners and refugees

The first order of business at the end of a campaign was to bury the dead. A conspicuous burial-mound is the dead hero's reward in the poems of Homer (*Iliad* 7.84-91) and Tyrtaeus (F 12.29 West), and it may have been common in archaic Greece to bury outstanding fighters separately from the other dead. In archaic Sparta, where the custom was to bury the fallen in collective graves on or near the battlefield, some men were given prominent graves of their own: Archias, the man who 'proved himself the best' in the siege of Samos of *c.* 525; Anchimolius, who had led an incursion into Attica *c.* 510;[44] and above all the best fighters at Plataea in 479 BC. Herodotus explains that after this battle the Spartans buried their 'holy ones' (*hirees*) in one tomb, the rest of the Spartiates in another, and the helots in a third (9.85.1-2). His list of men included among the 'holy ones' coincides exactly with his list of those proclaimed 'the best' and 'honoured' by the survivors of the battle (9.71.2-72.1): evidently the 'holy ones' were not priests but men of outstanding merit, and the honour awarded to these men consisted of separate burial.[45] The Athenians may have had a similar custom: a few years after the Persian Wars, when Hermolycus, who had distinguished himself as an athlete and as the best man in the battle of Mycale, died in action on Euboea, he was buried there in just the sort of spot envisaged in the *Iliad*, a conspicuous location on a headland for all passing ships to see (Herodotus 9.105).

Within a decade of Hermolycus' heroic burial, however, the Athenians stopped awarding such special honours and adopted the egalitarian practice of burying all the war-dead, regardless of status, in a common grave in Athens' public cemetery, just outside the city-gates, at an annual ceremony which featured a funeral oration delivered by a leading public figure. The cremated remains of rich and poor, general and private soldier, were placed together in a single coffin for each of the ten tribes, and the grave was marked with an inscription listing the names of all who were buried there. Similar casualty lists appear in many other Greek cities from the mid-fifth century onwards, which suggests that Athens was not alone in moving towards a more egalitarian treatment of the war-dead. The only

145

nod towards making social distinctions was to specify which of the men buried in the common grave were commanders or champion athletes, and which were non-citizens.[46] The burial of 13 Spartans where they had fallen in the fighting just outside Athens in 403 BC shows that in Sparta, too, the custom of awarding special funerary honours to outstanding men had by then been much diluted: all 13 casualties share the same grave, and the only sign of hierarchy is that two polemarchs and an Olympic champion are buried in a separate central section of the tomb, with their names and status inscribed on it (Fig. 11).[47]

Tyrtaeus promised that a war-hero's 'children, and children's children, and later descendants' would be 'conspicuous among people' (F 12.29-30 West), and this distinction too was given an egalitarian form not long after the Persian Wars, when several cities began to pay for the upbringing of all boys whose fathers had fallen in battle.[48]

The care of the wounded, on the other hand, apparently remained a haphazard process in which more prominent men had a much better chance than most of securing medical help. 'A healer is worth many other men when it comes to cutting out arrows and applying soothing drugs', according to Homer (*Iliad* 11.514-15), but only two men in the entire Greek army at Troy count as specialist healers (2.732; 11.833). Menelaus is lucky enough to have one of these physicians suck out the blood from his wound (4.190-219), but most of the casualties are dependent on the assistance of friends and attendants, who apply makeshift bandages and any remedies, pain-killers or 'incantations' which they happen to know.[49]

More or less the same situation prevailed in the classical period. The Spartan army had a number of physicians on its general staff, but other forces seem to have relied on whatever help happened to be available. Among Xenophon's mercenaries there were either no doctors or far too few, and in one crisis eight men had to be 'appointed as doctors' on the spot to deal with the many casualties.[50] Most soldiers could expect no more than the sort of amateur medical care vividly portrayed by Theophrastus in his portrait of the typical coward:

Fig. 11. Tomb of the war dead. Reconstruction, plan, and contents of the Tomb of the Lacedaemonians, containing the bodies of 13 or 14 Spartans who fell near this spot in 403 BC. The tomb was situated about 50 m outside the Dipylon Gate at Athens (see Fig. 8 above) in the Athenian public cemetery along the main road leading west. It was a large but simple rectangular enclosure *c.* 11 or 12 m long and about 3 m high, decorated only with an inscription along the top, which in large letters read 'LAKEDAIMONION', and in smaller letters inserted the names of each of the casualties, the first two of whom were given their title *polemarchos*. The inscription is unusual in running backwards, i.e. from right to left. (The slab in front of the tomb is a boundary stone added later.) The tomb contained no grave goods and the only distinction made between the bodies was that the three placed in the middle compartment of the tomb – presumably the two polemarchs and the Olympic victor – had slightly more room and were laid out with their heads resting on two stones, rather than one stone as in the case of the others (see photo). One of the dead had a spear-head between the ribs, and another had two arrow-wounds to the legs.

147

> When he sees from his tent that a wounded friend of his is being brought in,
> he runs towards him, tells him to hang in there, picks him up and carries
> him .... He nurses the man; washes him with a sponge; sits beside him to
> keep the flies from his wound – anything rather than fight the enemy. When
> the trumpeter sounds the charge, he sits in his tent. 'Go to hell!', he says.
> 'Will he ever let the poor man get some sleep, with his constant trumpeting?'
> Covered with blood from another's wound, he goes to meet the men as they
> return from battle and ... takes those from his deme and tribe to see the
> casualty. He tells every single one of them how he himself, with his own
> hands, brought the man to his tent. (*Characters* 25.5-6)

One Athenian, laid low by dysentery as well as injuries sustained in
combat during the Corinthian War, had himself carried all the way home
from Corinth to Athens, presumably in order to seek medical treatment
there. About halfway along, as he passed through the harbour of Megara,
he encountered a friend of his who made a point of walking with him for
several hours before turning around and walking straight back to Megara
(Plato, *Theaetetus* 142a-143b). The wounded clearly got all the moral
support they could wish for, but specialist help was in short supply, unless
one had the means to travel and hire a doctor.

Not that specialists were always much help. Surgery did not extend
much beyond sewing up wounds, and even when no vital organs were
damaged blood loss and infection claimed many victims. A dozen case
studies recorded in two fourth-century medical tracts present a.tally of
nine men who died agonising deaths between a few hours and a week after
receiving their wounds; two men who were saved owing to medical intervention; and one who survived despite the doctor's inability to help – he
lived for at least another six years with an arrowhead embedded deep in
his groin.[51]

The wounded receive little attention in the Greek sources. Battle scars,
such a source of pride in many warlike societies, hardly get a mention. In
archaic Athens, a few outstanding disabled soldiers were rewarded with
the right to dine at public expense, but the classical Athenian state made
no special arrangements for the wounded: crippled veterans were lumped
together with all other invalids when it came to awarding pensions, which
were small and granted only to the poorest citizens. Perhaps injuries and
scars were to the Greeks not so much marks of honour as uneasy reminders that in war not everyone either died a 'beautiful' death or escaped
unscathed to be 'admired by men and desired by women'.[52]

Prisoners of war might suffer any fate from execution to instant release,
depending on the circumstances of their capture and the interests of their
captors. Most commonly, they were ransomed or sold into slavery. Ransoms were normally paid privately: a prisoner relied on his family and
friends to raise and deliver the required sum; the role of the state in this
process appears to have been minimal. The high level of ransoms in
archaic Greece – 200 drachmas was a standard amount – meant that only

the wealthy had a chance of escaping captivity in this way. A rich patron might help poorer men regain their freedom, but at a price: by law, a man 'belonged' to his ransomer 'unless he paid back the ransom-money'. The much lower standard sum of 100 drachmas demanded in the classical period obviously allowed a much wider group of citizens to regain their freedom without falling into the clutches of a creditor, and the reduction is probably another sign of the trend towards greater equality in the Greek world. In democratic Athens, at any rate, the rich prided themselves on advancing ransom-payments free of interest or even as a gift.[53]

Prisoners not ransomed, released or killed were sold on the spot to slave traders.[54] Where large numbers had been captured, supply might well exceed demand, and in such circumstances it counted as an act of humanity to ensure that all prisoners were indeed sold, however difficult it might be to find buyers for them. Normally, the slave traders would simply abandon the smallest children and the aged by the roadside to die of starvation and exposure, if they were not killed by dogs or wolves first (Xenophon, *Agesilaus* 1.21-2).

The human cost of war was greatest in sieges, which not only took the highest toll in dead and wounded and prisoners executed or enslaved, but often also created huge numbers of refugees. Thousands might try to escape with a few possessions from a city under siege; when the city fell, tens of thousands might be forced to leave their country with nothing more than the clothes on their backs. Refugee populations usually scattered as smaller and larger groups were taken in by other communities and at least some upper-class families were put up by personal friends abroad. The charity extended by other communities should not be underestimated: the people of Troezen are said to have offered hospitality to great numbers of evacuated Athenians during the Persian Wars, and to have raised funds to pay for the education of these refugees' children. Some scattered populations were even lucky enough to be reunited after a few years in exile, restored to their home, or given a new home, by a powerful ally.[55] For the vast majority of refugees, however, the conditions of life can hardly have been much better than those familiar from newsreel images of dispossessed families trudging along dusty roads or eking out an existence in camps and slums:

> The most wretched of all things is for a man to leave his city and its fertile fields, reduced to the life of a beggar, wandering with his mother and aged father, his little children and wedded wife. Wherever he ends up, he will be as an enemy dwelling among them. He will succumb to need and detestable poverty, bring shame upon his family, disgrace his splendid looks. All forms of dishonour and misery will dog him.
> Since this is how it is and no one cares for or respects a wanderer or his offspring at all, let us fight hard for our land and die for our children without sparing our lives.

149

For this early Spartan poet, at any rate, the life of a refugee was a fate worse than death.[56]

*

Greek warfare had two faces, but its destructive side stands out most clearly. Agonal ideals had their place, of course: armies fought open battles if the odds were good enough; archaic communities occasionally tried to impose restrictions on warfare; rules governing classical infantry combat sprang up as victory in battle became a goal in itself. Yet throughout the archaic and classical periods city-states generally sought to do as much damage to the enemy as they possibly could, and if there were limitations to their search for honour or profit, these were imposed more by logistical than by ethical constraints. As and when Greek states acquired greater central resources and control, they wasted no time in finding ways to overcome their traditional limitations and wage ever more devastating wars.

Part V

The Experience of Combat

Blind terror is only a figure of speech to most of us, but some soldiers are so traumatised by combat that they are literally struck blind with fear. One such casualty was Epizelos, an Athenian militiaman who fought the Persians at Marathon:

> As he was fighting at close range and proving himself a good man, he was robbed of his eyesight although no part of his body was struck with a weapon or hit by a missile, and from that moment on he remained blind for the rest of his life.

He himself said that it happened when he saw the man immediately next to him killed by what appeared to be a giant hoplite with a huge beard (Herodotus 6.117.2-3). Ten years later, 300 picked Spartan fighters prepared to meet the Persians at Thermopylae. They were immortalised in tradition as preparing for death with complete composure, calmly doing their exercises and combing their long hair. Yet tradition also said that two of the men were 'laid up with extreme eye problems' and their temporary blindness too may well have been of a psychosomatic nature.[1] The Greeks were apt to stress how frightening it could be simply to see the enemy: Herodotus noted that the Athenians 'were the first who could bear to look upon Persian clothes and the men who wore them; until then the Greeks had been terrified at the mere mention of the name "Persian"' (6.112.3).[2] It may be no coincidence that we hear of soldiers losing their eyesight precisely when their cities for the very first time came under attack by a strange and dangerous new opponent.

The trauma of ancient Greek battle was different from the experiences which leave so many modern soldiers 'shell-shocked' or debilitated by post-traumatic stress disorder. Greek soldiers rarely came close to suffering the extremes of physical deprivation associated with trench or jungle warfare, and never saw their friends blown to pieces. On the other hand, hoplites suffered the devastating experience – almost unknown in modern warfare, dominated as it is by long-range fighting with guns, artillery and bombs – of standing at no more than arm's length from the enemy and laying into one man after another with spear, sword, and ultimately bare hands and teeth (Herodotus 7.225.3).

V. The Experience of Combat

Exactly how hoplites fought their fearsome battles is not immediately clear from ancient descriptions. All the most explicit evidence relates to the heavy infantry employed by the Macedonian and hellenistic kingdoms from Philip II and Alexander the Great onwards, rather than to the heavy infantry of the Greek city-states. Archaic and classical Greek authors assumed that their audiences were familiar with the experience of combat and, apart from recording the occasional striking detail, described battle only in the most general terms: armies advance, fight and 'push' until one side 'breaks' and runs. Much of the vague and limited evidence gives the impression that the clash of phalanxes was of unimaginable intensity: the hoplites, apparently drawn up in the tightest possible ranks, shoulder pressing against shoulder and shield rubbing against shield, charge at a run and appear to throw their bodily weight against the enemy front line, one rank after another, resulting in a massive pile-up of men pushing and shoving one another forwards until the opposing formation disintegrates under the sheer physical pressure.

The most influential modern interpretation of classical Greek battle holds that this is precisely what did happen. If so, the hoplite way of war was unique and must have been uniquely traumatic. A small but crucial body of evidence, however, does not fit this picture of a horrific 'hoplite scrum', as it has been dubbed, and we shall see that it is yet another modern myth about Greek warfare. Hoplites were notable for their close formations and close-range fighting, but their battles were a far cry from collective shoving matches.[3]

If any question has been more vigorously debated than the nature of hoplite tactics, it is the question of their origins. Here the sources offer no explicit guidance at all,[4] and we must deduce what we can from epic poetry, fragments of war songs, battle scenes in art, and the arms and armour found deposited in graves or dedicated in temples. Ever since Wolfgang Helbig first tackled the question almost a century ago, some scholars have dated the rise of hoplite tactics by the earliest finds of hoplite equipment, c. 725-700 BC,[5] while others have dated this development by what are thought to be the earliest representations of a hoplite phalanx in art, c. 650 BC.[6] On either view, the nature of infantry battle is believed to have remained essentially unchanged over the next three or four centuries, until the end of the classical period. Such stability in an age of social and political upheaval and incessant warfare would be quite remarkable, and should give us pause for thought. Once again there is reason to suspect that the consensus is wrong. It was, rather, a slow and steady process lasting throughout the archaic and classical periods which transformed Greek infantry tactics from the kind of fluid long-range skirmishing found in 'primitive' societies into the kind of close-order hand-to-hand combat found in more developed city-states and, beyond this, into the highly demanding and sophisticated manner of fighting practised by the armies of the most powerful hellenistic kingdoms.

11

The Deeds of Heroes

Battle in the Iliad

In the Highlands of Papua New Guinea, old warriors used to tell tales about the battles of their youth which went something like this:

> 'We met on the mountainside near Wihun. A man of our side, named Maigi, threw a spear at a man of their side, named Wea. He missed. Then a man of their side threw a spear and hit my cross-cousin from Ahalaseimihi. Then I was angry and threw a spear at Wena, a big man of their side, and missed ....' (Mead 1968, viii)

But for the names, their stories might have come straight from Homer:

> Antiphos cast his sharp spear through the crowd at Aias. He missed him, but hit Odysseus' fine comrade Leucos in the groin as he was dragging the body [of a dead Trojan] to the other side ... Odysseus was very angry at his death. He went forward through the frontline fighters, moved in very close, stood still, looked all around him, and cast his spear. The Trojans fell back before the man as he took aim ... but he hit Democoon, bastard son of Priam. (*Iliad* 4.489-99)

These narratives may at first seem baffling. 'I have often found the accounts of such warfare hard to credit', commented the anthropologist who reported the example from New Guinea. 'Listening to such a verbal account, one cannot help wondering what everybody else was doing.'[1] Most readers of the *Iliad* find it equally difficult to imagine what the cast of thousands are supposed to be doing on the battlefield while a handful of heroes trades blows.[2]

However, when ethnographers were able to witness Highlands battle for themselves, it emerged that the old warriors' stories were perfectly correct, if selective, accounts of the action. While hundreds of men engaged in combat, they fought in such open and fluid order that each warrior had the freedom to move around and pick his opponents. The war stories were selected highlights, each covering only some of the action and only a small section of the battle-lines. Homeric battle-scenes can be understood in the same way: they make sense when seen as highlights of a general engagement involving large numbers of men who fight in loose and fluid order. To say that they make sense is not to say that they are realistic. The epic battles are set in the distant past and are fought by heroes with super-human strength and divine helpers. The action features sensational wounds and spectacular death-dives which would not be out of place in a spaghetti Western. But the basic patterns of the heroes' battlefield behaviour are internally consistent and plausible. Whether or not Homeric combat is based on historical warfare (see Appendix 3), the *Iliad*'s picture of battle is by far the richest we have from ancient Greece, and, if nothing else, conveys to us an early Greek *ideal* of combat – which turns out to be, by our standards, surprisingly unheroic.

The shape of battle

The main obstacle to understanding how Homeric armies fight is the preconception that there are only two kinds of mass fighting: either a scattered light-armed crowd throws or shoots missiles at the enemy from a distance, or a heavy-armed crowd fights the enemy hand-to-hand in tight formation. The battles fought in Papua New Guinea show otherwise.

Before combat, Highlands warriors gather round their leaders in dense crowds (Plate XIV) and after a harangue set off at a run towards the battlefield, scattering as they do so (Plate XV) and slowing down as they draw closer to the enemy (Plate XVI), until they come within firing range of the opposing lines. At this point the warriors are widely dispersed (Plate XVII) and in constant movement, not only across the front line 'to avoid presenting too easy a target', but to and from the front: 'men move up from the rear, stay to fight for a while, and then drop back for a rest'. Warriors fight as archers or spearmen as a matter of personal preference, Spears, as in Homer, are used both for thrusting and throwing. At any one time, only about a third of each army takes an active part in battle, while two-thirds stand or sit well back and observe the action. In the course of a day's fighting, a man spends much time at the back, but he will also go forward several times to take his turn at doing battle.[3]

In the course of this open-order skirmishing, 'the front continually fluctuates, moving backwards and forwards as one side or the other mounts a charge'. 'As the early afternoon wears on, the pace of battle develops into a steady series of brief clashes and relatively long interruptions .... An average day's fighting will consist of ten to twenty clashes between the opposing forces', lasting between ten and fifteen minutes each.[4]

This is the normal pattern of combat on the open battlefield. The intense fighting required to break into an enemy settlement, however, may involve a denser and more organised formation. Spearmen equipped with shields, 'who usually number only about a tenth of the force, ... move together as a tight front line, keeping close together to protect one another's flanks.

Their archers fire over and around them.' As the action unfolds, the forces spread out into 'a loose skirmishing line' and contract again into close order as the situation demands. The spearmen take pride in forming an 'impenetrable' wall of shields; anyone dropping out of this front rank is obliged to warn his neighbours first.[5]

Combat in the *Iliad* follows essentially the same patterns. Before battle, leaders harangue their followers, who excitedly form dense crowds as they jostle to get to the front:

> The lines drew closer together when they heard their ruler .... Shield pressed against shield, helmet against helmet, man against man. They stood so close that the shining crestholders of their plumed helmets touched when they nodded. (16.211-17)

As they advance, this 'cloud of footsoldiers' in 'dense ranks, dark and bristling with shields and spears' (4.274-82) begins to 'swarm out like wasps' (16.259). Each band of warriors moves at its own pace: the most eager sweep forward 'one after another ... some ahead, close together, and others behind them', like the waves of a stormy sea (4.422-8; 13.795-800), but the less keen hang back (4.331-5, 347-8). Each man also moves at his own pace. Some move out far in front, 'walking ahead of the mass with great strides' (4.22) or driving their chariots 'ahead of everyone ... with only one thought – to fight in front' (16.218-20). Others linger among 'the hindmost ranks' and need to be spurred on by their leaders.[6]

As the armies move into action and the initial dense crowds dissolve, a distinction develops between the minority who go forward to within range of the enemy, the 'frontline fighters' (*promachoi*), and the 'multitude' (*plêthus*) who keep their distance. Even the men at the front generally venture only just within missile range to throw stones, shoot arrows, or hurl javelins, but from time to time they will dash forward to attack an enemy at close range with spear, sword or axe, before dashing back again to a safer distance.

The first scene of the first battle is typical. Antilochus opens the action by throwing a spear which catches a Trojan in the forehead. Another Greek runs forward and grabs the dead man by the feet in an attempt to drag him into the Greek lines 'away from the flying missiles' and plunder his corpse. By moving so close to the enemy, however, he makes himself vulnerable and as he bends down to take hold of the body, a Trojan stabs him at close range. Other men now join in a fight over both bodies, which involves the exchange of missiles already cited: Aias kills one of the Trojans 'coming forward', Leucos accidentally gets hit by a spear thrown 'through the crowd', and Odysseus charges forward 'through the frontline fighters' to take revenge by hurling his spear into a group of Trojans (4.457-99). The ten men named in this short sequence are surrounded by many unnamed others, as references to 'the flying missiles', 'the crowd', and further 'frontline fighters' remind us. As the fight intensifies, they are close enough for a spear which misses its target to hit another man, though at other times the gaps are larger and spears fly through the ranks without hitting anyone (13.502-5; 16.608-15), and there is always enough room for individuals to move around among the crowd. The main tactics are to run some way forward and throw a missile or run all the way up to the nearest enemy to attack at close range.

Most men retreat after only a short while at the front, or indeed run back immediately after launching their first missile or landing their first blow.

> Harpalion leapt out at Menelaus …. At close range he struck with his spear the centre of Menelaus' shield, but was unable to drive his weapon through it, and drew back again into the crowd of his comrades to escape death, looking all around him, concerned that someone might touch his skin with a weapon. (13.642-9)

In praise of Hector, it is said that he 'never stayed among the multitude, but used to run far forward' (22.458-9), but even this most energetic of fighters from time to time falls back 'towards the multitude' (11.354-60), 'interrupts the fight' (16.721), and does 'not fight as a *promachos*, but waits among the multitude, outside the turmoil' (20.376-7). The second greatest Trojan warrior, Aeneas, is particularly given to standing around 'at the very back of the crowd' (13.459), and on the Greek side, too, even 'the best men in the army' spend time 'in the rear, catching their breath at the ships' (13.83-4, 117). Some absent themselves for long periods of time, sitting in their quarters, talking and drinking, just as Highlands warriors take breaks to chew tobacco behind the lines while their friends carry on fighting.[7]

At the same time, no one can get away with hanging back among the multitude all the time. Leading warriors are forever telling others not to 'stand off without fighting, doing as they please' (14.132) or to 'shirk the fighting of their own free will' (13.234). Their exhortations are aimed at the entire multitude: 'the work of more is better', they say (12.410-12), reminding 'each man' to 'go forward and be eager to fight' (20.353-5). Two commanders 'rebuked whomever they saw shirking the fight completely' with the words:

> 'Friends! You who excel among the Greeks, you who are average, and you who are worse – after all, not everyone is equal in war – now there is a task at hand for *everyone*, as you yourselves know very well. Do not turn back towards the ships … but go forward and encourage one another!' (12.269-74)

Everyone is expected to take their turn at fighting among the 'frontline fighters', and everyone is entitled to spend some time taking it easy among the 'multitude'. How much time a man spends in the front or the rear of this highly fluid battle order is ultimately up to himself, as a matter of personal commitment, courage and stamina.[8]

Homer's battle narrative cuts back and forth between close-ups of the deeds of a few men somewhere along the front and panoramic images of the entire mass of men in action, exchanging missiles and trading blows. To the modern reader, unfamiliar with the kind of fighting described by the poet, the panoramic scene of 'shields clashing' at the beginning of the first battle (4.446-56) may suggest a collision of two close-order phalanxes, while the missiles which fly all morning at the beginning of the third battle (11.90-1) may sound like long-range skirmishing.[9] But to audiences who understood how the heroes fought it would have been obvious that such images simply represented two sides of the same coin. In the fluid, open-order action of the epic, mass fighting takes place at close range and long range at the same time, as nicely illustrated by the opening scene of the *Iliad*'s second battle:

> When the armies came together, shields clashed, as did the spears and spirits of bronze-cuirassed men; embossed shields struck one another and a great roar went up. Killers shouted in triumph as their victims screamed; the earth was soaked in blood. Throughout the morning, while the holy light of day grew stronger, missiles from both sides hit their mark and men fell. (8.60-7)

The absence of a regular formation does not prevent warriors from spontaneously joining forces at all levels. Homer stresses the effectiveness of 'two men standing together' (5.565-72; 17.721). 'We may do some good even if there are only two of us, for even the poorest fighters can display combined prowess' (13.236-7). Archers rely on comrades to provide cover (4.112-26; 8.266-72) and every man relies on others to rescue him when he is in trouble or wounded, or, should he fall in action, to save his body from falling into enemy hands. Often, it is not just a matter of a few men helping a friend, but of sizeable crowds running up from the rear or from another part of the frontline to 'stand close by him, leaning their shields against their shoulders, their spears levelled' (11.584-95; 13.477-88). In a few cases, several leaders join forces, and their bands of followers merge into an unusually large and dense mass (13.498-95; 17.246-61). The Greeks are portrayed as more aware than the Trojans of the tactical value of solidarity and cohesion: they advance 'eager in their hearts to defend one another' (3.8-9; 14.368-9) and fight with fewer casualties 'because in the mêlée they always remembered to protect one another' (17.364-5).[10]

As more and more men join in an attempt to rescue a wounded comrade or the corpse of a leading warrior, the action intensifies. The combatants venture further forward, increasingly fight hand-to-hand rather than with missiles, and begin to pack together 'like a wall' (13.152; 15.618), as tightly as they had done before 'swarming out' into battle (13.126-35). In the culminating struggle over the corpse of Patroclus, the Greeks temporarily abandon their usual mobile tactics and, instead of fighting as individual *promachoi*, form a fully closed and entirely stationary 'fence of shields' which the enemy is unable to attack (17.352-65). But this uniquely cohesive order soon crumbles, and even while it lasts it involves only part of the army. Elsewhere, long-range combat in open order continues to prevail:

> ... the *other* Trojans and Greeks did battle in comfort, under a clear sky .... They fought intermittently, avoided the other side's painful missiles, and stood far apart.[11]

Whether through collective effort, a single conspicuous killing or divine intervention, a breakthrough will eventually occur, and one side will run while the other pursues. The fight turns into a massacre, often described in a catalogue of how 'each of the leaders killed a man' (5.37-8). Eventually, the flight is halted, the scattered troops rally, the pursuers in turn draw back and regroup, and 'standing battle' starts all over again. The pattern is repeated time and time again, until nightfall puts an end to the fighting.[12]

Chariots in combat

On and off the battlefield, a Homeric hero is 'made resplendent by his chariot' (*Iliad* 12.114), a light wooden vehicle drawn by two horses.[13] The warrior and his charioteer, usually a kinsman or friend of lower status, stay in their chariot for as long as they hang back among the multitude, 'outside the missiles, the killing, the blood' (11.163-4). On rare occasions they may drive right up to the frontline, close enough to fight from the chariot, but normally the warrior 'jumps off' when he decides that the time has come for action and 'mingles with the *promachoi*' on foot. After a while, he will return to his chariot to store away spoils, nurse his wounds, move to another part of the field, or, most urgently, to escape or pursue the foe in a general rout. This use of the chariot as a 'taxi', as it has been mockingly described, has parallels among the Celts,[14] and according to Xenophon among the Assyrians, who 'left their chariots to fight as *promachoi*' and eventually 'remounted and withdrew towards the multitude of their own men' (*Education of Cyrus* 3.3.60).

The *Iliad*'s picture of chariots in combat is strikingly detailed. A good deal of attention is given to the question of the best distance at which the chariot should follow the fighter while he is on foot. The advantages of keeping the horses as close as possible to the fighting-man, 'breathing in his neck', are highlighted: when in danger, he will not have to 'run a long way back' and meet his death because 'his horses were not near enough'.[15] On the other hand, the deaths of drivers and horses who venture too near the combat-zone serve as warnings. The poet covers all eventualities: spare horses are taken into battle; men who lose their drivers retreat to find replacements; charioteers leave battle when their fighting-men are killed, since to attempt to carry on fighting alone is an 'unprofitable notion' (17.458-73). Remarkably, charioteers and fighting-men rarely try to avenge one another's deaths or rescue one another's bodies, but usually simply turn the chariot round and leave: the immediate safety of the horses takes precedence over normal obligations to a fallen comrade.[16] During flight and pursuit, chariots charge ahead of the mass ('the fast horses carried Hector and his weapons away; he left the men of Troy behind', 16.367-9), but they are reunited with their companions on foot when the enemy rallies: the infantry 'turned white in the shower of dust kicked up among them ... by the hooves of the horses which rejoined them, for the charioteers wheeled them round' (5.503-5).

Despite the richness and subtlety of Homer's portrait of chariot war-fare, and the known parallels in other societies, most scholars dismiss 'the nonsense we read in the poems about military chariots' (Finley 1977, 149). They believe that chariots *ought* to have been used quite differently in war, in specialist battalions, either carrying archers and serving as a missile arm, or carrying heavy-armed fighters with long lances and serving as a shock-force. The conclusion generally drawn is that Homer and his fellow-poets were trying to recreate the use of war-chariots which they knew had existed in the Bronze Age, but had no idea of how these had really been used and therefore simply made something up.[17]

Yet the Homeric use of chariots should not be dismissed as 'nonsense' just because it is not the most efficient use conceivable. Considerations other than pure military efficiency always play a part in determining the ways of war in any society. In the heroic world, chariots do not fight in battalions for the very good reason that they belong to *leaders*, who cannot unite in specialist mounted battalions because they are bound to fight alongside the footsoldiers who form their personal retinues.[18] Leading warriors travel in chariots wherever they can, because the chariot is a status symbol which sets them apart from their followers, not to mention a fast get-away vehicle. At the same time, they are acutely aware of putting their prized horses in considerable danger (5.192-203), so they rarely drive them into the thick of the action, but instead dismount to fight – a practice which minimises the risk to chariots and horses without entirely depriving the proud owners of their use.[19]

Occasional images of chariots crushing the corpses of fallen soldiers under their wheels as they speed along are sensational rather than realistic, and it would clearly be wrong to assume that the *Iliad*'s repre-sentation of chariots was drawn from life in every detail. But in outline Homer's portrayal of chariots is precise, coherent and perfectly plausible, whether he shows them hanging back among the multitude, edging forward through the crowd as they track the movements of the dismounted fighters, or racing ahead in flight and pursuit.[20]

Battlefield etiquette: the myth of the heroic code

With a black sense of humour, the heroes refer to combat as 'the intimacies of the front line' (*Iliad* 13.291; 17.228). In its way, face-to-face fighting *is* an intimate activity and, like all social intercourse, tends to follow certain rules. What is most remarkable about battlefield behaviour in Homer, and in Papua New Guinea, however, is how few rules there seem to be.

An ideal of open and fair combat does exist, but this appears only in the formal duels which may precede and follow battle, not in battle itself. When about to engage in single combat, Aias freely offers Hector the advantage of making the first move, and Hector repays the compliment by warning Aias to be on guard: 'I do not want to look for an opportunity to hit a great man like you by stealth, but will hit you openly if I can.'[21] Nowhere else in the *Iliad* do the heroes display such chivalry. Duellists who decline an advantage, therefore, are not simply obeying some universal 'heroic code',[22] but showing off their exceptional courage. After all, duels are primarily fought to display personal prowess.

Quite different behaviour is expected of warriors in a regular battle. Here, the first priority is to eliminate the enemy by all possible means, and no one is at all concerned that the fight should be open or fair. The only notable restriction is that leaders should concentrate on fighting enemy leaders. Just as in Papua New Guinea it is understood that ordinary warriors, 'rubbish men', should not attack 'fight leaders' or 'Big Men', so the Homeric elite tries to keep some social distance from commoners in the mêlée. Hector first kills as many leaders as he can, 'and after them the multitude' (11.299-305). Men of high rank are marked out above all by their chariots, so chariot-fighters pick out their opposite numbers, even as they mingle with *promachoi* of lesser status.[23]

Most fights take the form of hit-and-run attacks rather than face-to-face confrontations. Only about one in six of the fights described in the *Iliad* involve opponents who deliberately seek out one another, or at least stand their ground when they come face to face. They shake their spears and 'scream piercingly' at one another, 'like vultures on a rock'. Sometimes they shout threats and insults. 'What is the point of skulking around here for a raw recruit like you?' (5.633-4). 'I am telling you ... do not try to stand up to me, or you may have a nasty accident' (20.196-8). In some of the longest exchanges warriors try to frighten one another by boasting of their ancestry: the purpose is to show that they are close descendants of Zeus, who is sure to give them victory.[24] A few speeches end with a rhetorical challenge to the opponent – 'Let's fight!' (21.160) – but genuine challenges inviting an opponent to step forward from the crowd are rare, and never actually succeed. Paris challenges 'all the best men' but loses heart and

160

retreats when his invitation is taken up; two other Trojans are challenged by name, but refuse to pick up the gauntlet – instead, they retaliate later, without warning, by throwing a spear at the man who tried to provoke them.[25]

Both in their refusal to accept a challenge and in their attempt to catch the enemy off-guard when they do decide to fight, these Trojans behave like typical Homeric heroes. Never mind a verbal challenge, even a spear which misses a man by inches because he ducks in time is not enough to provoke a response. Warriors who strike a blow but fail to wound or kill the enemy do not feel obliged to finish the fight they started, but give up and retreat to safety.[26] No one is expected to stand his ground against the odds, and that includes not only fighting more than one opponent at a time ('Aeneas did not stand his ground when he saw two men making a stand side by side', 5.571-2), but also fighting a single opponent who is younger (13.476-86), stronger (7.104-21; 22.38-40), or otherwise somehow not equal (17.561-2; 20.100-1). A couple of heroes profess shame at the thought of running away from the enemy, but are advised not to be reckless, and end up running away after all (8.137-56; 22.33-137). Odysseus may say that 'a man who seeks to excel in fighting must by all means stand his ground firmly, to kill or be killed' (11.409-10), but it is clear that such bravery would indeed mark out a man as a quite exceptional warrior in the Homeric world, where the norm is for warriors to take no unnecessary risks. A refusal to fight is shameful only if the opponent is known to be a *weaker* man (17.582-90).

When a warrior does fight in the *Iliad*, five out of six times he attacks his opponent without warning, often catching him by surprise or at a disadvantage, as is common practice in Papua New Guinea, too.[27] The single most common action in the *Iliad* is a single shot or blow which kills an enemy who is evidently caught unawares. Some men are hit while still dismounting from their chariots; others struggle with one opponent only to fall victim to another who creeps up on them unnoticed. Archers jump out from cover to shoot at unsuspecting victims. Those who try to take possession of a dead body are not challenged but attacked from all sides and killed as soon as they take their eyes off the enemy. In retreat and flight men are hit and stabbed in the back without any attempt to make them stand and fight. A few are slaughtered while in a helpless state of shock.[28]

Adding insult to injury, a Homeric hero may mock a man he has just killed, and strip or even mutilate the dead body. Jokes about the manner of the victim's collapse ('What an acrobat! Such elegant somersaults', *Iliad* 16.745) or about what he can do with the spear which killed him (14.456-7) alternate with sarcastic remarks about his deluded hopes of victory and dire warnings that his corpse will be savaged by vultures and wild dogs.[29] Men will take great risks to drag dead bodies by the heels out of enemy lines and over to their own side, so that they can strip them at leisure.

161

Mutilation of the dead as an act of revenge is less common but quite spectacular when it happens. Severed heads are raised on a spear or hurled 'like a ball' through the ranks (13.202-5; 14.493-507). One man has his head and arms cut off and his torso sent rolling through the crowd 'like a log' (11.138-47). Such acts serve only partly to glorify the killer: just as men join forces to protect fallen comrades, so they team up to humiliate dead enemies for the greater glory of the entire army. The *Iliad*'s final battle scene significantly shows all Greeks taking turns to stab Hector's dead body and cracking jokes about how 'much softer to the touch' he is now.[30]

Fields of glory? The psychology of combat

At its most intense, Homeric battle can be as traumatic an experience as any classical or modern form of combat. Heroes may burst into tears at the sight of the enemy onslaught, or become paralysed with fear and allow themselves to be slaughtered without any resistance.[31] Much of the time, however, Homeric combat is not excessively demanding: the fighters keep at a relatively safe distance from the enemy, fight only in short bursts, and retire from the field altogether when they take fright or become tired. No one is expected to fight on an empty stomach; the men take food and drink, and have a wash, as soon as they are momentarily out of action. No one is under much pressure to control his emotions: there is no great shame in crying out in pain, or fainting, or even panicking. It is accepted that even the bravest man will lose his nerve once in a while. Wounded men are urged to leave battle at once, rather than make any attempt to carry on fighting.[32] In all these ways, Homeric combat is again close to the battles of Papua New Guinea, some of which are so undemanding that they seem to be fought merely 'for fun'.[33] There are times when the heroes go into action smiling (*Iliad* 7.212) and laughing (6.514), when 'the joy of battle' (13.82) seems 'sweeter' than the prospect of going home (2.453-4; 11.13-14). Even so, Homer's image of war, conveyed by a range of deeply negative epithets from 'tear-filled' to 'dreadful' via 'wretched' and 'baneful', heavily emphasises its miseries.[34]

The single positive epic epithet for battle is 'glory-bringing'. Fame (*kleos*) and glory (*kudos*) above all else make the suffering of war worthwhile. The heroes do not, however, seek glory selfishly and obsessively, at the expense of all else and to the detriment of their communities, as has often been claimed.[35] Personal fame goes hand-in-hand with communal glory in Homer, and many motives other than fame play a prominent part in combat.

The highest imperative of all is to 'defend the fatherland' (*patris*). Hector and other great warriors are praised not as inveterate seekers of glory but as great defenders of their cities. If the paramount importance of patriotism has not always been obvious to readers of the *Iliad*, this is perhaps because it takes the simple form of protecting the community's women, children and elderly – a more down-to-earth conception of the fatherland than one finds in modern expressions of patriotism. Moreover, in the heat of battle there are more immediate concerns than the defence of one's country, in Homeric as in modern warfare.[36]

In action, the heroes stand out as men determined to protect and avenge their fellow-soldiers.[37] 'They miss me mightily when I am away', says Hector (*Iliad* 6.361-2). Even Achilles, who rejects all appeals for help when he is angry, accepts in the end that a man who fails to 'bring light' to his comrades is no more than 'a useless burden on the earth' (18.102-6).[38] At the sight of a wounded or dead friend, men 'groan deeply', 'shudder', and are filled with rage and sorrow. The death of Patroclus makes Antilochus cry and lose his voice; it makes Achilles near-suicidal with grief and ultimately drives him to exact revenge without restraint. As if to refute the tradition that Achilles and Patroclus were lovers, the poet makes a point of telling his audience that these two slept in opposite corners of their shared quarters, each with a woman by his side (9.663-8), but even without a sexual dimension their relationship is intensely emotional. It represents an ideal of comradeship as a motivating force in combat. In Homer, moreover, men protect and avenge their friends not just for personal, emotional reasons, but because they under an *obligation* to do so. To help a comrade in battle is to do him a 'favour' (*charis*) which must be returned.[39]

The Homeric warrior is also driven by the desire to win 'respect' (*timê*) from his comrades and community. Tangible signs of respect include a fair share of the spoils and one or more 'prizes' (*gera*). Prizes are selected items of booty such as 'a tripod, or a two-horse chariot, or a woman' (*Iliad* 8.289-91), awarded 'to the best men and the princes' (9.334); in other words, not only to those who prove themselves 'best' in action, but also to all men of high rank, regardless of their performance in combat. Agamemnon gets a prize from the spoils of a raid in which he did not even take part. A warrior will withdraw his services if he believes that he is not being shown sufficient gratitude and respect. He may resentfully skulk in the rear, as Aeneas used to do 'because Priam showed him no respect' (13.459-61), or refuse to fight at all, as Achilles did when he fell out with Agamemnon over the allocation of two female captives as prizes.[40] Such shirking is deemed perfectly legitimate: a man who allows himself to be denied due respect is not a real man, but a 'worthless nobody' (1.293). When mutual respect among the men is lacking, Homeric armies literally fall apart, but conversely, where ties of friendship and reciprocity exist, they create a powerful solidarity.[41]

This solidarity is reinforced by the sense of shame (*aidôs*) to which commanders constantly appeal. 'Feel shame before one another in hard battles. Of men who know shame more survive than die' (15.562-3). Exhortations to 'be men' and taunts of being 'women, men no more' or 'little boys' show that a prime cause of shame is to fall short of standards of masculinity, but it is also shameful to fall short of higher expectations raised by one's own boasts, record or appearance, and to be compared unfavourably with the highest standards of warriorhood, especially if one's own father was a great fighter. Nestor even tries to shame the Greeks into action by holding up Achilles' father, Peleus, as a father-figure to them all, almost dying with embarrassment at the sight of their collective cowardice.[42]

The love of glory is thus only one motivation among many, but it does feature prominently. The gods compensate Hector for his impending early death by bestowing glory upon him 'and upon him alone among many men' (*Iliad* 15.610-14). Achilles, given the choice between a short but glorious existence and a long life in obscurity, opts for 'imperishable fame' (9.410-16). Communities are no less eager in pursuing collective glory. Scattered throughout the narrative are references to glory won by common effort: 'the ranks of the Trojans stood around Patroclus, intending above all ... to win glory', 'the Greeks through their own force and strength might have taken glory even beyond the destiny set by Zeus', and so forth.[43] Leading warriors are expected to seek fame for their communities as well as themselves. The king of Lycia says that he fights so that his subjects may say 'our princes and rulers are certainly not without fame' (12.316-19), and Hector is accounted 'a very great glory' to his city (22.435). Even Achilles, for all his devotion to fame and his insistence that only he may kill Hector (22.206-7), lets the whole army share in his success:

'Come, let us sing a *paian* as we return to our ships, young men of Greece ...
We have won great glory – *we* have killed Hector.' (22.391-3)

Patriotism, friendship, a sense of shame and the desire for respect and fame all feed into the 'spirit' (*menos*) which drives men into action. Whether through his own dedication or divine inspiration, a hero's spirit may reach such extraordinary levels that others think him 'mad'. When 'a spirit three times as a great as before' enters Diomedes in his quest for glory, he fights with such vigour that the Trojans denounce him as 'savage' and 'too crazed'; it takes divine intervention to put an end to his excesses. When Achilles, in search of revenge, is filled with 'a spirit like gleaming iron', he too is called 'savage' and said to be possessed by 'rabid rage' (*lyssa*). And Hector, in his utter determination to destroy those who have invaded his country, fights so hard that the Greeks not only call him 'a savage man' and 'rabid dog', but say that he 'stinks of *lyssa*' and 'has gone utterly crazy and ... has no respect at all for men or gods'. In this state of mind Hector ignores all omens and advice, and he pays a heavy price for these errors of judgement.[44]

A warrior in the grip of such 'madness' might be described as going 'berserk', in the modern sense of losing control. There is no hint in Homer of the howling, shield-biting antics of the original Norse berserkers, let alone of the bodily transformations of the Celtic hero Cu Chulainn in his 'warp spasm': the only physical sign of battle madness is 'blazing eyes', although Achilles once also grinds his teeth and Hector at one point 'began to foam at the mouth' – surely a result of extreme physical exertion rather than a symptom of rabies.[45] The heroes do not display even the characteristic feeling of invulnerability which makes modern soldiers lose all sense of fear and discard their body-armour when they run amok. However high their spirit, they continue to experience the occasional shiver of fear, and Achilles, furious as he may be, absolutely refuses to fight without his armour. Homer's berserkers remain quite sane by modern military standards, let alone by the standards of other heroic traditions: their behaviour is mad only by comparison with the rather low levels of courage and stamina expected in Homeric combat. Otherwise, the role of the berserker in epic warfare is much the same as his role in modern warfare: the few men who 'go mad' in battle provoke at least as much apprehension as admiration among their fellow-soldiers since they are as liable to make fatal mistakes as they are to perform great feats of valour. Fighters who become too fanatical are warned to 'think and retreat'.[46]

*

In a famous analysis of 'the warrior of epic and myth' Marcel Detienne argued that Homeric combat was characterised by 'two features: single combat and the state of *furor*'.

> Warlike activity is epitomised by the individual feat of arms, by combat between champions vying in challenges .... The exploit is accomplished in a state of exaltation, in which the warrior, beside himself as it were, is possessed by a furious madness.[47]

This reading of what happens in Homeric battle may seem attractive because it corresponds to common preconceptions of how 'primitive' and 'heroic' warriors *ought* to behave, and because it creates the sharpest possible contrast between the Homeric hero's single combat and 'rabid rage', and the collective efforts and 'complete self-control' of the classical hoplite, 'a wholly new type of man' (1968, 122-3).[48] But Detienne's picture is misleading, since it presents as the rule what was in fact the exception. A less selective reading of the *Iliad* reveals the hero as a less exotic figure, different from the hoplite by degree rather than by category. It may have been precisely because heroes and hoplites were *not* worlds apart that the *Iliad* remained an inspiration to later generations of Greek soldiers and generals.

165

12

The Archaic Phalanx

Infantry combat down to the Persian Wars

The warriors of Euboea shaved their foreheads, samurai-style. A local historian explained that they did so in order to prevent the enemy from grabbing them by the hair. The Euboeans were indeed among the first to gain a reputation for excellence in hand-to-hand fighting:

> Not many bows will be drawn, no great number of slings extended, when the god of war stirs up trouble in the plain: it will be the woeful work of swords, for that is the kind of fighting in which these men are experts, the spear-famed masters of Euboea.[1]

The emergence of soldiers like these, exclusively dedicated to hand-to-hand fighting, and the development of a close-order formation are the two main strands of the history of Greek infantry combat. The introduction of the hoplite shield and bronze body armour was an important step in this direction but only a first step on a long road. Vase-paintings and fragments of songs show that heavily armoured infantry long continued to fight in a loose formation and to mingle in action with horsemen and light-armed. Archaic infantry combat was in many ways closer to Homer's heroic clashes than to the battles of the classical period.[2]

Dark Age combat and the first hoplites, *c.* 720-640 BC

Hair-grabbing, sword-wielding warriors are among the earliest human figures to be represented in Greek art (Fig. 12), and the sword is the single most prominent weapon in battle scenes painted on Athenian vases from *c.* 850 to 700 BC. The size and number of swords found in graves of this period confirms that Dark Age warriors were no strangers to close combat, despite their light shields and lack of metal body armour.[3] At the same time, Dark Age swordsmen also fought at long range with throwing-spears or arrows.[4] Vase-paintings suggest that spearmen and bowmen stood side by side, and that the latter played a more prominent role than they were to do in later centuries. Archers make up about a third of all warriors,[5] and they stand in the front-line as the equals of spearmen: equipped with

12. The Archaic Phalanx

Fig. 12. Combat with swords on the leg of an Attic Middle Geometric stand, *c.* 850-760 BC (Toronto, Ontario Museum 957X245).

sword and helmet, and sometimes a shield, they are almost always face-to-face with an opponent, and are repeatedly shown killing an enemy with a shot in the head or throat (Fig. 13).[6]

Around 720-700 BC, a desire for greater protection in hand-to-hand fighting inspired the introduction of the bronze panoply and the large double-grip shield which created the hoplite. The new shield was so heavy that it needed to rest on the bearer's left shoulder as well as his lower arm. Hoplites therefore adopted a sideways-on stance, left shoulder and shield turned towards the enemy, left foot forward, right foot placed well back for balance (see Plate IV). Poets evoked the stance of soldiers 'leaning their shields against their shoulders' and exhorted men to stand 'legs well apart, both feet planted firmly on the ground, biting your lip'.[7] Hoplites would

Fig. 13. Archers and slingers in combat. *Above*: central part of a scene of combat on a late eighth-century amphora recently discovered on Paros. A light-armed and a heavy-armed archer fight a spearman (apparently armed with three javelins) and two slingers over a fallen warrior. The slingers shown here are unique in Greek Geometric art. Not shown in the drawing are a line of six or seven horsemen and three footsoldiers with pairs of spears and round shields standing behind the combatants on the left, and two footsoldiers with pairs of spears and round shields on the right. *Right*: fragment of an Attic Late Geometric I krater, *c.* 750 BC (Louvre A 528).

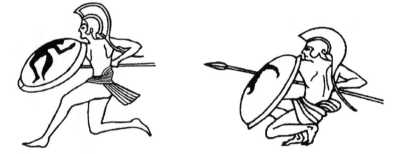

Fig. 14. Hoplites running and squatting with left shoulder turned forwards, torso almost at a right angle to the shield, on (*left*) a terracotta plaque from Athens, *c.* 520-510 BC (Acropolis Museum 1037) and (*right*) an Attic red-figure cup, *c.* 520-10 BC, from Chiusi (Louvre G25).

even squat and run with their left shoulders twisted forwards (Fig. 14).[8] Since the shield was tilted back against the shoulder, its lower edge projected a couple of feet in front of its bearer (Fig. 15; Plate IV) and provided cover not only for his upper body but for his 'thighs and shins below'.[9] Archaic poets speak of shields striking against one another with 'a terrible din' as the protruding lower rims of the shields clashed in accidental collisions and in deliberate shoving designed to expose an opponent or throw him off balance.[10]

The hoplite shield thus served as something of an offensive weapon as well as providing excellent protection. It is a common misconception that the shield failed to offer much cover for the bearer's right flank while offering too much cover on the left, so that hoplites were forced to stand close together and in effect shelter behind the redundant left-hand halves of their neighbours' shields (see Fig. 16). This would be true if hoplites had stood frontally opposed to the enemy, like wrestlers, but since they actu-

Fig. 15. Profile views of hoplite shields as carried in combat, tilted back against the left shoulder, on (*left*) a Middle Protocorinthian vase, the Berlin *aryballos* attributed to the Chigi/Macmillan Painter, *c.* 650 BC, from Kamiros (Berlin inv. 3773), and (*right*) a Siana cup by the Heidelberg Painter, *c.* 560 BC, from Boeotia (Athens, NM 435).

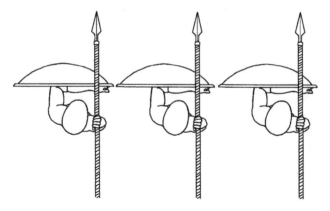

Fig. 16. Phalanx formation, assuming three-foot intervals and a frontal stance.

ally stood sideways-on, like fencers, they automatically found themselves behind the centre of their shields, well covered on both sides (Fig. 17; Plate IV). Of course the hoplite's right flank was relatively 'unprotected', as classical Greeks said, but only to the extent that *any* kind of shield carried on the left arm leaves the bearer's other side comparatively vulnerable. The hoplite shield did not presuppose or dictate a dense formation but could be used to equally good effect in open-order fighting.[11]

Indeed, for two generations or more after the introduction of the new shield hoplites must have fought in a quite open formation because they continued to use their spears as missiles, which requires a good deal of room for manoeuvre. Vase-paintings show that a pair of spears continued to be standard hoplite equipment until at least 640 BC. One or both of these weapons might be fitted with a throwing-loop – a string wound around the fingers so as to make the spear spin when thrown, giving it greater speed and force – which leaves no doubt that they were designed to be used as

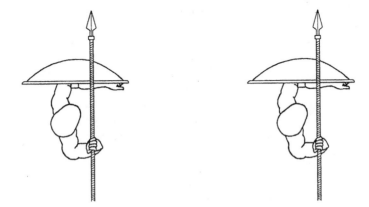

Fig. 17. Phalanx formation, assuming six-foot intervals and a sideways-on stance.

missiles.[12] Songs composed by Archilochus of Paros and Callinus of Ephesus between 680 and 640 BC alluded to battle as 'the thud of javelins', an expression (also used in the *Iliad*) which suggests that spears were used *primarily* as missiles.[13] Hence Callinus poignantly urged the young men of his native town to 'charge forward with raised spear' and 'throw your last javelin as you are dying' (F 1.5, 9-11).

Archers continued to fight alongside spearmen, but from the early seventh century onwards they were represented in art, not as independent fighters, but as unarmoured men kneeling or squatting behind hoplites (Fig. 18).[14] The *Iliad* vividly describes how this works: the archer 'stands under the shield' of a heavy-armed soldier, but every so often jumps out, 'looks around to see if he can shoot someone in the crowd', fires a shot, and quickly returns to the cover of the shield, 'like a child to its mother' (8.266-72; cf. 4.112-15; 15.440-4). Close co-operation between spearmen and bowmen, unattested in earlier art, must have been a new tactic, made possible by the large new shields and encouraged by the greater emphasis on close combat.

The number of archers in archaic art is minute compared to the number of hoplites – and much smaller than in Geometric art – but it does not follow that the archaic phalanx included only a handful of them. Their rarity in art was not a reflection of their small numbers in archaic armies, but of their lower prestige. As close combat came to be ever more highly valued, and as light-armed became dependent on hoplites for protection, their status fell, and artists began to represent them less often. Similarly, the *Iliad*, which contains some dismissive remarks about the effectiveness of archery (5.204-16, 11.385-95) features only a few named bowmen, but many 'arrows flying from bowstrings' are a constant presence in the background.[15] In any case, the large quantities of arrowheads which have been found in excavations prove that archery in some form continued to be a major part of archaic Greek warfare.[16]

Painted battle-scenes of this same period also feature other new themes, such as flight and pursuit and groups of hoplites charging into action. The latter in particular have often been seen as the first representations of close-order mass fighting in the manner of the classical phalanx, they show at best a single line of hoplites, who might be the front rank of a phalanx or merely a schematically rendered crowd.[17] The most elaborate battle scene appears on a Corinthian jug of *c.* 640 BC, the Chigi vase (Plate XVIII). In the centre of the scene are two small groups of hoplites raising short spears and holding a larger spear in reserve. It is clear from a picture of a pair of spears at the far left of the scene that they have throwing-loops attached. In other words, the two front lines are about to hurl javelins at one another, and contrary to appearances are evidently meant to be standing some way apart. On the right are seven running hoplites, the first few with spears half-raised as they approach the enemy. On the left, we find nine hoplites, also running, but apparently still at

Fig. 18. Squatting archers. *Top*: detail of Middle Protocorinthian aryballos, 690-80 BC, from Lechaion (Corinth Museum CP-2096). *Centre*: detail of Middle Protocorinthian aryballos, 675-650 BC, from Perachora. *Bottom left*: detail of Middle Corinthian pyxis, 600-575 BC, from Perachora. *Bottom right*: Laconian Lead II figurine of a kneeling archer, *c.* 620-580 BC, from Sparta (Sparta Museum).

some distance from the action since none of them have their spears at the ready yet. On the far left, two more men are putting on their armour and getting ready to join combat with a pair of throwing-spears. The groups in this scene are all different in size, move at different speeds, and make use of missiles, so they cannot represent close formations, let alone a phalanx organised in regular ranks.[18] The Chigi vase rather calls to mind the fluidity of the Homeric battlefield, where individuals and small groups advance at their own pace, and crowds come running up from the rear when embattled frontline fighters call out for help.[19]

Even in full armour, a hoplite was quite capable of moving back and forth across the battlefield in the Homeric manner. The equipment was not so cumbersome that it imposed a static form of combat.[20] Classical

171

hoplites charged at a run over at least 200 yards, and ran still further in flight and pursuit, even if some threw away their shields in order to go faster. Images of running hoplites, as on the Chigi vase, are common in archaic art (see also Figs 14, 21A). Running in armour actually became an Olympic sport in 520 BC.[21] But of course the weight of the panoply did slow a man down, and the persistence of the lighter Boeotian shield until *c.* 480 BC shows that some hoplites continued to opt for greater mobility rather than greater protection.[22]

In flight, the hoplite might be forced to discard his shield. For classical Greeks it was a disgrace and a crime to throw away one's shield, but not so in the early seventh century:

> One of those Saians is showing off with a shield, a perfect piece of armour, which I dropped beside a bush, unwillingly. At least I saved myself. Why should I worry about a shield? Let that thing go to hell! I'll get myself another one, just as good.

Judging by the tone of the poet, Archilochus (F 5 West), running away from the enemy, though embarrassing, was not wholly unacceptable behaviour in the fluid, mobile battles of his time.

Tyrtaeus' phalanx, *c.* 640-600 BC: close combat, missiles and mobility

The next crucial step in the development of the hoplite phalanx came soon after 640 BC, when, as countless images show, the majority of soldiers abandoned the use of throwing-spears and fought exclusively hand-to-hand with a single thrusting spear and sword.[23] The change is reflected also in the songs of Tyrtaeus, composed during Sparta's war of conquest in Messenia in the late seventh century BC,[24] which for the first time made an explicit distinction between the light-armed and the heavy-armed (FF 11.35; 23a.14). Tyrtaeus encouraged the light-armed to use missiles, while he constantly appealed to the hoplites to fight the enemy face-to-face:

> Go near, strike with a long spear or a sword at close range, and kill a man. Set foot against foot, press shield against shield, fling crest against crest, helmet against helmet, and chest against chest, and fight a man, gripping the hilt of a sword or a long spear.[25]

The poet also urged solidarity within the ranks. 'Stay together when you fight, lads', he said. 'Speak words of encouragement to the next man as you stand beside him.'[26] Exhortations to stand one's ground and warnings against running away formed another major theme.[27]

Tyrtaeus' songs may have advertised the virtues of hand-to-hand combat in close order – which is why they were still sung and cited in the classical period – but they reveal that late seventh-century hoplites remained far more mobile than their classical successors. They needed encouragement not just to hold their position in the line, but to make their way to the front in the first place. 'Dare to move into close range and towards the frontline fighters [*promachoi*].' 'Do not stand with your shield beyond the range of missiles.' A badly damaged fragment appears to describe a battle against the Messenians during which 'some stand face-to-face' with the enemy while 'others are beyond the range of missiles'. A soldier who 'remains among the frontline fighters without pause', rather than drop back from time to time, is praised. When and how far to charge forward or hang back was evidently a matter of individual choice.[28] The same freedom of movement is attested in the *Smyrneis* of Tyrtaeus' contemporary Mimnermus, which celebrated the deeds of a great warrior 'racing among the frontline fighters'.[29] Appeals to go in close, stick together, and stay at the front were urgent precisely because they were addressed to hoplites who did not have a fixed station in a tight battle order, but were quite mobile.[30]

Late seventh-century hoplites continued to fight in an order sufficiently open for light-armed men and mounted hoplites to mingle. When Greek mercenaries and hangers-on at the Lydian court first encountered the Medes, during the reign of Cyaxares in the late seventh century, they were struck by the separation of different types of fighting men in the Median army. The story grew up that Cyaxares had been 'the first to put spearmen, archers and horsemen in a separate formation each; before him, they were all indiscriminately mixed up together' (Herodotus 1.103.1). Evidently the Greeks themselves at this time did not yet differentiate tactical units in this way: heavy infantry, light-armed and horsemen still stood together in a single motley crowd.

How Greek light-armed operated at this time emerges from a few lines in which Tyrtaeus briefly turned aside from his habitual exhortations to the hoplites:

> You, light-armed, squatting under a shield here and there, must throw great rocks and hurl smooth javelins while you stand close by the heavy-armed. (F 11.35-8)

The light infantry was scattered 'here and there' among the hoplites, 'squatting' for cover behind the latter's shields, in the manner of archers as represented in Homer and archaic art.[31] Tyrtaeus' references to 'standing beyond the range of missiles' indicate that light-armed were present in large numbers. He highlights the 'great rocks' which clatter against soldiers' helmets (F 19.19-20; cf. 19.2), and in a very scrappy fragment he speaks of 'savage missiles', 'many men hurling sharp javelins' and 'light-armed fighters … running forward' (F 23a.10-14). At the end of the seventh century, Alcaeus, another poet with much combat experience, spoke of greaves as 'a defence against the forceful missile' (F 140.10 L-P), as if the greatest threat to a soldier were not the hoplites' spears and swords, but the arrows, stones and javelins of the light-armed.

Alcaeus, like Archilochus before him, was not ashamed to publicise the fact that he had dropped his shield in battle: a poem addressed, via a friend, to the people of his home town, said: 'Alcaeus is safe, but men from Attica hung up [his armour] in the sanctuary of Grey-eyed Athena' (F 428a L-P). Running away from the enemy was clearly still not the utter disgrace it would later become, because formations remained open and fluid, breaking and rallying with relative ease. The Spartans, desperate to force a decision in the Second Messenian War, found it necessary to station their troops in front of a deep trench, making it impossible for their men to run away, and forestalling the kind of undecisive surges back and forth across the battlefield familiar from the *Iliad*, which must have continued to characterise most contemporary battles.[32]

The hoplites' new exclusive concentration on close combat may have been accompanied by the first steps towards their organisation in centrally mobilised units – three tribes in Sparta (Tyrtaeus F 19.8-9) – rather than in privately raised war bands. There is perhaps also a hint of a more abstract notion of patriotic duty in war. Tyrtaeus remarks that a good performance in battle is 'a shared blessing for the *polis* and the entire people' (F 12.15). Otherwise, motivating factors were what they had been in previous generations: the defence of 'fatherland', family and friends, the avoidance of shame for oneself and one's family, and the quest for fame and respect for oneself, family and country.[33] The importance of individual fame, however, may have been toned down a little. In an early seventh-century battle exhortation, the poet Callinus had promised that 'the entire people' would regard a brave warrior 'as their bulwark, for by himself he matches the deeds of many', so that 'he will be the equal of the demi-gods during his lifetime' (F 1.18-21 West). Tyrtaeus, more modestly, promised immortality only after death (F 12.27-34); during his lifetime, the brave warrior would merely have everyone's 'respect' – meaning that his fellow-townsmen would not insult or injure him, and 'all will give up their seats for him – the young, the men of his own age, and even his elders' (F 12.35-42).

Images of combat in the sixth century

For four or five generations between Tyrtaeus and the Persian Wars the written record of military developments is a blank. Only a few scraps of poetry so much as mention war. On the other hand, thousands of painted and sculpted scenes of warriors and combat survive, the majority dating to the sixth century. Whether they illustrate episodes from heroic legend or show anonymous hoplites in generic battle scenes, these images usually feature heavy-armed men fighting in pairs or small groups, occasionally joined by an archer, a couple of horses or even a chariot. There is rarely any sign of regular order (Plates XIX, XX). Scholars who believe that the phalanx reached its classical form no later than about 650 BC dismiss sixth-century art as representing a heroic style of combat long since abandoned, if it ever existed.[34] As we have seen, however, the phalanx was still open and fluid in the days of Tyrtaeus, Mimnermus and Alcaeus, and it is entirely possible that it remained so through all or most of the next century. Sixth-century scenes of heroes and unknown soldiers in combat, therefore, may well be based on contemporary reality, and reflect a loose, mixed formation still in use at the time.

Two dozen or so images show hoplites in a line, running or marching into battle, standing ready to fight or running away, but they contain nothing to indicate that tactics had developed beyond their late seventh-century level.[35] An early sixth-century painting offers a rare glimpse of the rear ranks in action (Plate XXI): a fairly typical scene of six men fighting hard over a fallen comrade is enlivened by the addition of a second group behind them, consisting of five or more hoplites who strike a crouching pose, some almost down on one knee, others merely stooping slightly. They do not raise their spears for action, but hold their weapons horizontally or rest them on the ground pointing diagonally forward. The painter clearly had in mind the kind of scenario described by Homer and Tyrtaeus, in which the 'multitude' stand some way behind the 'frontline fighters'. Their unglamorous appearance, however, crouching behind their shields for safety, is never described in the surviving epics or exhortations, and the artist presumably drew inspiration from life rather than literature. Such scenes are rare, but it is hardly surprising that archaic artists usually did not bother to put nervously cowering crowds in their pictures.[36]

Crouching for safety, at a distance from the enemy, only makes sense if there is a danger of being hit by missiles. The occasional token archer still featured in sixth-century battle scenes, and very rarely a slinger or stone-thrower.[37] This was not just an artistic cliché, as is clear from the many figurines of archers in the familiar kneeling combat pose found among the countless lead figurines dedicated at sanctuaries in Sparta throughout the century.[38] In Athenian art, archers were an exceptionally popular subject, which featured on some 750 surviving vases, most dating to between 525 and 500 BC. These archers commonly stand, walk or run beside hoplites, and on about a hundred vases they take an active part in battle or ambush amongst the heavy infantry. Sometimes hoplites fight over the body of a dead bowman (Figs 19, 20). Nine out of ten archers are in Scythian dress, and their exotic appearance helps explain why they were popular with artists when ordinary archers were much more rarely portrayed: painters liked the contrast between 'barbarian' bowmen and Greek heavy infantry. Scythian archers had no precedent in epic poetry, nor is the idea of putting them among hoplites likely to have been an artistic fiction designed purely for symbolic effect – Thracian peltasts, equally exotic and also often represented in Athenian art, were not shown

Fig. 19. Archer fallen in combat between heroes, on a black-figure amphora showing Diomedes and Hektor fighting over 'Skythes', late sixth century BC (Musée Pincé, Angers).

mingling with hoplites in this way. In all probability, Athens did employ Scythian mercenaries at the time, and these did operate as shown, mixed in with a loose hoplite formation, rather than as a separate, independent force.[39]

Archaic vase-painters occasionally show hoplites followed into action by their chariots and charioteers, in the Homeric style, or more often by a pair of horses controlled by a squire, a practice which has no precedent in epic.[40] The heroic-looking chariots are represented with some concern for plausibility: whereas horses and squires stand facing battle and will have to turn

Fig. 20. Archers taking part in mass combat between hoplite armies, on a black-figure kylix of c. 550 BC (sold on the antiquities market in Basle).

round to retreat, the less manoeuvrable chariots are turned round already and stand facing away from the action, ready to leave in a hurry when their master remounts (Plate XX). Charioteers never carry hoplite shields, which would interfere with their control of the reins, but only Boeotian shields, slung across the back and leaving both hands free (Plate XXII). Such realistic touches support the literary evidence which suggest that even in the sixth century chariots might be used as transports in war (see above, pp. 59-60). Horses and chariots sometimes appear in the thick of battle, and one remarkable painting shows three lines of seven running hoplites, each group about to be joined by an eighth running hoplite whose horses are galloping beside him (Fig. 21A). The horses are clearly envisaged as mingling with the infantry in the epic manner.[41]

Some hoplites, especially mounted hoplites, are portrayed as carrying pairs of throwing-spears or light Boeotian shields, or both, until about 480 BC (see above, p. 50). Every single one of the two dozen Athenian vase-paintings of a hoplite arming himself in the presence of a Scythian archer, for example, has the hoplite picking up two spears (Fig. 22).[42] Throwing-spears and light shields are usually dismissed as unrealistic, heroising elements, but if the infantry formation remained as loose and open as the artists suggest, a minority of hoplites – perhaps the elite – may well have used such equipment and continued to practice a more mobile, missile-based style of fighting, long after the single thrusting spear and the heavy shield had become the norm.

So far as we can tell from the iconography, the Greek style of fighting throughout the sixth century remained much the same as in the time of Tyrtaeus. The first hints of change come only at the end of the century: mounted hoplites begin to fade from the vase-painters' repertoire, soon followed by hoplites with throwing-spears and Boeotian shields, and from about 500 BC Spartan archer figurines no longer kneel in combat pose, but instead stand up straight, with their bows unstrung. We know that for most of the fifth century there were indeed no bowmen in the Spartan army.[43] The strict separation of hoplites, light-armed, and horsemen characteristic of the classical phalanx, therefore, may not have emerged until the very end of the archaic period.

Herodotus' phalanx: the Persian Wars

The *Histories* of Herodotus contain the first surviving narratives of historical Greek battles, beginning with Athens' defeat of a Persian invasion force at Marathon in 490 BC. The battles of the Persian Wars, as described by Herodotus, in most respects sound much like later hoplite battles, but some surprising twists suggest that they were not fought in quite the same way.

By the time Herodotus collected second-hand stories about Marathon from people who had known veterans of the battle (6.117.3), Athens'

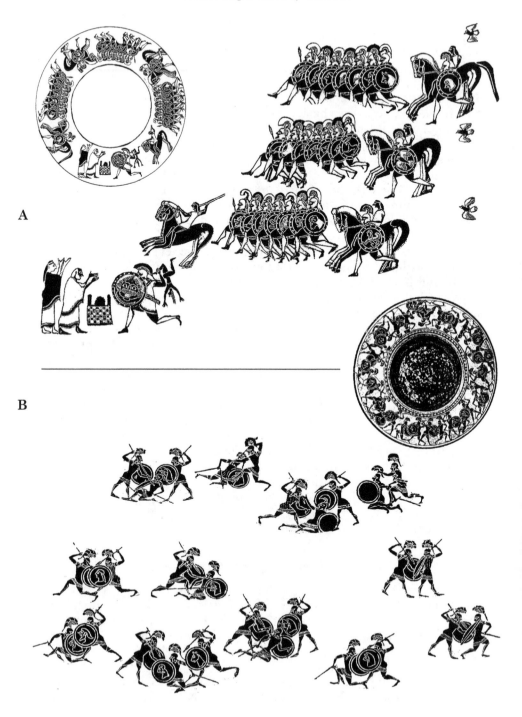

A

B

178

12. The Archaic Phalanx

Fig. 21 (*opposite*). Two mass combat scenes, after the C-Painter, *c.* 570-560 BC. The charge in (A) and the massacre in (B) were originally painted in a single narrow band on a circular vessel, as shown in the insets, but are here projected to give a more lifelike impression of what these scenes represented. (A), from the lid of a lekanis (Naples Museum), shows the sack of Troy. Neoptolemus swings the dead body of Hector's son Astyanax towards Priam and Hecabe or Andromache, who have taken refuge at an altar (cf. Fig. 6 above). Behind him, two cavalrymen lead a charge of three groups of eight hoplites, the eighth man accompanied by his horses and squire. (B), from a tripod pyxis (Louvre CA 616) shows the massacre of a routed army; the sequence of figures from top to bottom and left to right corresponds to the sequence from left to right in the original. In the majority of scenes (9 out of 12), a fallen warrior, whose spear is usually broken, is (about to be) killed by an enemy. The third figure in some of these scenes is either another enemy joining in the kill (bottom line, second left) or a comrade coming to the rescue (top line, second right, where the victim stretches out his arm in supplication). In the remaining scenes, the enemy still offers some resistance while running away or retreating.

Fig. 22. Late archaic hoplites equipped with pairs of spears. *Above*: a departure scene on a black-figure olpe of *c.* 510 BC (sold in the antiquities market at Freiburg). *Below*: a hepatoscopy, a reading of omens from the liver of a sacrificial animal, prior to departure for war, on a black-figure amphora of *c.* 530-510 BC (Brussels, Musées Royaux d'Art et d'Histoire, inv. R 291).

179

victory had been elevated to mythical status and ranked alongside such feats as defeating the Amazons and sacking Troy. Monumental paintings of these three triumphs were on display in the town square. Epiphanies of gods and heroes, and the haunting of the battlefield by the ghosts of fallen soldiers had all become part of the story.[44] Some of this mythologising rubbed off on Herodotus' account, which presented Marathon as an ideal version of a classical hoplite battle. The hoplites alone faced the Persians, he said; no horsemen or archers were present (6.112.2). Actually, the Athenians went so far as to mobilise their slaves for this battle, so there was surely a levy of all available manpower to meet the threat, as one would expect, including poor citizens who fought with any weapons they could lay their hands on. Within a generation, these non-hoplites had been written out of the picture.[45] Herodotus went on to make the Athenians inventors of the hoplite tactic of charging the enemy at a run ('the first Greeks known to us' to have done so, 6.112.3), which is blatantly untrue since running into battle had long been common practice. What is more, the Athenians allegedly ran eight times the normal distance: almost a mile instead of a 200-yard dash.[46]

No less remarkable was the course of battle itself. In classical hoplite clashes, it was quite common for one section of an army to pursue a routed enemy, unaware – or regardless – of the fact that their compatriots or allies elsewhere were being slaughtered. Sometimes a victorious wing retained enough cohesion and showed enough solidarity to leave their defeated opponents alone and instead turn back to help comrades in trouble, but this did not happen often.[47] Yet at Marathon, not one but *both* Athenian wings are supposed to have spontaneously abandoned pursuit of the Persians and turned round to help their friends struggling in the centre, managing to 'join forces' in the process (6.113.2). Nothing like it ever happened in classical Greek battle because hoplite armies did not have the degree of control and cohesion required.[48] Herodotus' account of Marathon does not tell us much about the realities of warfare at the time; it presents us with a story of ideal hoplite behaviour pushed to heroic extremes.

In his build-up to the battle of Thermopylae in 480 BC, Herodotus praised the hoplite virtues of the Spartans who '*together* are the best of all men', 7.104.4): their strength lay in solidarity. Yet in the battle itself, the Spartans proved themselves 'absolute experts' against the 'inexpert' Persians, not by superior cohesion in close-order combat, but by pretending to flee, then suddenly rallying to massacre their scattered pursuers (211.3). Neither the Spartan army nor any other hoplite force in the classical period ever executed such feints, which were regarded as the trademark tactics of light infantry. The select Spartan force at Thermopylae apparently fought in an order almost as fluid as that of the earliest hoplites. The culminating 'great push' (*ôthismos*) in which 'the Greeks, thanks to their excellence, drove back their opponents four times' to gain control over the dead body of king Leonidas (225.1) presents a scene that might have come straight out of the *Iliad*. If these Spartans came to be revered as perfect hoplites, it was for their exemplary spirit in refusing to surrender – not for their tactics (7.225.3).[49]

In preliminary skirmishes at Plataea the following year, 300 picked Athenian hoplites teamed up with a group of archers to face the Persian cavalry. When one of the archers shot the Persian commander, the hoplites 'were immediately on top of him' and seized his corpse, calling the rest of the Greeks to their aid (9.21-2). The scene is again more reminiscent of Homer and archaic art than of the hoplite ideals evident in the story of Marathon and shared by Herodotus.

The final victory at Plataea, by contrast, was won by a mass charge of Spartans and Tegeans. When they had broken through the barricade of wicker shields set up by the Persians,

> finally a hard-fought battle took place by the temple of Demeter, and it took a long time before they got to the final push [*ôthismos*], since the barbarians would grab hold of the Greeks' spears and snap them. The Persians were not inferior in courage or strength, but they were unarmed as well as unskilled and not equal to their opponents in intelligence. Dashing forward one by one, or banding together in groups of ten – more or less – they fell upon the Spartans and were destroyed .... What did them most damage was that their outfits lacked armour: they competed as light-armed against hoplites. (9.62.3, 63.2)

So the secret of the Spartans' success was their superior armour – a judgement which some in antiquity found outrageous[50] – with a bit of help from their superior cohesion in battle order.

Yet Herodotus believed that the Spartan army at Plataea incorporated vast numbers of light-armed: '35,000 light-armed helots protected the 5,000 Spartans', he said, 'seven of them stationed with each man'. He repeated this last phrase three times, adding for good measure that these light-armed belonged to 'the Spartiate formation' and that 'every single one was equipped for war' (9.28-9; cf. 9.61.2). This emphatic explanation of the role of the helots is remarkable, especially since they had been ignored at Thermopylae. Herodotus was evidently trying to describe something unfamiliar, an arrangement no longer used by the Spartans. It has plausibly been suggested that the Spartan hoplites formed a single rank, with seven helots drawn up behind each man.[51] Not only is this one of the few ways in which the hoplites could retain some cohesion despite being 'protected' by so many light-armed each, but about a decade later the Spartans are said to have fought a battle at Dipaea in a formation only 'one shield deep', presumably with many helots stationed behind them (Isocrates 6.99). At both Dipaea and Plataea, the Spartans were vastly outnumbered by their opponents, so they may have been forced to adopt the shallowest of hoplite formations in order to match the length of the enemy line, and to rely on a mass mobilisation of helots in order to fill out their ranks.

Among the other Greeks, the number of light-armed was roughly the same as the number of hoplites 'since there was one with each man'. Herodotus made it quite clear that these were 'combatant light infantry', not personal attendants,[52] yet somehow they were associated with individual hoplites. The most plausible scenario is that these light-armed attached themselves to hoplites and relied upon them for cover in combat, in the manner familiar to Homer, Tyrtaeus and archaic vase-painters, but no longer practised in Herodotus' own generation. If so, the Spartans were ahead of their contemporaries in segregating hoplites from light-armed, which may have contributed to their reputation for maintaining exceptional cohesion in the ranks.

Not even Spartan close order, however, entirely precluded displays of individual heroism in front of the thin red line. At Plataea, Aristodemus 'accomplished great deeds, *stepping outside the formation* and fighting in a rage' (9.71.3). The Spartans refused to reward his valour, not because he broke rank, but because they felt that he had been suicidal rather than truly brave.[53] Herodotus put this down to envy, and insisted that Aristodemus was 'by far the bravest man, in our opinion' (9.71.2-4; cf. 7.231). He clearly regarded charging ahead of one's comrades as acceptable behaviour, and implied that the Spartans normally also regarded it as acceptable.

It was said that the best of the Athenians, Sophanes of Decelea, tied himself to the spot with an iron anchor 'whenever he drew near the enemy and came within range, so that the enemy, when they dashed forward from their formation, would be unable to move him' (9.74.1). True or not, the story takes it for granted that it was normal for Greek hoplites – Boeotians at Plataea, Aeginetans earlier in Sophanes' career (6.92.3; 9.75) – to 'dash forward from the formation' (as opposed to dashing forward *in* formation) in combat, just as Aristodemus did.[54]

Herodotus' stories about Thermopylae and Plataea were no doubt influenced by the battle narratives of the *Iliad*, and by epic-inspired poems such as the recently discovered elegy on the Battle of Plataea composed by Simonides soon after the war.[55] But his account was not a purely literary heroic fiction, since it also drew on eyewitness testimony, at least for Plataea (9.16), and had to satisfy audiences which included many experienced militiamen and at least some veterans of the Persian Wars. If Herodotus occasionally sounded like Homer, it was probably because in some respects early fifth-century Greeks still fought like Homeric heroes. After all, Greek warfare at the time did still contain 'heroic' elements such as champion combat, mounted hoplites, and conspicuous warrior burials.[56] Booty was still shared out according to merit, as in the Homeric world, with spectacular prizes for the greatest men.[57] All these things point to a society which greatly valued individual achievement in combat, and which is likely to have continued practising a form of combat which left scope for displays of personal prowess.[58]

If hoplites of the Persian Wars could still drop back without shame and charge forward with honour, and if most hoplite formations still included light-armed troops, we can understand why Herodotus, unlike later historians, had no information about the precise depth of formations: there were no regular files.[59] Hence also Herodotus' failure to mention *tropaia*: trophies were not yet set up because battles were not normally decided by a single breakthrough but tended to swing back and forth in the Homeric manner.[60] Finally, a style of fighting which still gave scope to individual prowess explains why tradition remembered outstanding individual warriors and why Herodotus, unlike his successors, spent much energy on establishing which contingents and individuals performed best in battle.[61] If this is indeed how the Greeks fought, they can hardly have operated in much closer order than the Persians did. The superior cohesion of the phalanx in the early fifth century would therefore have been not so much a matter of greater physical density as of greater co-operation and solidarity among the soldiers – a quality praised as characteristically Greek already by Homer.[62]

*

The key stages of development of archaic combat were thus, first, the introduction of hoplite armour at the end of the eighth century, which produced a fluid mixture of missile- and close-range fighting of the kind portrayed in the *Iliad*,[63] and, second, the exclusive dedication of most hoplites to hand-to-hand combat in the late seventh century, which gave rise to the sort of battles envisaged in the exhortations of Tyrtaeus. When the next significant changes occurred is hard to say, but the artistic evidence suggests that it may not have been until *c.* 500 BC that hoplites, horsemen and light-armed began to be segregated, and Herodotus' *Histories* suggest that this development was still incomplete at the time of the Persian Wars.

The impact of the Persian Wars themselves was mainly ideological. It added two new dimensions to hoplite claims of superiority: the notion that Greeks fought of their own free will, in obedience to the law (Herodotus 7.104.4), while barbarians only fought 'coerced by the whip' (7.103.4; 223.3); and the idea that a hoplite never gave ground but fought to the death, lunging with his spear until it broke, slashing with his sword until it snapped, then punching and biting until the end (7.225.3).

13

The Classical Phalanx

Infantry combat transformed

Fifty years after the Persian Wars we finally have our first prose accounts of contemporary battles – and we finally have evidence for the kind of massed collision which is widely but wrongly assumed to have dominated battlefields ever since the introduction of the bronze panoply almost three centuries earlier. In the conflicts of the Peloponnesian War (431-404 BC) and the fourth century, hoplites were drawn up in regular ranks and files, strictly separated from the light infantry and horsemen. It had become a criminal offence for a hoplite to abandon his station. Battles no longer swayed back and forth indecisively but were won or lost in a single great 'push' (*ôthismos*).

What such a 'push' might have been like has been much debated. One view is that it involved a physical massed shove between two crowds of soldiers who crashed into one another at a run, as visualised in brilliantly vivid detail by Victor Davis Hanson:

> Both sides literally collided together, creating the awful thud of forceful impact at the combined rate of ten miles per hour .... The unusual size and bowl-like shape of the hoplite shield helped to create a feeling of absolute protection in the last seconds of the run .... Perhaps [the hoplite] thought that, if he ran with his shield chest-high and his head lowered, he might not even see the enemy upon impact .... Veterans of hoplite battle would have known that in the final rush into the enemy phalanx, ... rather than hitting a wall of wood and/or flesh, a point of iron, a plate of bronze, they might be forced into the small gaps *between* the running soldiers ... and begin stabbing at the second or third rank of the enemy phalanx. (1989, 157-9)

> In the initial moments after the two sides collided ..., each hoplite pressed with the centre of his shield against the back of the man to his front .... There are many references to men who were either trampled down or literally suffocated as they stood. Any man who stumbled or fell wounded was in danger of being ground up as the men in the rear lumbered forward, blinded by dust and the press of bodies. (1989, 174-5)

The other view is that classical battle consisted simply of intense hand-to-hand combat in a comparatively close formation which ultimately led to one side being figuratively rather than literally 'pushed' off the battlefield by the other. This prosaic view may lack the fascination of the image of a blind stampede followed by a suffocating crush, but it does seem to make better sense of the evidence which suggests that the violence of hoplite battle, great as it was, did not normally take quite such inhuman form.

Rank and file: the classical formation

'Everyone stand in a row, three shields deep ....' This line from Aristophanes' first comedy, *The Babylonians* (426 BC), is the earliest evidence for battlefield formations drawn up in regular ranks and files.[1] The command was probably a joke, not addressed to soldiers at all – the context is lost – but it implies familiarity with a practice of officers instructing their men before battle to form up in files of a certain length. Formations were normally 'eight shields deep' but precise depths varied from unit to unit: the decision was left to individual officers rather than decided centrally.[2] A formation shallower than eight might be adopted by an army stretched out in an attempt to surround a city, or on parade.[3] There are hints that by the late 370s the Spartans had adopted 12 as their normal depth, and the Thebans habitually fought in very deep formations – depths of 25 and 50 shields are mentioned.[4] Otherwise only forces which vastly outnumbered their opponents adopted average depths greater than eight, doubling the length of the file to 16 shields.[5]

Every hoplite 'brings his unprotected side as near as possible to the shield of the man drawn up on his right and believes that density of formation is the best protection', said Thucydides (5.71.1). His remark is often cited as evidence that files stood so close together that shields actually touched, allowing each man a space of only three feet,[6] but clearly what he meant by 'as near as possible' depends on how much room hoplites needed to wield their weapons effectively. A Macedonian phalangite, for instance did require only three feet, since he held his pike (*sarissa*) and small shield steady in front of him and needed minimal room to manoeuvre, but a Roman legionary, who actively wielded his shield on his left arm and his sword in his right hand, required 'at least' an additional three feet of elbow room, a total of six feet (Polybius 18.29.2, 30.6-9).[7] Ancient authors regarded the Macedonian phalanx as a much denser formation than its classical predecessor: Polybius compared it to Homer's jostling crowds rather than to the hoplite phalanx (12.21.3; 18.29.6) and it was even alleged that the Homeric model had inspired the creation of this new, tighter formation (Diodorus 16.3.2). Classical hoplites must indeed have fought more like Romans than like Macedonians, since they not only wielded their weapons energetically (see below), but instead of the Roman short sword used spears up to eight feet long, pointed at both ends.

The classical phalanx can therefore hardly have operated with intervals of much less than six feet (1.8 m; see Fig. 17), enough for neighbours in the ranks to swing their arms fully extended without hitting one another. The

185

'protection' of which Thucydides spoke was therefore not direct cover provided by a neighbour's shield, but the general protection of having a friend close by: at six feet a man was still within a spear's thrust from his neighbour which would have deterred enemy soldiers from trying to enter the gap.[8]

We often hear of hoplites drawing closer together, but even when 'joining shields' (synaspizein), they did not necessarily stand literally shield-to-shield. One could speak of soldiers 'with shields joined' when they marched at six-foot intervals, and to indicate the minimum three-foot interval one had to specify that they 'joined shields completely'.[9] By the standards of many later armies, the density of classical formations was not high, despite Greek pride in their cohesion. At six-foot intervals, the front line of a general levy of 9,000, eight-deep, stretched out over two kilometres, and even a small expeditionary force of 1,000 would have a front more than 200 metres long.

The individual files which made up these formations were only loosely organised. In the model army described by Xenophon in his Education of Cyrus, officers decided each man's place in line, from designated file-leader to file-closer (ouragos; 2.2.6, 2.3.22). This was presumably also Spartan practice. In most Greek forces, however, commanders might try to put the better fighters in front and reliable men at the rear – a tactic already known to Homer (Iliad 4.297-300) – but they probably had neither the necessary personal knowledge of their men to do so systematically nor the authority to impose their will. A soldier was as likely to choose his own place in line as to be assigned a place by an officer:

> Wherever a man stations himself in the belief that it is the best place, or wherever he is stationed by his commander, there he must stand his ground and face danger... and give no thought to death or anything else but shame.[10]

There must have been a good deal of shuffling around and jostling for places before battle. The Greek mercenaries who fought for Cyrus at the battle of Cunaxa began to form up in battle-order in mid-morning and when the enemy finally appeared mid-afternoon 'the formation was still being added to by those coming up' (Xenophon, Anabasis 1.8.1, 8, 14).

Armies on the move found it hard to stay in formation, since hoplites rarely marched in step. The start of the advance was co-ordinated by striking up a hymn, the paian, sometimes reinforced by a trumpet signal,[11] but essentially everyone moved at their own pace over half a mile or more of a wide stretch of terrain, some walking on roads and paths, others tramping across fields, orchards or rocky ground, still others negotiating ditches or small streams.[12] The pace gradually picked up, and the hymn-singing was replaced by invocations of the god of war, and yells of 'eleleu!' or 'alala!' Those who fell behind began to run to catch up. This set off a chain reaction, and by the time there were 200 yards to go, everyone was running. If both sides ran at a speed of five or six miles an hour the final dash would have lasted only 35-40 seconds, but that would have been enough to rip holes in an already disrupted battle-order.[13]

Experienced fighters might manage to keep from running until they were at a mere 100 yards distance (Xenophon, *Hellenica* 4.3.17) and reach the enemy with a less broken line. Better than average cohesion could also be achieved by deploying elite troops as a highly trained and disciplined front rank behind which the rest of the militia formed up, as the Thebans did for a long time.[14] But most formations – largely improvised on the spot by men thrown together for the first time on the battlefield, without prior training as a unit – were kept together by nothing but the hoplites' best efforts to stay 'as near as possible' to their right-hand neighbours for cover. This not only kept the battle-order roughly intact but even led to some 'bunching' during the advance: the cumulative effect of hundreds of men each drawing a few inches closer to their neighbours was a marked contraction of the front line.[15]

Only the Spartans managed not to run at all, but to march in step the whole way. They sang hymns and moved 'slowly, to the music of many pipers stationed among them, not for religious reasons, but so that they might advance smoothly as they walked to a rhythm and their formation was not torn apart, as tends to happen with large armies during the advance' (Thucydides 5.70). They also wore garlands, at least up to the point where they halted to perform – much later than anyone else, and deliberately within sight of the enemy – their pre-battle blood sacrifice. This last-minute halt provided a chance to dress the ranks again. At Nemea in 394 BC, the Spartans sacrificed when the enemy was a mere 200 yards away: in other words, they stopped at the exact moment that their opponents began to run.[16] Apart from having the practical advantages stressed by Thucydides, the slow march, hymns, pipers and garlands could not fail to remind onlookers of a religious procession. The Spartans' disciplined march was an all the more unnerving sight because it suggested that they saw themselves as serenely advancing to the ritual slaughter of their enemies.

If most classical Greek hoplite formations were loose by Spartan standards, they were nevertheless very much tighter than anything the archaic age had seen. Generals and a few other high-ranking figures might still be accompanied by their shield-bearers or even their horses in the battle-line,[17] but otherwise attendants were banished to the rear, and horses were confined to the cavalry, normally stationed on the wings. Light-armed no longer had a place within the phalanx, but stood before, beside or behind it.[18] Above all, the classical hoplite had lost his individual mobility: once he had taken his place, he was supposed to keep to it as closely as possible, for as long as he could.

Fighting and pushing: the mechanics
of combat

'He crashed into the Theban army head-on – and as they threw shield against shield they pushed, they fought, they killed, they died' (Xenophon, *Hellenica* 4.3.19). Laconic as it is, this description of king Agesilaus and the Spartan army at Coronea in 394 BC is among the more detailed classical accounts of what exactly happened when charging armies met. Elsewhere, in his eulogy *Agesilaus* (2.13-14), Xenophon was happy to elaborate:

> There were no screams, yet there was no silence either, but the kind of sound made by fury and combat .... When battle ceased, the place where they had fallen upon one another was a sight to behold: the earth red with blood, the corpses of friend and foe lying side by side, shields shattered, spears smashed, the naked blades of daggers taken from their sheaths, some on the ground, some stuck in bodies, some still held in hands.

Such graphic detail, however, was not something that classical Greeks looked for in a sober historical account. As a result we hear little of the actual experience of combat, and there is plenty of room for disagreement in piecing together what happened in a clash of phalanxes.

Xenophon's picture of the clash between Thebans and Spartans at Coronea is sometimes taken as evidence that hoplite battles began with a full-speed, shield-to-shield collision.[19] It was not, however, a normal opening charge, but occurred late in the battle. The Theban and Spartan armies had each already been victorious on their own wing, and then turned round to face one another: the Spartans must have walked in step as usual; the Thebans 'tightened their ranks and advanced forcefully' (4.3.19). Neither side ran. This particular 'crash' must have involved simply marching towards one another and engaging in hand-to-hand combat.

When armies did charge at a run, it was certainly not in order to give greater force to the first thrust of spear or shield. A hoplite would have needed a run-up of 15 metres at most to reach his optimum speed, and running more than ten times as far would only have weakened his impact. In any case, human psychology suggests that very few hoplites would have charged blindly onwards until their shields or spears hit an immovable object, and human physiology suggests that those who did would have ended up sprawling on the ground, if not skewered on an opponent's weapon. A hoplite ran, rather, to relieve his pent-up emotions, to minimise his exposure to missiles – and, with any luck, to frighten the enemy.[20]

Most soldiers must have slowed down in the last few seconds and ground to a halt 'within spear-thrust' (*eis doru*; Xenophon, *Hellenica* 4.3.17; 7.1.31). The moment was caught in Euripides' version of the legendary duel between Eteocles and Polyneices:

When the roar of the Tyrrhenian trumpet gave the signal for blood-red battle, like a fire-beacon, they flew towards one another at a terrifying run. Their beards wet with foam, they engaged, like boars whetting their savage tusks. They lunged with their spears, but ducked behind their round shields to make the iron spearheads glance off harmlessly. If one man noticed the other raising his eyes above the rim, he wielded his spear hoping that the tip would catch him. (*Phoenician Women* 1377-85)[21]

The running charge does not end in a collision, but leads to cautious yet forceful hand-to-hand combat. Soon Eteocles lands a blow so hard that his spear snaps on impact (1396-9).[22]

The first two ranks of the phalanx could reach the enemy with their weapons, but what the rear ranks were supposed to do is not immediately obvious. If allusions to battles being decided by a 'push' or by the 'weight' of armies were meant literally, the rear ranks must have piled into the backs of those in front and physically shoved them forward. On the other hand, in ancient Greek, as in English, one could describe a drive forward as a 'push' even if it did not involve bodily pushing,[23] and speak of the 'weight' of pressure even if it was not physical: for example, 'the weight of courage' might win the day.[24] If these expressions were meant figuratively, the other ranks might simply have stood by, waiting their turn.

If classical hoplite battle was a concerted physical shoving-match, front-rank soldiers could have done no more than lunge blindly at the enemy while being almost crushed to death by their comrades.[25] What little evidence we have for conditions in the front line paints a different picture. Men who fall are able to get up again without being trampled, and there is enough room for the dead and wounded – from generals to ordinary soldiers – to be carried out of battle by men from the rear ranks or attendants.[26] Hoplites carry their spears either lowered in an underarm position or levelled overarm above their shields, and they are able to alternate between the two in combat – not an easy manoeuvre and one that certainly requires a good deal of elbow-room.[27] Combat actions mimicked by war-dances, normally performed in hoplite armour, included

the avoidance of all blows and shots by sideways dodging movements, by yielding completely, by jumping up in the air and by ducking low, as well as the opposite, postures relating to offensive action which try to imitate the launching of arrows and javelins, and all kinds of blows. (Plato, *Laws* 815a)

In these dances the hoplite shield was 'extended this way and that', just as Sophanes was said to have fought 'always swinging his shield around, never keeping it still' during the Persian Wars, and a Homeric hero took pride in his skill in wielding a shield 'to the right and to the left'.[28] The variety of ways of striking the enemy and the range of movements designed to parry blows or avoid being struck once more imply a good deal of elbow-room.

Another indication that weapons were wielded actively and freely is the fact that weapons training was said to pay off not only during flight and pursuit but brought 'some benefit also in battle proper, when one needs to fight in formation alongside many others'. If some dismissed such training, it was not because in the crush of hoplite battle one needed no skill with weapons, but because the Greeks subscribed to a strong ideology of amateurism.[29]

A soldier in the front rank might also use his shield for physical pushing. As he delivered blows with spear or sword, he could force his shield against that of his opponent in an attempt to drive him back or knock him off balance. One manoeuvre, the 'Thessalian feint', involved suddenly pulling back one's left side and shield, so that the pushing opponent would lose his balance and tumble forward. This trick, of course, required space to step back and could not have been pulled off with the rear ranks pushing one forward.[30] When we read that 'they pushed, they fought' at Coronea, or that 'a hard fight and pushing of shields' took place at Delium, we should presumably envisage *this* type of individual pushing, which occurred regularly in the course of close combat, rather than a tactic of concerted pushing by the entire front rank, let alone by the entire formation.[31]

The big 'push' which decided battle by driving one side or the other off the battlefield was the culmination of all these individual efforts of fighting and pushing. Conceivably, close combat degenerated into a collective shoving contest as more and more weapons broke and the rear ranks thrust themselves forward. But if battles were really decided by the physical pressure of the crowd, it is hard to see how certain armies could hold out against an opponent drawn up in a much deeper formation. At Delium, 25 ranks of Thebans did not overwhelm the eight ranks of Athenians but only slowly 'pushed' them back (Thucydides 4.96.4). At Leuctra 50 ranks of Thebans were initially being beaten by 12 ranks of Spartans, although the latter were ultimately 'pushed back by the mob' (Xenophon, *Hellenica* 6.4.12-14). Like a tug-of-war in which one team is three or four times as large as the other, these battles should have been over in seconds if they had been decided by the weight of the masses.

Xenophon believed that a phalanx only two deep could in theory stand its ground against any number of opponents. In his view, 'phalanxes too deep to reach the enemy with their weapons' were a waste of manpower since 'all but a very few' were inactive.[32] To illustrate his point, Xenophon described a fictional battle in which a two-deep Persian phalanx easily defeated an enemy drawn up thirty deep, and was only slowly driven back by an Egyptian force which was not only a *hundred* deep but for good measure equipped with large shields specifically designed for physical pushing (*Education of Cyrus* 7.1.33-4). Of course this was an unrealistic scenario, because in practice casualties would soon create large gaps in a phalanx so shallow and heavily outnumbered. Nevertheless, the fact that

190

an experienced and thoughtful soldier like Xenophon could believe that theoretically a phalanx which kept its formation and suffered no casualties could hold its ground even when it was outnumbered fifty-to-one shows that he did not envisage the 'push' as a concerted mass shove. He assumed that pushing was confined to the front rank and fighting to the first two ranks.

While the front line remained intact, the rear ranks will thus have remained largely passive, but as the men ahead of them began to fall, or perhaps retreated wounded or exhausted (see below), they moved forward to close the gaps. The 'weight' of a formation was therefore not the physical but the psychological pressure which it brought to bear: the deeper the enemy's formation, the larger the number of soldiers ready to take the place of casualties, and the slimmer one's chances of breaking through. The prospect of having to fight one's way through not just eight, but 16, 25 or 50 ranks was deeply demoralising.[33] The final 'push' was the moment when the army's collective and sustained fighting efforts caused the opponent to run, otherwise described as 'breaking' and 'turning' the enemy.

Battles might be over quickly or last until nightfall.[34] When an entire army broke, battle was over: it was almost unheard of for beaten troops to rally and charge again. The fluid formations of earlier centuries had been able to regroup, but the tight order of the classical phalanx was impossible to restore once it had been lost.[35] Victorious troops, on the other hand, did try to maintain cohesion in pursuit, which meant that they could not pursue very fast or very far, but also that they were able to resume fighting if necessary. It happened often enough that only one wing – usually the right wing – broke through, while other sections of the army were broken by the enemy. The successful troops might then turn round to help their beleaguered comrades or, if these were beyond rescue, to attack enemy contingents returning from pursuit in disorder, as for instance the Spartans did in the battle of Nemea (394 BC). The behaviour of the Athenians in the same battle was probably more typical of armies which lacked the Spartans' discipline: four regiments broke through the ranks of their opponents and pursued them at length, oblivious to the fact that behind their backs the other six Athenian regiments were being massacred.[36]

For victorious troops on *both* sides to maintain their battle-order, turn round, and fight a second full-scale engagement was almost unknown. When this happened between Spartans and Thebans at Coronea, an amazed eyewitness called it 'a battle like no other fought in our time'. Even on this unique occasion only one trophy was set up: the expectation that battles were decided in a single clash had become too ingrained for exceptions to be made.[37]

V. The Experience of Combat

Andreia: the mentality of the classical hoplite

Without a chance to run or recover, without second chances of any kind, combat in classical Greece was a physically and psychologically draining experience, far more so than Homeric or archaic combat had been. No hoplite could sleep well or enjoy his food before battle. A few were so nerve-racked that they lost control over their bladder and bowels.[38]

Preparation for battle required much confidence-building. The careful maintenance of equipment helped to steady nerves: 'he who whets his spear, whets his spirit'. Apart from sharpening their blades, hoplites might polish or repaint their shields. Spartans made a point of carefully dressing their long hair.[39] Everyone anxiously watched the skies for divine signs in the flight of birds, or in sudden thunderstorms and other unusual natural phenomena. Seers offered animal sacrifice to propitiate the gods and read the omens. In addition to more usual offerings, just before the hoplites marched into action the throat of a ram or goat was cut, in a blood sacrifice (*sphagia*) symbolic of the occasion.[40] Generals rode along the ranks to harangue the troops, reminding them of what was at stake and talking up their chances of winning. The long, polished speeches which we find in most sources must be literary fictions: real harangues apparently consisted of series of short pep-talks, and might be abruptly cut short when the enemy began to advance.[41] Meanwhile, a watchword such as 'Zeus the Saviour and Victory' was passed down the line like a Mexican wave – repeatedly, if there was a delay before action. Collective yelling, like singing and whooping during the charge, no doubt helped to get soldiers in the right frame of mind.[42]

No amount of morale-building could suppress fear enough to ensure that hoplites would fight as tenaciously as they were meant to. 'Citizen armies will stand their ground to the death ... for they regard flight as shameful and death as preferable to that kind of survival', Aristotle claimed (*Nicomachean Ethics* 1116b18-21), but in practice they rarely did. No Spartan army ever again fought to the death after the archetypal last stand at Thermopylae – one force notoriously surrendered when surrounded at Sphacteria in 425 BC – and we hear of more Greek armies turning tail before battle had even begun than of armies which fought to the bitter end. The only Greek state which could claim to have lived up to the ultimate hoplite ideal on more than one occasion was Thespiae, a small Boeotian city. Seven hundred Thespiaeans shared the Spartans' fate at Plataea, and their feat was matched by Thespiaean contingents at Delium in 424 and Nemea in 394 BC.[43] Indeed, hoplites were not always expected to fight to the death: a man who fell and got up to fight again three times was regarded as exceptionally brave even for a Spartan (Xenophon, *Hellenica* 5.4.33), which suggests that the badly wounded or exhausted would normally retire, without loss of face.

In classical hoplite combat, it was vital that soldiers contained not only their fear, but all their emotions. Anger in particular could be a threat to the cohesion of the phalanx. Thucydides hinted that the 'keyed-up and angry', and by implication disorderly, advance of the Argives was a factor in their defeat at Mantineia (5.70), while the death of Teleutias in an angry charge inspired Xenophon to warn that 'to proceed against enemies in a rage but without good sense is an utter mistake' (*Hellenica* 5.3.7; see above, p. 25). Fighting under the influence of anger was positively excluded from the definition of 'courage' (*andreia*, literally 'manliness') offered by Aristotle's *Nicomachean Ethics*:

> People feel pain when they are angry, and pleasure when they take revenge: those who fight from these motives are aggressive, but not brave, for they do not act for the sake of what is noble or according to reason, but are driven by emotion. (1117a6-9)

Aristotle also felt that drunks can never count as brave because they 'become optimistic' about their chances of victory (1117a14-15), a philosophical observation matched by a more pragmatic critique in Xenophon, who blamed Sparta's defeat at Leuctra in part on alcohol. King Cleombrotos had convened a war council after breakfast, and 'people say that they continued drinking until noon and that the wine made them a bit keen'.[44] The ideal hoplite was sober and in control of his emotions, a happy 'medium between fear and recklessness'.[45]

If in these respects greater demands were made on classical hoplites than on their archaic or Homeric predecessors, basic combat motivations remained much the same. A love of honour (*timê*) and a sense of shame (*aidôs*) were the key ingredients of true *andreia*, which

> stems from a sense of shame, from striving for what is noble, namely honour, and avoiding reproach, because it is disgraceful .... Citizens stand their ground in the face of danger on account of the punishments imposed by law and the reproaches of fellow-citizens, and for the sake of honours.[46]

Shame remained as powerful a force as it had ever been. 'I shall not shame these sacred weapons' were the opening words of the oath sworn by Athenian ephebes when they became eligible for service.[47] Legal sanctions for cowardice were only haphazardly enforced in Athens, but the social consequences were severe. We get an idea of the relentless verbal abuse hurled at cowards from the treatment in Athenian comedies of Cleonymus, a politician who allegedly dropped his shield in the battle of Delium. For many years afterwards, every single surviving comedy by Aristophanes contained a couple of jokes about Cleonymus the 'coward' and 'woman'. Ten years after the battle, Aristophanes was still mocking the 'Cleonymus tree' which 'in winter sheds its shields' (*Birds* 1473-81). An earlier play featured Cleonymus' son singing Archilochus' famous song about leaving behind his shield (see p. 172): when he gets to 'At least I saved myself', another character cuts in: 'and brought shame on my parents' (*Peace* 1295-1304).[48] The boundaries of shameful behaviour had been redrawn since the archaic period, but the role of shame as such was undiminished. In Sparta, too, the social ostracism of 'tremblers' and their public humiliation as half-men, obliged to shave off half their beards, was no less painful than their loss of citizen rights.[49]

The main honours attainable for a classical hoplite were shared with the whole army: the respect of fellow-citizens for the living; a public funeral for the dead (see pp. 145-7). This did not mean that love of honour became a less important motivation, merely that honours were more equally distributed. The Homeric and archaic custom of awarding 'prizes' of booty according to merit had been abandoned in Athens by the start of the Peloponnesian War. Instead, a single olive wreath or 'crown' was designated as *the* prize (*aristêion*) and awarded by the generals to the man judged bravest of all.[50] The very existence of this prize is further confirmation that classical battle still allowed scope for individuals to stand out in man-to-man combat and had not become an anonymous scrummage. At first, this symbolic prize probably did still come with an item of booty, as in the case of the wreath and panoply presented to Alcibiades, wounded in action at Potidaea in 432 BC, but by the mid-fourth century crowns were awarded on their own.[51] Beyond this, there was no regular system of military decorations, although one-off rewards might be offered – sums of 3,000 and 10,000 drachmas for being the first to scale a city-wall are mentioned.[52] A more egalitarian ethos appears to prevail, although, as in previous centuries, social rank continued to be a factor alongside merit: the very rich and powerful Alcibiades was happy to admit that he had been awarded the prize 'on account of my status', when it really should have gone to the man who had saved his life, the brave but poor Socrates (Plato, *Symposium* 220e).

With honours came fame, which extended to soldiers' families as well. 'The whole earth is a grave monument for famous men', Pericles is supposed to have said in his Funeral Oration, as he told parents of fallen Athenian hoplites to 'lighten your spirits with the thought of their good reputation, for love of honour is the only thing that does not grow old'. He also assumed that competition for fame would drive some people to resent and reject praise lavished on the war-dead out of sheer envy.[53] In Sparta, after the battle of Leuctra,

> one could see the relatives of the dead parading around in public, bright and beaming, while few relatives of reported survivors were to be seen, and those few walked around disgruntled and dejected. (Xenophon, *Hellenica* 6.4.16)

Such fanatical family rivalry is chilling testimony to the continuing importance of honour and fame on the battlefield, even if these things were now to be won collectively.

Solidarity among peers continued to count for more than obedience to officers in maintaining discipline, and was extended to all fellow-soldiers: 'I shall not abandon the man beside me, *wherever* I stand in line,' Athenian ephebes swore.[54] In practice, the next man in line was still quite likely to be a kinsman, friend or lover, and these primary loyalties will have been a major force in combat. Certainly, homosexual relations were seen as a powerful means of creating cohesion and spurring soldiers on to fight their hardest, as demonstrated by the institutionalisation of homosexuality in Thebes' elite Sacred Band, which proved its value by fighting to the death at Chaeronea in 338 BC.[55] A less dramatic but perhaps more typical illustration of the important informal role which erotic ties between men could play in combat is Plato's half-joking suggestion that the ideal reward for an outstanding fighter would be a kiss from all the younger men and boy-attendants in the army (*Republic* 468bc).

Patriotism, of course, was also always a factor:

Go forward, sons of Hellas, set free your fatherland, set free your children, wives and ancestral gods, and the graves of your forefathers!

Gaze upon the true power of our city every day, and become her lover.[56]

These feverishly nationalistic slogans represent a still higher key of intensity than anything found in Homer or archaic poetry, and in this respect they are characteristic of developments in battlefield mentality: the classical hoplite was not 'a wholly new type of man' (see p. 165), but in many ways a more intense and more controlled version of the Homeric hero.[57]

The transformation of the phalanx

Almost all modern interpretations of Greek warfare assume that the hoplite mentality and battle-order described by Thucydides, Xenophon and their contemporaries had existed for centuries. The contrary evidence from archaic poetry, archaic art and Herodotus is variously explained away as unreliable, untypical or irrelevant, and the classical model is projected back 200 years or more. If we take the early evidence seriously, however, we find significant differences between archaic and classical combat, and we must conclude that the formations and tactics of the Peloponnesian War were not much more than a generation old.

We have no explicit evidence for this transformation, and it may seem strange that such dramatic changes should have occurred in the early classical period without leaving a record. But our information on institutional military change is limited and haphazard. The epoch-making creation of the Macedonian phalanx, for example, at a period for which we have otherwise abundant evidence, is attested by only a single sentence in a much later source.[58] It is therefore not so surprising if developments taking place in the far less well-attested first half of the fifth century can only be inferred from indirect evidence.

There are in fact good reasons why the classical phalanx could only have emerged in the classical period. When hierarchical personal ties bound men together, as they did in archaic Greek society, horsemen operated alongside their followers on foot, while heavy- and light-armed men fought in unequal pairs.[59] As we shall see (pp. 233-5), drastic social and cultural changes in the late sixth and early fifth centuries BC established greater state control in political and military institutions, while promoting more egalitarian as well as more exclusive citizen communities. Only at this stage did it become possible and desirable to separate horsemen from their former followers and organise them into distinct elite units, and to separate hoplites from light-armed. By 480 BC this development was still going on – hoplites continued to be mobile and accompanied by light-armed in their battles against the Persians – but it was quite far advanced in Sparta, where it may have been completed with a reform of military organisation soon after the Persian Wars. Elsewhere, classical hoplite tactics probably took rather longer to become established. In Athens, the final segregation of heavy and light infantry may have taken place as late as the mid-fifth century, with the creation of two large specialist corps of cavalry and archers.[60]

The transformation of the phalanx did not stop here. Commanders tried out new roles for their newly specialised troop types. Cavalry and light-armed soon found their niche in protecting the flanks of the phalanx in action and the backs of hoplites in flight; they also chased the enemy in pursuit, something which hoplites now found hard to do effectively without abandoning their denser, more static formations.[61] Much ingenuity was expended on compensating for the tendency of the phalanx to drift to the right during the advance. While this drift had the advantage that it often allowed an army to outflank and encircle the enemy on the right wing, it also meant that armies were vulnerable to being overwhelmed in turn on their left. Strategies to cope with such a turn of events ranged from the simple expedient of setting of troops in ambush at a point where they could attack the encircling enemy wing in the rear, to the complicated and nearly disastrous sideways troop movements attempted by the Spartans at Mantineia in 418 BC. The most successful solution was found by the Thebans: their successes at Leuctra in 371 BC and Mantinea in 362 BC owed much to a 'slanted' advance, in which a strong left wing moved forward fast to force a quick breakthrough while a weak right wing held back to avoid being broken in turn.[62]

The radical tactics of the Thebans were not the only innovation of the 370s, a dynamic decade in the history of hoplite warfare. The Spartans increased their standard depth to 12 men, as well as adding another level to their already sophisticated command structure.[63] The Athenians, meanwhile, took the first steps towards a system of regular training and more efficient methods of mobilisation,[64] and may also have experimented with an entirely new troop type: towards the end of the decade, the general Iphicrates appears to have created a hybrid soldier, equipped with a version of the light shield, light body-armour and light boots of the peltast, yet armed not with javelins but with a long sword and – crucially – a heavy spear, one-and-a-half times or even twice as long as the normal hoplite weapon.[65] Spears of such length, 10-15 feet, could only be wielded with both hands and would have necessitated a still more static style of fighting: only straight-ahead underarm thrusts could be delivered, without the possibility of overarm thrusting or active manipulation of the shield, which would have had to be suspended from the shoulders rather than carried on the arm.[66] This style of fighting would have made a much denser formation possible, and indeed necessary.

The experiment failed to take off in Athens, which continued to arm its citizen hoplites in the conventional manner, but some fifteen years later, in 356 BC, Philip II of Macedon created a force almost identical to the one pioneered by Iphicrates. Macedonian infantrymen carried a small shield suspended from the shoulders and a pike 12 to 16 feet long; they stood in a tight phalanx, almost literally shoulder-to-shoulder with their neighbours, leaving just enough room for the levelled pikes of the rear ranks to pass between them, protruding well in front and overlapping with their own. Instead of running into battle Macedonian soldiers had to march in step, and instead of fighting with one hand and pushing with the other, they simply pushed and stabbed with the pike alone.[67] This type of fighting required a professionalism which not even the Spartans could match, and was made possible only by a total transformation of the Macedonian army. The infantry became a standing force, subject to constant formation-drills and 35-mile training marches in full gear – including a heavy load of provisions and tools since personal attendants were banned.[68]

The Macedonian phalanx, in its extreme density, was the logical culmination of centuries of slow development towards ever more exclusive close combat in ever closer formation. Its superiority became self-evident when in little more than 30 years it conquered the Balkans, Greece and the Near East as far as Pakistan. Yet Greek city-states did not even try to adopt its tactics until a century or more later, when first the cities of Boeotia, then Sparta, and finally the Achaean League formed their own Macedonian-style phalanxes in an attempt to match the armies of the Hellenistic kings and become major players on the international stage.[69] The other Greek cities could not follow suit, for the same reason that Iphicrates' experiment had not worked earlier: even states which were in principle prepared to abandon their traditional ethos of amateurism and elitism, such as Athens, lacked the manpower and money to maintain standing armies – and the Macedonian way of war made demands on skill, stamina and co-ordination which only fully professional forces could meet.

Part VI

Ruling the Waves

A few weeks before he fell overboard and drowned, the Spartan admiral Callicratidas sent a short message to his opposite number in the Athenian fleet: 'I will stop you screwing my sea.'[1]

Callicratidas' choice of words was startling, but everyone knew what he meant. The sea was something to be controlled and fought over, no less than territory or women. The ultimate aim was to establish lasting thalassocracy (*thalassokratia*), 'sea-power', over the whole Aegean or even the entire eastern Mediterranean. Polycrates of Samos was 'the first Greek known to have conceived the ambition to rule the sea', in the 530s BC, according to Herodotus (3.122.2), but Thucydides could think of two or three earlier naval powers in Greece (1.13-14), and long before Polycrates came to power the Samians themselves were already making demonstrations of sea-power by means of calculated insults to rivals. Their ships seized precious diplomatic gifts passing between Sparta and the kings of Egypt and Lydia; they intercepted a cargo of boys sent by Corinth, a major naval power, to become eunuchs at the Lydian court; and they once launched a full-scale, highly destructive naval expedition against Aegina, another aspiring thalassocrat.[2] When Polycrates 'captured numerous islands and many cities on the mainland' (Herodotus 3.39.4), he merely raised an old game to new levels.

After the Persian Wars, the Athenians took sea-power further still. With the largest and most effective navy yet seen in Greece, they not only extended their domination over a much wider area, but claimed to police the seas under their control. By the middle of the fifth century, the Athenians were sending out ships on patrolling missions and advertising their efforts to 'put down piracy' in the common interest of the Greeks and to the benefit of trade.[3] By the end of the century, they refused to acknowledge that anyone else had a right to sail the Aegean in warships at all.[4] Without modern communications and surveillance technology, the sea could not be policed very successfully, but the mere attempt – indeed the mere claim that they were trying – added a new dimension to thalassocracy.

When the Spartans with Persian help built up their own naval resources in the last phase of the Peloponnesian War, their commanders were falling over themselves to be the first to claim naval hegemony for their country. On the strength of a minor victory at Notium in 407/6, Lysander received his successor in naval command, Callicratidas, with the words 'I hand over to you as ruler of the sea' (Xenophon, *Hellenica* 1.6.2). Callicratidas was as quick to mock that claim as he was to follow up his own short-lived success with the boast already cited. Such ambitions were not new: Sparta's reputation as a land-based power has tended to obscure the fact they had been thalassocrats of a sort ever since the sixth century. Their own navy was small, but as leaders of an alliance which included both Corinth and Aegina they could mobilise a large coalition fleet. During the Persian Wars even the Athenians, who provided more ships than all the Peloponnesian cities put together, deferred to Spartan naval command. As early as 525 BC Sparta launched a large fleet against Samos, forced a landing and began an ultimately unsuccessful siege of the city. Officially, this was in retaliation for the gifts stolen twenty years earlier, but the scale and ambition of the enterprise were remarkable for its time and suggest that Sparta intended to oust Samos as the dominant sea-power of the day.[5]

'It is obvious', said Aristotle, that any city needs 'naval power up to a certain level' in order 'to inspire fear and be able to defend not only itself but also some of its neighbours', while any city aiming at international leadership needs a large navy 'in proportion to its activities' (*Politics* 1327a40-b6). Yet the upper classes in classical Greece resented and despised the so-called 'naval mob', the tens of thousands of people – mostly poor men, foreigners, and slaves – required to build, maintain and man the fleet. Even in plays written when the Athenian fleet was as its most successful, Aristophanes could barely muster a few back-handed compliments to its crews for the 'sore bottoms' and blisters they had suffered in the battle of Salamis (*Wasps* 1118-19; *Knights* 784-5, 1366-8). No sooner had they been beaten by the Spartans in 405 BC than he let rip: the oarsmen at Salamis had been a rabble 'good for nothing but shouting "Bread!", calling "Yo-heave-ho!" ..., farting in the face of the rower on the lowest bench, crapping on their mess-mates, and going ashore to mug somebody'. In his own day, they also dared talk back to their captains and refused to row, leaving the ships to drift all over the place (*Frogs* 1071-6). Aristotle felt that the presence of such people was a necessary evil which could be contained by excluding them from political rights (*Politics* 1327b7-9). Plato suggested that renouncing sea-power altogether would be preferable to having to deal with 'helmsmen, pursers, rowers, and all sorts of quite disreputable people' (*Laws* 707ab).

The contrast between the prestige of hoplites and the disrepute of naval personnel could not be sharper. Classical representations of war in art and public monuments concentrated heavily on hoplite imagery, with sailors and rowers nowhere to be seen.[6] It was not just the low social status of most of its personnel which made the navy distasteful to the elite, but the fact that its ethos and principles of organisation were inimical to hoplite ideals: the classical navy was largely a world of lower-class professionals rather than leisure-class amateurs.

14

The Wall of Wood

Ships, men and money

The graves of men buried in Athens' cemeteries in the late eighth century
BC were often marked with a large vase, decorated with a battle-scene. As
often as not, the battle takes place around a ship on a beach. Sometimes
the dead lie piled up beside the vessel (Fig. 23). These vases must be the
memorials of men who had made their reputation as raiders, who, in
Homer's words, 'wandered across the sea at random in the manner of
freebooters' in search of plunder and slaves. So long as sea-raiders chose
their targets with care and did not risk exposing their communities to
retaliatory strikes, their activities made them not only rich but 'respected'

Fig. 23. Fragment of a scene of battle around a ship on an Attic Late Geometric Ia krater, *c.*
760-750 BC (Louvre A527). Amid the corpses of his comrades, a warrior carrying a Dipylon
shield attacks the prow of a beached ship. Other fragments indicate that the ship was shown
with several defenders on board, and several other attackers standing 'behind' it, evidently
surrounding the vessel.

by everyone but their victims.[1] In sixth-century Athens, raiding and trading were still regarded as complementary and equally legitimate ways of making money: a law of Solon's granted legal validity to agreements made by private groups of men 'who travelled in search of booty or for the purposes of trade' (Ulpian in *Digest* 47.22.4).

By the middle of the fifth century, however, Athenians thought of private raiding and piracy as 'shameful' activities, practised only in the more backward parts of Greece (Thucydides 1.5). What had happened in the meantime was that such enterprises had become subject to a greater degree of central control, until it got to the point where, in Athens at least, the state nearly monopolised naval resources. A key element in this process was the widespread adoption of the *triêres* or trireme, a faster and larger type of warship – but the rise of the trireme was itself only part of broader social and political developments which transformed naval organisation.

Sea-raiders and navies in early Greece

Early Greek raiders normally travelled in a *pentekontoros*, a galley powered by 50 oarsmen and equipped with sails as a secondary means of propulsion, capable of reaching even the most remote corners of the Mediterranean and the Black Sea. Smaller 20- or 30-oared ships were also used. A ship-owner could raise a crew from among his friends and peers, as Telemachus does in the *Odyssey* when he goes around town inviting 20 young men of his own age to join him 'out of friendship' (2.383-5, 3.363-4). Additional manpower might be raised from volunteers, such as those apparently recruited in one of Odysseus' tales by a Cretan raider who offered lavish feasts for six days while 'crews quickly gathered' (14.248-51). Thucydides certainly assumed that crews in the old days included many needy volunteers: he said that Greeks used to raid 'under the leadership of the most powerful men, who sought to make profit for themselves and provide a livelihood for the weak' (1.5.1). A third possibility, evidently regarded as a last resort, was for the ship-owner to mobilise 'his own hired labourers and slaves; for he might be able to do even this' (*Odyssey* 4.643-4). All crew members were armed – whether at their own expense or the leader's – and both rowed and fought.

Fleets of warships owned by the state did not yet exist. In time of war, communities relied on private ship-owners to make themselves and their vessels available. The Cretan raider in Odysseus' story recalls how he came under heavy pressure from public opinion to join his country's expedition against Troy; he might even have suffered penalties if he had refused.[2]

A more formal arrangement existed in archaic Athens, where local government was in the hands of the so-called *naukraroi*, 'ship-captains'. Fragments of the laws of Solon show that there were administrative units called *naukrariai*, to each of which belonged several of these ship-captains who were responsible for 'the silver of the naukraric fund'.[3] An oral tradition reported by Herodotus and confirmed by an early fifth-century graffito adds that it was the 'chiefs [*prytaneis*] of the ship-captains' who had led the citizens in their resistance against the attempted *coup d'état* by Cylon in *c.* 630 BC.[4] Classical authors explain that there were 48 *naukrariai*, which until the reforms of Cleisthenes played a role in local administration much like the later demes, and that after the reforms the *naukrariai* were reorganised to form 50 units similar to the later sym-mories, groups of wealthy men who pooled their resources to pay for the cost of a warship each.[5] Later sources fill in a few details: the original ship-captains collected revenue from public property and taxes; their military duty was to provide one ship and two horsemen per *naukraria* and serve under the supreme commander, the *polemarchos*.[6]

In other words, in each of the districts of Attica the rich men who owned 50-oared ships were organised into a group of ship-captains, led by a chief, who were collectively required to make available one of their own ships when the community needed to assemble a fleet. In order to meet the cost of feeding the crew, they collected revenues from public property in the district and taxes from the local population, in particular from rich men who did not have ships of their own to contribute. The ship-captains and their chiefs branched out from these central roles into related areas of administration, such as arranging for so-called sacred ambassadors to travel by ship to major sanctuaries in Attica and abroad,[7] and mobilising local militias. In 508 BC, Cleisthenes transferred most of these responsi-bilities from the rich ship-captains to the elected officials of the demes and other institutions, and in his new, more democratic, system, the ship-owners were left only with the duty to provide 50 ships between them.[8]

The local administration of archaic Attica would not have been in the hands of ship-owners if it had not been of vital importance to the Atheni-ans to be able to raise a fleet. Wars and raids between Athens and its island neighbour, Aegina, occurred throughout the archaic period; the Athenians after a long war conquered the island of Salamis around 600 BC. From the late seventh to the mid-sixth century, they tried to occupy remote overseas territory just south of the Hellespont, and in the late sixth century they also fought at least semi-public campaigns on the other side of the Hellespont, in the Chersonese.[9] By contrast, we have no record of Athenian campaigns by land until 519 BC when Athens occupied Plataea and Hysiae in Boeotia, allegedly at the instigation of the Spartans who aimed to 'cause trouble' for the Athenians by embroiling them with their neighbours. The story implies a belief that there had been no previous enmity over territory.[10] When the Boeotians tried to recover their lost territory in 506, the Athenians defeated them again, in a battle celebrated by Herodotus as evidence of the superior virtues of the new democracy, since previously the Athenians had been 'no better than any of their neighbours in war' (5.77-8). We may conclude instead that until the end of the sixth century Athens' military ambitions had simply not been directed against their Boeotian neighbours but primarily against overseas targets, which had made their ability to raise a public fleet from private resources indispensable. The idea that the Athenians had been landlubbers until Themistocles' naval programme turned them into a seafaring nation is clearly a myth.[11]

Tantalising clues suggest that elsewhere in Greece navies may have been organised along similar lines. Miletus was governed for some time by a wealthy elite known as 'the permanent sailors', *aeinautai*, and inscriptions show that Eretria and Chalcis in Euboea had groups of *aeinautai* as well. We have no other useful information about them, but they were probably the counterparts of Athens' *naukraroi*: men who were required to keep their ships permanently available for collective military use, and who derived political power from this role. In late sixth-century Eretria naval organisation was certainly subject to enough state control for a law to stipulate that crews sailing beyond the Gulf of Euboea were entitled to pay, and to oblige all inhabitants of Eretria to make a contribution towards this expense.[12] A puzzling Corinthian law which decreed that ships could not be given away as gifts may be evidence that archaic Corinth also tried to exercise some control over the privately owned ships on which its navy depended. Perhaps the law sought to prevent private individuals 'giving' their ships in loan to others, as envisaged in the *Odyssey*, in order to prevent a ship-owner from dodging his obligations to the navy by alleging that he had lent his ship to someone else as a favour, and to prevent powerful men from forcing others to lend them their ships and so creating private fleets for raiding expeditions over which the community had no control.[13]

Even the sea-power of Polycrates of Samos seems to have rested on privately owned ships: 'he had 100 50-oared ships and 1,000 archers', according to Herodotus, with which 'he plundered and pillaged everyone, making no distinctions, for he said that one did a friend a greater favour by giving him back what one had seized than by not seizing anything in the first place' (3.39.3-4). It makes no sense, of course, for Polycrates' navy to raid a friendly city and then return the spoils. His witticism is meaningful only if it refers to a policy of not restricting *private* raiding: he ostentatiously allowed Samians to plunder whomever they liked, showing that he was prepared to make enemies and occasionally to make restitution to friends. Specifically, Polycrates may have allowed Samians to raid Egypt, long a favourite destination for plundering expeditions, but ruled by Polycrates' most powerful friend, the pharaoh Amasis. His 100 warships were no state-built navy, but a collection of privately-owned raiding vessels which he was able to mobilise also for his public campaigns of conquest.[14]

Early Greek cities thus devised ways of harnessing the naval resources of their citizens: they imposed some measure of control and provided some public funding.[15] Ultimately they did rely on private resources, however, and this limited naval power in two ways: fleets remained small – Athens' 50, Alalia's 60 and Samos' 100 ships represented forces of only 2,500-5,000 men[16] – and it was impossible to suppress raiding and piracy because no citizen would have had an incentive to acquire a warship if he was not allowed to go plundering in it.

The rise of the trireme

Into this world entered the trireme, a vessel of a highly sophisticated design which naval architects have only recently been able to replicate, and even then only with limited success: the modern trireme *Olympias* performed about 30% below ancient levels. This long, narrow and shallow ship – 35 metres long, less than 6 metres wide, only 3 metres in height – carried a crew four times as large as the *pentekontoros* did: 200 men, including 170 rowers packed tightly onto the three tiers of benches (Plates XXIII, XXIV).[17] Its extra manpower and sleek design made the trireme much faster, so that it could cover longer distances – up to 130 sea-miles (240 km) in a day – and was harder to catch, escape or outmanoeuvre; in short, as one admirer put it, the trireme was 'terrifying to enemies, for her friends a sight to behold'.[18]

When this type of ship was invented is unclear, but it probably originated in the Near East and was first introduced to the Greeks in the late sixth century by the Persian empire. The earliest mention of a trireme comes in a poem by Hipponax of Ephesus, *c.* 540-520 BC, soon after Ephesus and the rest of the Greek cities in Asia Minor had been subjected by the Persians and forced to contribute naval forces to subsequent Persian campaigns of conquest. In 540 BC the major Greek sea-powers were still using only *pentekontoroi*, yet by 500 BC six Ionian cities and three Greek islands between them could muster more than 350 triremes. Chios alone had as many triremes as Polycrates had had 50-oared ships. This explosion in ship-building must have been directed and paid for by the conquerors, keen to create a modern imperial navy for themselves. Towards the end of his reign, Polycrates himself may have acquired 40 triremes from Persia, on condition that the Samians would join the Persian invasion of Egypt.[19]

Outside the Persian sphere of influence, the Greeks took much longer to adopt the trireme. However much they might have appreciated its tactical advantages, the difficulty and cost of recruiting and feeding a crew of 200, rather than 50, put the new ship beyond the reach of all but the very richest and most enterprising ship-owners. The first two Greeks known to have owned private triremes, both in the decade 520-510 BC, illustrate the type of rare individual able and willing to invest in a trireme. Philippos of Croton, an Olympic victor, 'the most beautiful Greek of his time', who was at one point engaged to marry a daughter of the ruler of Sybaris, sailed with 'a private trireme and a crew paid from private funds' to join a colonising venture in Sicily, where he fell in battle. Miltiades, son of Cimon, whose family was among the most powerful in Athens and had a record of multiple Olympic chariot victories, sailed 'in a trireme' to the Chersonese where he established himself as ruler and conquered Lemnos before eventually returning to Athens with five triremes to his name and going on to lead the Athenian army to victory at Marathon.[20] Men of such wealth and ambition were few and far between, and the majority of ship-owners necessarily continued to sail in *pentekontoroi*.

Greek city-states could therefore not rely on private individuals to acquire triremes in sufficient numbers to match the navies being constructed elsewhere in the Mediterranean – not only in the Persian empire and Egypt, but also in Carthage – and the only way to upgrade and expand their naval forces was to begin building and maintaining triremes at *public* expense. 'The first to handle naval matters more or less in the modern way' were the Corinthians, according to Thucydides, 'and triremes were built in Corinth before anywhere else in Greece' (1.13.2).[21] By about 490 BC, triremes were used 'in number' by Corcyra and Syracuse, and in the late 480s a naval arms race between Athens and Aegina led these two states to abandon their old-fashioned *pentekontoroi* and construct trireme fleets (1.14). Herodotus' catalogues of Greek ships in the Persian Wars confirm this picture and flesh it out: in 480 BC Aegina, Corinth and Corcyra had more than 30, 40 and 60 triremes respectively, while Athens and Syracuse had a staggering 200 each. No other Greek state apparently owned more than 20 triremes, and many smaller cities still made do with 50-oared ships.[22]

In a community which had always relied in war on the weapons and ships of its citizens, the establishment of a publicly owned navy was a radical step. It meant building not just the ships themselves, but also a military harbour with dockyards and fortifications, setting up a central organisation to supervise their construction and maintenance, and creating central funds to pay for all this: in short, it meant a great extension of the role of the state. Athens, driven by its violent rivalry with Aegina, made this transition in little more than a decade. In 493 BC work began on a new fortified harbour at Piraeus. A couple of years later, in order to match the size of the Aeginetan fleet, the Athenians bought 20 triremes from Corinth to complement their naukraric fleet: these triremes were Athens' first public ships.[23] With this precedent, Athens began its own ship-building programme, funded by revenue from the silver mines. In 483 BC 100 of the richest citizens – no doubt *naukraroi* already – were given public money to build a trireme each, and soon still more ships were commissioned. Within another couple of years, responsibility for the building and maintenance of warships was transferred directly to a central body of government, the 'trireme-makers', a subcommittee of the Council.[24]

These rapid developments put an enormous strain on Athens, partly because ship-building materials were scarce and costly and partly because an entire branch of government had to be created almost from scratch, but primarily because it was hard to find and fund the number of men needed to operate the ships. The modest initial purchase of 20 triremes almost trebled the number and cost of naval personnel, as 4,000 men were added to the 2,500 already employed. When the first 100 home-built triremes replaced the old naukraric fleet, Athens needed 24,000 men, the absolute maximum that could be levied from its own population at the time. When the fleet expanded further, there was simply not enough local manpower to go round: in the general levy of 480 BC, when every man of suitable age – from the most aristocratic youth to the lowliest foreign resident – took to the ships, only about 120 men were available for each of the 200 triremes. This left the oar-crews at a mere 60% strength, and in order to cover as much as possible of the shortfall the Athenians must have mobilised thousands of their slaves.[25]

Raising the money to pay these crews was equally hard: at the lowest rate, the fleet at Salamis would have swallowed up more than 10,000 drachmas a day. Mining revenue did not stretch to this, and an anecdote told of payments falling so far behind that one crew mugged their own captain, snatching the food from his table. Later accounts hotly disputed how enough money was found in the end: the upper-class version was that Athens' richest citizens had made generous private donations, while the popular story was that the supreme commander, Themistocles, had searched the luggage of the rich when their property was carted to safety, and had confiscated the money which they were desperately trying to hide.[26]

A few weeks before the battle of Salamis, Cleinias, son of Alcibiades, who 'paid from private funds for 200 men and his own ship', had won recognition as 'the best man' in the battle of Artemisium, perhaps as much for his lavish spending as for his heroism in action.[27] Cleinias may have been the last man to contribute a private ship to the Athenian fleet, indeed one of the last men in Athens to own a warship at all. The Athenian state quickly established a monopoly over naval warfare and raiding, which was always carried out in publicly owned ships under the direction of an appointed commander. Not coincidentally the suppression of piracy became a professed goal of Athenian sea-power at the same time.[28] When a certain Makartatos in the fourth century enterprisingly sold his estate and bought himself a trireme, his action was so unusual that it threw his fellow-citizens into a mild panic (Isaeus 11.48).

The other states which developed public navies in the early fifth century must have faced strains on their resources and manpower similar to those experienced in Athens, and probably arrived at similar solutions. Most did not, however, impose levels of central control as high as they were in Athens. Even in the fourth century and later, prominent navies such as the Rhodian and Macedonian relied to some extent on private ships and funding,[29] and throughout the classical period most states allowed their citizens to own warships and go raiding, especially in time of war. Stray references to such figures as Theopompus 'the Milesian raider' are only the tip of the iceberg. Raiders from the Peloponnese operated so widely that it was only natural for an Athenian general to mistake a small Spartan fleet sailing to Sicily for a private raiding party. Even Argos, a highly developed state with no known naval tradition, had its raiders: the unfortunate merchant Lykon, sailing from the Black Sea to Libya, made it safely all the way across the Aegean only to lose his life to an Argive pirate's arrow.[30]

The navy in classical Athens

Classical Athenian warships had very rich captains and very poor crews. Serving as a trireme captain, trierarch (*trierarchos*), was a public service, a so-called liturgy (*leitourgia*), which only the wealthiest 2-3% of citzens, some 800 men, were liable to perform. After 340 BC, trierarchs were selected from an even more exclusive group of the richest 300 citizens.[31] Captains were picked by the generals and served for a term of one year. If they were at sea in active service when their term of office expired, a newly appointed batch of captains would sail out from Athens in passenger ships to catch up with the fleet and take over. We hear of trierarchs forced to continue in post while they sent go-betweens to plead and negotiate with their designated successors to stop dragging their feet, and take charge of the trireme.[32]

Apart from commanding the ship, the captain was responsible for hiring the crew and for maintenance of the vessel. Among the sounds and sights of the city preparing to launch a fleet were 'shouts around the trierarch, pay distributed' (Aristophanes, *Acharnians* 546-7), as captains and their agents went around town trying to attract crews. Although the state provided pay at a fixed rate, captains might offer advance payments and 'big bonuses' to attract 'the best possible sailors', or indeed any sailors at all if competition for manpower was intense. Classical navies hired crews from all over Greece: many men appear to have made a living as itinerant rowers, flocking to any city that was known to be hiring. It was only rarely necessary for generals and captains to take the initiative and go out recruiting abroad, but at least one expedition was delayed because the captains had to scour the Cycladic islands for extra men.[33] Even when a general levy was ordered to man the ships, trierarchs might have to hire rowers if the levied citizens proved incapable of doing an effective job, or simply failed to turn up.[34]

A captain might have his allotted ship overhauled and fitted with new sails and rigging, instead of the equipment provided by the state, in order to make the vessel as fast as possible. He might also splash out on 'expensive emblems and gear' (Thucydides 6.31.3) and boast of 'the most beautiful decoration possible, more magnificent than any other trierarch's' (Demosthenes 50.7). A less ambitious captain was still liable to pay for damaged or missing equipment and for repairs to the hull – or indeed the cost of a new hull if his ship was captured or sunk. The total cost of a lavishly performed trierarchy might add up to some 5,000 drachmas if the ship came home safely; if the ship was lost, replacement costs might amount to another 5,000 drachmas or so.[35] Even the rich rarely had this sort of money in ready cash, and many would have to borrow, or mortgage their land, in order raise the necessary sums. No wonder that the strain of public duties was a staple of conversation among anti-democrats: 'When will we get a break from liturgies and trierarchies wiping us out?'[36]

In order to lighten the burden, an appointed captain could get a relative or friend to share his trierarchy with him – whether by taking turns or by dividing responsibilities – presumably on the understanding that the favour would one day be returned. Around the middle of the fourth century, captains began to share their responsibilities with two or more associates. On at least one occasion, a joint trierarchy was divided between 16. The reform instituted by Demosthenes in 340 BC put a stop to this not only by restricting the trierarchy to the richest 300 men, but by making their financial contribution proportionate to their property, so that the very richest would pay for more than one ship and the less rich for only part of a trireme. This broke the traditional link between paying for a ship and acting as its commander: naval records mention trierarchs who paid for, say, a third of one trireme, another third of a second vessel, and a quarter of a third ship; they obviously could not actively captain all three. This system must have encouraged trierarchs to hire trained sailors to take their place on board, a practice in any case already common enough for a naval defeat in the late 360s to be blamed on the fact that too many appointed captains had hired substitutes and stayed at home.[37] The role of the amateur gentleman naval captain thus shrank gradually, turning the rich trierarch into little more than a taxpayer while leaving more and more ships in the hands of professionals.[38]

Unless the ships were manned by a general levy, the only other amateurs on board, if any, were the ten hoplites and four archers who served as marines (*epibatai*, 'passengers'). Like the rest of the crew, they were paid 'volunteers', and leisure-class hoplites could in principle offer their services. Thucydides would probably not have singled out the marines of one fleet as 'the best men' who fell in the Peloponnesian War if they had not been men of some standing.[39] Normally, however, the volunteers were working-class hoplites, who were more likely to need the money as well as more likely to be available, because they were not already liable to regular hoplite service. Since fighting from the deck of a moving ship required special skills, most soldiers employed in the navy were probably men who made their living as marines. Despite their relatively low social status, they were next to the captain in the ship's hierarchy: unlike the rest of the

210

I. Gender roles in a city under siege: hoplites fight under the wall and throw stones from the towers and battlements, while a woman shows signs of distress.

II. Classical hoplite equipment: double-grip shield, spear, *pilos*-helmet and tunic.

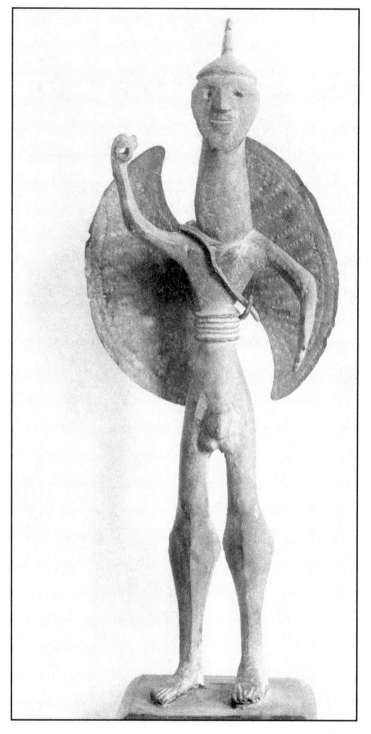

III. Pre-hoplite equipment: 'Dipylon' shield, spear (lost), helmet and metal belt.

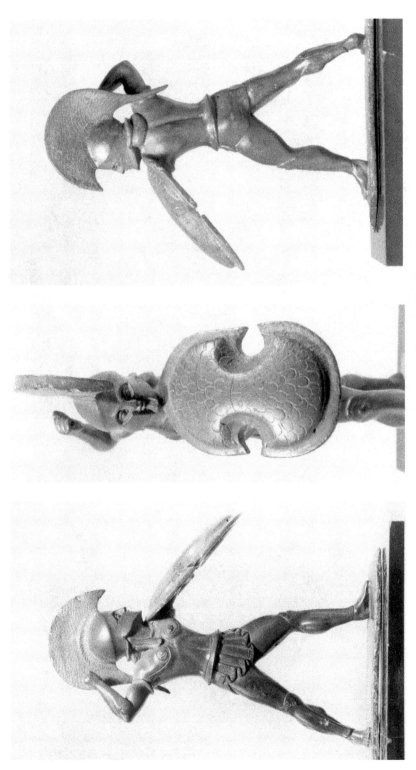

IV. Hoplite in full panoply, with 'Boeotian' shield, bell-cuirass, Corinthian helmet, greaves, and short tunic, adopting characteristic sideways-on combat stance.

V. Peltast with crescent-shaped *pelta* and spear or javelin. His pointed hat is probably the *alôpekis*, made of fox-skin, characteristic of Thracian peltasts (Herodotus 7.75.1).

VI. Cavalrymen in short cloaks and sun-hats riding horses without saddles, stirrups or armour, and throwing javelins at a target in a contest at the Panathenaic Games.

VII. Early sixth-century cavalrymen (*above*), helmeted but otherwise unarmoured, preparing to throw their javelins at a group of fighting hoplites, including an archer (*below*).

VIII. An attendant in short cloak and sun-hat, carrying a spear, stands beside a young hoplite, who is handed his helmet by a woman at the moment of departure for war.

IX. Archaic departure scene: a four-horse chariot carrying a charioteer and a hoplite with two spears is surrounded by three archers and a hoplite with double-crested helmet.

X. Classical departure scene: a hoplite makes a libation in the presence of an older man (presumably his father), a woman (his mother, wife or sister) and his dog.

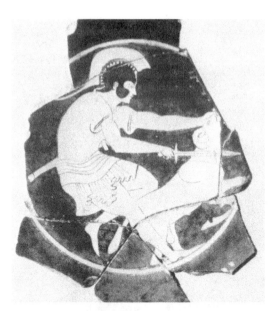

XI. *Sphagia*: a hoplite sacrifices a ram as a blood sacrifice before battle.

XII. Ambush: four hoplites and an archer squat behind some bushes as they lie in wait.

XIII. *Tropaion*: A winged goddess of victory attaches a captured set of arms to a tree trunk, in one of the earliest representations of a battle-field 'trophy'.

XIV. 'Dense ranks, dark and bristling with shields and spears' (*Iliad* 4.281-2): the Dani of the Highlands of Papua New Guinea crowd closely together before battle.

XV. The men advance into battle, in no particular order and each at his own speed.

XVI. Some men fight at close range, while the majority remain passive and at a distance.

XVII. Men are far apart in combat, and continually run back and forth as well as across the field, but the two sides remain separated by a strip of no man's land.

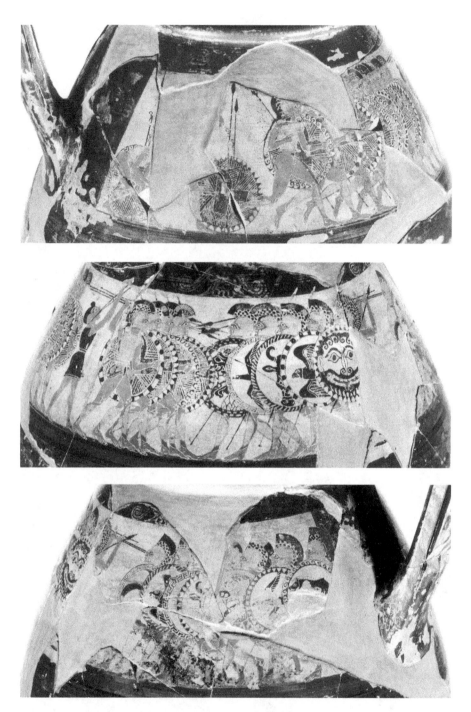

XVIII. Chigi Vase: two groups of hoplites are about to throw javelins at one another while a piper plays (*centre*); behind them more hoplites come running up, some raising their own weapons (*below*), others still holding their spears upright or putting on armour (*top*).

XIX. Sixth-century Corinthian battle scene, showing twelve hoplites fighting hand-to-hand in a dense mêlée.

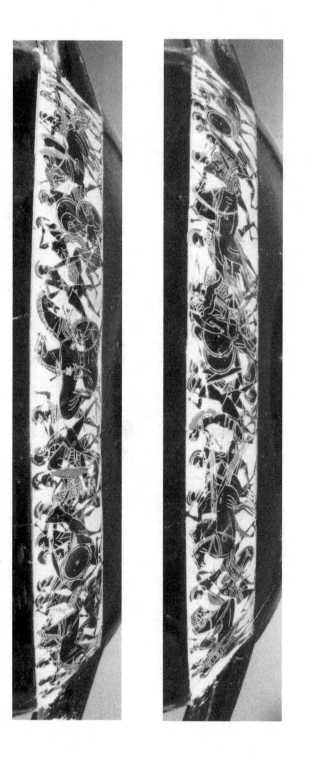

XX. Sixth-century Athenian battle scene, showing horses and chariots, some facing away from the action (below), in the midst of numerous hoplites engaged in hand-to-hand fighting.

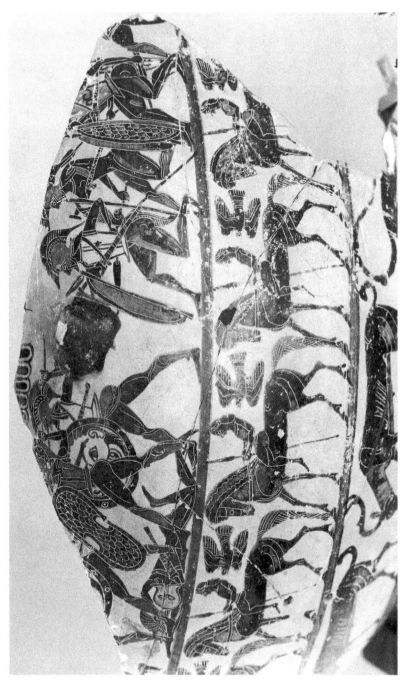

XXI. Above: fight over a dead body, which shows rear ranks keeping their distance from the action and ducking behind their shields to avoid (unseen) enemy missiles. Below: youths on horseback, possibly representing cavalry.

XXII. Fifth-century clay model from Boeotia showing a hoplite with double-grip shield mounted beside a charioteer with a Boeotian shield slung behind his back.

XXIII. The reconstructed trireme *Olympias*.

XXIV. The three levels of rowers aboard *Olympias*, illustrating the cramped conditions, especially for the *thalamioi* on the lowest bench.

XXV. Sixth-century triremes under sail, navigated by helmsmen and look-outs. The ships have rams in the shape of boars' heads and carry disembarkation ladders in their sterns.

ΒΑΣΙΛΕΟΣΕΛΘΟΝΤΟΣΕΣΕΛΕΦΑΝΤΙΝΑΝΨΑΜΑΤΙΧΟ
ΝΑΥΤΑΕΓΡΑΨΑΝΤΟΙΣΥΝΨΑΜΜΑΤΙΧΟΙΤΟΙΘΕΟΚΛΟΣ
ΕΠΛΕΟΝΗΛΘΟΝΔΕΚΕΡΚΙΟΣΚΑΤΥΠΕΡΘΕΙΝΙΣΟΠΟΤΑΜΟΣ
ΑΝΙΗΒΑΛΟΓΛΟΣΟΣΟΘΗΕΠΟΤΑΣΙΜΤΟ ΑΙΓΥΠΤΙΟΣ ΔΕ ΡΜΑΣΙΣ
ΕΓΡΑΦΕΔΑΜΕΑΡΧΟΝΑΜΟΙΒΙΧΟΚΑΙΠΕΛΕΡΟΣΟΥΔΑΜΟ

a

ΚΑΙΧΕ

ΚΡΙΘΙΣΕΓΡΑΛΛΕΜΕ   ΓΥΘΟΝ ΑΜΟΙΒΙΧΟΥ

XXVI. Graffito carved by Greek mercenaries into a colossal statue flanking the entrance to the mortuary temple of Ramesses II at Abu Simbel (for translation, see p. 232).

crew, they took part in ceremonies at departure, were addressed in battle harangues, and were even engaged in political discussions by their captains and commanders.[40]

Next in ranking order came the sailors, collectively known as 'the staff' (*hypêresia*). They were led by the helmsman (*kubernêtes*), an experienced sailor who navigated the ship from his seat by the steering oars in the stern, with the help of a look-out who stood in the bow (*prôiratês*). The helmsman gave instructions to the rowing-master (*keleustês*) who by means of shouts and whistles gave orders to the oarsmen, assisted by a piper (*aulêtês*) setting the rhythm. Each ship carried its own shipwright (*naupêgos*) to make emergency repairs and a purser (*pentekontarchos*) to distribute pay and rations. Ten deck-hands completed the team. Athens prided itself on having enough citizens trained in naval skills to provide expert sailors for the entire fleet, but 'staff', like rowers, might be hired from anywhere in Greece. One of the few trierarchs to get away unharmed from the disastrous Athenian defeat at Aigospotamoi took credit for having 'attracted with money' Phantias, the best helmsman in Greece.[41] As members of the working classes, the sailors were generally looked down upon, but the upper classes grudgingly acknowledged the importance of a professional staff, and the helmsmen in particular enjoyed a good deal of influence and even prestige.[42]

On the lowest rung of the naval ladder stood the 170 oarsmen, with their own internal hierarchy: the 62 top-bench *thranitai* rated above the 54 middle-bench *zygioi* and the 54 *thalamioi*, who were seated lower still in the hold, physically and socially at the bottom.[43] Rowing was so much a lower-class occupation that the richer citizens were excused this duty even in emergency mobilisations, and it was so typical a lower-class occupation that the common people of Athens could be flatteringly described as 'the *thranitai* who saved the city' or sneeringly called 'the yo-heave-hos' (*to rhuppapai*), after the rowers' rhythmic call.[44]

Even so, the sheer number of men employed by the navy meant that Athenian citizens in fact formed only a minority of rowers. In a famous phrase, Athens' naval power was described as 'bought rather than home-grown', meaning that the bulk of crews normally consisted of mercenary rowers hired from abroad (Thucydides 1.121.3; cf. 143.1-2). Another large group of oarsmen were metics, foreigners resident in Athens, many of whom will have moved to Athens precisely because they hoped to find semi-permanent employment as rowers. Indeed, the rowers of the Athenian fleet during the Sicilian expedition are collectively described as metics, 'regarded as Athenians, although they are not, because they know our dialect and imitate our ways' (7.63.3). Moreover, many oarsmen brought one or more slaves to row beside them – or rather below them – on the same ship. An inscription which partially preserves a set of rosters from the late fifth century shows that anywhere between a fifth and two-thirds of a trireme crew might consist of slaves. Oar-crews were

211

evidently constituted in the same way as the crews of construction workers building a temple on the Acropolis at the same time: they were hired in small teams of citizens, metics and slaves who worked alongside one another.[45]

The superior quality of trained rowers, sailors and marines became painfully evident when, in a crisis, the rest of the citizens were mobilised for naval service in a general levy. With these inexpert crews normal battle-tactics could not be executed (Xenophon, *Hellenica* 1.6.31), and, as we have seen, some trierarchs simply dismissed their levied crews and hired professionals instead (Demosthenes 50.7). Even the most skilled rowers, however, needed further training before they could operate effectively, because crews were assembled from scratch each time a fleet was launched and they had no experience of rowing together as a team. A commander who trained his crew *en route* to battle was a rare example of efficiency; as a rule, it would take a week or so before a new crew had had enough practice of various drills to be ready for action.[46]

This level of training was of course vital to the navy's success, but it was quite at odds with the amateur ideals of gentlemen hoplites and horsemen and fuelled their contempt for the 'naval mob'. During the Ionian Revolt, according to Herodotus, the citizens' reaction to being forced to train every day, all day, for a week, 'worn out by hard work and the hot sun', was to mutiny against such 'intolerable insults' and refuse to put up with this kind of 'slavery' (6.12).

Above the level of the trierarch and his ship, very little naval organisation existed. The fleet was normally commanded by one or more of the same ten generals who were elected to lead the army, and in a general levy the commanders of the ten tribal regiments would also join the fleet. Sometimes naval detachments were sent out under a specially elected 'admiral' (*nauarchos*), whose authority ranked below that of a general. None of these officers had their own ships: they simply sailed on any of the regular triremes they chose, competing for places on the fastest and best-looking ships. One trierarch proudly recalls an occasion when all ten generals engaged in a 'long slanging-match' as they fought over a place on his splendid ship.[47] Otherwise, the only specifically naval officials were the supervisors of the dockyards – an elected committee responsible for the storage of naval equipment and the maintenance of ships and ship-sheds, a huge complex of buildings which dominated Piraeus – and the committee in charge of ship-construction. The manual labour required for all this must have been carried out by hundreds of citizen, metic and slave workers. The chief shipwright involved in building a trireme was deemed important enough for his name to find its way into the naval records occasionally, but of the rest we know nothing.[48]

So far as we can tell, the organisation of other classical navies in some ways followed the Athenian pattern. In the Spartan navy, captains and marines were citizens and *perioikoi*, but the rest of the crew were 'either helots or hired men'. One such hired man was Hermon, a non-citizen resident of Megara, who served as helmsman under successive Spartan commanders at Arginusae and Aigospotamoi, and was so highly regarded that the Spartans included a statue of him in their victory monument for the latter battle.[49] The helots were not the only serfs to be used as rowers: so were the Thessalian *penestai* and the native Mariandynians who formed the subject population of Heraclea-on-the-Black-Sea. Aristotle recommended the employment of barbarian serfs as naval personnel as a model of good practice. In the absence of a serf population, Corcyra mobilised huge numbers of chattel slaves to row their warships: in the naval battle of Sybota, almost 80% of captured Corcyraeans were slaves. Crews which consisted predominantly of slaves or serfs must have been recruited and managed differently from Athens' mixed complements, and the title 'master seamen' (*desposionautai*) for one category of helots offers a tantalising hint of their internal organisation, but beyond that we can say little, except that all classical Greek fleets were associated with the lowest social classes.[50]

*

Why were classical Athenian triremes manned by lower-class professional rowers, whose fighting role was limited to some light-armed raiding at best, rather than regularly manned by 'self-rowing' soldiers, as they sometimes were in emergencies and as archaic warships always used to be?[51] A simple answer is that the trireme was adopted for its superior speed, manoeuvrability and ramming power and that it took a highly trained crew to maximise these advantages. But technological and tactical progress do not add up to a full explanation, because triremes were, after all, not widely used in Greece until at least a generation after their introduction in Ionia, and even when and where they did come into use, old-fashioned naval tactics which failed to make the most of the trireme's virtues often continued to prevail, as we shall see. For some time Greek cities were content to reinforce their fleets of 50-oared ships with the few triremes which could be raised by conventional means, as privately owned ships manned by the captains' own friends, dependants and neighbours. Things might have stayed this way, if fundamental political and social changes had not transformed the navies of Greece.

The decline of personal power and the growth of central power from the end of the archaic period onwards made it difficult for local elites to mobilise large numbers of personal followers, and this affected naval crews no less than infantry bands. In Athens, Cleisthenes' transfer of local power from the ship-owners to elected officials was a major step in this direction, a quarter of a century before the city even started building triremes. Just as personal followers finally stopped playing a role in infantry warfare in the first half of the fifth century, so the traditional

213

bonds between naval crews and their captains were broken at the time, leaving the trierarchs little more than agents of the state whose only tie to their crew was a temporary responsibility for ensuring that they received their wages and rations. And just as on land these changes made possible dramatic tactical advances – the use of massed hoplite formations in classical phalanx tactics (see pp. 195-6) – so at sea they paved the way for the use of professionals capable of executing sophisticated naval manoeuvres which had been far beyond the abilities of the 'self-rowing' soldiers of earlier generations.

War at Sea

Classical naval campaigns

The punishment of being thrown into a ravine and having one's body lie rotting away unburied at the bottom of the precipice was normally reserved for serious criminals. During the Peloponnesian War, however, the Spartans meted out the same treatment to all 'traders from Athens and its allied states whom they caught sailing round the Peloponnese in merchant ships'. In fact, 'at the start of the war, the Spartans killed every single person they caught at sea, treating them as enemies whether they fought on the side of the Athenians or were neutral' (Thucydides 2.67.4). The indiscriminate brutality of this small-scale naval activity early in the war was matched by the Spartans' wholesale massacre of captives after the final naval battle, when they killed in cold blood all their 3,000 Athenian prisoners and left the bodies unburied. To justify this atrocity, the Spartans pointed out that the Athenians had recently drowned the crews of two captured triremes, and had threatened to cut off the right hand of any prisoner they might take.[1]

The war at sea was waged with the same ferocity as the war on land (Fig. 24), but, like infantry warfare, it did recognise a few conventions and rituals. A notable example is the care taken by the Spartans to mark a scrappy victory over a small Athenian fleet in 411 BC: the day after the battle, they rowed 50 miles to the site of their victory and back, just to set up a trophy.[2] Naval warfare had its own peculiar characteristics and problems, but the fundamental parallels with land warfare are striking. The tactics and strategies of Greek fleets, like those of hoplite armies, were shaped by a mixture of logistical constraints, weak discipline, agonal ideals and 'total' objectives.

In the navy: mobilisation, logistics and discipline

A Spartan in a canoe seizing a puppy-dog from a trading ship belonging to one of Athens' tiniest allies was all the provocation Athens needed to launch an armada, Aristophanes joked:

VI. Ruling the Waves

All over the city there would be raucous cries of soldiers, shouts around the trierarch; pay distributed, images of Pallas gilded; colonnades groaning, grain measured out; wine-skins, oar-loops and a jar bought; garlic, olives and onions in nets; garlands, anchovies, girl-pipers, black eyes. And then, all over the dockyards, oars planed, dowel pins tapped, bottom oars fixed, pipes, rowing-masters, whistles, trills. (*Acharnians* 541-55)

Rowers are recruited, go shopping for essential supplies, get out of hand in last-night parties, prepare their places on board and start their training, all in apparently quick succession. In practice, however, mobilisation of a fleet took a long time and a lot of effort.

When the Athenians decided to fight the Persians at sea in 480, they needed to recruit all their naval personnel from scratch. The board of generals started by appointing 200 ship's captains 'from among those who own land and a house in Athens, have legitimate sons, and are no more than 50 years old' (ML 23.18-22). In order to speed up this process, the generals later began making an annual selection of 400 men liable to serve during that year, from among whom they could then at short notice pick captains for active service. The selection, however, remained a cumbersome business because anyone put on the list could challenge his appointment by finding someone richer than himself who had not recently served. The latter was then be obliged either to take the place of the original appointee or, if he denied that he was the richer man, to accept a

Fig. 24. Prisoners being drowned, on a black-figure lekythos by the Beldam Painter, *c.* 490-480 BC (Athens, NM 487). This is generally believed to represent a scene of torture of prisoners by pirates (see Ducrey 1968, 214), but it may represent a regular method of drowning prisoners of war: they are tied to ropes to prevent them from getting away, and pushed under with sticks or spears. This is clearly not the most efficient or humane way of executing prisoners, but that is no reason to associate it with piracy rather than legitimate naval warfare.

so-called 'exchange' (*antidosis*) whereby he traded his own estate for the estate of the challenger. Inevitably, this gave rise to mutual recrimination, bad blood, and rounds of litigation.[3]

In order to minimise such trouble, the annual lists were replaced in 358/7 BC by a single permanent register of 1,200 liable estates – reduced to 300 in 340 BC. This register still needed to be periodically revised, of course, and up to 40% of estates included might at any time be unable to provide a captain, but it did help to streamline the mobilisation process.[4]

The generals allocated by lot to each captain a ship and its 'wooden gear' – 200 oars, two rudders, masts, spars, poles, ladders – and the supervisors of the dockyards handed out from their storerooms sets of 'hanging gear' – two sails, a range of cables, ropes, screens and awnings of canvas and leather, and a pair of anchor-stones. Ships and gear varied greatly in quality and state of repair, so to forestall complaints of unfairness they were allocated at random, but the process was nevertheless regarded with suspicion. Aristophanes has a general threaten:

'I will make sure that you become a trierarch and spend your own money, with an old ship on which you cannot stop spending however many repairs you make, and I will fix it so that you get a rotten sail.' (*Knights* 912-18)

The biggest problem was that the ships' gear, worth thousands of drachmas per set, vanished from the naval stores at an alarming rate. The meticulous naval records which survive show that every effort was made to keep track of the whereabouts of naval equipment, but trierarchs often failed to return or replace items, and some supervisors themselves engaged in large-scale misappropriation of everything from oars to anchors.[5] The unreliability of the naval stores drove some trierarchs to buy their own sets of equipment, but that led to complications when handing over ships in mid-campaign: new captains were reluctant to pay their predecessors for sets of gear which they could get from the state for free.[6]

The reforms of 358/7 BC tried to improve matters by making the 1,200 potential trierarchs more directly responsible for ships and gear. Those liable to serve as trierarchs were organised into 20 groups called symmories, among which all available ships were distributed, and each of these groups was charged with the duty of retrieving the equipment used on its ships. The immediate result was not overwhelming: the next year saw a series of confrontations, punch-ups and court-cases as trierarchs still failed to hand over equipment to their successors, and the naval records still contained dismal entries such as the following, for the trireme *Europa*:

Europa, in need of repair   Symmory of Pythodoros of Thria

Present rudders – unusable; big sailyard – unusable; ladders – one unusable

Owed Demophilos' heir, Sostratos, son of Euxitheos, of Acharnae – a full set
   of oars
Strombichos of Euonymon and Dorotheos of Anagyrous – mast supports
Stephanos of Myrrhinous and Demonicos of Laciadae – a mast[7]

Further debt-clearing measures and reform proposals followed, including the further subdivision of the symmories into 100 small groups by 340 BC and the creation of new ship-sheds, a vast new naval arsenal, and an emergency reserve of 100 sets of hanging gear on the Acropolis by 330 BC. Still the efficiency of the fleet continued to be impaired by missing equipment.[8]

The mobilisation of crews could take a long time. Even in Athens at its peak it cannot have been easy to hire on the open market the 17,000 rowers needed for a medium-sized fleet of 100 triremes, and it is not surprising that generals and trierarchs were sometimes forced to make recruiting trips abroad (see p. 209). General citizen levies, too, were harder to organise for the fleet than for the army: instead of simply raising the alarm and waiting for soldiers to come running up, the generals had to raise specific numbers of men and assign them to particular ships. Crew lists were drawn from citizen registers and advertised on whiteboards. If many men failed to turn up it could well be because the message had not reached them in time.[9] Between 362 and 347 BC the previously exceptional use of citizen levies to man the fleet was so common in Athens that it was almost the norm. In the middle of this period Demosthenes proposed that certain blocks of ship-sheds should be designated embarkation points for each tribe and *trittys*, so that in the event of a general levy everyone would know where to go (14.22-3). That he should have felt the need to make this simple suggestion shows not only that such levies were now common, but also that their organisation was still far from smooth. Athens' reliance on citizen levies appears to have been temporary and was surely a response to an acute shortage of money and manpower, but it is a sharp reminder of how hard it could be to man a fleet.

In short, it took even longer to launch a fleet than it did to raise an army. The whole process from selecting the first captain to hiring the last oarsman must have taken several weeks, and then it was another week or so before the crews had had enough training to risk going into action.[10]

Once the ships were underway, of course, they moved much faster and ranged much further than any army could. The speed of a trireme fleet, however, came at a cost. Little storage space was available on the tightly packed ships. A crew needed an estimated 300 kg of grain and 500 litres of water a day, not to mention the wine-skins and the nets of garlic, olives and onions featuring in Aristophanes, and there was no room for more than two or three days' supply. Nor was there enough space for more than a part of the crew to sleep on deck. The trireme therefore normally made land at midday for a meal, and again at nightfall.[11]

Finding a place which could offer food and drink for thousands of men was hard, and crews might have to travel several miles from their landing places to gather enough food, reach an adequate water supply, or get to a market. More than once, a cunning enemy exploited the lengthy absences of rowers on provisioning trips to strike a major blow, as we shall see. These problems were partly alleviated by the flotilla of trading ships that usually followed in the wake of any sizeable expedition, and for their most ambitious naval ventures states might go so far as to include dedicated grain-transports carrying weeks' or months' worth of food. But such extensive logistical support was rare, a sign of the kind of exceptional wealth and commitment that made the Athenian state go so far as to recruit even a team of bakers for the Sicilian expedition.[12]

Naval warfare was as much a seasonal activity as infantry warfare. Sea-travel was deemed safe only during a period of less than five months in spring and summer, and although triremes could certainly be found at sea outside the season, fleets did avoid sailing in winter. It was in any case essential for the maintenance of triremes that they were regularly taken into dock and dried out, as the Athenians found to their cost when their ships became waterlogged during a protracted naval blockade of Syracuse. When fleets did not return home at the end of the season but spent the winter in another port, the lack of logistical support meant that rowers were in danger of starving and liable to mutiny.[13] The quick retreat of the Persian fleet after Marathon and Salamis may therefore not have been due solely to Athenian prowess: in each case the battle came right at the end of the sailing season and it would have been time for the Persian triremes to go home or find winter quarters even if they had not been defeated.[14]

Upper-class opinion held that rowers were liable to mutiny even at the best of times. The typical rower talked back to his captain and refused to do any work, according to Aristophanes (cited above, p. 200). When the commander of a fleet from Thurii was threatened with a beating by his Spartan superior, his long-suffering crews 'erupted' and started throwing things at the Spartan – 'since they were sailors, after all', Thucydides could not resist adding (8.84.2-3). One might have thought that discipline would be less of a problem within the hierarchical organisation of a trireme than within the egalitarian citizen militia, and it is true that Thucydides singled out the 'free men' among the crew as the 'boldest' in dealing with their captains (ibid.). However, the hired foreigners among the crew had an option unavailable to citizens: they could desert to another fleet which promised better conditions. One broke trierarch noted:

> My crew, confident in their ability to row, went away to wherever they would receive the most money again; they regarded their present prosperity as more important than the fear of what might happen if I ever got my hands on them. (Demosthenes 50.16; cf. 44)

The same trierarch observed that it was 'a universally agreed truth' that citizen and metic rowers would also desert in droves, or demand higher wages to stay on, if they had a chance to go home early when the ship put in at Piraeus 'halfway through' (50.11). For slave rowers, of course, it was always tempting to abscond, and when they did, their masters would also tend to leave the ship to run after their property (Thucydides 7.13.2).

The trierarchs themselves were not exactly docile in their relations with naval commanders. The captains who deserted the Ionian rebel fleet in 494 BC because they could not tolerate the 'slavery' of regular training imposed on them by their commander were in good company. A Persian expedition against Naxos in 500 BC is said to have fallen apart when the commander of the Greek contingent refused to accept Persian authority, and in particular sabotaged an attempt to impose some discipline by releasing a negligent Greek captain who had been tied to the lowest rowing bench with his head sticking out of the oar-hole. The Greek coalition against Persia fell apart when the Spartan commander Pausanias was rude to his captains and punished indiscipline by having men flogged or forced to stand holding an iron anchor.[15] Less momentous, but no less telling, was the behaviour of Apollodorus, who presented himself as a rare example of a trierarch who would obey his general's command to sail even if he were not given the wherewithal to pay his crews, but was nevertheless quite capable of refusing to appear before the general when summoned for disobeying a direct order: 'I said to his servant: "If there is something he'd like to discuss with me, I'll be in the market place!" ' (Demosthenes 50.51).

Since generals and other officers did not have their own ships but were dependent on the ships provided by the trierarchs, the balance of authority aboard such vessels could be precarious. Apollodorus' refusal to obey an order which he regarded as illegitimate (50.47-8) led to a quarrel with the officer stationed on his ship, as both men tried to give orders to the helmsman. Eventually, the helmsman announced that he would obey the trierarch alone, since it was he, not the general, who was 'accountable' and who paid him (50.50). The general was ultimately able to carry out his order only by having his officer *pay* another captain to give up his trierarchy, so that he finally had full control of a ship (50.52). The command structure at the highest level thus involved a triangular relationship between the helmsmen, who had no formal authority but had to be consulted on tactics and enjoyed great influence, the captains and the naval officers. It was far from clear who was in control. Alcibiades once left a helmsman in command of the entire fleet, with strict orders not to engage the enemy; not untypically, his orders were ignored.[16]

Weak control meant that captains were able to divert their ships from the fleet for a spot of private raiding or piracy. Weak logistic support meant that they were often positively forced to do so, in order to find food or raise money for pay. At one end of the scale, Themistocles allegedly sailed ahead of his own fleet and privately extorted vast sums of money from various cities by threatening to steer the entire Greek armada in their direction. At the other end, rich captains were not above petty depredations like rustling cattle and stripping woodwork for re-use as fence- and door-posts on their own farms or as pit-props in their mining concessions. The hiring out of trierarchies to professionals aggravated the problem, since those who made a living from captaining warships were naturally keen to spend as little as possible of the money they received and to cover most of the running costs of ship and crew with the proceeds of plunder. The resentment and retaliation to which these activities exposed the whole fleet almost justified the rhetorical claim that 'such ships do not sail *for* you, but *against* you'.[17]

From sacrifice to salvage: agonal and total warfare at sea

A naval expedition began with ritual and agonal displays. The sacrifice before departure was felt to be of great importance. The decree of mobilisation for Salamis stipulated that it should be 'a placatory sacrifice to Zeus the Omnipotent and Athena and Victory and Poseidon the Steady' (ML 23.38-40), and the Spartans inaugurated a great naval expedition against the Persians with a sacrifice at Aulis, in imitation of Agamemnon's legendary sacrifice before the Trojan War. A Boeotian cavalry raid which disrupted the latter sacrifice was cited as a cause of war a few years later. Prayers and libations were customarily performed ship-by-ship, but before the Athenian expedition to Sicily they were impressively stage-managed: a trumpet called for silence, a herald recited the prayer to be repeated in unison by the crews and the crowd of spectators on the quays, wine was poured by captains and marines from golden and silver vessels, a *paian* was sung. Then the agonal spirit kicked in and the ships raced one another all the way to Aegina.[18]

In the course of a single expedition, a fleet often had to play both of its two essential roles: as warships battling for control over sea-routes, and as transport vessels carrying armies overseas. These functions were difficult to reconcile, since triremes were at their most effective in combat if they carried few soldiers, too few to produce a respectable invasion army. There was room on deck for some 30 soldiers in addition to the regular 14 marines and this maximum number was often carried even by ships primarily intended for combat, despite the adverse effect on their mobility and stability. Hulls might be modified and decks extended to carry still greater numbers.[19] Thucydides derided such practices as 'archaic and quite ignorant' (1.49.1); the smart, modern alternative was to distinguish between 'fast' combat triremes which carried only the standard number of marines and 'army' triremes (*stratiôtides*) or 'hoplite-carriers' (*hopli-*

221

tagôgoi) which probably carried fewer marines but up to 100 additional soldiers.[20]

Expeditions which intended to fight at sea, or to engage in small-scale raiding, like the 100 Athenian ships which made landings in the Peloponnese in the first year of the Peloponnesian War, needed no soldiers other than the marines. The problem was that such lightly manned fleets could not exploit certain opportunities: during this particular expedition, the Athenians briefly occupied the strategically vital port of Pheia, but had to leave as soon as the locals fought back (Thucydides 2.23, 25, 30). Expeditions which intended to wage major land battles or attack cities overseas, on the other hand, like the 100 Athenian ships which tried and failed to capture Epidaurus and Potidaea in the next year, might bring up to 4,000 extra hoplites, as well as cavalry in old triremes converted to horse-transports. The problem here was, of course, that heavily manned fleets might find themselves forced to fight a naval battle, in which they would be hopelessly disadvantaged. A small, fast Athenian fleet could decimate a troop-transporting Corinthian fleet more than twice its size, but when forced to sail with large numbers of soldiers on board even a vast Athenian fleet could be destroyed in battle by a competent opponent.[21]

Attackers tried to exploit the element of surprise to effect unopposed landings, and the speed of the trireme was such that even large fleets – unlike large armies – often reached their destinations before their victims could organise any resistance. If the defenders were ready, however, they would fight on the beaches: the agonal spirit did not extend to allowing an enemy to deploy his forces on land before engaging in a pitched battle. At Pylos, the Athenians held the coast so effectively that the Spartans were forced to crash their ships onto the shore in a doomed attempt to land. Given more time to prepare, the Syracusans spiked their landing places with an artificial reef of sharp stakes, which the invaders were not able to dismantle even with the aid of hired divers. To avoid such desperate struggles, landings were often made at night, and sometimes involved elaborate deceptions – disinformation, decoys, and disguised ships.[22] Nor did any agonal convention say that beaten invaders should be allowed to depart unhindered: on the contrary, every effort was made to capture or burn their ships. For the Athenians, one of the most memorable things about the battle of Marathon was that Aeschylus' brother had had his hand cut off while grabbing the stern of a Persian ship, trying to set it on fire.[23]

Plato observed disgustedly that the hoplites involved in naval raids, instead of feeling duty-bound to stand their ground as they would in infantry combat, 'are in the habit of constantly leaping down from their ships and then quickly retreating to their vessels at a run, and they see nothing shameful in this' (*Laws* 706c). Maritime raids were governed by the hit-and-run tactics associated with the light-armed – including the marine archers and the masses of haphazardly armed rowers who fought and pillaged alongside them[24] – and had no place for hoplite ideals.

The other main role of the navy was to ensure that key sea-routes were as safe as possible for friendly traffic, and as dangerous as possible for those who would bring help and supplies to the enemy. In peace-time, this was a routine matter of deterring pirates with a few triremes on stand-by in a nearby port, or occasional patrols. In war, the control of sea-routes became an almost impossible task. Loose blockades by naval detachments stationed along key routes could fairly easily be circumvented by travelling at night or in bad weather. Nevertheless, much naval activity concentrated on controlling merchant and military traffic in this way, especially along the major channels of grain supply, from the entrance of the Gulf of Corinth towards the west and from the entrance of the Black Sea towards the east. Close permanent blockades, such as Lysander's siege of Athens with a massive fleet of 150 ships, could be successful, but triremes were ill-suited to such tactics: they were too vulnerable to be kept at sea in stormy weather, became waterlogged if they stayed at sea too long, and were abandoned by most of their crews at mealtimes. Even the tightest blockade could be breached by divers and small craft, especially if their captains were prepared to crash-land their boats on the shore during a stormy night.[25]

Sea-lanes which could not be fully controlled could at least be exploited or terrorised. In peace time, cities had an informal right to deal with acute food-shortages by forcibly 'bringing down' to their port passing grain-ships, and where traffic was easy to monitor they might use their warships to exact tolls, as in the straits of the Hellespont and Bosporus.[26] In war, merchant shipping was in no way protected by law or convention, and one could resort to indiscriminate seizures, as Sparta did. Ships carrying diplomatic or religious missions were not safe either, since their distinguished passengers could be used as pawns in negotiations, or at least command high ransoms. Indeed, diplomatic missions might engage in opportunistic piracy themselves: a trireme carrying Athenian emissaries to Mausolus captured a 57,000-drachma cargo from Naucratis, a seizure retrospectively ratified by a willing popular assembly.[27]

Many expeditions passed without the fleet ever having to wage a pitched naval battle. Just as in land warfare, outnumbered opponents did not feel honour-bound to fight against the odds. For the best part of two years in 412 and 411 BC, for example, Spartan and Athenian fleets stationed opposite one another at Miletus and Samos, respectively, engaged in a cat-and-mouse game of one side sailing out to offer battle and the other side declining to fight.[28] The Spartan admiral who, in 375 BC, set up a naval trophy just because his opponent had failed to come out and fight was overcompensating outrageously for his previous defeat by the same opponent; normally, even a superior fleet could repeatedly refuse to fight and suffer at worst a slight loss of face.[29]

When one did decide to fight a pitched battle to prevent an enemy from landing, contest his control of the sea, or challenge him for the title of 'thalassocrat', it was wholly acceptable to catch him at a disadvantage. Apart from waiting for a favourable wind, a common ploy was to attack when the enemy's crews had scattered for their midday meal. The Athenians suffered a disastrous defeat at Syracuse because their opponents had established a market so close to their ships that their rowers could shop, eat and be prepared to fight again long before the Athenian crews were ready. Two years later, they suffered an even worse blow at Eretria because their supposed allies deliberately provided no market at all, so that the crews had to scour houses on the edge of town for food and could not get back quickly enough when the Spartan fleet charged: almost two-thirds of their ships were captured. And the shattering Athenian defeat at Aigospotamoi which effectively ended the Peloponnesian War was also the result of a surprise attack when the bulk of the crews were on their way to the nearest market, several miles away: 95% of their ships were captured severely under-manned, or unmanned.[30]

Naval night-fights were rare, but not unknown. Callicratidas planned to attack the Athenian fleet at Arginusae during the night, but bad weather meant that he had to wait until daybreak. Another Spartan commander, Gorgopas, had better luck in the early 380s, when he spotted the lights of an Athenian squadron on its way to Cape Zoster in the dark and tailed it with his own fleet, observing the ancient equivalent of radio silence: his rowers moved their oars as quietly as possible, and his rowing masters signalled their orders by clapping stones together instead of shouting. When the Athenians were halfway through disembarking, he pounced.[31]

Outright deceptions are also reported, including several instances of disguised identity. Crews were put on board captured ships which then sailed towards or past the enemy, sometimes towing their own ships as if these had been captured, pretending to be on the same side. Decoys were sometimes used to create diversions. Themistocles became a national hero for allegedly spreading disinformation and manipulating the Persian fleet at Salamis into an engagement at a location which favoured the Greeks.[32] Whether or not he did, the story shows that deceit was thoroughly acceptable in naval warfare. Ships often invited battle by lining up in the open sea, just as armies did by drawing up in the plain, which creates the impression of a courtly challenge, but no agonal code of honour dictated such behaviour. If navies often awaited the enemy in plain sight on the open sea, it was not because they felt obliged to fight openly and on equal terms, but because they believed that this place and time offered them the best chance of victory.

The parallels with land warfare extend also to the conclusion of naval battle, which was marked by the near-ritual actions of singing a victory paean, setting up a trophy, and concluding a truce for the retrieval of bodies – but not before some of the most brutal violence seen in Greek warfare had been inflicted on the defeated enemy. When a fleet broke and fled, the victors gave chase and tried to catch as many ships as possible. Captured crews were taken prisoner or slaughtered at the discretion of the captain who seized them, and a gruesome mopping-up operation followed as ships searched out and killed those who had fallen or jumped overboard:

> with splintered oars and planks from wrecked ships they beat them and broke their backs, as if they were tunnies, or fish caught in a net. Moans and shrieks sounded across the sea.[33]

Fleets were less constrained than armies by the need to stay in formation while giving pursuit, and at the same time it was harder for shipwrecked sailors to swim to land fast enough than it was for hoplites to run to safety: casualty figures in the thousands were therefore more common in naval combat than on land. Sometimes troops were stationed on nearby shores and islands to intercept anyone who made his escape to land – and ensure that no one got away alive.[34]

The buoyancy of triremes meant that they did not sink, however badly damaged, so the battlefield was always full of floating wreckage, which the victors towed away. Ships damaged beyond repair were burnt, though their prows might be cut off as trophies, and a ship might be dedicated to Poseidon near the battle-site. Captured ships which were still serviceable or could be patched up were towed to a friendly port, and might become the target of a rescue mission by the defeated fleet. If the battle was fought in shallow water near the coast, infantry soldiers sometimes waded into the water and tried to drag the ships back to their own side.[35] Naval battle would not bring many spoils other than the ships, but lucky beachcombers might later find 'gold and silver drinking vessels, money chests ... and other property' washed ashore, and some even employed divers to dredge up what had sunk to the bottom of the sea (Herodotus 7.190; 8.8).

The recovery of the dead and shipwrecked was a difficult operation: bodies would drift and sink; adverse weather might prevent rescue and salvage. Men clinging to pieces of wreckage, cursing their commanders for taking so long to come to the rescue, and drowning before help arrived, must have been a common sight (Xenophon, *Hellenica* 1.7.11). The losing side had to wait for the winners to clear the battlefield and then ask permission to pick up their dead, who by that time, usually a day or more after the battle, might be irretrievable or indeed unrecognisable. Practical difficulties aside, officers were perhaps not as determined to retrieve the dead after a sea battle as after a land battle. The historians never record numbers of naval casualties, and even if citizen rowers were included in casualty lists – which is not certain – foreigners and slaves were not.[36] True, the Athenian generals who won the battle of Arginusae were notoriously condemned to death for failing to recover the dead and wounded, but this battle was fought by a general levy of citizens, not by the usual hired crews. It would not be surprising if there was less pressure to retrieve the bodies of non-citizens. After the battle of Sybota, the Corcyraeans, whose fleet was manned mostly by slaves, left their casualties drift for two days until the wind blew them in their direction, rather than ask for permission to collect them, and so admit defeat.[37]

In situations like this, when the debris and the dead drifted into the hands of the side which had had the worst of it in the fighting, both fleets might proclaim themselves the victor. Normally, however, the winner was whichever side controlled the corpses and wreckage, and they marked their victory by singing a paean and putting up a trophy on a headland or island near the site of battle. If this was impossible on the day of battle, they would come back for it next day, rowing long distances if necessary – a rare element of competitive display in a form of warfare which otherwise knew very few 'agonal' rules, and was constrained only by practical necessity.[38]

Ramming and rowing: the experience of naval battle

Sore bottoms and blisters seemed the essence of the naval experience to some (see p. 200), but such dismissive attitudes should not make us forget that rowing warships was highly dangerous as well as hard work. An early fourth-century oration over the war dead imagined in a more empathetic vein how the trireme crews felt at the battle of Salamis:

> They must so often have grabbed one another by the hand and lamented for themselves ... when they heard at the same time the mixed sounds of Greek and barbarian paeans, the exhortations on both sides and the screams of the dying; when the sea was full of corpses and the wrecks of their own and the enemy's ships were clashing together ....
> The terror that was all around them must often have made them think that they saw things which they did not really see, and heard things which they did not hear. What pleading prayers to the gods and reminders of sacrifices there must have been, what pity for children, longing for wives, sorrow for fathers and mothers, and what calculations of future misery if they should fail .... (Lysias 2.37-39)

Combat at sea did not have very much in common with combat on land, apart from the preliminaries and aftermath, but its terrors were as great – and its deprivations worse

In preparation for combat, triremes took down their main sails, which were left ashore along with valuables and supplies, to ensure that the ships went into action as light as possible, despite the risk that the enemy might do serious damage simply by snatching this equipment.[39] Generals harangued their assembled crews before boarding, and when all had taken their stations the ships moved out in a single long column, then turned their prows ninety degrees to form a single line abreast, facing the enemy. A fleet would only adopt a formation two or more lines deep if there was not enough room, or if they were manned by inexperienced crews whose manoeuvring skills were thought to be inferior to the enemy's. A heavily outnumbered force might resort to a circular formation with the sterns in the centre and the prows facing outwards in order to prevent the enemy from attacking in the rear.[40] Then the vessels launched into action at a trumpet signal, while the crews sang paeans, shouted and whooped, just as in infantry combat.[41]

The triremes needed to be close enough in line to make it hard for the enemy to break through, but they also needed to keep enough distance to prevent their oars from clashing: if ships came too close together, the crews 'pushed them apart with poles, and shouted and warned and cursed one another so that they could not hear their officers or rowing-masters' (Thucydides 2.84.3). Each trireme needed at least 15 metres, and a large fleet in battle formation could therefore easily stretch out over more than a mile. Each ship picked an opponent and tried to crash into the hull of the enemy vessel with the heavy bronze ram which was attached to the prow at water-level. Ramming was aimed at the flank, though there was some experimentation with reinforced prows and head-on crashes. After a hit, the ramming ship either pulled back quickly, to attack again or wait for the victim to capsize, or else used grappling irons to hold the other ship in place while the marines tried to enter and capture it. Stationary deck-to-deck fighting was 'archaic' in Thucydides' book, but was nevertheless practised by some of the greatest navies of his time; the more sophisticated mobile ramming tactics, relying on the manoeuvring skills of helmsmen and the speed and timing of rowers, were associated above all with Athens.[42]

While the ships manoeuvred, the archers on deck shot at their opponents and the hoplite marines threw javelins and stones. Since the balance of the ship and the rhythm of the rowers could easily be upset by movements across the deck, the marines launched their missiles from a seated position, which took some practice. Even trained javelin-throwers could not be effective marines unless they were also trained in this particular technique: 'they will not even be able to work out how you are supposed to throw a missile while sitting down' (Thucydides 7.67.2). The aim was to clear the deck of opposing marines and then jump or clamber onto the enemy ship with the aid of boarding-planks, and take control. This required some agility and it seems likely that marines were generally quite young, perhaps no older than 30.[43]

Some marine fighting would be hand-to-hand, but even this was of a kind which seemed faintly ludicrous to admirers of hoplite combat. Plato poked fun at a weapons-instructor serving as a marine with a weapon of his own devising, a spear-scythe ('a different kind of weapon for a different kind of man'). As the trireme moved past its target, a trading ship, his weapon got caught in the rigging and he ran along the deck trying to hold on to it, letting it slip further and further from his grip until he was holding it by the butt-spike, and finally had to let go altogether: 'and then even the trireme crew could not contain their laughter any longer, when they saw that spear-scythe-thing dangling from the merchant ship' (*Laches* 183d-184a). Marine combat would more often be a deadly serious affair, with much 'stabbing and slipping on … bloody decks'.[44]

The rest of the crew, meanwhile, tried to outmanoeuvre the enemy ship and ram it without being rammed in turn. Smooth co-operation between all members of the crew was vital: information and orders needed to pass quickly and clearly from the bow-officer to the helmsman, from the helmsman to the rowing-master, and from him to the rowers. 'Order and silence' were therefore vital aboard a trireme, and noise interfering with the chain of command could have catastrophic consequences.[45] The two chief manoeuvres, *diekplous*, 'sailing through and out', and *periplous*, 'sailing round', are usually mentioned in the same breath and were probably two stages of a single tactic: a trireme would sail through the narrow gap between two enemy ships, pass beyond the enemy line, then turn about sharply to ram its target from behind. The other key manoeuvre was *anakrousis*, 'pulling back', reversing fast after ramming to disentangle the trireme from the enemy ship. All along the line, triremes would engage in duels of speed and skill, circling one another in a two-dimensional version of an aerial dogfight.[46]

Sooner or later the manoeuvres and crashes led to the dissolution of a regular formation, and ships found themselves ramming one enemy vessel only to be rammed in turn by another, or being attacked by two opponents at the same time. It was nevertheless possible to distinguish friend from foe, because fleets were small enough for officers and others to be able to identify individual ships and captains if they came close enough, and to call across to one another by name in the middle of battle. In any case, triremes which carried generals were distinguished by some mark – not necessarily a flag – and national emblems decorated the top of the high, curved sterns of warships: Athenian triremes displayed gilded images of Pallas Athena.[47]

Some naval battles carried on without a decisive result until dark, or until the two sides drew apart, but most ended with a rout when too many trierarchs gave up hope and left battle. The winners then rowed in pursuit, shouting triumphantly and singing victory paeans.[48]

The decisive factor was the fear and determination of the officers, captains and helmsmen, the only men with the power to turn the ship around. Rowers in particular had no control over, and little idea of, what was happening. They were to some extent insulated from the action, because they faced away from the enemy when attacking, and insofar as they could see outside the ship at all – the lower-bench oarsmen could not

– their view was restricted in combat by protective canvas or leather screens. For them, it was the *sound* of battle which was the greatest 'terror', as Thucydides noted (7.70.6). The floating wreckage and dead bodies 'gathering around the prows of the ships and interfering with blades of the oars' added to their fear (Herodotus 8.12). Missiles were not normally a great threat to the rowers, but a ram breaking through the hull could crush men on the bottom bench, which was barely above the water-line. Above all, rowers were in as much danger as anybody else of being massacred if their ship were captured. Fear might ultimately drive them to desert or even simply refuse to board their vessels.[49]

The entire crew thus had every reason to be afraid, and Lysias' funeral oration was probably right to imply that the 'apparition of a woman' urging the Greeks into action at Salamis, reported by Herodotus (8.84), was a stress-induced hallucination. And perhaps Aristophanes' obscure comment about rowers 'crapping on their mess-mates' alludes to a problem which he elsewhere attributed to cowardly soldiers: a nervous loss of bowel-control.[50] The decoration of early triremes was designed to make the sight of the ship approaching at ramming speed even more fearsome: its sides were painted with images of snakes and monsters, in the much the same way as hoplite shields were, explicitly designed to face and frighten the enemy (not, as Hipponax mocked, face the other way and 'bite the helmsman on the shin', F 28 West). Sometimes the lower part of the prow and the ram were given the shape of an animal, as in the case of the impressive boar-headed triremes used in the late sixth century (Plate XXV). Classical ships, like classical hoplite shields, were less flamboyant and individualistic in their decoration.[51]

Competitiveness did much to counter to fear. In the final naval battle at Syracuse in 413 BC, 'every single man tried to prove himself the best in the particular sphere assigned to him', said Thucydides. Rowers displayed 'dedication'. Rowing-masters did not stop at giving 'technical orders' but shouted exhortations 'from an acute desire to win'. Helmsmen 'matched their skills and pitted themselves against one another'. Marines made sure that 'what happened on deck did not fall behind the other branches of expertise' (7.70.3, 7). These rivalries are a matter of skill rather than courage, as befits the professional status of most classical naval personnel.

Rivalry between captains appears to have been a major force in early naval battles, but declined in the course of the fifth century. Herodotus tells stories which suggest that in 480 BC captains competed for the honour of being the first to capture an enemy ship, and that a regular 'prize' (*aristêion*) was awarded for this feat – at a time when the award of prizes in infantry battle was still very much an irregular, *ad hoc* business. The extraordinary bounty of 10,000 drachmas put on the head of Artemisia, the only female commander in the Persian fleet, 'because they thought it a terrible thing that a *woman* should attack Athens', also suggests that captaining a trireme was seen as a warlike, masculine activity, rather than merely or primarily a financial role.[52] Such sentiments did not disappear overnight: Thucydides had Nicias urge his captains to live up to their own and their families' reputations in combat, and he reported that a Spartan trierarch killed himself, presumably in shame, when his ship was sunk (2.92.3, 7.69.2). Yet in the fourth century even trierarchs who saw active duty, rather than hiring substitutes, prided themselves only on how much money they spent on their crews and ships, not on any specific feats of war. The only naval prize attested at this time is a wreath for the captain who got his ship manned and fitted out most quickly. Amateur bravery, it seems, had become an irrelevance at sea.[53]

*

The rise of the navy in Athens has often been linked to the rise of democracy, as we have seen, and it has been argued that the experience of naval service itself fostered attitudes which were essential to the functioning of democratic politics. Working as part of a large, well-drilled team, within which everyone had an equally vital role to play, might indeed seem likely to encourage egalitarian sentiments and close co-operation among citizens.[54] But in practice trireme crews were, if anything, more hierarchically organised than militia infantry and there were sharp social distinctions between trierarch, marines, 'staff', and citizen, foreign and slave rowers. Service on a trireme might actually reinforce, rather than help overcome, these distinctions.

The experience of rowing was clearly not the same for everyone. The *thranitai* on the top bench had a clear view of what they were doing, enjoyed 'ample' ventilation, and often drew a higher rate of pay. The *thalamioi* on the bottom bench, seated deep in the hold, were rowing blind, soaked in the sweat dripping off the rowers above them, and suffered 'barely adequate' ventilation in the stinking bottom of the hull, which in the reconstructed trireme *Olympias* needed 'to be washed out with sea water at least once every four days' to remain tolerable. They were also the only members of the crew in direct danger of being crushed by ramming. In all likelihood, the *thranitai* were mostly citizens and the *thalamioi* were mostly slaves.[55]

An even greater contrast, however, was evident between the rowers and sailors, who toiled constantly throughout every journey, and the trierarch and marines who sprang into action only during battle. In Aristophanes' *Frogs*, the god Dionysos incongruously pretends to have recently returned from service as a marine, and after a bit of boasting about sinking a dozen or so ships ('and then I woke up', interjects his attendant) he reveals how he has spent the rest of his time on deck: 'I was reading Euripides' *Andromeda* to myself' (48-53). The tradition that among the few survivors of the Sicilian expedition some had escaped death or captivity by being able to recite parts of recent works by Euripides for their captors suggests that reading might have been a not unusual pastime for soldiers and marines. Compared to the captain, marines were generally poor men, but while they were on board they temporarily joined him in his upper-class lifestyle, as he let them pour libations from his golden cups, engaged them in conversation, and let them spend the voyage in leisure pursuits. While they were on board, they might well be tempted to see the rowers from the superior perspective of an Aristophanes or Isocrates as 'the laziest of people, who do all sorts of mischief' (8.79), and regard above deck and below deck as worlds apart.[56]

Conclusion

The Development of Greek Warfare

War and the state

Far down the Nile, at Abu Simbel, eight Greek soldiers in the service of pharaoh Psamtik II marked their safe return from an invasion of Ethiopia in 591 BC by leaving some graffiti. A man called Archon took an axe, clambered up one of the colossal seated statues of Ramesses II flanking the entrance to the temple, and cut the following message into its leg:

> When king Psamatichos came to Elephantine, the men who sailed with Psammatichos, son of Theocles, wrote this. They went beyond Kerkis as far as the river allowed. Potasimto led the foreign-speakers, Amasis the Egyptians. This was written by Archon, son of Amoibichos, and Axe, son of Nobody.

His comrades, including Python, son of Amoibichos, presumably his brother, added their names, and on the leg of a second colossus, another man wrote: 'Anaxanor of Ialysos ... when king Psamatichos first marched out the army' (ML 7; Fornara 24; Plate XXVI).

We may be impressed by Archon's literacy, wit, explorer's curiosity and sense of history, but we should not forget that his inscription was also an act of brute vandalism – its large, deep letters, easily readable from the ground, were hacked into the pristine façade of one of the most awe-inspiring sacred places in the world. The Greeks normally treated sacred sites with respect, so defacing this ancient temple was a remarkably aggressive show of pride in having sailed as far down the Nile as possible.[1] These graffiti may stand as a reminder of some constant elements in Greek history: the competitiveness which often spilled over into acts of aggression, and the social and economic conditions which drove men like Archon to seek their fortunes as soldiers in the remotest corners of the world. These pressures were also fundamental causes of war, and remained so throughout the archaic and classical ages.

The way in which wars were fought, by contrast, was subject to constant change – most dramatically so in the late archaic and early classical period. The trends towards more centralised military organisation, ever closer combat in infantry battles, and more sophisticated technology in naval and siege warfare were gradual and on-going, but saw a quantum

232

leap between *c.* 550 and 450 BC: armed forces were re-organised, siege techniques began to develop, the hoplite phalanx took its classical form, and the trireme changed the face of naval warfare. The cause of this transformation was the development of the Greek state.

'Their master is the Law': the power of the state

The formal institutions of government in archaic Greek city-states were weak, and even classical city-states might not strictly qualify as 'states' on a narrow definition of the term.[2] Nevertheless, there was a distinct growth in central control by the state, or perhaps rather in collective control by the community. The informal and personal power of the elite, based on networks of friends, followers and dependants, competed increasingly with formal positions of power and public institutions, and was gradually whittled away. Inequality and hierarchy did not disappear, of course, but the late sixth and first half of the fifth century saw many Greek cities transformed from overtly hierarchical to ostensibly egalitarian societies in which the interests of the community came first – in war as in politics.

Archaic cities were generally dominated by two or three large networks of prominent men and their personal followers. This is well illustrated by the events of 508 BC, when the Spartan king Cleomenes could mobilise enough personal supporters to mount a private invasion of Athens to help his friend Isagoras, who had at least 300 supporters, against the dominant faction – the Alcmeonid family – which allegedly included 700 households.[3] Followers were recruited through kinship, friendship and various forms of patronage from regular dinner invitations to gifts, loans and employment.[4] Political office was controlled by the more prominent members of these factions. The Athenian *naukraroi*, in charge of local administration be-cause they were the richest men in their areas and had the means to provide warships and raise crews, are a good example of how in the archaic period public and private power tended to coincide, and how this affected military organisation.[5] Wealthy men in archaic Greece no doubt consid-ered it a matter of prestige to lead their friends and followers in war. Mounted hoplites were certainly accompanied by upper-class young squires, and judging by departure scenes in art the elite liked to imagine itself travelling to war in chariots, surrounded by a band of hoplites and light-armed men, very much in the Homeric manner.[6]

The introduction of sworn bands and messes in Sparta, sometime between 550 BC and the Persian Wars, attempted to replace such private power with public, formal institutions, and to substitute an egalitarian for a hierarchical culture. Membership of a mess-group was decided by a collective ballot of its members, who were all called 'Equals' (*homoioi*), dressed the same, made by-and-large identical mess contributions and shared the same, ample but notoriously unappetising, diet. Personal patronage and inequalities of wealth certainly persisted, but every attempt was made to restrict their scope and play down their importance.[7]

The control of the Spartan community over its office-holders was remarkably strong. Quite a few Spartan kings, regents and other commanders tried to strike out for themselves, mounting expeditions unsanctioned by the other Spartan magistrates or the assembly, but such behaviour was not tolerated and many a highly successful military leader ended up in prison or exile. It may not be a coincidence that according to tradition some of the most successful figures of the late sixth and early fifth century, precisely in the transitional period, came to particularly gruesome ends: king Cleomenes placed under house arrest, and mutilating himself with fatal consequences; the regent Pausanias seeking refuge in a temple and being starved to death. Sparta sent out a stern message: all individuals and all private interests were supposed to be subordinate to be the law of the community.[8]

In Athens, formal public power also grew stronger at the expense of informal private power. A turning point was the reform of Cleisthenes, begun in 508 BC, which among other things deprived the *naukraroi* of their power; they still provided warships but no longer enjoyed local political privileges, which were divided between some 140 demes, which elected their own local officials, the demarchs, and their own representatives to serve on the national Council. Factional loyalties were broken up by creating new and more administrative units at all levels, and by uniting groups of demes from different parts of Attica in a single tribe. An egalitarian climate was encouraged by the rule that for official purposes citizens were to be known by the name of their deme, rather than their family: all were 'fellow-demesmen', not unlike the 'citoyens' of the French Revolution or the 'comrades' of the Russian Revolution.[9]

As at Sparta, the community in Athens began to exercise a remarkable degree of control over its elected and appointed officials. Not even the most successful generals were safe from prosecution for misconduct in office in classical Athens, and a large proportion of known generals were condemned to death. Miltiades the Younger, having won the battle of Marathon but botched a campaign in the following year, was found guilty of 'deceiving the Athenian people' and died in prison of a gangrenous wound (Herodotus 6.136). Even more notoriously, the whole board of generals was condemned to death by the assembly, in effect for having shown insufficient concern for their citizen soldiers and rowers, and failed to pick up the shipwrecked and the dead after the battle of Arginusae in 406 BC.[10]

In the fourth century, Athenian military expeditions were chronically underfunded, and it has been suggested that this was a matter of policy in the popular assembly – a way to keep generals on a short leash. Despite complaints about Athenian generals serving foreign powers as mercenary commanders, this was in fact a rarity in the fourth century, and insofar as it did happen, it was nothing new – Miltiades the Elder had in effect been a mercenary leader in Thracian service already in the mid-sixth century. The significant point is that such behaviour had now become unacceptable.[11]

These changes were not confined to Sparta and Athens, nor were they achieved purely by political reform. Archaeological evidence suggests a broad movement towards a culture of greater social equality across Greece around 500 BC.[12] This trend may have been mirrored in international relations by a move from overtly hierarchical rule over conquered serfs and *perioikoi*, via hegemony over unequal alliances, to ostensibly egalitarian forms of leadership and conquest.[13] The new political and social regimes established in Sparta and Athens may be seen as two expressions of this trend, very different is almost every detail, yet fundamentally similar in advancing the process of state-formation.

Sparta's sworn bands cut across the private friendships and obligations which had shaped archaic war-bands by demanding an oath of loyalty to the officers appointed to command the units. Athenian men swore loyalty to any fellow-citizen who might happen to stand beside them: the tribal regiments were commanded by elected officials who were as likely as not to be strangers to their men; select expeditionary forces were hand-picked by the generals from among all citizens liable to serve – if not already under Cleisthenes, then from 457 onwards at the latest – leaving no room at all for personal ties to shape such armies.[14] Only when the community was able to command this level of loyalty from its citizens did the state gain enough control to impose the segregation of troop types required for classical phalanx tactics and to impose the centralised organisation required to man a trireme fleet.

'Greece grew up with poverty': the resources of the state

Archaic city-states had even less control over financial resources than they did over their citizens. An anecdote relates how in 525 BC a group of Samian rebels requesting Spartan aid in their war against Polycrates came into the assembly 'carrying a bag, and said "The bag needs flour". The Spartans answered that the business with the bag was redundant, but decided to help them.' So they decreed a one-day fast for themselves, their slaves, and their beasts of burden, and gave the Samians the food saved from their own mouths.[15] The story is too good an illustration of Laconic speech and Spartan austerity to be true, but it nevertheless points to an important general truth: Greek states had few means of funding their wars.

A horror of taxation was one problem. Greek states did not fund their armies from regular, annual taxes, but relied on collecting compulsory 'contributions' (*eisphorai*) or voluntary donations (*epidoseis*) if and when the need arose.[16] Another problem was that regular taxes would not have covered the cost of major campaigns even if they had been raised. Classical Athens had a total taxable wealth of about 36 million drachmas, from which at most one million drachmas a year in taxes might have been squeezed, but the nine-month siege of Samos in 440 BC cost more than seven million, and the long siege of Potidaea swallowed up 12 million.[17]

A third problem was specific to the archaic period: states which did have surplus revenue – from booty, or tolls and taxes on trade, or in a few cases from gold- or silver-mines – did not channel this into public treasuries. Common archaic practice is exemplified by the sixth-century Siphnians, who converted one-tenth of the revenue from their gold mines into dedications at the temple of Apollo at Delphi and distributed the rest amongst themselves. The major stores of wealth were therefore temple treasuries, and the use of sacred funds for military purposes, while not inconceivable, was inhibited by serious religious scruples. A proposal to fund the Ionian Revolt from the treasures of Apollo at Branchidai, for instance, was quickly scotched.[18]

A lack of central funds thus always limited the scale and duration of the wars of the Greek city-states, but imposed particularly severe constraints in the archaic period. The first signs of change occur from about 550 BC onwards, when several tyrannical rulers temporarily concentrated resources in their own hands and even imposed regular taxes in order to maintain their standing forces and other *epikouroi*, while the introduction and spread of coinage marked the beginning of a more lasting financial role adopted by Greek states.[19]

The greatest structural changes occurred in the early fifth century. We can trace these developments in detail only in Athens, but they were clearly widespread. First of all, surplus revenue was no longer distributed to private citizens, but accumulated in public treasuries. A defining moment was the Athenian decision in 483 BC to stop sharing out the revenue from the silver mines and create the city's first large and steady stream of public income.

Equally momentous was the decision no longer to share out booty among soldiers and citizens. During the Persian Wars, booty was still distributed in the Homeric manner, with each soldier getting 'what he deserved' according to status and merit, and outstanding men receiving 'selected pieces'. At Plataea, the Spartan general Pausanias was awarded 'ten of everything: women, horses, talents, camels, and the rest'. The gods received a tithe, but otherwise there was no surplus. The same Homeric pattern of complete and direct distribution of booty is still found occasionally even in the fourth century.[20] The norm, however, became to provide the troops with sustenance or pay at a regular rate, or both, while any money raised from booty and ransoms over and above the required sum was retained for the public treasury. This practice is first attested from *c.* 470 BC onwards, when Cimon's naval campaigns raised more money than he needed to sustain his fleet and the treasury received the surplus.[21]

Naval expeditions may well have produced such surpluses even at an earlier date, since rowers already received pay by 480 in Athens, and by the late sixth century in Eretria, and probably were not also given a share in booty. Hoplites, on the other hand, presumably continued to be rewarded with shares of booty for as long as they did not receive pay: the introduction of hoplite pay in the 450s marked the final step in the centralisation of military revenue in Athens. The Spartans also began to retain central control of booty, and were notably efficient in raising money through instant sales by the public booty-sellers (*laphyropolai*) who accompanied their armies.[22]

Attitudes towards temple treasuries changed as well. By the mid-fifth century at the latest, the Athenians regarded it as perfectly acceptable to borrow money from the gods, at interest, publicly or privately. The very image of Athena in the Parthenon, a huge cult statue, was covered with a metric tonne of gold plating which was 'designed to be removable' so that it could be converted into coin. Many temples became money lenders, and public borrowing from the gods came to be widely regarded as legitimate, although some states felt greater scruples than others: Sparta and Mantineia took a strong line against what they saw as inappropriate use of the treasures at Delphi and Olympia by their allies.[23] Under financial pressure during the Peloponnesian War, the Athenians rationalised borrowing by consolidating smaller sacred funds into a single Treasury of the Other Gods (i.e. other than Athena), and increasingly concentrated revenue in secular treasuries, so that they could spend without having to borrow at all.[24]

This transformation of public finance transformed warfare by making it possible to mobilise more manpower for longer periods of time and so wage war at sea and on land with an intensity and persistence which had rarely been feasible in earlier generations.[25] The spiralling effect of putting public resources to effective use in war was most spectacular in Athens. Six years after first spending their mining revenue on building a vast trireme fleet, the Athenians were able to put themselves at the head of an innovative form of alliance, in which many members, instead of providing manpower, paid a tribute in silver (*phoros*). This soon amounted to 3.6 million drachmas a year. Athens immediately led its allies into campaigns aimed at securing access to gold mines in Thrace, and in 462 BC confiscated the mining and other revenues of Thasos, worth a handy one or two million drachmas a year. By the middle of the century, the total accumulated surplus in Athenian treasuries was almost 60 million drachmas.[26] By that time, Athens had also begun to transcend the traditional limitations of Greek warfare. The introduction of pay for hoplites and horsemen – a drachma a day for every man, plus another drachma for his servant – made it possible to keep troops in the field as long as it took to complete even the lengthiest sieges. Siege engines were built for the first time. Miles of fortification wall were constructed. The state paid for a standing force of 1,600 archers and heavily subsidised a cavalry force of 1,200. And by offering a full drachma as a standard wage for rowers, the Athenians were able to hire far more and better naval crews than anyone else.[27]

Almost equally dramatic military developments occurred at the beginning of the fourth century in Sicily, where Dionysius I made himself sole ruler of Syracuse and campaigned against the Carthaginians. He was accused of imposing outrageous taxes, fraudulently manipulating coinage, extorting money from friend and foe alike, and robbing temples. Whether or not one believes this hostile tradition, Dionysius undoubtedly raised enormous sums of money, which he used not only to equip a great mercenary army, but also to develop new military technology. His engineers invented siege towers and artillery ('catapults'), copied the Carthaginians' super-trireme, the quadrireme (*tetrêres*), and topped it with an even bigger and more manpower-guzzling quinquereme (*pentêres*) of their own devising.[28]

The other Greeks tried to keep up. Aristotle mocked the emptiness of Sparta's treasuries and the reluctance of its citizens to pay taxes ('their lawgiver has made the city destitute and the people greedy', *Politics* 1271b11-17), and the one surviving list of contributions does not make for impressive reading (ML 67; see p. 31), yet even Sparta hired rowers and mercenary soldiers, like many other states, and in 424 BC created a standing force of cavalry and archers, none of which would have been possible without substantial public funds.[29]

However much money a Greek state managed to accumulate, the sheer and always rising cost of warfare soon exhausted its funds. Only three years into the Peloponnesian War the Athenians were reduced to paying 'contributions' themselves, and towards the end of the war, rowers' and soldiers' pay was halved to three obols a day, a mere subsistence wage.[30] In 405 BC the Spartan fleet was so short of funds that the rowers hired themselves out as farm labourers to make money. When work dried up in winter, their commander Eteonicus averted a mutiny only by extorting a month's wages from the local, allied, population. Seventeen years later, the same commander faced another mutiny brought on by a lack of pay, and this time it was left to his successor to find the money through petty piracy against merchant ships, fishing boats and passenger ferries (Xenophon, *Hellenica* 2.1.1-5; 5.1.13-24). In the 370s BC, Athenian rowers, too, were hiring themselves out as farm hands, and the city was twice forced to make peace simply because it had no money for war.[31] A late fourth-century treatise on *Economics* had no trouble compiling a long list of desperate money-raising schemes – none more desperate than the Athenian general Timotheus' idea of funding his siege of Samos by selling the food plundered from the countryside to the very Samians he was besieging.[32]

A measure of the precariousness of military funding in Greece is the way in which Persian financial backing could instantly swing the balance. Undignified as it may have been to 'suck up' to barbarians (Xenophon, *Hellenica* 1.6.7, 11; 5.1.17), both Sparta and Athens tried from the start of the Peloponnesian War to persuade Persian governors and generals to bankroll their campaigns. In 407 BC the Persian prince Cyrus, as a personal favour to their naval commander Lysander, gave the Spartans funds which enabled them to outbid Athens by offering rowers four obols a day instead of three. Within months, Lysander was able to increase his navy from 70 to 90 ships, while the Athenian fleet shrank from more than 100 to 70 triremes. Next year, thanks to vigorous fund-raising and contin- ued Persian support, the Spartan fleet grew to 140, then 170 ships, while the Athenians were reduced to manning their fleet with a compulsory levy of citizens and slaves. Then Lysander was replaced and Cyrus withdrew his backing, sparking off the financial crisis and near-mutiny already mentioned. As soon as Lysander was reinstated and funding restored, the Spartan fleet was brought up to 200 ships within months, and Athens was comprehensively defeated. After the war, subsidies stopped and Greek fleets rapidly contracted to dozens rather than hundreds of ships. They only expanded again as and when a Greek state regained Persian support.[33]

Every effort was made in fourth-century Athens, and no doubt else- where, to escape dependence on personal favours from Persian dignitaries and other erratic sources of support. Grand schemes of financial reform became almost routine: Demosthenes proposed one in his first public speech and Xenophon in his old age came up with a radical pamphlet on *Ways and Means*. The reforms of Euboulus and Lycurgus in fact succeeded in raising Athens' annual revenues to more than seven million drachmas, which may have been nearly as much as the city's income at the peak of its empire.[34] A small, but symbolically significant step was the melting down of all the golden wreaths with honorific inscriptions which had been dedicated in Athens' temples over the years: they were converted into anonymous, identical golden bowls for ease of record-keeping and future use. One way or another, public finance was constantly rationalised and maximised. As a result, Athens was able to acquire, belatedly, some of the outsize warships invented in Sicily half a century earlier, and military training for all citizens finally became viable in the 330s.[35]

This story of a permanent struggle to overcome financial difficulties may create an impression of decline, especially in comparison with the wealth of fifth-century Athens. But Athens' temporary success in extract- ing huge imperial revenues was something of a blip, which masked the economic weakness which remained a structural problem for all the city-states throughout Greek history. From a broader perspective, the story is one of growing centralisation of financial resources and maximisa- tion of revenue from the early fifth century onwards, a process which made new forms of warfare possible, even if it never produced quite enough to allow warfare on the scale to which the city-states aspired. Poverty may have stimulated Greek martial valour, as Herodotus had it (7.102.1), but ulti- mately it also sharply inhibited Greek military ambitions.

*

The growing power and resources of the community reshaped the pursuit of honour through warfare. Archaic battle had allowed the pursuit of personal as well as communal glory: some men fought single combats, and individual prowess was acknowledged with prizes, shares of booty and special burials. Classical battle, by contrast, concentrated purely on the honour and glory of the community: inviolable battlefield trophies began to mark the collective achievement while the collective burial and commemoration of the war dead became the highest priority. Hoplites fought anonymously and as equals in a dense, uniform formation; only one man was singled out for the award of a token prize for valour. The features most closely associated with hoplite combat in our imaginations were classical innovations, not relics of the archaic past. Hoplites were not 'dinosaurs' by the time of the Peloponnesian War.[36] On the contrary, they were only just coming into their own.

But the pursuit of honour had never been confined to a show of courage within the bounds of a more-or-less regulated pitched battle. An injury or insult required above all a show of strength, a demonstration of the ability to harm the enemy: the massacre or mutilation of men, the devastation of farmland, the sacking of cities. When honour demanded it, all these forms of what one might call 'conspicuous destruction' were goals of war in their own right.[37] As the power and resources of communities grew, such destructive goals could be pursued with an intensity that had been an ideal of sorts ever since Homer's heroes razed Troy and wiped out the Trojan race, but had rarely been feasible in practice. In other words, the sieges, naval warfare, distant campaigns, and mercenaries which are so often cited as signalling the end of the golden age of the hoplite are in fact part and parcel of the same growing dominance of the community in warfare which created the tactics and rituals of the classical hoplite phalanx.

At the end of the Peloponnesian War, there was a period when not a single crow was to be seen anywhere in the Peloponnese or Attica because, according to Greek birdwatching lore, the birds had all flown north to Thessaly to scavenge on the unburied bodies of thousands of mercenaries massacred at Larisa.[38] At about the same time, 13 Spartan soldiers who had fought in support of an oligarchic reign of terror in Athens were given a monumental burial in Athens' public cemetery (Fig. 11). Despite the deep resentment towards Sparta felt in Athens, their grave was treated with complete respect. In extreme form, the two faces of Greek war once again appeared side by side. This was one constant, through all the changes: Greek communities sought to display their courage in 'agonal' warfare, demonstrate their strength in 'total' warfare, and make a profit where they could, with all the power and resources they could muster.

240

Appendices

1. Athenian manpower in 480 and 431 BC

The key evidence is the survey of manpower in 431 BC provided by Thucydides (2.13.6-7):

> There were 13,000 hoplites, not including 16,000 in the garrisons and manning the battlements. For that was how many served as guards at first when the enemy invaded, drawn from the oldest and the youngest and the metics insofar as they were hoplites.

Diodorus (12.40.4) gives slightly different figures of 12,000 and 17,000, respectively. A little later Thucydides tells us that 'not less than 3,000' of the metics (resident foreigners) were hoplites of a suitable age to join the field army, if necessary, rather than play their normal role in defending the fortifications (2.31.2).

The simplest, and I believe correct, interpretation of these passages is that the total number of hoplites in Athens, including metics, was 29,000, and that among them 13,000 (or 12,000) citizens and 3,000 metics were of the right age to serve in the hoplite field army, while the remaining 13,000 (or 14,000) citizen and metic hoplites counted amongst the 'oldest and youngest' and stayed behind as a home-guard. To the numbers of citizen in the field-army category, we must add 1,000 cavalry (Thucydides 2.13.8).

The total number of men of hoplite and cavalry status of an age to serve in the field army was thus 17,000 (or 16,000) of whom 3,000 (17.6% or 18.8%) were metics. Assuming that the proportion of metics among the 'oldest and youngest' hoplites was roughly the same, Athens had 10,700 citizens and 2,300 metics in that category, on Thucydides' figures (or 11,400 citizens and 2,600 metics on Diodorus' figures). In total, Athens in 431 BC thus had 24,700 citizen hoplites and cavalry according to Thucydides, or 24,400 according to Diodorus.

Mogens Hansen has argued, however, that the number of troops attributed to the 'oldest and youngest' age classes is demographically impossible (1981, 19-24; 1988, 23-5). He assumes that 'the oldest' could only refer to those aged 50-59 at most, and this small age group, together with 'the youngest' (aged 18 and 19), could not have amounted to 10,700 men when the 20- to 49-year-olds amounted to the only slightly larger number of 14,000 (let alone 11,400 against 13,000 if one follows Diodorus). His solution is to argue that those left behind on the walls include *all* 'oldest and youngest' citizens, even those who were too poor to serve as hoplites, and that the phrase 'insofar as they were hoplites' applies only to the metics. By his calculations, the number of citizen hoplites in Athens was only about 18,000.

It is grammatically possible to interpret the passage as Hansen does, but since the first sentence implicitly includes the 16,000 in the number of hoplites, it is odd if the second sentence is taken to mean that many of the 16,000 were not hoplites at all. Moreover, Thucydides generally gives numbers only for hoplites and cavalry (and ships), not for citizens too poor to serve as hoplites; he accordingly gives the number of hoplites and cavalry only for the field army, which the poorer classes would have joined as light-armed (see pp. 61-2). So why would he make an exception and include non-hoplite citizens in his figures for troops guarding the walls? And if he did include non-hoplites in his figures for these troops, why did he exclude non-hoplite metics? Were poorer metics not expected to help in the defence at all?

The simpler solution is to accept the force of the demographic arguments, but to conclude instead that the 'oldest' age group must have included the 40- to 59-year-olds, and not just the 50- to 59-year-olds (so Jones 1957, 165). The ages of 40 and 45 were in fact common dividing lines in Athens between those deemed fit for front-line service and those left to play a less active role. In 346 BC, a fleet was manned by citizens up to the age of 40 (Aeschines 2.133) and the hoplite army up to the age of 40 was mobilised in the Lamian War of 323 BC (Diodorus 18.10.2); the same cut-off point is used by Xenophon's mercenaries (*Anabasis* 5.3.1). In 353/2 BC, a fleet was manned by citizens up to the age of 45 (Demosthenes 3.4; cf. Xenophon, *Anabasis* 6.5.4). It seems likely that the main reason for this low age limit for active service (in comparison to Sparta's: see p. 46) was that Athens needed a large home-guard because it had several miles of fortification walls to man, as Thucydides himself went on to indicate (2.13.7). Some men older than 45 did serve in the field on occasion, perhaps as volunteers (see pp. 46, 100, and Hansen 1988, 23 n. 12), but this was clearly not the norm.

Our figures for hoplites make demographic sense if the 'oldest' were indeed those over 40. The proportion of 'oldest and youngest' hoplites among citizens was 43.3% or 46.7% by Thucydides and Diodorus' reckonings, respectively. On the modern 'model life table' used by Hansen as the most appropriate for comparison with ancient Greece (Coale & Demeny's Model West, mortality level 4), the 18- to 19-year-olds and 40- to 59-year-olds account for 40.1% of all males between 18 and 60. The discrepancy of a few per cent is a perfectly acceptable margin of error for these model tables, or our sources, or both.

What proportion of the total citizen population of Athens did hoplites constitute? By means of careful calculations (which do not rely on his estimate of the number of hoplites), Hansen arrives at a total of *c.* 60,000 Athenian citizens in 431 BC (especially 1988, 14-28). On my view of the number of citizen hoplites, they would therefore have constituted just over 40%.

This matches very well what little information we have for the period of the Persian Wars. The so-called Decree of Themistocles (ML 23; Fornara 55), which was inscribed much later, but which I believe to record accurately the procedures used to mobilise the Athenian fleet in 480 (see pp. 208, 216), envisages that apart from about 20 sailors and marines only about 100 citizens and metics will be available for each of the 200 triremes to be manned (lines 28-35). The total number of citizens and metics in 480, of all classes and of a suitable age – probably 40 or 45 again; the maximum age for marines was 30 [line 25], for captains 50 [line 22]) – was thus estimated at 24,000. Assuming a proportion of metics similar to the situation in 431, or slightly lower, we arrive at a figure of *c.* 20,000 citizens of fighting age. The year after Salamis, Athens sent out a field-army of 8,000 hoplites to fight at Plataea (Herodotus 9.28.6). Assuming, as seems very likely, that these represent citizen hoplites of roughly the same age-group as the men mobilised to row and fight at Salamis, hoplites thus represented 40% of citizens.

2. Changes in Spartan military organisation from 480 to 371 BC

In a succession of ever more ingenious theories, one scholar after another has tried to reconcile the various bits of ancient evidence for the organisation of the Spartan army. The debate has now become unmanageably convoluted (see the surveys of theories and scholarship in Anderson 1970, 225-51; Gomme et al. 1970, 111-17; Lazenby 1985, 5-10, 41-54; Cartledge 1987, 427-31; and most recently Singor 2002). In offering yet another interpretation, I will (a) introduce into the debate a source for the Spartan organisation at the time of the Persian War which has so far been ignored; (b) go back to basics by showing what the classical sources do and do not tell us.

The oath sworn by the Greeks before the battle of Plataea, mentioned in several sources and recorded in a fourth-century Athenian inscription (Tod II.204, lines 21-46), contains an odd clause which not only supports the cause of those who argue that the oath is genuine, rather than a later historical fiction (see Siewert 1971, for the debate and for other arguments in favour of authenticity), but also throws light on Spartan military organisation in 479 BC.

After pledging to fight to the death for freedom, the swearers promise:

'I shall not desert my *taxiarchos* or my *enômotarchês* whether he is alive or dead, and I shall not leave unless the *hêgemones* lead us away, and I shall do whatever the *stratêgoi* may command, and I shall bury on the spot those of my fellow-fighters who die, and I shall leave no one unburied.' (lines 25-31)

This oath is called in the preface 'the oath which the Athenians swore', and the reference to doing what the *stratêgoi* command is indeed appropriate for Athenians, whose armies were led by these 'generals'. The preceding clauses make no sense in an Athenian context, however. In Athens, it would be the *stratêgoi* who led the army away, so why they are described as *hêgemones*, or indeed why this separate clause is included at all, is unclear. The reference to *hêgemones* is meaningful, however, in a Spartan context, since this is what the Spartans called their kings (e.g. Tyrtaeus F 19.11 West). The *enômotarchês*, moreover, is a purely Spartan figure, without Athenian parallel, and Herodotus mentions *taxiarchoi* in the Spartan army (9.53.2), although the Athenian army also had officers called *taxiarchoi*. Finally, there is a notable contrast between the oath sworn by Athenian ephebes, recorded in the same inscription (lines 5-20), who say: 'I shall not desert *the man next to me* wherever I may be stationed in the ranks' (lines 7-8), and the promise at Plataea not to desert one's *officers*. The latter pledge again sounds more appropriate to the hierarchical Spartan army than the egalitarian Athenian.

This part of the oath thus looks as if it consists of a Sparta-oriented pledge ('I shall not desert my *taxiarchos* or my *enômotarchês* whether he is alive or dead, and I shall not leave unless the *hêgemones* lead us away') and an Athenian addendum ('I shall do whatever the *stratêgoi* may command'). Given that Sparta was the unchallenged leader of the Greek alliance, it seems likely enough that the Spartans dictated the bulk of the oath, which was then suitably adapted for each ally by adding the necessary clauses. Fourth-century Athenians aiming to glorify the deeds of their ancestors (as those who inscribed and cited the oath did) would hardly have invented this curious, bolted-together form of oath. In fact, the sources which cite it gloss over the entire awkward Spartan-sounding section, which they paraphrase as 'I shall not abandon the leaders (*hêgemones*) whether alive or dead' (Lycurgus, *Against Leocrates* 80; Diodorus 11.29.2). This seems to me a strong argument for its authenticity.

The most obvious source for the specifically 'Spartan' clauses of the Oath of Plataea is the oath taken by members of the sworn band, the *enômotia*, as I suggested above (p. 98). Whatever their source, these clauses show that there were only two levels of officers below the kings in the Spartan army of 479 BC: the *taxiarchoi* – in charge of units described by Herodotus as *lochoi* (9.53.2) – and the leaders of the *enômotiai*.

*

The Spartan army at Mantineia in 418 BC is very clearly described by Thucydides. His account has nevertheless caused many problems and has been endlessly re-interpreted, primarily because it does not fit with the information provided by Xenophon a generation later.

Thucydides described the Spartan order of battle as follows (5.67.1):

on the left wing, the Skiritai, *perioikoi*, 'the only ones among the Lacedaemonians' who traditionally formed a distinct unit by themselves

next, 'the soldiers who fought under Brasidas in Thrace, and the *neodamodeis* with them'

next, 'the Lacedaemonians themselves stationed their *lochoi*, one next to the other'

next, three contingents of Arcadians (Heraeans, Maenalians and Tegeans)

on the right wing, 'a few Lacedaemonians'.

Thucydides goes on to say that he cannot give accurate numbers for either side, because people made exaggerated claims. The Spartans, unlike the others, were secretive, rather than boastful, so they revealed no numbers at all. Thucydides, however, believed that he could work out 'the number of Lacedaemonians' by means of calculation (5.68.2). He explains that 'seven *lochoi* fought, not including the Skiritai, of whom there were 600, and there were four *pentekostyes* in each *lochos*, and four *enômotiai* in each *pentekostys*'; the average *enômotia* was drawn up four wide and eight deep, so that 'the front rank, not including the Skiritai, in total consisted of 448 men' (5.68.3). Each *lochos* consisted of 32 x 16 = 512 men at Mantineia, when they were at five-sixths strength (5.64.2-3), or just over 600 men at full strength.

Thucydides' sums clearly concern only the central force of 'the Lacedaemonians themselves' in 'their *lochoi*, one next to the other': he not only excludes the Skiritai explicitly, but implicitly excludes the 'few Lacedaemonians' on the right wing, since their front rank was not contiguous with that of the other units (separated as they were from the main body of Spartans by three contingents of Arcadians). Contrary to a common modern view (e.g. Cartledge 2002, 218; Hodkinson 2000, 421; Lazenby 1985, 42-3; Gomme et al. 1970, 112; Anderson 1970, 230, 235), these seven *lochoi* cannot possibly include Brasidas' soldiers and the *neodamodeis*: Brasidas' force originally consisted of 700 helots and 1,000 Peloponnesian mercenaries (4.80.5), who were not 'Lacedaemonians', probably not organised in *enômotiai* or *pentekostyes*, and definitely not comparable in size to the *lochoi* (especially not when an unspecified number of *neodamodeis* is added; cf. Lazenby 1985, 42). Excluding the Skiritai, the regular Spartan army according to Thucydides thus consisted of seven *lochoi*, not six (or five: Singor 2002, 254-5) *plus* the 'few Lacedaemonians' on the right wing.

In the course of the battle narrative, it emerges that these 'few' actually amounted to at least two more *lochoi*. As a result of the drift to the right which all hoplite armies experienced, Thucydides explained (5.71.1), the Tegeans and Lacedaemonians on the right wing extended far to the right of the Athenians stationed opposite them, just as on the left the Skiritai found that their opponents, the Mantineians, extended far beyond them (71.2). Agis, the Spartan king, was afraid that the Mantineians outflanked the Skiritai too far and would surround them. He therefore attempted an unusual manoeuvre, telling the Skiritai and Brasidas' men to move further to the left to prevent being outflanked. This left a gap between them and the seven *lochoi* of the main Spartan force, so he ordered the polemarchs Hipponoidas and Aristocles to fill this gap with 'two *lochoi* from the right wing, thinking that there would still be more than enough men on their own right' (71.3). The polemarchs disobeyed the order, the gap remained open, and the enemy poured in, inflicting heavy casualties upon the nearest Lacedaemonians (5.72.1-3).

Thucydides could not have described the situation more clearly: the Spartans have a surplus of men on one wing and are in danger of being surrounded on the other, so they try to transfer two redundant units from the right to the beleaguered left. The implication is that the 'few Lacedaemonians' on the right consisted of at least two *lochoi*, more than 1,000 men, and that Thucydides thought that there were at least nine Spartan *lochoi* at Mantineia.

Modern scholars have been deeply reluctant to accept this, and have resorted to arguing that the *lochoi* transferred from right to left were two of the seven *lochoi* which formed the main body of Spartan troops (e.g. Lazenby 1985, 43). This is utterly implausible: it implies that, in order to fill the gap between the Spartan main body and Brasidas' men on their left, the king was planning to open up a second gap, between the main Spartan body and the Arcadians on their right – a gap which he apparently had no intention of filling. Opening up a gap on the more vulnerable right-hand side to close a gap on the better-protected left-hand side makes no sense (so e.g. Anderson 1970, 235). Especially not when, all the while, the redundant troops on the far right wing were left to do nothing. We cannot read Thucydides' account in this way unless we attribute suicidal motives to Agis and incompetence to the historian.

It remains peculiar that Thucydides spoke of a 'few Lacedaemonians', rather than specify the number of *lochoi*, as he did for the main body, particularly since he knew that they amounted to at least two *lochoi*. The explanation is presumably that he simply had no information on how many units were stationed on the right wing: he only knew that two polemarchs were found guilty of cowardice for disobeying an order, from which he inferred that there had been at least two *lochoi*. In order to gloss over his ignorance on this point, he spoke vaguely of 'a few' and restricted his calculations to the main body of Lacedaemonian troops.

Thucydides' uneven knowledge surely reflects the unevenness of his sources: his detailed information on the left and centre of the Spartan army presumably derives from the Argives stationed opposite them, whereas (as an exile from Athens at the time) he had no comparable information from the Athenians stationed opposite the right wing. Apparently neither Thucydides nor his sources knew how many *lochoi* the Spartan army had in total – or else he and they could have worked out, without being told, how many units were stationed on the right. The total number of units, then, was evidently the point on which the Spartans were 'secretive'; certainly Thucydides claims to know everything else about the Spartan army.

One may reject Thucydides' information as unreliable, or one may accept that the Spartan army in 418 BC did indeed consist of nine or more *lochoi*, plus a unit of 600 Skiritai. This, at any rate, is what Thucydides believed. He cannot be made to say anything else.

*

It is ironic that scholars have tried so hard to reinterpret Thucydides' account in order to make it fit with the information provided by Xenophon, since Xenophon's information itself appears to be inconsistent: most importantly, the explicit description of Spartan military organisation in his *Spartan Constitution* does not match the organisation implied by his account of the Corinthian War in *Hellenica*. Rather than propose emendations of the text of the *Spartan Constitution* (e.g. Lazenby 1985, 7; Gomme et al. 1970, 115) or cast doubt on its authorship and accuracy in general (e.g. Lazenby 1985, 175 n. 7; Chrimes 1949, 490-9), it is possible to explain the differences by assuming that the Spartan army underwent a reorganisation after the Corinthian War, and that the *Spartan Constitution*, almost certainly written after the Corinthian War (but before 371 BC: Sparta is portrayed as no longer free from corruption but still powerful) reflects the new structure.

Hellenica provides information about the organisation of the Spartan army in the period 403-390 BC, in the year 371, and in a few years after 371. During the first period, the largest unit is called *mora* (2.4.3; 4.3.15; 4.5.12; cf. *Agesilaus* 2.6) and it is commanded by a polemarch (e.g. 4.4.7; 5.4.46). One such *mora* consisted of 600 men in 390 BC (4.5.12), a figure which does not necessarily include men of all age groups, and certainly does not include the men from Amyclae who happened to belong to this unit (so e.g Lazenby 1985, 9). The number of *morai* is not specified for this period. The *mora* is subdivided into an unspecified number of *pentekostyes*, whose commanders rank immediately below the polemarchs (3.5.22; 4.5.7). Xenophon does not mention the *enômotia* until 371 (6.4.12, 17), but it surely existed throughout. During the period 403-390, therefore, the only difference between Xenophon's and Thucydides' picture of the Spar-

247

tan army is that the largest unit, consisting of about 600 men under the command of a polemarch according to both authors, is called *mora* by one and *lochos* by the other. The difference is easily explained by assuming that Thucydides used the generic Greek word for such units while Xenophon used the technical Spartan term. Both authors have only two levels of subdivisions, the *pentekostys* and the *enômotia*.

For the period after 390 (and presumably after the end of the Corinthian War in 386) until 371 BC, we have the description in *Hellenica* (6.1.11; 6.4.12, 17) of the Spartan army at Leuctra and the information provided by the *Spartan Constitution* (11.4, 13.4). Both tell us that there were six *morai*, led by polemarchs. The *Spartan Constitution* adds that these were each subdivided into four *lochoi*, eight *pentekostyes* and 16 *enômotiai*. *Hellenica* confirms only that the smallest units were *enômotiai*, and that these consisted of up to 36 men. If we accept the accuracy of this information, we must posit a major organisational change: the largest unit is still called *mora*, and still consists of 16 *enômotiai*, but there are now fewer such units (taking it from Thucydides that there were nine or more in 418 BC), with a more elaborate system of subdivisions. The *lochos* has replaced the *pentekostys*, which is downgraded to a third level of command, comprising only two *enômotiai* each. In other words, the army has shrunk in size and grown in complexity – two plausible developments given Spartan manpower problems and the growing sophistication of military organisation in general from the 380s onwards.

One may object that Xenophon should have mentioned such a significant reform if it had taken place during the period covered by his *Hellenica*, but the fact is that our historical sources are extremely haphazard in recording institutional reforms, and indeed Xenophon himself failed to mention another Spartan military reform which must have taken place immediately after the disaster at Leuctra. In subsequent years, he never mentions the *morai* again, but speaks only of 'the twelve *lochoi*' (7.4.20; 7.5.10; cf. 7.1.30). What must have happened seems obvious, and is generally accepted (e.g. Anderson 1970, 226): the great number of casualties at Leuctra – 1,000 men, probably almost a third of Sparta's total manpower at the time (see below) – meant that the army had to shrink in size and organisation, so that the number of *lochoi* was halved from 24 to 12 and the level of the *mora* simply abolished altogether.

*

If the assumptions made here, and the idea that the Spartan army underwent three reforms in the course of a century, are acceptable, we need not explain away any of the evidence.

The implications for the decline of Spartan manpower are worth spelling out. The Spartans could allegedly mobilise 8,000 citizens (not including *perioikoi*) in 480 BC, and in 479 BC did mobilise 5,000 citizens, which perhaps represented roughly a two-thirds levy (Herodotus 7.234.2, 9.10.1; see p. 84 with n. 28).

By 418 BC, assuming that the Spartan army had ten *lochoi* (not including the Skiritai), each consisting of 600 men (now including both citizens and *perioikoi*), the numbers had dwindled dramatically. Citizens at the time constituted 40-50% of each unit (see p. 84 n. 29), so there were only 2,400-3,000 Spartiates, to which we should probably add the elite band of 300 Hippeis as a separate unit (5.74.2). A full levy of Spartan citizens thus consisted of somewhere around 3,000 men: a reduction in manpower of about 60% in the course of two generations.

By 371 BC, there were only 96 *enômotiai* of up to 36 men each, or a total force of *c.* 3,400. At the battle of Leuctra, only four *morai* (or 64 *enômotiai*) were present, a force of 2,300 (with only the 55- to 59-year-olds absent). Of these 2,300, only 700 were Spartan citizens, i.e. 30% – although they accounted for 40% of the casualties (see p. 84 n. 29) – which means a total Spartan citizen body of about 1,100 men, another reduction of more than 60% over a span of rather less than two generations.

3. The historicity and date of Homeric warfare

The *Iliad* and *Odyssey* are set in a remote heroic age, and it is not immediately obvious whether or how their picture of warfare relates to any historical period. Some argue that the poems contain a mixture of elements from different periods, ranging from the early Mycenaean age to the late eighth century; others assume that Homer by and large reflects Dark Age patterns of warfare; yet others believe that Homeric warfare is entirely unrealistic, a poetic fiction designed only to show heroic ideals in action. Because the Homeric evidence is controversial, I have discussed it separately from the other literary and archaeological sources, and avoided making assumptions about its historicity or date. On my interpretation of war in Homer, however, it is in fact very similar to Greek warfare of the archaic age, as the reader will have noticed. Specifically, Homeric battle corresponds exactly to the type of fighting depicted in art and poetry of the first half of the seventh century – no earlier and no later.

The *Iliad* envisages its heroes as generally equipped with bronze armour: 'it blinded eyes, the glare of bronze from shining helmets, newly polished cuirasses and bright shields, as they advanced in their masses' (14.240-3); 'the brightness lit up the sky, and all around the earth beamed with the shine of bronze' (19.359-63). Helmets are frequently said to be made of bronze (e.g. 4.495, 5.562, 681, 6.116, 369, 17.3, 20.111); only two helmets are explicitly not made of bronze (10.257-71) and at least one of these is clearly exceptional, requiring detailed description. 'Bronze-cuirassed' (4.448; 8.62) and, more poetically, 'bronze-tunicked' (e.g. 1.371, 4.537, 5.180, 15.330, 17.485, 24.25) are common epithets for both Greeks and Trojans, used 31 times in the *Iliad* and twice in the *Odyssey*. The epithet 'bronze-greaved' is used only once, but 'well-greaved', which must refer to bronze greaves as well, is again very common (e.g. 1.17, 24.800; 31 times in the *Iliad*; ten times in the *Odyssey*). Parallels for all these items of bronze armour are known from the Mycenaean period, but they disappeared during the Dark Age and only re-emerged when the hoplite panoply was introduced, *c*. 720-700 BC.

A further item of body armour regularly mentioned is the metal(-covered) belt, the *mitrê* (5.538-9, 615-16; 6.219; 7.305; 10.77-8; 11.234-7; 16.419; 17.519), which in at least one case is worn under the cuirass (4.132-3). These belts were a common item of Dark Age armour and continued in use until the mid-seventh century (see the statuette in Plate III); the first hoplite in the first group on the left on the Chigi vase, *c*. 640 BC, is shown wearing a bronze belt under his cuirass (see Plate XVIII). The only time when Homer's picture of body armour corresponded to reality – give or take the odd golden or ornate cuirass – was thus 720-640 BC.

Homeric shields are round ('well-rounded': 5.453, 797, 12.426, 13.715, 14.428; 'circles': 11.32-7, 12.294-7, 20.280-1; 'equal everywhere': e.g. 3.347, 356; in total 17 times in *Iliad*) and 'bossed' (e.g. 4.448, 8.162; total 11 times in *Iliad*; cf. 6.267, 13.192). They are made of several layers of hide, covered with an outer sheet of bronze (7.219-23, 12.294-7, 12.405-7, 13.804, 17.492-3, 20.275-6; bronze also 3.348, 11.65-6, 14.9-11, 17.268) and carried with a strap around the shoulders (5.795-8, 11.38-9, 12.401-2, 14.404-5, 16.802-3, 18.480; implicit also at 8.94, 11.545), which suggests that they had a single central grip. Round, bossed, leather, single-grip shields were used throughout the Dark Age, but bronze facing was not added until *c*. 700 BC. They went out of use by 650 BC (Snodgrass 1964, 51-7).

Moreover, three passages describe a group of warriors standing close together 'leaning their shields against their shoulders' (11.593; 13.488; 22.4). These phrases have puzzled scholars (e.g. Hainsworth 1993, 287, ad 11.593-4; Lorimer 1950, 188) because it would be difficult to carry a single-grip shield leaning against one's shoulder: the length of extended lower arm means that in order to reach the shoulder the shield would have to be very large and held at an extreme angle. But the texts make perfect sense if – and only if – they refer to the double-grip hoplite shield. Resting the top edge of the shield on one's shoulder, so that the bottom half of the shield points diagonally forward, while raising a spear (as 11.594 adds) is the standard hoplite pose in archaic art. Its earliest unmistakable representation features on the so-called Berlin aryballos of *c*. 650 BC (Fig. 15; cf. Fig. 14; Plate IV). These passages thus confirm a date after 700 BC, when the hoplite shield first appeared.

Hector and Periphetes are said to have carried shields which reached their feet (6.117-18, 15.645-6). It has often been pointed out that round shields could hardly have had such a large diameter, and since Aias' shield is sometimes described as 'like a tower' (e.g. 11.485, 527), many have argued that Aias and the others carry tall rectangular or oblong shields of lighter materials (hide or wicker), perhaps like the Mycenaean figure-of-eight shield. However, Hector's shield is elsewhere described as round and bronze-faced (13.803-4), and Aias' shield, too, is bronze-faced (7.219-23, 245-6). Other comparisons with 'towers', moreover, make it clear that Homer associates towers primarily with impenetrability (13.152, 15.618, 16.211-17), not with height, and Aias' eight-layered shield is indeed exceptionally thick. The simple solution is that Homer, whose heroes are equipped with shields of different sizes (14.371-82; 15.616), attributes enormously large round shields to some of them. Their size is clearly not realistic, but then neither is the superhuman strength of the heroes who carry them.

Fantasy size (and decoration) aside, we thus have two types of shield in Homer: both must be dated after 700 BC, and the single-grip version before *c.* 650 BC. Vase paintings of this period do indeed sometimes show both types used side by side in a single battle (notably on an aryballos from Lechaeum, *c.* 690-680 BC: Snodgrass 1964, pl. 15ab).

The weapons used by Homeric warriors are not described in sufficient detail for us identify clear archaeological parallels, especially since some indications of size and decoration clearly belong to the realm of fantasy, as in the case of the shield (see in detail van Wees 1994, 133-4, 138-9). The way in which weapons are used, on the other hand, does allow us to pin down a date. Spears, normally carried in pairs, are the dominant weapon in Homer – 166 out of the 206 times anyone uses a weapon in the *Iliad* (i.e. 80.5% of the time), it is a spear – and it is used almost as often for thrusting (79 times) as it is for throwing (87 times). As we saw in Chapter 12, the poetry of Archilochus and Callinus, and early seventh century vase-painting, show precisely the same predominance of the spear and the same use for both thrusting and throwing. This pattern is different both before 700 and after about 640-625 BC. Before 700, the sword was a far more prominent weapon than the spear: it accounted for 44% of weapons represented in use on Attic Geometric vases, while the spear accounted for only 24%; scenes of men 'duelling' with spears, so common in archaic art, are unknown in the eighth century when sword-duels do feature. Archaeology confirms the prominence of the sword in the Dark Age (see in detail van Wees 1994, 143-6). In the late seventh century, by contrast, the poetry of Tyrtaeus and vase-paintings show that most hoplites fought with a single spear, used for thrusting only.

The spear clearly developed from being primarily a missile in the eighth century, via becoming as much a thrusting weapon as a missile in the early seventh, to taking on its classical role as exclusively a hand-weapon by the end of the seventh century – and what we find in Homer corresponds to the middle phase of the evolution, to be dated *c.* 700-640 BC.

Finally, the bow was also a more prominent weapon in the eighth century than it was in Homer: it accounted for 32% of weapons shown in use on Attic Geometric vases, but only for 10% of weapons shown in use in the *Iliad*. A related and even more telling change was in the battlefield role of archers. We saw in Chapter 12 that in eighth-century art archers fight standing up, independently, in the front line, while in seventh- and sixth-century art they are shown squatting or kneeling behind the shield of a hoplite: with the rise of the heavy infantry and close combat, archers began to take on a secondary role. The *Iliad* illustrates both roles: a few bowmen stride around in the front lines and fight independently (3.15-20; 13.576-92), but others shelter behind a comrade's shield (4.112-14; 8.266-72; 15.436-44) or other cover (11.369-94), and it is significant that archers, unlike other heroes, never run up to their victims to finish them off or take spoils, but keep their distance. Homer, in other words, is aware of the older, more prominent, role of archers, but is also familiar with the archaic practice (also first illustrated on the Lechaeum aryballos mentioned above). Yet again a date not long after 700 BC seems to fit best.

*

A range of clear, objective dating criteria thus point to 700-640 BC as the period which best corresponds to Homer's picture of warfare. Other aspects of Homeric warfare – the fluidity of formations, the mobility of fighters, the intermingling of light-armed and horses – remained features of Greek warfare throughout the seventh century, and probably throughout the archaic period. There is thus every reason to regard Homeric warfare as a larger-than-life version of military practice of the early seventh century – a date which is in any case increasingly favoured by a number of scholars on the grounds that many aspects of the Homeric world at large can plausibly be dated to this period, and an independent case can be made for the 'freezing' of the oral tradition at about the same time (see van Wees 2002c; West 1995).

Notes

Part I. War and peace

1. Herodotus 1.87; cf. Thucydides 2.61.1.

2. See Crane 1998, 61-71; Constantineau 1998, 103-12.

3. See Howard 1983, 7-22, who explicitly says that there is little to add to Thucydides' analysis.

4. Hartmann and Heuser (eds.) 2001.

5. Loenen 1953, 80-1. This myth was established as the consensus view by Bruno Keil's study *Eirene* (1916, 7-10); cf. e.g. Martin 1940, 393-9, 577-94; de Romilly 1968, 207-10; Finley 1985, 67-71. Finley's emphatic and influential defence of the consensus (see e.g. Sage 1996, 129; Hanson 1999, 18) in fact established only that war was *common* (75) and regarded as *legitimate* in many circumstances (71). This falls a long way short of demonstrating that war was regarded as *the* 'natural condition' of mankind, in the sense of the *normal*, default, state of affairs. Wilhelm Nestle (1938) attacked the myth at length, but ineffectively; better discussions in Bravo 1980, esp. 981-2, and Baltrusch 1994, 92-4; the myth is dismissed in passing also by Ducrey 1968, 3-4; Adcock and Mosley 1975, 12; Bauslaugh 1991, 194 n.55.

6. Many of the scholars cited in n. 5 mistakenly assume that the speaker's view is Plato's own, but Plato himself, through his Athenian speaker, argues against it: the constitution of a state ought to be geared towards peace, not war (*Laws* 628de). So too Aristotle, *Politics* 1333a31-34a16.

7. Keil and others (n. 5) adduce the temporary nature of classical 'peace treaties' (*spondai*) as evidence that the war of all against all was a political reality; against this see pp. 17-18.

8. Herodotus 1.1-4; an allegedly Persian story, but constructed from Greek myths and concepts.

9. See van Wees 2002a, 343-8, for Herodotus' views on the causes of war. Although there was no single word for 'neutrality' in Greek, the concept did exist: Bauslaugh 1991, 13-16.

10. Connor 1988, 3-8, and Shipley 1993, 18-23, point out that our sources probably give an exaggerated impression of the omnipresence of war: if classical Athens was at war two out of every three years between 490 and 336 BC, as Garlan calculated (1975, 15), it was hardly typical.

1. Kinsmen, friends and allies

1. A later source claims that they were friends because the Sybarites wore clothes of Milesian wool (Timaeus *FGrH* 566 F 50, cited by Athenaeus 519b), but there was presumably more to it than that.

2. The concept of a 'society of states' was applied to the modern world by Hedley Bull, *The Anarchical Society* (1977).

3. Herodotus 5.22; 8.137-9.

4. *Panhellenes*: *Iliad* 2.530; Hesiod, *Works and Days* 526-8; cf. F 130 M-W; Archilochus F 102 West; cf. Hall 2002, 131-4, who argues that early usages of the term do not refer all of Greece; *Panachaeans*: e.g. *Iliad* 2.404; *Odyssey* 1.239; cf. van Wees 1992, 330 n. 48. Languages: 2.803-4; 4.437-8; 'barbarian': 2.867; cf. pp. 71-2. Greek military superiority: van Wees 1996, 59-60, and see p. 108. Scholars often play down the extent of Homer's awareness of the Greeks as a distinct 'ethnic' group: e.g. Hall 2002, 118; Taplin 1992, 110-15.

5. The distinction is most explicitly made by Plato, *Republic* 469b-471c; *Menexenus* 239a, 242a-d, 245cd; the theory of Greek natural superiority is found for example in Euripides, *Iphigeneia in Aulis* 1400-1; the Hippocratic treatise *Airs, Waters, Places* 12-24; Aristotle, *Politics* 1327b20-33; cf. 1252a24-1255b40. Lonis 1969, 31-70, points out, however, that there is not much evidence to suggest that the Greeks *in practice* treated 'barbarians' much more harshly than fellow-Greeks.

6. Aristotle *Politics* 1256b23-7; cf. 1255b37-8. The earliest explicit expression of this form of 'Panhellenism' appears in Gorgias F 82 B 5b D-K (= Philostratus, *Lives of the Sophists* 1.9.1); also Lysias 33.6; Isocrates (e.g. 4.173-4; 12.158, 163, 219) and Xenophon (see Dillery 1995, 54-63).

7. Concept of autonomy: Ostwald 1982; Hansen 1995, 21-43.

8. 'Evil twin': Wickersham 1994, 23. Herodotus uses *hêgemonia* and *archê* interchangeably: 3.65.6 and 3.73.1-2 (Persian empire; cf. 7.8, 9.122), 7.148.4, 149.2, 150.3 (Argos); so does Xenophon, e.g. *Hellenica* 7.1.33, 40. A speaker in Thucydides speaks of the leadership of Sparta and Athens as '*archê* and *hêgemonia*' (6.82.3). Wickersham 1994, e.g. 83-4, unconvincingly argues that there was an original distinction which later 'weakened'.

9. Agamemnon's legendary leadership partly reflects the power of Mycenae in the Bronze Age, but also the existence of a *concept* of a 'leader of all Greeks' already in the early seventh century. Bones of Orestes and appeal to Agamemnon: Herodotus 1.67-8, 7.159.

10. Xenophon, *Hellenica* 7.5.27, 5.2.35; cf. Dillery 1995, 27-38. For the privileges of, and rivalry for, 'leadership', see pp. 23-4. See Strauss 1997 for obstacles to hegemony in Greece.

11. Herodotus 1.141; 5.49; Xenophon, *Hellenica* 3.1.3.

12. See pp. 22 (liberation, autonomy), 28-9 (annihilation).

13. Herodotus 5.97, 9.106. Thucydides acknowledged that the Athenians were asked to get involved on the basis of kinship (1.95.1), but characteristically (see below) hints that they accepted out of self-interest: it gave them a chance to arrange this 'in the best way for themselves' (1.95.2).

14. See further Hall 2002, esp. 213-14; Jones 1999; Mitchell 1997, 23-8; Hornblower 1996, 61-80.

15. E.g. 3.86.2, 7.58.3, and 5.80.2 (the king of Macedon abandoned his alliance with Athens because Argos had already done so 'and he himself was originally from Argos', i.e. by descent; see p. 7).

16. For other instances of Thucydides' contrast between self-interested Athenians and kinship-respecting other Greeks, see also the passage cited above, n. 13; the Melian dialogue, in which the Athenians argue that the Melians are foolish to think that kinship ties will carry more weight than self-interest (5.84, 89, 104-9); and the evidence discussed by Hornblower (1996, 61-80).

17. Delos: Herodotus 1.64; Thucydides 3.104, 5.1 and 5.32.1 (all three passages mention only religious motives; Diodorus 12.73.1 looks for a political explanation).

Cow, panoply, phallus: ML 46.41-3, 49.11-12, 69.56-7 (translated in Hornblower and Greenstock 1983, nos 76, 85, 135); see Meiggs 1972, 291-305.

18. Delphic (or Pylaean) amphictyony: e.g. Sanchez 2001; Davies 1994. Calaurian: Strabo 8.6.14. Argive: Pausanias 4.5.2 (a very unreliable story, but the existence of the amphictyony as such was probably not invented and seems in any case implied also by Herodotus 6.92, see below, n. 19). Aeolian, Ionian and Dorian leagues in the East: Herodotus 1.141-51. For the possibility that such leagues were a dominant feature of early Greece: Forrest 2000; Singor 1988, 288-91.

19. Xenophon, *Hellenica* 2.4.20-1. Melia: Vitruvius 4.1.4, with *Inscriften von Priene* 37 (Ager 1996, no. 74), which lists several classical and hellenistic authors who wrote about the 'Meliac War'. Argos: Herodotus 6.92: there is no explicit mention of the amphictyony, but it is hard to imagine under what other conditions a defeated state could (with some success) have demanded a fine from its enemies. Sparta: Diodorus 16.23.2-3, 29.2; there is a tradition about a Spartan counter-charge against Thebes in Cicero, *De Inventione* 2.23, 69-70.

20. Greek text of treaties: Bauslaugh 1991, 57; for Sybaris and the Serdaioi, see also ML 10 = Fornara 29. Distinction between *philia* and alliance: see Adcock and Mosley 1975, 206-9; Bauslaugh 1991, 56-64, 88-91; Baltrusch 1994, 3-15. Examples: Herodotus 1.22 (Alyattes and Miletus, *c.* 600 BC), 1.69 (Croesus and Sparta), 1.141 (Cyrus and Miletus), 3.39; cf. 2.182 (Amasis and Polycrates); Thucydides 3.70.2, cf. 1.31.2 (Corcyra remains an 'ally' of Athens and a 'friend' of Sparta); *IG* I² 87 (= *SV* 184; Athens and Halieis, 424/3); *IG* I³ 83 and Thucydides 5.47 (= *SV* 193; Athens, Argos, Mantineia and Elis, 420); Isocrates 14.33 (Athens and Boeotia).

21. Sworn friendship in *Iliad* 3.73, 94, 256, 323; ritual: 3.268-301; 4.158-9. Contrast the less formal short-term truces at 7.408-12 and 24.656-70, 778-81.

22. Thucydides 1.41-2; quoted phrases at 42.1, 41.1, 42.3. See Missiou 1998, 184.

23. Herodotus 3.47; other examples: 1.18, 5.99.

24. Thucydides 6.83.2; at length e.g. 1.73.2-75.1; Herodotus 7.139 (supporting Athens' claim to have saved Greece), 9.27 (appeal to role at Marathon). Fourth century: e.g. Isocrates 4.85-100.

25. Herodotus 9.27 offers a list of the myths to which Athens liked to appeal (see p. 23). For the Athenian self-image, appeals to past, and presentation of Theseus, see especially Mills 1997, 34-86. Bones of Theseus: Plutarch, *Theseus* 36; *Cimon* 8.3-7.

26. Thucydides 5.89; 6.83.2. Reciprocity in interstate relations and Thucydides' realist attitude towards it: Crane 1998, 36-71; Constantineau 1998, 103-12. Xenophon, by contrast, presents Athens (after the Peloponnesian War) as motivated by an unselfish concern with justice: see p. 21. For the concept of reciprocity and its significance in other cultures, see van Wees 1998a.

27. E.g. Neapolis (in Thrace: *IG* I³ 101 = ML 89 = Fornara 156) and Samos (*IG* I³ 127 = ML 94 = Fornara 166; a relief added above the decree shows Athena and Hera of Samos clasping hands).

28. Thucydides 2.27.2, 4.56.2. Around the time of the composition of the *Odyssey*, Sparta supposedly in the same way resettled its allies from Asine (Pausanias 2.36.5; 3.7.4; 4.14.3) and Nauplia (4.24.4, 27.8, 35.2). See also pp. 28-9.

29. *Odyssey* 16.424-30; cf. *Iliad* 3.56-7. Usage of *arthmios*: Bauslaugh 1991, 59-62. On *oikeios*: Hornblower 1996, 64-70.

30. Kinship: 11.221-30, 13.171-6. 'Helpers': see pp. 71-3.

31. Agreements: *Iliad* 2.339-41; 4.266-7. Recruitment: 11.765-82; cf. 1.158; *Odyssey* 24.115-19.

32. *Symmachia*, as well as *philia*, between Lydia (Alyattes) and Miletus: see n. 20 above, with other sixth-century examples. Sybaris' *symmachoi* are mentioned in the treaty of *c*. 550 BC, cited above; according to Strabo (6.1.13) 25 cities and four 'tribes' were 'subordinate' to Sybaris. Sparta must have made most of its allies between the end of the Second Messenian War (*c*. 600 BC, see e.g. Parker 1991, 34-42) and their alliance with Tegea not long before 550 (according to Herodotus 1.68.6). Chalcis and Eretria are said to have brought in many allies to fight their 'Lelantine' War, which most modern scholars believe may have taken place *c*. 700 BC (see especially Parker 1997): if this date is right, these 'alliances' were presumably of the *ad hoc*, Homeric kind: although Thucydides speaks of a *symmachia* (1.15.3), Herodotus before him spoke of the help extended between them as a 'favour' (*charis*), repaid in 499 BC (5.99).

33. Greek text: ML 17 and *SV* 110, also Bauslaugh 1991, 58.

34. Originally published in Peek 1974 (dated to 500-470); see also e.g. Cartledge 1978 and Baltrusch 1994, 21-4, who suggest much later dates. Summaries of two classical treaties, in Xenophon, *Hellenica* 2.2.20 (with Athens, 404) and 5.3.26 (with Olynthus, 379), indicate that these were made on the same terms. That Peloponnesian allies already swore to follow Sparta 'by land and sea' before 480 BC is evident from their total acceptance of Spartan leadership in that year, while they absolutely refused to accept Athenian leadership at sea, despite the fact that Athens provided the bulk of the fleet (Herodotus 8.2). Hints of Spartan naval ambitions in the sixth century suggest that the full clause was part of the treaties even then (see p. 200). A clause about not receiving refugees was already part of Sparta's treaty with Tegea, *c*. 550: Aristotle F 592 Rose (Plutarch, *Moralia* 292b; cf. 277c). See further Cartledge 1989, 9-13.

35. This is particularly clear from Thucydides 1.44.1.

36. The treaties with Athens, Olynthus and Tegea were made after these communities had been defeated; Herodotus' comment that the Spartans by *c*. 550 had '*subjected* most of the Peloponnese' (1.68) suggests that this had been the normal pattern. See de Ste Croix 1972, 108-12.

37. As in the Athenian alliances with Corcyra in 427 (Thucydides 3.70.3, 6; 3.75.1, where the promise is one-sided – unlike in the equal treaty proposed six years earlier: see n. 39 – since its opponents object that it would 'enslave' Corcyra to Athens), with Perdiccas (*IG* I³ 89 = *SV* 186.20), the Bottiaioi (*IG* I³ 76 = *SV* 187.19-20), and probably Thurii (Thucydides 7.33.6), or again in the alliance between Thebes and Macedon in 368 (Plutarch, *Pelopidas* 27.3).

38. Apart from the Delian League (see below), the only example is the proposed alliance between Athens and Corcyra in 433, which the Athenians rejected precisely because they did not want to commit themselves to an offensive pact (Thucydides 1.44.1).

39. This was the limited extent of, for example, Athens' commitment in 433 BC to its distant allies in Corcyra (Thucydides 1.44.1), Rhegium and Leontini (*IG* I³ 53-4 = ML 63-4 = Fornara 124-5; evidently renewed in 433 and so going back at least to the mid-fifth century). Athens made the same commitment to Sparta and Argos during Peloponnesian War (Thucydides 5.23.1-2 and 47.3-4, featuring the clause quoted in the text), and, so far as we can see, to all the allies it acquired subsequently (for a list, see Adcock and Mosley 1975, 191). Note also the defensive alliance between the Acarnanians, Amphilochians and Ambraciots of 426: Thucydides 3.114.3.

40. The *Athenian Constitution* (23.5) says explicitly that the Athenians reciprocated the promise: on their behalf Aristides 'swore to the Ionians that they would have the same friend and enemy' (see esp. de Ste Croix 1972, 298-307; Baltrusch 1994, 58); cf. Plutarch, *Aristides* 25.1. Athens' demanding leadership and the goal of the League (cf. p. 121): Thucydides 1.96, 99.

41. So e.g. Adcock and Mosley 1975, 189-92. Elsewhere they rightly note that *symmachia* is the official, technical term used for all sorts of alliances; a purely defensive treaty is sometimes called *epimachia*, but that was a colloquial rather than formal designation (1975, 121).

42. See pp. 23-4.

43. Cretan treaty: ML 42 = Fornara 89. Delian League and later alliance: Thucydides 1.96, 5.47.6. See Garlan 1989, 41-55, and p. 237.

44. 50 years: Thucydides 5.23.1 (Athens), 5.79.1 (Argos). 100 years: 5.47.3 (Athens and Argos), 3.114.3 (Acarnians and Amphilochians), and the alliance of Eleans and Heraeans, cited p. 13. 'Forever' is common in many fourth-century Athenian alliances (e.g. *IG* II^2 97, 105, 116 = Harding 42, 52, 59) and has been plausibly restored in the much earlier alliances with Rhegium and Leontini (n. 39 above). Permanence of Delian League: *Athenian Constitution* 23.5; Plutarch, *Aristides* 25.1. There is no evidence for a time-limit on alliances within the Peloponnesian League, and it seems likely that unequal treaties were generally imposed in perpetuity.

45. *Iliad* 11.123-5, 139-41; cf. 3.205-24. Other embassies: 24.234-5; *Odyssey* 3.366-8. Homeric international relations: Wéry 1979; van Wees 1992, 168-72; Raaflaub 1997a.

46. 'Giver of justice' (*dosidikos*): Herodotus 6.42.1; cf. 6.92.

47. See further p. 239. On the roles of *xeinoi*, see Herman 1987; Mitchell 1997.

48. The earliest known *proxenos* is attested through a memorial in the city he represented (Corcyra) of *c.* 625-600 BC (ML 4 = Fornara 14). See further Herman 1987, 130-42; Marek 1978.

49. Herodotus 7.133-7. The murder of heralds also caused the sack of Sybaris: Athenaeus 521d. Diplomacy in ancient Greece: Adcock and Mosley 1975; Olshausen and Billet (eds.) 1979.

50. See references in n. 29 above.

51. Herodotus 5.95 (Periander of Corinth); Plutarch, *Solon* 10 (Spartans): in both cases Athenian claims are said to have relied on 'evidence' from the *Iliad*. Sparta backed up at least one arbitration judgement by force during the Peloponnesian War: Thucydides 5.31.3-4. The nomination of the city of Posidonia as 'guarantor' of the treaty between Sybaris and the Serdaioi (see p. 10) is probably another instance of an arbitrator chosen for their power. See Adcock and Mosley 1975, 210-14.

52. As proposed by Corcyra: Thucydides 1.28.2; in an earlier dispute with Corinth, Corcyra had agreed to arbitration by Themistocles (Plutarch, *Themistocles* 24.1), chosen perhaps both for his authority and his (informal) power at the time. For other arbitrations, see Piccirilli 1973; Ager 1996.

53. Some early examples: *IG* I^3 10 = ML 31 = Fornara 68 (Athens and Phaselis); Tod 1.34 = Fornara 87 (Oianthia and Chaleion), both probably *c.* 450 BC. See Adcock and Mosley 1975, 186-9; Gauthier 1972.

54. Contra Keil 1916 and many others: see p. 4 with n. 5 above. For the evidence, see n. 57 below.

55. On such 'goal-oriented' armistices, see e.g. Baltrusch 1994, 99-154.

56. Thucydides quotes the Spartans as offering 'peace' when they mean *spondai* in 425 (4.19.1: 'peace and alliance') and himself calls the *spondai* of 421 'peace' (5.17.2), which suggests that the conventional name for this treaty, 'the *Peace* of Nicias' (Plutarch, *Nicias* 9.8, *Alcibiades* 14.2) was not a late invention. Aristophanes' *Acharnians*, of 425, also repeatedly equates *spondai* with 'peace' (39, 278, 1020-1, 1029, 1053), as does his *Peace*, of 421 (211-18, 1199).

57. Long-term *spondai* without alliance: Herodotus 7.149 (Argos and Sparta in 481: rejected), perhaps implied also at 5.89 (Athens and Aegina, 491: rejected); Thucydides 5.14.4 (Argos and Sparta, 451), 1.23.4, 1.112.1, 5.18-19 (Athens and Sparta, 451, 446, 421, the latter soon followed by an alliance: 5.23-4). Long-term *spondai* with simultaneous alliance: e.g. Thucydides 3.114.3 (Acarnania and Amphilochia, 426), 5.47 (Athens and Argos, 420), 5.79 (Sparta and Argos, 418). There is no reason to think that *spondai* (or formal *philia*) were a pre-requisite for *every* alliance, since most surviving treaties of alliance do not mention either (contra Baltrusch 1994, 5-11, 192-3).

58. Evidence and discussion: Ryder 1965; Jehne 1994.

59. Polybius 12.26.2 and Plutarch, *Nicias* 9.2, quoting Gorgias; Herodotus 1.87; cf. Garlan 1989, 7-8, and on attitudes to war and peace generally Spiegel 1990; Arnould 1981; de Romilly 1968.

2. Justice, honour and profit

1. Thucydides 1.25.4; discussion of the episode in Crane 1992; 1998, 93-124.

2. Momigliano 1966, 113 ('silly'; cf. 'the prevailing tendency was to be frivolous and anecdotal about causes of war', 118); de Ste Croix 1972, 218 ('oddities').

3. The *Guardian* newspaper, 11 April 2001, p. 1.

4. Thucydides 1.75.3, 76.2 ('honour, fear and profit'); Plato, *Protagoras* 354b ('security, rule over others and possessions'); Xenophon, *Hellenica* 3.5.12 ('leadership, honour, and possessions'); Demosthenes, *Against the Rhodians* 15.17 (territory, rivalry, leadership, and defence of constitution and freedom); similarly Aristotle, *Politics* 1266b38-9, on civil war, cited p. 34.

5. Athens-Megara: Thucydides 1.139.2 (431); Demosthenes 13.32; 23.212 (*c.* 350); cf. Pausanias 3.4.5-6; Herodotus 6.75.3 for the importance attached to the sacred land at Eleusis by the Athenians (de Ste Croix 1972, 254-5). Phocis-Delphi: see n. 7 below.

6. Aeschines 2.115; cf. 3.109, 120. A 'powerful curse' added that offenders' land and flocks would bear no fruit, that they would always be defeated, and that their women would give birth to monsters (3.110-11). There is a close parallel to these formulae in the oath of Plataea: see n. 9 below.

7. 'Sheep-walk': Isocrates 14.31. First Sacred War: Aeschines (see n. 6); Athenaeus 560bc; Plutarch, *Solon* 11; and other texts assembled under Fornara 16; with Davies 1994 for the tradition. Later (Third) Sacred War: Diodorus 16.23.3-28.4.

8. Herodotus 8.144; Diodorus 11.29.2; cf. Meiggs 1972, 504-7.

9. Oath of Plataea: Tod II 204, lines 31-3; see also Appendix 2. Cynical manipulation: e.g. Plutarch, *Themistocles* 20.3-4 (by Sparta); Herodotus 6.133.1 (by Miltiades), 8.112 (by Themistocles).

10. *Ways and Means* 5.5-10, written at a time when more aggressive Athenian strategies had failed. Emphasis on Athens' moral disapproval of Thebes' actions: *Hellenica* 6.3.1, 5, 10, 13. Earlier Athenian concern to defend the 'wronged': 3.5.10, 14 (395 BC), 6.5.38-38 (in legend); see also pp. 11-12, and 199, 208 for the suppression of piracy.

11. Xenophon, *Hellenica* 3.5.3-4; see pp. 10-15 for obligations to friends and allies.

12. Sixth-century intervention: Herodotus 3.46-56; escalation in fifth century: Thucydides 3.82.1. Spartan hostility to tyrants: Thucydides 1.18.1; Plutarch, *Moralia* 859be. Athenian support for democracies: pseudo-Xenophon, *Athenian Constitution* 1.14, 3.11; Thucydides 3.47.2.

13. See p. 254 n. 11. Also Brasidas' appeals to liberation of the Greeks: Thucydides 4.85.1, 5. Sparta's 'liberation' of Elis' subject neighbours (Xenophon, *Hellenica* 3.2.23).

14. 'Freedom and autonomy' in Common Peace treaties: e.g. Xenophon, *Hellenica* 5.1.31; cf. Jehne 1994; Ryder 1965. Also in the 'Charter' for the Second Athenian League: Cargill 1981, 14-47.

15. On *timê*, see esp. Riedinger 1976; van Wees 1992, 69-77; Lendon 2000, 3-11.

16. Parke-Wormell no. 1. Other versions substitute 'Megarians': e.g. *Anthologia Palatina* 14.73. On ranking of states, see further Lendon 2000, 13-15.

17. Athens cited its autochthony (cf. Loraux 1986, 148-50) and legendary generosity (see pp. 11-12). Corcyraeans prided themselves on descent from the mythical Phaeacians (Thucydides 1.25.4).

18. Pausanias 1.15 for the Painted Stoa in Athens. For war monuments, see Rice 1993.

19. Herodotus 1.82.7-8 and 5.88: the defeated party in each case also changed its hairstyle or costume. Even if these stories are untrue, they tell us much about Greek attitudes to warfare.

20. Thucydides 1.75.3; and Herodotus 9.26-7 (Plataea); Xenophon, *Hellenica* 7.1.12-14 (naval command). Note also how the twin goals of war are often said to be 'freedom and to rule over others': Herodotus 1.210; Thucydides 3.45.6; pseudo-Xenophon, *Athenian Constitution* 1.8; Plato, *Gorgias* 452d5; Aristotle, *Politics* 1333b39-34a2.

21. Xenophon, *Hellenica* 3.2.21-2, 26; cf. Thucydides 5.31, 43-50; Diodorus 14.17.4-6; Pausanias 3.8.3. Elis was forced to relinquish control over its *perioikoi*, so Sparta also lived up to its claim to fight for their liberation. For Sparta's motives, see Lendon 2000, 1-2, 21; Roy 1998.

22. Xenophon, *Hellenica* 3.5.5 (and 7.1.34); cf. *Hellenica Oxyrhynchia* 13.1; Diodorus 14.18.1; Pausanias 3.9.3-10; Plutarch, *Agesilaus* 27.

23. 1.23.6, 33.3, 86.5, 88, 118.2-3

24. Thucydides 5.95-97, 116.2-4.

25. E.g. Thucydides 1.68.2 (Athens); Xenophon, *Hellenica* 3.5.5, 24 (Thebes), 5.2.38 (Olynthus). The ancient meaning of *hybris*, as explained Fisher 1992 (see also Lendon 2000, 14-17), is not to be confused with the modern sense of 'over-reaching arrogance'.

26. Vehement hatred (*misos*): Thucydides 1.103.4. Anger: e.g. Xenophon, *Hellenica* 3.2.21, 23; 3.5.5 (*orgê*), Herodotus 8.31 (*cholos*); resentment (*mnêsikakein*): e.g. Herodotus 3.49.2; enmity (*echthos*): e.g. Herodotus 5.89.1; envy (*phthonos*): e.g. Xenophon, *Hellenica* 5.2.1 (cf. Walcot 1978); shame (*aischron*): e.g. Thucydides 5.111.3, 6.11.6 (cf. Cairns 1993). On revenge (*tisis* or *timôria*), see Lendon 2000; Gehrke 1987; de Romilly 1971. The purpose of the Delian League was explicitly defined as revenge on Persia: see p. 121.

27. Herodotus 3.49; cf. Thucydides 1.25 (see n. 17 above).

28. Phocis: Herodotus 7.176, 215; 8.29-30. Athens and Aegina: Herodotus 5.81-9. For the extreme violence of these feuds, see esp. p. 131.

29. Xenophon, *Hellenica* 3.2.26; cf. Argos' raiding of Cynouria which brought in

25 talents (Thucydides 5.95.1). Plundering in countryside: pp. 121-3; provisioning: pp. 105-6.

30. *Iliad* 21.40-1, 58, 78-80; 23.741-7; [Demosthenes] 53.6-10.

31. 200 drs: Herodotus 6.79.1; cf. 5.77.3 (Athens). 100 drs: Androtion *FGrH* 324 F 44 (408/7 BC); *SEG* 33.17 (405/4 BC); Diodorus 14.102.2 (390 BC), 14.111.4 (386 BC; rough equivalence between ransom and sale price implied); Aristotle, *Nicomachean Ethics* 1134b (general rule). Retail prices of slaves ranged from 100-200 dr. in the late fifth century: they will have been cheaper when sold in bulk to slave traders; given 'inflation', prices must also have been lower *c.* 500 BC. Ducrey (1968, 252) points out that the sources for the sack of Thebes in 336 BC imply a plausible average sale price of 88 dr. (see n. 35 below). For other sums, see Pritchett 1991a, 245-97; Ducrey 1968, 238-54. See further pp. 148-9.

32. Herodotus 6.132; also Samians demand 100 tal. from Siphnians (3.58); Thessalians demand 50 tal. from Phocians (8.29); Themistocles demands 'large sums' from Andros, Paros, Carystos, etc. (8.111-12). That this was common practice emerges also from the Thebans expectation that they will be able to buy off their besiegers (9.87, see p. 21).

33. See Xenophon, *Education of Cyrus* 7.5.73; cf. 3.3.45; 4.2.26; *Memorabilia* 4.2.15; *Dissoi Logoi* DK p. 410; Aristotle, *Politics* 1255a6-7; Polybius 2.58.9-10.

34. See Ducrey 1968; Garlan 1989, 83-8; 1975, 68; Karavites 1982. Qualms: see p. 7.

35. Thebes: Diodorus 17.14.4 (cf. n. 31 above); Cleitarchus *FGrH* 137 F 1 (Athenaeus 148df) claimed that 440 talents included the value of all property in Thebes as well, but given his mockery of the Thebans for their alleged meanness this is hardly reliable. Lysander: Diodorus 13.106.8 (1,500 tal., but how much of this was booty and how much Persian subsidy? Cf. 13.104.3-4); Agesilaus: Xenophon, *Hellenica* 4.3.21 with 3.4.24. The sack of Hykkara in Sicily (Thucydides 6.62.4) and the campaigns of Chabrias in 376 (Demosthenes 20.77) fetched 120 talents each. Few if any of the other known figures are useful or reliable: see for the evidence Pritchett 1971, 53-84; 1991a, 68-541.

36. Diodorus 16.57.2. Also 15.14.4 (Dionysius I) and 16.24.3-25.2 (Phocis seizes Delphic oracle).

37. See p. 236.

38. *Hellenica* 3.2.26 (invasion of Elis) and 5.2.19 (in general); belated leadership ambitions: 7.1.24-5.

39. Aristotle F 576 Rose (= Plutarch, *Moralia* 296ab); Ager 1996, nos 26, 74, 99, 160, 171 (*Inschriften von Priene* 37 and 41); for some time in the classical period, Samos had the upper hand to such an extent that they were no longer fighting Priene over the disputed plain, but fighting Miletus for control of Priene: Thucydides 1.115.2; Plutarch, *Pericles* 25.

40. Tacitus, *Annales* 4.43; *IG* V 1.1431; see Ager 1996, nos 50, 150, 159, and esp. p. 450.

41. Herodotus 1.82; Thucydides 5.14.4, 41.2, 6.95.1; Pausanias 7.11.1; 10.9.6. See e.g. Kelly 1970. 'Conflicts between equals over land boundaries' as the rule: e.g. Thucydides 1.122.2; 1.15.2-3; cf. de Ste Croix 1972, 218-20.

42. Pasture: *Hellenica Oxyrhynchia* 18.3. See Ma 2000, 350, for other natural resources contested by cities in the hellenistic period.

43. Giving away of Cynouria: Thucydides 2.27.2 (see p. 12). Symbolic value of disputed borderland: Sartre 1979; Ma 2000, esp. 353. It seems to me to be going too far to describe such wars as 'ritual' and argue that their main function was to offer young men a chance to be 'initiated' as warriors (so Garlan 1975, 26-31;

Brelich 1961), because they were not as a rule fought subject to any special restrictions, let alone confined to the youngest age classes: see pp. 133-4.

44. The 'clothes on their backs' meant, depending on gender and local costume, one or two garments: Plutarch, *Virtue of Women* 3 (*Moralia* 244f-245a) (Chios); Thucydides 2.70.3 (Potideia; also allowed 'travel money'); Xenophon, *Hellenica* 2.3.6 (Samos); Diodorus 16.34.5 (Methone). Other forced evacuations: e.g. Thucydides 1.103.1, 114.3, 2.27.1.

45. Strabo 6.1.13. The territory of Cirrha conquered in the First Sacred War was said to not to have been occupied but dedicated to Apollo: Aeschines 3.109. (cf. Lecythos, next note).

46. Thucydides 3.68.2-3; Brasidas similarly dealt with Lecythos (a fortress at Torone) by pulling down its walls and dedicating it to Athena (ibid. 4.116.1-2). Sparta sacked quite a few places for the sake of booty alone: Hysiae (in 417: 5.83.2); Iasos (in 411: 8.28.4); Cedreae and Lampsacus (both in 405/4: Xenophon, *Hellenica* 2.1.15, 18-19); Caryae (in 367: *Hellenica* 7.1.28).

47. Cities sacked and replaced with 'cleruchies': Lemnos (and Imbros, *c.* 500): Herodotus 6.140. Eion and Skyros (*c.* 476/5): Thucydides 1.98.1-2. Hestiaea (446): Thucydides 1.114.3; Diodorus 12.7 and 12.22.2; Strabo 10.1.3; Plutarch, *Pericles* 23.4; scholion on Aristophanes, *Clouds* 211-13. Aegina (431), Potidaea (429), Melos (416): Thucydides 2.27.1; 2.70.4; 5.116.4. Lesser territorial concessions were demanded of Chalcis in 506 (Herodotus 5.77) and 446 (Plutarch, *Pericles* 23.4; Aelian *VH* 6.1), Thasos in 463 (Thuc. 1.101.3), and Mytilene in 427 (Thuc. 3.50.2-3). Salamis, first occupied *c.* 600 BC, also had a cleruchy (ML 14 = Fornara 44). The status of the sixth-century settlers in Sigeum (see p. 28) and in the Chersonese under Militades (Herodotus 6.34-40) is not clear. Cleruchies were also established in the Chersonese, Andros and Naxos, *c.* 450, but perhaps not as a result of conquest: see esp. Plutarch, *Pericles* 11.5-6; Isocrates 4.107.

48. Thucydides 4.130 (Mende), 5.3.4 (Torone), 5.32.1 (Scione). Torone and Skione as examples of Athenian aggression: Xenophon, *Hellenica* 2.2.3. Athens gave away recently conquered Naupactus to Messenian refugees, *c.* 455 BC: Thucydides 1.103.3.

49. The brutal treatment of the Hestiaeans was also attributed to anger: they had executed the crew of a captured Athenian warship (Plutarch, *Pericles* 23.4). The destruction of Sybaris was also attributed to anger at a series of outrages committed by the Sybarites: Diodorus 12.9.1-10.1; Strabo 6.1.3; Athenaeus 521d. On anger and greed, see further pp. 32-4.

50. Archilochus F 102 West; fighting Thracians: T4, FF 92-8; disparagement of Thasos' agricultural resources: FF 21-2. Gold mines: Herodotus 6.46.3-47.2; Thucydides 1.100.2, 101.3.

51. Herodotus 4.159. On overseas settlement generally, see e.g. Graham 1964; 2001, and, for the violent expulsion of natives, Rihll 1993; see also n. 55 below.

52. State-organised colonies: e.g. Brea (ML 49 = Fornara 100); Thurii (Diodorus 12.10f.); Amphipolis (Thucydides 4.102). Relations between 'colony' and mother-city: Graham 1964; Osborne 1998.

53. Main evidence: Herodotus 6.83; Aristotle, *Politics* 1303a6-8; Socrates of Argos *FGrH* 310 F 6 (Argos); Theopompus *FGrH* 115 F 176, 311; *P. Oxy.* 1241, col. iii.2-12; Pausanias 7.26.2, 6 (with Herodotus 5.68; Sicyon). This interpretation of the evidence is advanced in van Wees 2003.

54. Ancient tradition attributed the creation of the *penestai* to conquest, but implausibly dated this back to the so-called Dorian migration; one tradition also attributed the creation of the Laconian helots to Dorian conquest, another to conquest in the late eighth century. See van Wees 2003. The extent and frequency of territorial conquest is generally underestimated by modern authors, who treat the Spartan conquest of Messenia as a unique exception: Connor 1988, 16; Anderson 1970, 2.

55. Fisher 1993, 33. Main evidence: Herodotus 7.155; Aristotle F 586 Rose (Syracuse); Phylarchus *FGrH* 81 F 8 (Byzantium); Plato, *Laws* 777c; Aristotle, *Politics* 1327b12-15; Athenaeus 263ce; Strabo 12.3.4 (Heraclea).

56. Herodotus 4.148 (conquest); Thucydides 5.31.2 (Lepreon); cf. 2.25.3; Xenophon, *Hellenica* 3.2.30 (Epeion); Strabo 8.355. We have very little evidence for the history of *perioikoi* elsewhere.

57. Crete: Chaniotis 1996, 160-8 and texts 64 (early third century BC) and 69 (late third/early second century BC). Elis: n. 21 above. Thessaly: Xenophon, *Hellenica* 6.1.9 and 19 (going back to Scopas, sixth century). Sparta: [Plato], *Alcibiades I* 123a; cf. Xenophon, *Spartan Constitution* 15.3. In general, see Larsen 1937. For military service, see pp. 83-5.

58. Special levy by Sparta: ML 67; Fornara 132; see Loomis 1992. Sums of tribute: Thucydides 1.96.2; 2.13.3; Diodorus 11.47.1-2; Plutarch, *Aristides* 24; ML 69 = Fornara 136. Sparta later also allowed substitution payments: see p. 75.

59. Herodotus 7.156; Thucydides 6.4.2, 6.5.3; Diodorus 11.49.1-2.

60. Pausanias 8.27.1; cf. Strabo 8.6.10-11. Also Diodorus 11.65 and Pausanias 2.15.4, 16.4, 7.25.3 (Mycenae); Herodotus 6.83, 7.137 and Pausanias 2.17.5 and 25.7 (Tiryns); Thucydides 6.7 and Pausanias 2.25.4-5, 8.27.1 (Orneai).

61. For the latter, see Ma 2000, 352-3, and Austin and Vidal-Naquet 1972, 350.

62. Messenia: Pausanias 4.4.1-5.5. Lemnos: Herodotus 6.137-40.

63. Material compensation rejected in favour of violent assertion of honour: *Iliad* 6.45-65; 9.645-8; 18.498-501; 21.99-105; 22.111-28; *Odyssey* 22.54-64. See van Wees 1992, 131-5; Wilson 2002.

64. So Ma 2000, 353; Garlan 1975, 183; cf. 1989, 28-30. See also n. 20 above for 'ruling others'.

65. Tod II no. 204; cf. the oath sworn in hellenistic Cos: *Tituli Calymnii*, test. xii.26-7 (Ma 2000, 352).

66. See e.g. Xenophon, *Hiero*, esp. 7.1-4. The same hierarchy of values is implied by the Athenian claim in Thucydides that they had acquired their 'rule'/empire *for the sake of* honour and profit.

67. See e.g. Fornara 1983, 76-86 and Sealey 1957 for discussions of causation in Greek historians; and van Wees 2002a, 343-8, for Herodotus. I would insist that Thucydides' 'truest' should be taken to mean that he regarded all causes cited as true, but this one as most true, i.e. most important; modern scholars generally but wrongly simplify this into a categorical distinction between one 'true' explanation and a series of (false) pretexts.

68. 'Profit' as most important: e.g. Finley 1985, 75-7; Garlan 1989, 33-40. 'Honour' as most important: e.g. Lendon 2000, esp. 21-2.

3. Pleonexia

1. *Politics* 1266b38-9, 1267a14; cf. Fisher 2000, 84-90, on the significance of 'honour' here. See Garlan 1989, 24-30, for Plato's and Aristotle's views on the causes of war, although he overemphasises the economic aspects: e.g. Aristotle's remark that 'even warfare is in some way a natural form of acquisition' (1256b24-

6) means only that acquisition was part of warfare, not that this was its main rationale. See also Balot 2001 on *pleonexia*.

2. Solon F 6.3 West; Theognis 153; see further Fisher 1992, 201-46.

3. Herodotus 1.66; 5.81; Thucydides 1.25.4, 38.6; 3.39.4-5; Xenophon, *Hellenica* 5.2.16-18, 38; 7.1.23-6, 32.

4. See Fisher 1993, 42-5 on slaves, and Finley 1973, 40-1, on the definition of poverty.

5. Theognis 173-8, 181-2, 267-8. See van Wees 2000b, 65-6.

6. See the full analysis in Fisher 1998.

7. Xenophon, *Ways and Means* 1.1; 4.33; 6.1. Isocrates: esp. 4.131; *Letter* 3.5.

8. *Politics* 1264a14-18, arguing that Plato's scheme of having 5,000 Guardians was unworkable; it is an exaggeration because he elsewhere claims that even Sparta's territory could maintain 31,500 hoplites and cavalry (1270a29-31). Aristotle is quite evasive on the number which he himself thinks it is feasible to sustain: 1325b40-26b26.

9. For the archaic evidence, see esp. van Wees 1999b; Fisher 1992, 201-46. Classical civil war and its causes: esp. Fisher 2000; Lintott 1982; Asheri 1966.

10. See van Wees 1999a, 1-13 (seventh-century crisis in Sparta), and 1999b, 10-18 (land in Athens).

11. Finley 1985, 74-7, and Garlan 1989, 38-9, both cite Ciccotti 1901, 75-6, for the idea that the frequency of war was due to the 'limited development of productive forces' which meant that 'new needs' could not easily be satisfied by applying labour to available natural resources. 'Violent appropriation' took the place of 'economic growth', as the 'path of least resistance'.

12. See Foxhall 1997, 122-9.

13. See p. 164 with n. 42.

14. *Politics* 1269a34-6; cf. 'the land must belong to those who own arms and armour and who constitute the political community ... and those who cultivate the land must be a different group from the owners' (1329b36-9). Aristotle argued that the serfs in Sparta and Thessaly were too liable to revolt, although he conceded that the system in Crete worked well (1269a37-b12; 1264a20-3). His main objection to previous theories was that they had not gone far enough in subjecting the farmers to the warriors. Hippodamus allowed farmers to own land and enjoy citizen rights alongside the warriors, which Aristotle thought unjustifiable, unnecessary and unworkable (1268a16-b4). Plato failed to make it clear what the political and military status of the cultivators was to be, but he did allow them to own the land and merely pay 'tributes' to the warriors, giving them a degree of independence which would probably make them 'much more unmanageable and full of big ideas than the helots and *penestai* and slaves which they have in some places' (1264a33-6; b34-7).

15. Skolion 909 [*Song of Hybrias*] Page. For serf populations, see e.g. van Wees 2003. Spartan ban on crafts: e.g. Xenophon, *Spartan Constitution* 7.1-2; Plutarch, *Agesilaus* 26.2; other sources cited in Hodkinson 2000, 177-8, noting that this may have been a development of the classical period. Thessalian ban: Aristotle, *Politics* 1331a31-b14.

16. See pp. 55-7, 77-85.

17. Swords: e.g. *Odyssey* 2.2-14, 4.307-11, 8.403-6, 20.124-7. Spears: e.g. *Odyssey* 2.10, 20.127. Odysseus' hall: *Odyssey* 1.127-9; 22.109-86. See van Wees 1998b, 335-6, 363, and Gröschel 1989, 75-9, on weapons, and van Wees 1992, esp. 148-52, on early Greek ideals of masculinity.

18. Archaic and classical evidence: van Wees 1998b, 344-66.

19. See Dover 1974, esp. 164-6; on *andreia*, see pp. 192-5 and Rosen and Sluiter (eds) 2003.

20. 2.148, with 147 (father), 149 (brother), 151 (brother-in-law), 167-9 (self). Other examples include Demosthenes denouncing Meidias as a coward (21.110, 132-5, 148, 161-4) and the speaker of Lysias 10 praising the valour of his father (10.27-8) while denouncing the cowardice of his opponent (10.23). See further Burckhardt 1996, 157-256; Roisman 2003.

21. *Seven Against Thebes* 78-281, esp. 181-95; cf. Just 1989, 198-203, and especially Powell 2003, who notes the importance of the ritual cry here; that the women utter it from the roofs of their houses is not explicitly said, but seems implied. See also p. 144.

22. Telesilla: Plutarch, *Moralia* 223b, 245cf; Pausanias 2.20.8; cf. Herodotus 6.76. She has a parallel in the history of my home town, Haarlem, in the Netherlands, where during the Spanish siege of 1573 a woman played a prominent role in the defence. Her first name, Kenau, came to denote a virago in Dutch. Powell 2003, n. 32, cites a Welsh parallel for the Sinopean stratagem (see p. 144).

23. Aristotle, *Politics* 1269b37-39; for the correct interpretation of this passage, and general discussion of this theme, see Powell 2003. This view of Spartan women is part of Aristotle's unusually critical line on Sparta: others felt that Spartan women were actually quite strong: see e.g. Ducat 1999, 44-5.

24. '*Kinaidos*': Aeschines 2.151 (referring to Demosthenes). 'Woman': see pp. 109, 134, 163-4, 193-4.

25. 4.168; cf. 146 (of 380 BC), 5.120-2 (346), 8.24 (355).

26. Cf. Menander's *The Shield*: a young man serves as a mercenary to raise a dowry for his sister.

27. See further Humphreys 1978, 161-9; Strauss 1993, 110-29.

28. Raiders: see e.g. the career of the Samian exiles of Herodotus 3.57-9, with the comments of Jackson 2000, 143-4. Dorieus: Herodotus 5.42-6; cf. 6.64-70 (Demaratus) and Cartledge 1987, 110-15 (including Agesilaus). Exiles: Seibert 1979. Pattern of factional rivalry in archaic Greece: Stahl 1987.

29. Parke 1933, 20; Griffith 1935, 3-4; Adcock 1957, 20; Miller 1984; Marinovic 1988.

30. Arcadians and Achaeans made up more than half of the Ten Thousand: Xenophon, *Anabasis* 1.1.6; 6.2.10; cf. Roy 1967; 1999; Trundle 1999; Fields 2001.

31. Gelon: see p. 73 n. 38. Cyrus: see n. 30 above.

32. Herodotus 2.151-4 (Ionians); 5.44-5 (Dorieus). Mercenaries (or 'volunteers') turning settlers: e.g. Miltiades and followers in the mid-sixth century: Herodotus 6.34-6. Xenophon considered settling down with his Ten Thousand (*Anabasis* 5.6.15-7.6; 6.4.3-7); Isocrates recommended colonisation as the solution to the mercenary problem (5.122; 8.24), and the conquests of Alexander made it possible to do this on a large scale: e.g. Billows 1995, 146-82. Cf. Garlan 1989, 156-61 (esp. 160: 'mercenary service deserves to be treated as an aspect of the Greek colonisation movement'), 194-8.

33. On the likelihood that many early 'colonies' were effectively private enterprises, see Osborne 1998. Widespread international participation even in classical public colonising ventures: e.g. the 10,000 colonists from Athens and many allies who tried to settle at Amphipolis in 465 (Thucydides 1.100), and the similarly ambitious 'panhellenic' settlement at Thurii twenty years later (Diodorus 12.9-11).

Part II. Citizens and Soldiers

1. Thucydides 7.58.3 (Gylippus sole Spartiate, with *neodamodeis* and helots; cf. 6.91.4), 6.104.1 (two Spartan ships, i.e. 400 men; cf. 7.1.3, 5: armed), 7.19.3 (reinforcements). Cf. Hornblower 2000, 58.

2. Brasidas in 424 took 700 helots and 1,000 mercenaries to Northern Greece: Thucydides 4.80.5. Later expeditions: Xenophon, *Hellenica* 1.3.15 (Clearchus, 'some *perioikoi*, a few ex-helots', allies), 3.1.4-6 (Thibron, 1,000 ex-helots, 4,300 allies; cf. Diodorus 14.36.2, 37.1: joined by another 2,000 allies, 5,000 mercenaries), 3.4.2 (Agesilaus, 30 Spartiates, 2,000 ex-helots, 6,000 allies; takes over mercenaries as well), 5.2.24 (Eudamidas, 2,000 ex-helots and *perioikoi*), 5.3.8-9 (Agesipolis, 30 Spartiates, *perioikoi*, *trophimoi* foreigners, bastard sons). Xenophon's comment that people everywhere obey 'even a single Lacedaemonian' (*Anabasis* 6.6.12), and the fact that Thucydides could not take it for granted that the Spartans would send even a single Spartiate (6.91.4) show how common it was for Spartan forces to contain only one full citizen.

3. Thucydides 4.90.1, as explained by Hornblower 1996, ad loc.

4. Thucydides 4.94.1 with 4.93.3. According to Thucydides, in 431 BC 16,000 men were needed to guard the city walls and other fortifications, leaving 13,000 heavy infantry available to serve as a field army (2.13.6-7; 2.31.2); see Appendix 1. Between 430 and 426 4,400 men, or about 30%, of the field army died of the plague (3.87.3), and assuming a similar proportion of losses among the remainder of the troops, the total forces available would have been reduced to about 20,000. A levy of 7,000 heavy infantry thus left only 13,000 men, rather than the required 16,000, to defend the walls, and must have been the largest number Athens could spare. The total adult male citizen population of Athens at this time was probably about 60,000 (see again Appendix 1).

5. Thuc. 4.101.2; for further discussion of the role and status of baggage carriers see pp. 68-71.

6. Thuc. 2.31.3; 4.66.1 (431-425 BC); also 1.106.2 for a precedent (458 BC).

7. For the size of modern armies, see Townshend (ed.) 1997, 140 (by my calculation, the figures for 1977 amount to 1.5% of the population in the USSR, 1% in the USA, 0.8% in West Germany and 0.6% in the UK). First World War: ibid., 247.

8. Age range: e.g. Xenophon, *Hellenica* 6.4.17; pseudo-Aristotle, *Athenian Constitution* 53.4. Modern figures: Black 1994, 222; Best 1982, 86-91.

9. Thuc. 5.64.2-3: the oldest and youngest constituted 'a sixth part' of the levy, i.e. presumably seven of the 42 year groups, or those aged 18-19 and 55-59. The levy for the Battle of Leuctra in 371 also went up to 54 (Xenophon, *Hellenica* 6.4.17). Old warriors in poetry: Homer, *Iliad* 13.361, 484-5, 512-15; Tyrtaeus F 10.19-27 West.

10. See Appendix 1.

11. Herodotus 1.30. Other evidence for elderly soldiers: Hanson 1989, 89-95.

4. Men of bronze

1. True excellence: Tyrtaeus F 12 West (although it should be noted that his hoplites did not yet fight in the classical manner, see Chapter 12). Men of bronze: Herodotus 2.152; cf. 9.62 on the superiority of Greek armour. See further pp. 108, 192-5, and Pritchard 1998, 44-53.

2. This common idea has been argued most fully and eloquently by Victor Hanson (1995).

3. The modern view that hoplites formed a middle class relies heavily on a few passages in Aristotle's *Politics* which imply that the hoplites and the middle class were the same group, or overlapped (esp. 1297b16-28; see Hanson 1995, esp. 115-19; Prost 1999, 71-2, 86). These passages, however, are almost meaningless since for the purposes of his argument Aristotle resorts to a uselessly broad definition of 'middling' when it suits him, stretching the term to include everyone between 'extremely rich' and 'extremely poor' (1295b2-4); see further p. 60. Aristotle elsewhere pointedly does not identify the hoplites with the middle classes: in any community 'some are necessarily rich, some poor, and some middling, and the rich are hoplites while the poor are unequipped' (1289b30-2). See Hammer (forthcoming) for warnings against uncritical use of Aristotle's analyses of the 'middle'.

4. See Lazenby and Whitehead 1996, who effectively debunk the common notion that the heavy infantry was named after their shields (Diodoros 15.44.3), rather than after their 'equipment' at large. Note the expression 'those who provide/own the equipment' (*ta hopla*), which meant 'the hoplites'.

5. See Hanson 1991 for the shield and spear; also the surveys cited in n. 6.

6. Xenophon: *Anabasis* 1.2.15-16; 3.3.20. Syracuse: Diodorus 14.43.2-3 (all soldiers have shields and helmets; no mention of greaves). The best surveys of classical equipment are still Snodgrass 1999 (1967), 89-113, and Anderson 1970, 13-42; see also Hanson 1989, 57-60, for variation in armour.

7. Snodgrass 1999 (1967), 49-58, 90-8.

8. The best study of early Greek arms and armour remains Snodgrass's book of that name (1964); for belts, in literature and archaeology, see the (over-)imaginative study by Bennett (1997). On chariots and horses in early Greek warfare, see pp. 57-60, 158-60, 176-7.

9. See again Snodgrass 1964, and 1999 (1967), 35-47. Snodgrass's original late date for the introduction of greaves has had to be revised in the light of Kunze 1991; see Snodgrass 1993, 58-9; 1999 (1967), 137; van Wees 1994, 138-9 n. 78.

10. For the figures, see Jarva (1995, 111-12, 124-8), who counts *c*. 350 helmets and 280 shields, as compared to only about 225 greaves and a mere 33 cuirasses. Since a full set of armour includes two greaves but only a single spear, helmet, or cuirass, the number of captured greaves must be divided by two to be comparable to the numbers of other captured armour, i.e. it must be treated as the equivalent of about 112 pairs (as Jarva himself fails to bear in mind). Even if some types of armour are probably over- or under-represented in dedications, they offer a more reliable indication of proportions of actual use than representations in art do (so also Storch 1998, 3-5).

11. Additional armour: see Jarva 1995, 51-60, 72-84, 100-6; he suggests that some of these pieces go back to the seventh century, but the evidence for this is inconclusive. Development of types of cuirass: Anderson 1970, 20-3; Jarva 1995, 20-47; Snodgrass 1999 (1967), 90-2; the growing number of appearances in art of the non-metallic corslet may of course reflect greater artistic interest rather than more common use. Decline of Corinthian helmet: Anderson 1970, 28-9; Snodgrass 1999 (1967), 93-4.

12. Boardman 1983, 27-33; see also van Wees 2000a, 134-5. For the argument against the historicity of the Boeotian shield and for pairs of spears as merely an 'extraordinarily persistent theme' in art, see e.g. Snodgrass 1999 (1967), 55, 97.

13. Custom-made: Xenophon, *Memorabilia* 3.10.9-14. Shield-factory: Lysias 12.19. Sword-factory: Dem. 27.9. Retail sales: Aristophanes, *Peace* 1209-64 (although the characters are often designated as 'helmet-*maker*', etc., the dialogue makes it clear that they *buy* and sell military equipment).

14. The estimate of their cost is based on the figures of under two drachmas for a spear auctioned (and thus presumably relatively cheap) in 415, at a time when one dr./day was a standard wage for soldiers and skilled workers (Pritchett 1956, 253), and of three to four obols for spears and 20 dr. for a shield offered as a prizes (and thus presumably rather expensive) in a competition in the early third century (*IG* XII.5, 647, lines 27-31), when a rate of four obols/day is attested as a soldier's wage (Plutarch, *Moralia* 233c).

15. See Hanson 1995, 294-301; Jarva 1995, 148-54.

16. See Blythe 1977, summarised and confirmed by Jarva 1995, 141-3; also Franz 2002, 355-61.

17. Gilded armour: Xenophon *Memorabilia* 3.10.9-14. Crests and tunics: Aristophanes, *Acharnians* 1074, 1103-11; *Peace* 1172-8. Xenophon: *Anabasis* 3.2.7. Homer: *Iliad* 8.192-3; 18.613; 21.592.

18. Most famously, the *aigis* of Zeus (used as a kind of shield), but also the golden panoplies of Achilles (*Iliad* 19.14-15) and Athena (*Homeric Hymn* 28.5-16).

19. Quotations from Xenophon, *Spartan Constitution* 11.3; Aristotle F 542 Rose; Aelian, *Varia Historia* 6.6; also Plutarch, *Moralia* 238f – all referring to Spartan military dress, for which see further below. For the red tunic as a common part of military dress: Aristophanes, *Peace* 303.

20. On shield emblems, see Chase 1902 and Anderson 1970, 17-20. Emblems are known mainly from their appearances in art, but also from literary evidence: the Gorgon already features in Homer (*Iliad* 11.32-40); the anchor is mentioned in Herodotus (9.74); the fly and Eros are both mentioned by Plutarch, *Moralia* 234cd and *Alcibiades* 16.1-2. We can only make educated guesses at the meaning of most blazons (my interpretation of the meaning of the fly is based on Homer, *Iliad* 17.570-2, and differs from Plutarch's); for the principle that they express personal qualities, see references in n. 21.

21. Aeschylus, *Seven Against Thebes* 90-1, 385-648; Euripides, *Phoenician Women* 1099, 1107-38.

22. The vase is a late black-figure amphora in the British Museum (BM B173; see *CVA* 3, pl. 45, 1b). General trend in vase-painting: Anderson 1970, 17 (with references). Mantineia: Bacchylides F 21 (*c.* 480-450); Thebes: Xenophon, *Hellenica* 7.5.20. Initial letters: M(u) for Messenia (Photius, *Lexicon*, entry under *Lambda*); S(igma) for Sicyon (Xenophon, *Hellenica* 4.4.10); Ch(i) probably for the Chalcidian League (see Chase 1902, no. 151); L(ambda) for Lacedaemon (see below).

23. Xenophon, *Spartan Constitution* 11.3; see also Xenophon *Agesilaus* 2.7; Plutarch, *Agesilaus* 19.5; and references in n. 19 above. The idea that Spartans wore a red *cloak* as well as (or instead of) a red *tunic* is found in e.g. Cartledge 1977, 15 n. 38; Lazenby 1985, 32; Hanson 1989, 98, 186. Most ancient texts speak of the 'red garment' (*phoinikis*) without saying what it was, except Valerius Maximus, who calls it a *tunica* (2.6.2). The *phoinikides* worn by Persians in Xenophon (*Cyropaedia* 6.4.1) certainly, and those worn by Macedonians in Plutarch (*Aemilius Paullus* 18.7; cf. 18.5) almost certainly, are tunics (*chitones*). Cloaks worn over armour would have impeded movement and must have been removed before battle; if in action the *phoinikis* became stained with blood (Aelian, *VH* 6.6) or excrement (Aristophanes, *Peace* 1175-6) it must surely have been a tunic. Against this, only a late commentary on Aristophanes, *Acharnians* 320, suggests that the *phoinikis* is a cloak, and somehow this has become the standard dictionary definition. The confusion probably stems from the fact that Spartans were indeed famous for wearing a peculiar type of short and simple cloak, the *tribôn* (worn *without* a tunic in civilian life) – but there is no reason to think that this was red, or worn in combat.

24. Farmers: Xenophon, *Oeconomicus* 4.2-3; 5.5, 7, 14, 16; 6.6-7. Shepherds: Aristotle, *Politics* 1319a20-4. For detailed discussion of the questions addressed in this section, see van Wees 2001.

25. For the scattered but convincing textual, archaeological and comparative evidence, see Burford 1993, 67-72, 113-16; Gallant 1991, 82-7; Jameson 1978, esp. 125 n. 13.

26. Xenophon, *Oeconomicus* 4.2-3; 6.5-8. Craftsmen: Plutarch, *Agesilaus* 26.4-5 = *Moralia* 214a.

27. Help from friends: Lysias 16.14, cited p. 105 n. 13. Socrates' property: Xenophon, *Oeconomicus* 2.3. His hoplite service: Plato, *Symposium* 219e-220e; Plutarch, *Alcibiades* 7.2-3. A fictional Constitution of Draco assumes that large numbers of men who own less than 1,000 drachmas can serve as hoplites (*Athenian Constitution* 4.2), but perhaps this reflects the situation in the late fourth century, when Athens had started supplying shields and spears at public expense.

28. The political dimensions of the Athenian property-class system are set out in pseudo-Aristotle, *Athenian Constitution* 7.3; Aristotle, *Politics* 1274a16-22; Plutarch, *Solon* 18.1-2; Pollux 8.130. The only direct and reliable evidence for their military dimension is a passage in Thucydides which distinguishes categorically between hoplites mobilised 'from the list', on the one hand, and *thêtes*, on the other (6.43.1): the implication must be that only *thetes* were not 'listed', i.e. not under an obligation to serve (see pp. 103-4). Harpocration's *Lexicon*, in the entry under *thêtes kai thêtikon* (followed by *Etymologicum Magnum*, under *thêtikon*), based on Aristophanes' lost comedy *Banqueters* (F248 Kassel-Austin), goes further and claims that *thêtes* did not serve in the army at all, which, as we shall see, cannot be true. Presumably Harpocration misinterpreted a comic reference to the fact that *thêtes* were not *obliged* to serve. Rosivach 2002 argues that the property class had no military dimension at all, but fails to explain away Thucydides 6.43.1; see also Gabielsen 2002, 95-8.

29. Calculations: van Wees 2001; cf. the brief but important discussion in Foxhall 1997, 129-31, and the comments of Raaflaub 1999, 138, 150-1 n. 49.

30. For volunteering, see p. 100; for marines, see pp. 210-11.

31. An attempt at calculating the proportions may start from the fact that Athenian territory had room for no more than 10,000 farms of each 22 acres (9 ha), the zeugite minimum: see the further calculations in van Wees 2001. For the process of levying 'from the list', see pp. 103-4.

32. On this reform, see pp. 93-4. Property classes *must* have remained the basis for military service until this moment, since (a) hoplite service could not have been made a general obligation until and unless the poor were provided with funds – a fifth-century suggestion 'to make all the *thêtes* hoplites' (Antiphon F B6), which presumably aimed to extend compulsory service somehow, was evidently not acted upon – and (b) the only alternative would have been to abolish compulsory service altogether and rely entirely on volunteering from all classes, which is ruled out by the evidence that military service always continued to be obligatory for some (see pp. 99-100).

33. Mess contributions: Plutarch, *Lycurgus* 12.3, in Peloponnesian measures, translated into Attic measures by Dicaearchus *FHG* ii.242 (cited in Athenaeus 4.141c); see Foxhall and Forbes 1982, 48-9. (For the role of messes, see p. 97.)

Spartan citizen allotments, according to Plutarch, produced annually '70 measures of barley for a man and 12 measures for a woman, and a quantity of liquid produce in proportion' (*Lycurgus* 8.7). Assuming that this means 82 measures of barley for a married couple, and that Plutarch is again giving the figures in Peloponnesian measures, this would translate into 123 Attic measures of barley. The proportion of measures of barley to wine in the men's rations is 3:2, so the total proportion of liquid produce ought to have been 82 measures, giving a total of 205. These measures probably apply only to Hellenistic Sparta (so Hodkinson 2000, 126), but still give a good indication of the economic level associated with leisure-class hoplites. Estimates of the size of the average Spartiate citizen estate vary between *c*. 15-20 ha (Hodkinson 2000, 382-5), larger than those of Athenian *zeugitai* because they supported serf families as well.

34. Aristotle, *Politics* 1297a29-35. Aristotle does *not* say that the poor are excluded from the ownership of weapons, as H. Rackham mistranslates the text in the Loeb Classical Library series.

35. *Politics* 1297b2-6. Accordingly, he criticises Plato's *Republic* for failing to make clear whether the disenfranchised classes in this ideal state 'must own weapons and fight in war alongside [the elite], or not' (*Politics* 1264b34-7).

36. Price: *Anabasis* 7.8.6. Before battle: 1.8.15, 17. Trading places: 3.4.46-9. Xenophon does not give up his own horse even when the army is desperate to find horses for a cavalry troop: 3.3.19-20.

37. Price of 300 drachmas: Isaeus 5.43; other prices and costs: Spence 1993, 272-86.

38. Chariots in Homer: van Wees 1994, 9-13. Eretrian parade: Strabo 10.1.10; 'the horsemen': pseudo-Aristotle, *Athenian Constitution* 15.2. Archaic mounted hoplites in art: Greenhalgh 1973, 84-145. Another reference to sixth-century mounted hoplites is probably the story of Peisistratos 'making his sons mount horses' after battle in order to overtake the fleeing enemy (Herodotus 1.63). Scholars agree that mounted hoplites were prominent, but they are deeply sceptical about the use of *chariots* in achaic warfare; this scepticism is probably unfounded: see Chapters 11 and 12.

39. Herodotus 8.124. In a story about one of the *Agathoergoi*, set in the mid-sixth century, Herodotus (1.67) notes that these officials were selected from among ex-*Hippeis*, but that may simply reflect the situation in his own day, and does not prove their existence at this date.

40. For the *Hippeis* fighting on foot before or beside the king, see Thucydides 5.72.4; Xenophon *Hellenica* 6.4.14 (where *hippoi* must be a mistake for *hippeis*); Diodorus 15.32.1 (confusing *Hippeis* with the so-called Skiritai) and Strabo 10.4.18, both apparently drawing on the fourth-century historian Ephorus. Competitive selection: Xenophon, *Spartan Constitution* 4.1-6; cf. Plutarch, *Lycurgus* 25; *Moralia* 191f. Discussions: Anderson 1970, 245-9; Lazenby 1985, 10-12, 53-4.

41. The fact that Thucydides fails to mention its role in his account of the battle of Delium is no reason to deny the existence of the Charioteers and Chariot-fighters, as some scholars do.

42. Plutarch, *Pelopidas* 18.1-5, 19.3; *Moralia* 761b-d; Athenaeus 561f, 602a; Polyaenus 2.5.1. Discussion: DeVoto 1992. Scholarly scepticism about the original use of the Sacred Band as the front rank of the larger formation is unwarranted, see p. 187 n. 14.

43. Diodorus 11.30.4; Plutarch, *Aristides* 14.3-15.1; Pausanias 1.27.1.

44. Argos: Thucydides 5.67.2; 5.81.2; Diodorus 12.75.7 (first raised in 421/0); 12.79.4, 6; 12.80.2-3. Syracuse: Diodorus 11.76.2; Elis: Xenophon, *Hellenica* 7.4.13,

16, 31. It is important to distinguish between the permanent elite bodies discussed here, and troops picked *ad hoc* for a particular mission (such as the 300 Spartans at Thermopylae); see further Pritchett 1974, 222-4; Tritle 1989.

45. Pausanias 1.27.1. Tbe other sources (see n. 43) say nothing about the nature of the 300. Herodotus does, however, mention Athenian and Spartan 'horsemen' who carry messages (9.54, 60); neither side has cavalry, so these riders *might* be members of elite mounted infantry bands.

46. References: see n. 44. Elis' unit of 300, along with the Elean cavalry, in civil war fought on the side of the oligarchs against the democrats, which is proof enough of their economic and social status.

47. The speeches (Andocides 3.5; closely followed by Aeschines 2.173) do not say whether the 300 'horsemen' were regular cavalry or mounted hoplites. Their chronology is vague and confused: they clearly imagine that the 300 horsemen were instituted sometime *after* the Persian Wars and before 446 BC, yet they also date to this period the first fortification of Piraeus, which according to Thucydides (1.93.3) was begun well *before* the Persian Wars, in Themistocles' archonship, 493 BC. Scholars usually interpret the speeches as evidence for a regular cavalry unit established after the Persian Wars (see Bugh 1988, 39-40; Spence 1993, 9-15), but it is perfectly possible that they refer to the earlier establishment – in, say, the 480s – of the unit of mounted hoplites (and the unit of archers) alluded to by Herodotus. See further Chapter 12, pp. 176-7.

48. See pp. 80-2 for the political implications of this conclusion.

5. The other warriors

1. In the same way, Thucydides set out in detail his calculations of the size of Sparta's heavy infantry at Mantineia (see Appendix 2), but said nothing about the number or role in battle of the helots who, he knew, had been part of the general levy (5.64.2, 68.2-3). See also Hunt 1998; van Wees 1995b. For the role of hoplite *perioikoi* at Thermopylae, see pp. 83-4.

2. A bow and quiver worth 15 drachmas were offered as first prize and a javelin was sold at auction for 2 dr. 5 ob., on the occasions mentioned on p. 267 n. 14.

3. The evidence is catalogued in detail in Pritchett 1991, 1-67.

4. For the terminology, see e.g. Xenophon, *Hellenica* 2.4.12, where javelin-throwers who do not have shields count as 'light-armed' (*psiloi*) whereas those with light shields are *peltastai*.

5. See Thucydides on the invasion(s) of Megara, as cited immediately above, on the general levies at Delium, cited pp. 45-6, and on the (light-armed) helots in the general levy at Mantinea, n. 1 above. For earlier light-armed, see pp. 154-8 (Homer), 173-4 (Tyrtaeus).

6. Denied by e.g. Morrison et al. 2000, 115; Gabrielsen 2002, 86. For crews of warships, see Chapter 14.

7. Sphacteria: Thucydides 4.32.2; the passage gives no indication that this use of rowers was unusual. Formal arming of rowers: in 412, 500 rowers from a Spartan fleet of five ships (Thucydides 8.15, 17.1); in 409, 5,000 rowers from an Athenian fleet of 50 ships (Xenophon, *Hellenica* 1.2.2).

8. For their presence on Cythera (4.56.2), I can see no other explanation. In the attack on Spartolus, it is possible that the 'Athenian' light-armed were the 'allies from Krousis' mentioned immediately afterwards (so Gabrielsen 2002, 86 n. 11), but it seems to me that the text makes better sense if the light-armed from Krousis were in fact allies of Spartolus and the Chalcidians (2.79.1, 3-5). In the expedition

against Syracuse, all the allusions to 'light-armed' on Athens' side (6.52.2, 64.1, 69.2, 100) *may* refer to the 480 archers, 700 Rhodian slingers, and 120 *psiloi* from Megara explicitly mentioned (6.43), but more probably include also the thousands of rowers present, since they are evenly matched against the general levy of the Syracusans (6.69.2), which must have included many thousands of light-armed.

9. Aetolia: Thucydides 3.97-98. Sphacteria: Thucydides 4.32-38. Civil war: Xenophon, *Hellenica* 2.4.2-19, 25; for Aristotle, see also p. 78. Mercenary peltasts: Xenophon, *Hellenica* 4.4.17, 4.5.11-17. On the tactics and successes of light-armed, see Best 1969; Anderson 1970, 111-38.

10. See Appendix 1.

11. Spartan contempt for 'spindles': Thucydides 4.40.2; cf. Herodotus 7.226.2. Also Euripides, *Madness of Heracles* 157-63 (coward's weapon); Aeschylus, *Persians* 237-8 (barbarian weapon).

12. Commanders trying to ensure that their horsemen are 'beautifully equipped': Xenophon, *The Cavalry Commander* 1.22-3. For details of equipment, Spence 1993, 49-56, 60-5.

13. *Anabasis* 3.1.2. See further Thucydides; 2.79, 4.42-44, 5.10.9-10 (cavalry and light-armed defeat hoplites, presumably by attack on flank). In detail, see Spence 1993, 56-60 (mounted archers, *hamippoi*), 121-63 (role in battle).

14. Spence 1993, 40-9 (practical difficulties), 97-102 (numbers); cf. Greenhalgh 1973, 79-81.

15. For the iconography, see Greenhalgh 1973, 84-136 (esp. 98-100, with important comment on vase shown here in Plate VII), and Bugh 1988, 14-20. Athens' early cavalry force, organised by the districts called *naukrariai* (on which see pp. 96, 203-4): Bugh 1988, 4-6; Spence 1993, 9-11.

16. Main evidence: Herodotus 5.63 (Thessalian cavalry, 510 BC), 7.154 (Gela, *c.* 490 BC), 7.158 (Syracuse, 481 BC), 9.68-9 (Boeotian cavalry, 479 BC).

17. Bugh 1988, 3-78; Spence 1993, 9-17. Both assume that the 300 *hippeis* mentioned by Andocides and Aeschines were a first expansion of the cavalry force soon after the Persian Wars, rather than an elite unit of mounted hoplites created just before the Persian Wars, as I have suggested on pp. 59-60.

18. Sparta: Thucydides 4.55.2. None of the Peloponnesian states provided cavalry at Plataea in 479 (Herodotus 9.29-30) or for the invasion of Attica in 431 (Thucydides 2.9.3). Corinth still did not have cavalry in 425: Thucydides 4.42-4, with Spence 1993, 5; and ibid. 1-33 for the evidence generally.

19. Lysias 14.7; 16.13; see Spence 1993, 165-79 (views on cavalry tactics).

20. Hoplite ideal: see pp. 47, 192-5. In Athens, the cavalry was also suspect as a potentially anti-democratic force: see Spence 1991, 180-229, on attitudes towards cavalry.

21. Terms for 'attendants' include *hypêretai, therapontes, opaones*. Discussions of the nature and role of attendants: Sargent 1927; Anderson 1970, 29-30, 46; Pritchett 1971, 49-51; Hunt 1998, 55, 167-8.

22. The evidence for the hoplites' attendants, therefore, should not be used to argue that everyone who owned a hoplite panoply also owned a slave. Assessments of how far down the social scale slaves were owned in Athens vary widely, see e.g. Fisher 1993, 37-47, for a summary of the arguments.

23. Isaeus 5.11. Attendants in vase-paintings: Anderson 1970, 275 n. 88; also e.g. *CVA* Brussels, Musées Royaux 1, III.1.c, pl. 7.1b; III.1.d, pls 1.1a; *CVA* Syracuse III.1, pls 5.1, 9.1, 13.2, 17.2, 20-21. Helot attendants: Herodotus 7.229;

Thucydides 4.19. Slave attendants in Athens: Aristophanes, *Acharnians* 1099-1101, 1136-7; Demosthenes 54.4; Theophrastus, *Characters* 27 (25) 4.

24. For the images in art, see n. 23; for scholarly scepticism, see references in n. 21.

25. See Hunt 1998, esp, 102-15, on the reluctance of Greek states to encourage the enemy's slaves to desert, let alone promise them freedom.

26. See van Wees 1986, 288-90; 1992, 333-4 n. 61, and here, pp. 95-6.

27. For mounted hoplites and attendants in art, see Greenhalgh 1973, 84-145. Spartan youths carrying corpses: Lazenby 1985, pl. 6. Homosexual relationships in warfare: p. 195.

28. See further pp. 233-5.

29. Ethnicities: 2.840-77; 10.428-31. Languages: 2.803-4, 4.437-8. Separate unit: 12.101-2. Separate camp: 10.420-35. Far from home, nothing at stake: e.g. 5.472-92; 10.420-2; 16.538-40; 17.144-55.

30. *Anabasis* 1.1.10-11 (*xeinoi*); 7.2.38 (marriage). Other marriages: Parke 1933, 56, 132. Lavelle 1997, however, argues that the high status of Troy's *epikouroi* clearly separates them from mercenaries

31. See pp. 13-15.

32. See pp. 96-7 for personal ties, and p. 100 for the use of volunteers.

33. Typical *epikouroi*: Archilochus F 216. Saying: scholiast on Plato, *Laches* 187b. Greeks also served together with Carians as *epikouroi* abroad, but this circumstance cannot explain why they thought it was typical of Carians, rather than themselves, to serve others in war. Invention of hoplite shield (and helmet crests): Herodotus 1.171.4; Strabo 14.2.27-8; cf. Lavelle 1997, 247-50; Bettali 1995, 109-11.

34. So e.g. Herodotus 1.61.4 (on which see p. 73); Thucydides 1.60; 2.96.2; 4.80.5.

35. *SEG* 37 (1987) 994; cf. Bettali 1995, 69-70.

36. Aristotle (*Politics* 1311a7-8) says that tyrants' bodyguards were foreign mercenaries, a claim widely accepted by modern scholars; yet Hippocrates of Gela's guard, for one, may have included members of prominent local families (Herodotus 7.154); cf. Bettali 1995, 92-3; Luraghi 1994, 177.

37. *Athenian Constitution* 17.4, 19.4: they were led by Hegesistratos, Peisistratos' son by an Argive woman; cf. the troops sent to Kylon's by his father-in-law (Thucydides 1.126.5); Bettali 1995, 87-92.

38. Victory ode: Pindar, *Olympian* 6 (Agesias). Monuments at Olympia: Pausanias 5.27.1-7 (Phormides); *IG* V.2, 47 (Praxiteles). Another Olympic victor associated with Gelon was Astilos of Croton: see Bettali 1995, 92-9; Luraghi 1994, 291-4; Parke 1933, 10-13. Grants of land and citizenship: esp. Diodorus 11.62.3 (10,000 mercenaries made citizen by Gelon).

39. Herodotus 5.70.1 (Cleomenes as *xeinos*; that his army is a private force is suggested by its small size [72.1] and the fact that Herodotus pointedly excludes it from his list of Dorian and Peloponnesian invasions of Attica [76]). Cf. the band of Athenian volunteers led by Miltiades who join a Thracian tribe in their fight against the Apsinthians: Herodotus 6.36.

40. So e.g. Parke 1933, 7; Adcock 1957, 20; Baker 1999, 240.

41. Peisistratus: Herodotus 1.61, 1.64, 5.94; *Athenian Constitution* 15.2, 17.4. We are not explicitly told what kind of troops fought the latter campaigns, but it seems obvious (contra Parke 1933, 9) that *epikouroi* must have played a major part (perhaps Hegesistratus, who became ruler of Sigeum, brought his Argive troops: see n. 37 above). Polycrates: Herodotus 3.45, 54, 145-6.

42. See p. 45; cf. pp. 83-5.

43. Thucydides 3.97.2 (Acarnania); 4.28.4, 32.2 (Sphacteria); 4.129.2 (Northern Greece); 6.43 (Sicily); 7.27.1-2 (latecomers).

44. For the pattern of development, see pp. 95-100 and 233-5. For the sociology of classical mercenary service, see Dalby 1992; Nussbaum 1967.

45. *Anabasis* 1.3.21 (pay negotiations), 7.1.33-41 (Coeratidas; cf. Xenophon, *Hellenica* 1.3.15 and Diodorus 13.66.5 on Coeratidas' earlier career as commander of a mercenary garrison).

46. Substitution: Xenophon, *Hellenica* 5.2.21. For Athens' peltasts, see Parke 1933, 48-55; Best 1968, 85-97. For Spartan imperialism, see Andrewes 1978; Cartledge 1987, 77-98; Hodkinson 1993.

47. Surveys of fourth-century use of mercenaries: Parke 1933; Burckhardt 1996. The rising use of mercenaries is clearly led by demand rather than supply, see pp. 41-2.

48. Isocrates, *Letter* 9.8-10 (356 BC) and *To Philip* (5), 96, 120-1 (of 346 BC); cf. 8.46; Demosthenes 23.139. Note that the worst mercenary crises occurred when great imperial powers, rather than Greek city-states, sacked thousands of mercenaries: Isocrates' first complaint was probably sparked off by the simultaneous discharge of 10,000 mercenaries by the Persian king Artaxerxes' Ochus in *c.* 360 BC (scholion on Demosthenes 4.19; see Parke 1933, 122). The 8,000 mercenaries 'hanging around at Cape Taenarum' in the late 320s had been sacked *en masse* by Alexander the Great (Diodorus 17.111.1-3; 18.9.1-3, 21.1) and were thus not at all typical of the normal level of mercenary unemployment.

49. *Cavalry Commander* 9.3-4; see also pp. 192-3 on courage in citizens and mercenaries.

50. Olynthus: Philochorus *FGrH* 328 F 49-51; Demosthenes himself later claimed that 10,000 mercenaries and 4,000 citizens had been sent (19.266). Euboea: main source Plutarch, *Phocion* 12-13; cf. Burckhardt 1996, 121-3. Large campaigns: p. 222. Generally, at time when these complaints were made, citizen levies to man the fleet were very common: p. 218.

51. Thermopylae: Diodorus 16.37.3; cf. Burckhardt 1996, 119-20. Chaeroneia: Burckhardt 1996, 129-30. Lamian War: Athens provided 5,000 citizen hoplites and 300 cavalry, plus 2,000 mercenaries (Diod 18.10.2-3, 11.3); the Aetolians provided 7,000 citizens (Diod 18.10.5, 11.1-2); the total number of citizen troops may have been 30,000 (Justin 13.5). Hellenistic citizen militias: see Ma 2000.

6. Politics and the battlefield

1. Note that the phrase need not mean *all* those who own hoplite panoplies: see p. 81.

2. E.g. *Politics* 1297b2-6, 1320b22-30, and see pp. 55-7 and 80-3.

3. *Politics* 1297b16-22; cf. 1289b35-40. He adds as a secondary explanation that in the old days the numbers of hoplites were small, 'so that even when hoplites did fight in formation, they were more inclined to put up with being ruled' (1297b23-8).

4. For mounted hoplites, see pp. 58-60 and 176-7. On Aristotle on war and politics, see further van Wees 2002b, 72-7, and 1995a, 154-6; cf. Lintott 1992 on Aristotle and democracy.

5. The most influential and sophisticated version of this argument is presented by Victor Hanson (1995); see also Cartledge 1996; Detienne 1968, 120; Forrest 1966, 94-7; Andrewes 1956, 34-8; Nilsson 1929a, 2; 1929b, 247. Contra: Raaflaub 1997; 1996, 150-2; Salmon 1977, 84-101; Snodgrass 1965, 110-22.

6. Strauss 1996; Murray 1993, 142; Jordan 1974, 221; Finley 1963, 74. Contra: Ceccarelli 1993; Welwei 1974, 4-6; Forrest 1966, 216.

7. Parke 1933, 20 ('at once a symptom and a secondary cause of the downfall of the city-state'), 153-4. See also Finley 1963, 87-93; Marinovic 1988; Runciman 1998.

8. For power relations in Homeric society, see van Wees 1992, 31-6.

9. Archilochus F 114 West. For criticisms of chiefs, see van Wees 1999b, 2-10; 1992, 78-89. For roles of chiefs and masses in Homeric battles, see pp. 154-8, and van Wees 1995b, 165-9; 1988.

10. See pp. 55-7 and 268 n. 28, on the obligation to serve.

11. As suggested on p. 100.

12. So Lysias 20.13; cf. van Wees 2001, 56-9. In my view, Athens had 24,700 hoplites and cavalry in 431 BC (see Appendix 1): from this figures one needs to deduct about one-third to account for losses in the plague, and about 4,000 hoplites lost in the Sicilian expedition, as Hansen has shown (1988, 20-8: other losses would have been compensated by population growth), leaving *c*. 12,500.

13. Informal lower-class access to office: *Athenian Constitution* 47.1. The regime of 3,000 ('those most able to serve with horses and shields', Xenophon, *Hellenica* 2.3.48) instituted after the next oligarchic coup in 404/3, however, was denounced as too restricted: ibid. 2.3.19, and *Athenian Constitution* 36.2.

14. It is not clear whether he means to exclude the poorer hoplites where the hoplites amount to a majority of the total citizen population (a situation which was rare, but had recently been created at Athens as a result of the reform of the *ephebeia*), or to exclude just under half of the hoplite population, regardless of their proportion of the citizen population, along the lines of the constitutions of Solon and the 5,000.

15. Note the hoplite service performed by Athenian metics: Whitehead 1977, 82-6.

16. See Chapters 11, 12 and 13.

17. So e.g. Page in the Oxford Classical Texts edition of the play.

18. In Aeschylus, they occur after the battle; the hoplites are evidently the marines 'jumping out of their ships'; and it is the sight of this massacre which leads Xerxes to order the retreat. In other accounts, the hoplites are a separate force commanded by Aristides, the massacre takes place during the battle (Herodotus 8.95) or even beforehand (Plutarch, *Aristides* 9.1-2 with *Themistocles* 13.2-5), and the whole affair is little more than a side-show. See also Prost 1999, 75-6.

19. Strauss 2000b, 320-3, interestingly suggests that Cimon's decision to modify old triremes and carry large numbers of soldiers on deck for the campaign which included the battle of Eurymedon, *c*. 467 BC (Plutarch *Cimon* 12.2) was a political choice, designed to transfer credit for success as much as possible to hoplites: 'an attempt to reverse the Themistoclean revolution at sea' (323). More probably, however, this was simply an attempt to combine as large as possible a trireme fleet with as large as possible an invasion army: see pp. 221-2.

20. Also *Acharnians* 181, 694-8 (Marathon soldiers), 677 ('sea-battles we fought'); *Knights* 567-8 (land- and sea-victories of 'our forefathers'), 781-5 (Marathon, Salamis as achievements of 'the people'), 1325-34 ('the people' restored to their prime, at Marathon), *Clouds* 985-6 (Marathon soldiers), *Wasps* 1077-1100 (hoplite battles against Persians, naval campaigns to take cities from Persians and raise tribute). Note also Herodotus' view that the battle of Salamis was the decisive event of the Persian Wars (7.139).

21. *The Athenian Constitution* 1.2 (cf. Plutarch, *Themistocles* 19.4; *Aristides*

22.1). The date of this work is uncertain: see Hornblower 2000b, who suggests a fourth-century date.

22. Cf. Plato, *Laws* 707c; Plutarch, *Themistocles* 19.4.

23. See pp. 210-13.

24. So e.g. Cartledge 1987, 37-43; Hodkinson 2000, 420-2; cf. Mertens 2002, 288, 292-3, 295.

25. Herodotus (7.202) gives 300 Spartiates and 2,800 other Peloponnesians, but the epitaph quoted at 7.228 gives 4,000 men from the Peloponnese; cf. 8.25 for the corpses of helots (and p. 61). The 1,000 Lacedaemonians are twice mentioned in flattering terms by Isocrates 4.90 (cf. 92), 6.99-100 (*c.* 380 and *c.* 366 BC), and by Diodorus 11.4.2, 5. It is most unlikely that later historians invented a contingent of heroic *perioikoi* simply in order to make the numbers add up.

26. So Herodotus 9.28; also 49 ('Lacedaemonians only' stationed at spring), 54 (Lacedaemonians, Tegeans isolated), 61 (50,000 Lacedaemonians, including light-armed, still isolated). The (only) evidence that *perioikoi* and Spartans fought in separate units during the Persian Wars is Herodotus' reference to a 'Spartiate formation' within the body of Lacedaemonian troops at Plataea (9.29.1; cf. 28.2). Separate mobilisation of Spartiates and *perioikoi* (Herodotus 9.10.1, 11.3) remains a feature of later, fully integrated armies (Thucydides 4.8.1; Xenophon, *Hellenica* 3.5.7, 5.1.33).

27. See esp. Cartledge 1987, 37-43, and n. 24 above. Thucydides and Xenophon clearly show that the Lacedaemonian army included both citizens and *perioikoi* (see esp. n. 29 below), yet their descriptions of the Spartan army (see pp. 98-9 and Appendix 2) mention no separate perioikic units.

28. Herodotus 9.11.3 (picked troops, *logades*). The 5,000 Spartans levied correspond to nearly two-thirds (62.5%) of the total number of 8,000 Spartiates at the time (7.234.2); a levy of two-thirds was normal at the time of the Peloponnesian War (Thucydides 2.10, 47.1).

29. Sphacteria: Thucydides 4.38.5 (120 Spartiates among 292 Lacedaemonian prisoners = 41%, but see below on Leuctra). At Leuctra, Xenophon (*Hellenica* 6.4.15) tells us that there were 400 Spartiate casualties among 1,000 Lacedaemonian dead, i.e. 40%, but he also says that 700 Spartiates had been present, when the total force probably consisted of 2,300 men, so that they amounted to 31%. If the Spartans lived up to their reputation, it would not be surprising if they were overrepresented among the casualties – and if so, it is possible that they were correspondingly underrepresented among the survivors at Sphacteria, and may have originally constituted as much as half of the force there.

30. Xenophon, *Hellenica* 3.3.6. Revolts: ibid. 6.5.32, 7.2.2, and Thucydides 1.101.2.

31. Nothing new: by contrast, Thucydides points out that the creation of forces of cavalry and archers in the same year *was* an innovation (4.55.2). Ex-helots at Lepreon: at 5.31.1-5 and 5.49.1 Thucydides relates how the Spartans sent 1,000 hoplites to Lepreon during an Olympic truce in either 428 or 424, and at 5.34.1 the hoplites at Lepreon turn out to be *neodamôdeis*; they are joined by Brasidas' newly liberated helots. Surely the ex-helots settled at Lepreon had proven their loyalty in hoplite service already and could thus be trusted to garrison the town, rather than being specially-created new hoplites.

32. The story is undated but 'the wars' in question might have been the series of conflicts within the Peloponnese fought by Sparta in the 470s (so Hamilton 1987). The view that *neodamôdeis* were created only after 424 (Andrewes 1978) rests on the notion that Brasidas would have taken ex-helots, not helots, if any had been available. But Thucydides explicitly says that the Spartans were keen to get rid of a few hundred helots as potential troublemakers (4.80.5), so they would not have sent ex-helots of proven loyalty even if they had been available.

33. We simply have no information on the composition of the forces sent out by Sparta on the few overseas campaigns which it undertook before 424 BC, such as the Samian expedition of 525 or the series of small trireme fleets launched in 480-478 BC. It seems likely enough that the latter, at least, were manned by at most a dozen Spartiates and *periokoi* and up to 200 helots or mercenary rowers per ship, as in the fourth century: see pp. 212-13.

34. As many modern scholars do tacitly, and e.g. Berent 2000, 273-6, does explicitly.

7. Bodies of men

1. So Pritchett 1974, 208, in his useful compilation of material on training (208-31).

2. As is confirmed by the passages from Xenophon quoted pp. 87-8 and p. 94.

3. For evidence and discussion, see Wheeler 1982, 1983; and see pp. 227-8.

4. Recommended by Plato, *Laws* 814d-816b; see further Ceccarelli 1998; Rawlings 2000, 248-9.

5. See especially Xenophon, *On Hunting*; and further Anderson 1985, 17-29; Barringer 2001, 10-69.

6. See van Wees 1996, and briefly here, pp. 160-1.

7. See [Xenophon] *Athenian Constitution* 2.10, with discussion in Fisher 1998, 86-94. The Thebans' enthusiasm for wrestling was regarded as a factor in their military success: Plutarch, *Moralia* 639f-640a; Diodorus 15.50.5; cf. 17.11.4; Pritchett 1985, 64-5.

8. For a critical analysis of the evidence for Spartan education, especially Xenophon's *Spartan Constitution* 2-3 and Plutarch's *Lycurgus* 16-18, see Kennell 1995.

9. Xenophon, *Spartan Constitution* 12.5 (running track); *Hellenica* 4.8.18 (discus).

10. Dismissal of athletics: Tyrtaeus F 12 West; Xenophanes F 2; Euripides F 282 Nauck[2]. Debate on athletics and war: Mann 2002 and 1998; Golden 1998, 23-28; Pleket 1998; Poliakoff 1987, 93-103.

11. For the (implicit) distinction see van Wees 1997, 15-16.

12. Vidal-Naquet 1986, 106-56, and already Jeanmaire 1939; cf. Ogden 1996, 128-31; Ma 1994, 49-57.

13. Crete: Ephorus *FGrH* 70 F 149, 21 (= Strabo 10.4.21). Sparta: Plato, *Laws* 633bc, with the scholion on this passage; Aristotle F 538 Rose; Plutarch, *Lycurgus* 28.2-5, 7; Justin 3.3.6-7; P. BM clxxxvii; discussions in Lévy 1988; Meier 1998, 151-83. Kennell 1995, 71, suggests that the term 'fox time', which occurs in Hesychius, under the entry *phouaxir*, was a later name for the *krypteia*.

14. For discussions of the *ephebeia*, see e.g. Burckhardt 1996, 26-75; Vidal-Naquet 1986, 106-56; Ma 1994, 49-57. For the ephebes' rosters and their demographic signifcance, see e.g. Hansen 1988.

15. See van Wees 1995a, 166-74; contra the widespread view that Homeric war bands were feasting groups, whether hierarchical (e.g. Qviller 1981, 116-17, 124-5; 1995; Welwei 1992, 487-8; Whitley 1991, 348-52; Raaflaub 1991, 235-6; Ulf 1990, 131-3) or egalitarian (Murray 1993, 47; 1983a, 196-8; 1983b, 259-62; Andreev

1988, 46-59), and contra the less common view that they were age-classes (Bremmer 1982, 142-3; Jeanmaire 1939, 85-111).

16. Five attack columns: 12.86-7; 16.155-220. For this reconstruction of Homeric military organisation, see van Wees 1986; 1997a, 669-73, and further Donlan 1980, 1994, especially for the parallels with 'chieftains'. See below for the role of 'tribes' in Homer.

17. The remark quoted is somewhat obscure, but seems to me to make sense only as an allusion to the penalty for desertion, rather than (as it is usually taken) a suggestion that those who worry too much about their property should give it away.

18. Potsherd: ostrakon Agora P16873, as explained by Figueira 1986; see further pp. 203-5. Contra Frost 1984, who argues that archaic Athens had no central or formal military organisation.

19. Property classes: see pp. 55-7. Obligation to equip oneself: see *IG* I³.1 (ML 14; Fornara 44b). Volunteers for overseas expeditions: e.g., Solon occupied Salamis with 500 volunteers (Plutarch, *Solon* 8-9). See further Frost 1984.

20. Cimon's friends, see p. 100. Private warships, see pp. 203-6.

21. Departure scenes: Wrede 1916, with figs 2-7, 10-11, and plates 15-34 (chariot groups); Lissarrague 1990, 35-53, with figs 8-22 ('family' groups); see further pp. 196, 233-5.

22. Tyrtaeus F 19.8 West. I was sceptical of the value of this passage in van Wees 1986, 301 n. 74, but recanted in van Wees 1997a, 691-2 n. 28; the supposed evidence for a subdivision of the army into phratries (Athenaeus 4.141ef; see e.g. Forrest 1968, 44-5) still seems to too tenuous to be accepted.

23. Aristotle said that the Spartan army had once consisted of 5 *lochoi* (*Spartan Constitution* F 541 Rose; see Anderson 1970, 237-9); the army of Argos still did in the late fifth century (Thuc. 5.59.5, 72.4). The single *lochos* named by Herodotus (see below), however, does not correspond to Aristotle's *lochoi*, which may therefore represent an earlier form of the Spartan army, unless either Aristotle's or Herodotus' information was simply inaccurate (or imprecise: Cartledge 1987, 428-31).

24. The references in Alcman, *c.* 600 BC, to Spartan dining customs (esp. F17) are incompatible with the egalitarian and austere *syssitia* known from the classical period (Hodkinson 1997, 90-1; van Wees 1999a, 2-3); and the same is true of representations of drinking, *symposia*, and *komoi* throughout Laconian vasepainting (i.e. at least until *c.* 540 BC; see Powell 1998, 128-38); cf. Nafissi 1991, 206-24). On the sixth-century Spartan military developments, see Finley 1981, 24-40, and Trundle 2001. Cretan cities, like Sparta, had mess-groups (see e.g. Link 1994, esp. 9-29), but we know nothing else about Cretan military organisation.

25. For the organisation of *syssitia*, see esp. Hodkinson 2000, 216-18, 356-8; Singor 1999.

26. Thucydides gives the size of the unit as on average 4 x 8 = 32 men in 418, when one-sixth of the levy remained at home (5.68.3; cf. 64.3); Xenophon gives the size as at most 3 x 12 = 36 men in 371, when the oldest one-eighth of soldiers had been left behind (*Hellenica* 6.4.12 and 17). What in modern usage is called the 'Spartan' hoplite army was in antiquity more commonly called the 'Lacedaemonian' army, which points the important fact that it included a large proportion of non-Spartiate hoplites recruited from other towns in Lacedaimon, Sparta's so-called *perioikoi*: see above, pp. 45, 83-4.

27. This is part of the oath sworn at Plataea (Tod II, 204, lines 25-8): see Appendix 2.

28. See further pp. 90-2 on training, and pp. 185-7 on combat.

29. For instance, *lochos* is applied to the largest units within armies, consisting of more than 1,000 men, by Aristotle and Thucydides (see n. 23), but to the smallest units of the (idealised) Persian army, consisting of 100 men, by Xenophon (*Education of Cyrus* 6.3.21). Cf. Anderson 1970, 97.

30. The existence of *taxiarchoi* is confirmed by the oath cited above (n. 27). Thucydides (1.20.3) denied the existence of the Pitanate *lochos*, but that need mean only that it no longer existed in his day.

31. Thucydides 5.68.3. See Appendix 2 for the numbers of *lochoi* and men.

32. For the evidence, see Appendix 2.

33. For the evidence, see Appendix 2.

34. This scenario is explained and defended in more detail in Appendix 2. Alternatively, one could argue that our sources are unreliable and cannot be reconciled, but Herodotus evidently got his information from Sparta itself, where he visited the town of Pitana; Thucydides claimed to know enough about Sparta to do the sums while admitting that he did not have sufficiently reliable information to even guess at the size of the other contingents; and Xenophon had close and enduring Spartan connections.

35. On shortage of manpower, see pp. 83-5 and Appendix 2.

36. Apart from the figures in Thucydides and Xenophon, we have those of the fourth-century historians Ephorus who claimed that there were 500 men in a mora (presumably in the context given by Diodorus, who refers to five *morai* of 500 men taking the field in 377 (15.32.1)) and Callisthenes who claimed that there were 700 (Plutarch, *Pelopidas* 17.2). From much later sources, we also have a figures of 900 (Polybius, as cited by Plutarch, ibid.) and '500 or 1,000' (Photius, s.v. *mora*).

37. The main texts for classical Athens' military organisation are *Athenian Constitution* 21.1-22.2 and 61.1-3. The latter passage refers to the system as it existed in the late fourth century, when it was surely no longer exactly the same as in Cleisthenes' day. See further Fornara 1971, 1-39; Hamel 1998, 59-99; and, for military magistrates in general, Fröhlich 1999.

38. Trials for *astrateia* and *lipotaxia* judged by army: Lysias 14.5; 15.1; Plato, *Laws* 943a. Penalty of disenfranchisement: Andocides 1.74 (without loss of property); Lysias 14.9; Aeschines 1.29; 3.175-6; [Demosthenes] 59.27. Additional penalties: Aristophanes, *Knights* 443 (fine); Lysias 14.9 (confiscation and fines); cf. Plato, *Laws* 943b. See also pp. 108-12, 193-4.

39. For instance Tolmides' own invasion of Boeotia in 447 (Plutarch, *Pericles* 18.2; cf. Thucydides 1.113), for which he appears to have been allocated no Athenian hoplites, but only allied troops.

40. For military pay and new political rights, see also pp. 81, 237.

41. Aristotle, *Athenian Constitution* 61.1-3; see also Aristophanes, *Acharnians* 575 (cf. Plutarch, *Moralia* 186f); Xenophon, *Memorabilia* 3.1.5, 3.4.1. (In Xenophon, *Hellenica* 1.2.3, we cannot be sure that the *lochoi* in question are subdivisions of the tribes.)

42. The same was true of Athenian cavalry organisation: three cavalry commanders (*hipparchoi*), subordinate to the hoplite generals, were in charge of the whole force, which was divided into ten tribal troops of up to 100 horsemen (Aristotle, *Athenian Constitution* 61.4-6).

43. See pp. 109-12 for Athenian (in)discipline, and p. 195 and Appendix 2 for the ephebic oath promising loyalty to comrades: this oath may have been introduced only in the fourth century.

44. Demosthenes 21.103; Aeschines 1.172, 2.148. In the speeches *Against*

Alcibiades, the speaker stresses that his prosecution for draft-evasion and desertion is motivated by personal enmity (Lysias 14.2, 15.12).

8. The bare necessities

1. Pandion was the hero of Aristophanes' own tribe, and his statue was where
Aristophanes would have seen his own name posted, so perhaps he spoke from
experience (Olson 1998, ad 1181-4).

2. Demosthenes, *On the Crown* 169 (also Diodorus 16.84.3), as explained by
Usher 1993, ad loc.

3. *Iliad*: 18.207-13 (fire beacons), 219-20 (trumpet). For trumpets, see also
Bacchylides F 18.1-10; Plutarch, *Cimon* 16.5-6 (in Sparta); with Krentz 1991,
113-14. Messengers: Andocides 1.45.

4. Gathering in demes: Lysias 16.14; Isaeus 2.42; see Whitehead 1986, 224-6;
Osborne 1985, 82-3; van Effenterre 1976. Cf. the earlier 'general levy from the
countryside', led by the 'chiefs' of the *naukraroi* (see pp. 26 and 203-4). In
Sparta, *perioikoi* gathered in their towns before joining the Spartiate forces:
see p. 84 n. 26.

5. Lysias 3.35; Theophrastus, *Characters* 27 (25).

6. Aristophanes, *Peace* 1180-6; also *Knights* 1369-72 (changes 'from partisan
motives'); Lysias 9.4, 13-15, 20 (soldier selected before his turn because of personal
enmity); Lysias 15.6 (retrospective approval of transfer to cavalry 'as a favour').
See Christ 2001; Hamel 1998, 23-8.

7. Pseudo-Aristotle, *Athenian Constitution* 53.4, 7 explains the system of year-
classes, which is first mentioned, along with service by 'sections', by Aeschines
(2.167-8) as the normal form of mobilisation from *c.* 370 to *c.* 350. The last known
mobilisation by 'listing' occurred in 362, when it was, exceptionally, applied to a
naval levy (Demosthenes 50.6, 16); the latest references, around 350, refer to it
only as a possible means of mobilisation (Demosthenes 39.8; Plato, *Laws* 943a).
The interpretation of 'by sections' as merely another way of saying 'by listing (in
turn)' (Andrewes 1981, 1-2) cannot stand, because Plato, in the passage cited,
explicitly draws a contrast between being 'listed' and serving 'in a section'. That
'sections' are parts of armies seems likely from the fact that selection by unit is the
only other attested form of mobilisation (first found in an expedition to Megara in
446 BC, which involved only three of the tribal regiments: *IG* I^2 1085 = ML 51 =
Fornara 101), and confirmed by the terminology applied to Spartan armies (see
below).

8. Leuctra: Xenophon, *Hellenica* 6.4.17 (and 6.1.1). Two-thirds: Thucydides
2.10; 2.47.2; 3.15.1. Age restrictions: Thucydides 5.64.3; Xenophon, *Spartan Constitution* 11.2.

9. Aristophanes, *Peace* 1181-4 (cited p. 102), 312 (standard three-day ration; cf.
Acharnians 197; *Wasps* 243; cf. Pritchett 1971, 32-3); also Aristotle, *Rhetoric* 1411a
('come with your own provisions, as in the decree of Miltiades'). *Opsa*: Xenophon,
Education of Cyrus 6.2.30; Aristophanes, *Acharnians* 1099, 110; *Peace* 563. Bags
of flour, jars (or sacks) of wine and water, and *opsa* as travel rations appear in
Homer, *Odyssey* 2.349-80; 5.265-7; 6.76-80. There are remarkably few references
to soldiers carrying water. Smell of war: Aristophanes, *Peace* 527.

10. Shovels, hoes, axes, and sickles: Xenophon, *Education of Cyrus* 6.2.34
(which assumes that animals and carts are privately owned). Tents, see pp. 107-8.
Pack animals: Xenophon, *Anabasis* 1.3.1; 5.8.5 (several soldiers sharing a mule);
4.3.30, 6.4.22.

11. So Anderson 1970, esp. 45, 58 (contra Pritchett 1971, 34-5, 48, who assumes that state-supplied provisions were the norm). Exceptional state-organised supply trains: 500 pack animals (probably representing 250 wagons: Hammond 1983, 29) carrying supplies from the Peloponnese to Plataea, where the largest-ever Greek coalition army had been stationed for many days and where all neighbouring territory had already been plundered by the enemy (Herodotus 9.39.2); Diodorus 11.80.3-4 (Tanagra, 457 BC); Thucydides 4.26.4-9 (Sphacteria). When Xenophon, *Cavalry Commander* 6.3, advises officers to concern themselves with 'fodder, tents, water, firewood, and the other necessities', he evidently means not that they should directly supply all these but that they should try to put their forces in a position where the men could most easily look after themselves.

12. Train and officers: Xenophon, *Spartan Constitution* 11.2; 13.4. Wagon camp behind the lines: Thucydides 5.72.3. Sparta's baggage train: also e.g. Thucydides 6.7.1; Xenophon, *Hellenica* 5.4.17.

13. To Haliartos, in 395: Lysias 16.14. Some imagine that the money paid for arms or armour as well, but that is not what the text says: see the brief discussion in Pritchett 1971, 33-4 n. 16.

14. Inflated prices: Xenophon, *Anabasis* 1.5.6 (the equivalent of 30 drachmas for a *medimnos* of wheat charged by Lydian traders when all other supplies had been exhausted – between five and ten times the normal price in Athens), 3.2.21; pseudo-Aristotle, *Economics* 1347a32-b1.

15. See e.g. Xenophon, *Education of Cyrus* 6.2.38-9, where private traders are the only source of supply mentioned other than plunder and provisions brought from home, and deemed important enough to be offered incentives by the commander. The stories in the Aristotelian *Economics* in which governments and generals strike deals with merchants to meet an emergency also show both that private traders were important and that any interference in their business by central authorities counted was exceptional, a special 'stratagem'. Contra Knorringa 1926, 64-7; Pritchett 1971, 41-4 (whose references to 'market mobs' do not distinguish baggage-carriers from traders).

16. See Anderson 1970, 54-8; Pritchett 1971, 38-41, on living off the land.

17. Xenophon, *Education of Cyrus* 6.2.26-29; *Anabasis* 4.4.9; *Hellenica* 6.2.6 (fine wines).

18. For more on plundering and the role of cavalry in containing it, see also pp. 66, 121-3.

19. So Xenophon, *Anabasis* 3.2.27, and Philip II (Frontinus 4.1.6; Plutarch, *Moralia* 178a).

20. *Anabasis* 3.3.1; 4.1.12-13. Similar measures: see Engels 1978, 14-24 (Philip and Alexander), with his nn. 18 and 38 for Roman parallels. The unsuitability of pack animals (and especially of ox-carts) for many kinds of terrain was of course another limiting factor. Hammond 1983 argues that classical Greek armies preferred wagons to pack-animals, but his evidence relates only to Sparta, Macedonia and Persia, states with well-developed public supply systems: in most Greek cities, by contrast, the transport of provisions was a private matter, so that wagons were rarely a viable option.

21. *Spartan Constitution* 15.6. Water is not mentioned in either Anderson's (1970) or Pritchett's (1971) discussions of provisioning. I am obliged to David Harthen (Liverpool) for letting me read a chapter of his thesis which collates much evidence for the role of the availability or lack of water in Greek warfare, including Thucydides 3.88.1 (Aeolian Islands invaded in winter because they did not have enough water in summer) and 7.13.2 (letter of Nicias about fuel and water supplies in Sicily).

22. Critias F 34, D-K, cited by Plutarch, *Lycurgus* 9.4 and Athenaeus 483b; also Suda, s.v. *kôthôn*.

23. Anderson (1970, 61-2) offers a rare discussion of Greek camps. Cutting down trees for shelters: Polyaenus 2.1.20. More built shelters than tents: Thucydides 6.75.2; Plutarch, *Moralia* 177e.

24. Shape: Polybius 6.42. Central assembly space: *Iliad* 11.806-8 (cf. 8.249-50); cf. *Anabasis* 3.2.1 (meeting *eis meson*); *Iliad* 7.337-43, 436-64: trench and improvised wall; cf. Anderson 1970, 62-6; Pritchett 1971, 133-46, on fortification. *Ta hopla*, 'the place of arms' means simply 'camp' (e.g. *Anabasis* 2.2.20, 4.15; 3.1.33, 40), not (as some translators have it) an arms depot in camp.

25. Alcibiades (of Scambonidae, tribe Leontis) and Socrates (of Alopece, tribe Antiochis) 'shared meals' in camp before Potidaea (Plato *Symposium* 219e; Plutarch, *Alcibiades* 7). Note also the sons of Konon sharing a tent in camp, and confronting another group of 'mess-mates' (Dem. 54.3-4). For informal *suskênoi*, see also Xenophon, *Anabasis* 5.8.5-6.

26. See p. 97. Xenophon prefers the term 'tent-fellowship' (*suskania*: Spartan *Constitution* 5.2-4; 9.4; 13.1, 7; *Hellenica* 5.3.20), perhaps emphasising their role on campaigns.

27. Cf. [Hippocrates] *Airs, Waters, Places* 16; Aristotle, *Politics* 1327b23-33; also *Nicomachean Ethics* 1116a29-33 (superiority of citizen soldiers to those who fight under coercion); Xenophon, *Anabasis* 1.7.4 (stereotypical noisiness of barbarians), 3.4.25 (fighting 'under the lash').

28. See pp. 98-100 for officers, and 109-12 for Greek ideas of discipline.

29. Death threats: 2.346-9, 357-9, 391-3; 12.248-50; 15.348-51; cf. 16.722-3. Aristotle, *Politics* 1285a8-14 cites 2.291-3 with an extra half-line 'for in my hands is death', which does not appear in our text of the *Iliad*. His claim that generals once had power over life and death is based only on this phrase, and is probably to be rejected. Beatings and 'gentle words': 2.185-210, 243-9.

30. Withholding of services as proper thing to do when offended: *Iliad* 1.229-32; 2.235-42; 9.524-99; 13.107-10, 459-61; 14.49-51, 131-2. See further van Wees 1996, 19-21, 27-8; Donlan 1979.

31. Power to fine: also Lysias 15.5. Power to 'bind' (i.e. to hold in custody until trial): also Demosthenes 50.51. Generals executing soldiers for treason: Lysias 13.65; Xenophon, *Hellenica* 1.1.15; Polyaenus 3.9.56. See further Hamel 1998, 59-63. Given that generals were granted this much power in democratic Athens, they surely had it in most other, less egalitarian, states as well.

32. Quotation: *Anabasis* 5.7.21-8. Clearchus: ibid. 1.5.11-17; cf. Plutarch, *Aristides* 23.2 (with Thucydides 1.95.1) on the disciplinary 'blows' delivered by Pausanias, said to have cost Sparta the leadership of the Greek coalition. Stoning provoked by the mere raising of a stick: Thucydides 8.84.2-3 and Diodorus 14.7.6-7. Note also the attempted stoning of an Argive general for having made a poor decision (Thucydides 5.60.6) and the rebellion sparked by a Spartan general's 'rough handling' of a civilian (4.130.4); further Hornblower 2000a. The Athenian Iphicrates, who had a reputation as a disciplinarian, is said to have caused an outcry by stabbing with his spear a sentry asleep at his post: Frontinus 3.12.2-3; cf. Polyaenus 3.9.56; Xenophon, *Hellenica* 6.2.34.

33. Demosthenes 54.3-5. The speaker called witnesses to the incidents, so there was probably some basis in fact for his claims. If the generals had subsequently taken any further action, it would have helped the speaker's case to say so: his silence must mean that this was the end of the affair.

34. Xenophon, *Spartan Constitution* 12.5-7; cf. Herodotus 6.78. The Ten Thousand used a series of three horn signals for bed-time (Xenophon, *Anabasis* 2.2.4), perhaps modelled on Spartan practice.

35. Xenophon, *Hellenica* 3.1.9. Beatings: Xenophon, *Spartan Constitution* 9.5: cowards who behave with insufficient shame at home may be beaten (also ibid. 2.2: whip-bearers punish boys; Herodotus 6.75: Cleomenes hits citizens with his stick). For other Spartan officers threatening to beat non-Spartans, see Hornblower 2000a, citing e.g. Plutarch, *Themistocles* 11.3; *Moralia* 185b (Eurybiades v. Themistocles); *Lysander* 15.7 (Callibius v. Autolycus). Note the Spartan oath of loyalty to officers: see p. 98 and Appendix 2.

36. Thucydides 5.65.2-3 (Spartans); Xenophon, *Hellenica* 4.2.22; Plutarch, *Phocion* 25 (Athenians); cf. Hamel 1998, 71-5.

37. On Sparta, see Xenophon, *Spartan Constitution* 9.4-5; Plutarch, *Agesilaos* 30.3-4; the latter plausibly fleshing out the former's vague references to a ban on looking 'well-groomed' (*liparos*) and 'imitating irreproachable men'; cf. Powell 1989, 179-89. Also Thucydides 5.34 and Plutarch, *Agesilaos* 30.2 on *atimia* as the penalty for cowardice after Sphacteria and Leuctra; Herodotus 7.231-2 on the extreme ostracism of the survivors of Thermopylae. In the light of this evidence it is difficult to accept Diodorus' claim that the punishment for throwing away one's shield was death (12.65.5). *Atimia* in Athens: Andocides 1.74; Aeschines 1.29; 3.175-6; see also p. 99 with n. 38. On Cleonymus and shield-dropping, see pp. 193-4.

38. This is the implication of the response to events at Sphacteria, Mantinea and Leuctra (see above, with n. 37), though the exact procedure is not explained (cf. Pritchett 1974, 235).

39. E.g. Xenophon, *Anabasis* 5.4.16, 20; 5.7.13-17.

Part IV. Agonal and Total Warfare

1. So, for example, Anderson 1970, 1-5; Pritchett 1974, 147-50, 179-87; Ober 1985, esp. 35-6; 1991, 179, 188-9; 1996; Connor 1988, 19-24; Hanson 1995, esp. 327-55; 2000; Mitchell 1996, 91-7.

2. Demosthenes says that during this old war the Spartans were masters of land and sea and had the support of the Persian king (9.47): this did not happen until the last few years of the Peloponnesian War. He also claims that the Athenians successfully defended themselves (ibid.), which is not true of the Peloponnesian War, so he may be thinking of the Corinthian War (395-386) or still later wars.

3. See also *Iliad* 6.242-3 (Hector disdains advantage); 11.384-95 (Diomedes disdains ambush); Herodotus 1.212.2; Thucydides 4.86.6; Xenophon, *Hellenica* 4.3.19; 6.5.16.

4. Spartan pride in absence of fortifications: Plutarch, *Moralia* 190a, 210e, 212e, 215d, 230c. On walls, see further pp. 126-8.

9. Rituals, rules and strategies

1. Xenophon, *Hellenica* 4.7.2-7; see Goodman and Holladay 1986 for religious scruples in Greek war.

2. Evidence assembled by Pritchett 1971, 121-6; contra Pritchett (124-5), it is clear that in Argos the taboo applied to whole month of Carneios, not just to the

Carneia festival: the Argives postponed the first day of the month rather than the festival (Thucydides 5.54.3), and Xenophon refers to Argos' use of appeals to 'the months', not just the 'sacred periods' (*Hellenica* 4.7.2 and 5.1.29).

3. Carneia: Thucydides 5.54.2; Herodotus 7.206, 8.72. Hyacinthia: Herodotus 9.7; Xenophon, *Hellenica* 4.5.11; cf. Pausanias 4.19.4. Gymnopaidiai: Thucydides 5.82.3.

4. Sacred truces: see e.g. Thucydides 5.49.1 (Olympia); *IG* I³ 6, B 8-47 (Eleusis); Isocrates 4.43. See further Baltrusch 1994, 117-20.

5. Evidence assembled by Pritchett 1971, 116-21. Main sources: Herodotus 6.106.3-107; Pausanias 1.28.4 (Sparta); Hesychius and Suda, s.v. *entos hebdomês* (Athens). It may be that both rules were abandoned after the Persian Wars, which would explain why we hear so little of them.

6. Thucydides 4.97-99 (with Hornblower 1996, 308-15); cf. Herodotus 9.65 on divine intervention to keep the fighting at Plataea outside the precinct of Demeter.

7. *Iliad* 1.68-108, 12.237-43; *Odyssey* 2.178-82; cf. van Wees 1996, 11-12.

8. See Pritchett 1971, 109-15; Jameson 1991, esp. 205 (fall of victim, flow of blood), 208-9 (flames); Parker 2000. See also Lissarrague 1990, 55-69, for evidence from art.

9. E.g. Herodotus 9.41.4, 45.2 (Mardonius ignores omens), 61-2 (Spartans wait under fire); Xenophon, *Anabasis* 6.4.12-5.1 (mercenaries wait, but one unit ignores omens and is wiped out).

10. As shown by Thucydides 6.69.1-2. See Parker 2000, 303-4, for the historical developments.

11. Agesipolis' determination: Xenophon, *Hellenica* 4.7.5; cf. 3.2.24 for a Spartan campaign stopped by an earthquake, and Thucydides 5.116 for a campaign aborted on account of unfavourable omens.

12. See Parker 2000, 304-7. Efforts to contract *manteis*: esp. Herodotus 9.33-7, 92-5. Subordination of *mantis*, and general's ability to read omens: Plato, *Laches* 199a; Xenophon, *Anabasis* 5.6.28-9; Onasander 10-25-7. Overriding considerations: e.g. Aristotle, *Rhetoric* 1395a10-14 (quoting *Iliad* 12.243), and several hellenistic examples cited by Parker (ibid.).

13. Uniqueness of Spartan border-crossing sacrifices: Pritchett 1971, 113; Jameson 1991, 202. Sparta awarded the rare privilege of citizenship to the diviner Teisamenos and his brother in exchange for his services: Herodotus 9.33. Sacrificial herds: Pausanias 9.13.4.

14. The most comprehensive and best studies of agricultural devastation are Hanson 1998 and Garlan 1974, 1-86; but pertinent criticisms have been made by Thorne 2001. See also Ober 1985, 32-50; Osborne 1987, 137-40; Spence 1990; Foxhall 1993. On devastation, revenge and the Delian League, see Jackson 1969; Bellen 1974.

15. Evidence for evacuation and harvesting of crops before invasion is assembled by Hanson 1998, 103-21, 229-31; also Garlan 1989, 101-3. Livestock: Xenophon, *Hellenica* 4.5.1 (peninsula), 4.6.4 (mountains); Thucydides 2.14.1 (Euboea). Aeneas Tacticus advises against taking livestock into the city (10.1), but it may be that Mantineia in Arcadia had a river running through the middle (Xenophon, *Hellenica* 5.2.4-5) in order to have a water supply for its cattle in time of war. The vocabulary of devastation emphasises destruction rather than plunder: see Hanson 1998, 185-94, 250-1; Pritchett 1991, 73-152; Jackson 1969.

16. For all this, see Hanson 1998, 42-76, 213-26; Foxhall 1993, 138-9, suggests that he may have underestimated the damage done by 'great fat feet'; other criticisms in Thorne 2001.

17. See again Hanson 1998, 131-76, 231-50. The role of cavalry in containing devastation is noted by Spence 1990; Ober 1996, 72-85.

18. *Epiteichismos*: Hanson 1998, 28-30, 202; Ober 1985, 36-9; Garlan 1974, 33-8. On the significance of slave desertion as a tactic, see also Hunt 1998, esp. 102-15.

19. Spartan concentration on Acharnae, and avoidance of Pericles' estate: Thucydides 2.13.1, 20; Plutarch, *Pericles* 33. On such tactics, see especially Foxhall 1993, 142-3; Garlan 1989, 110-12.

20. Spartan campaigns: evidence listed by Hanson 1998, 132-7; Athenian devastations of Megara: Thucydides 2.31. Note also the token ravaging of Mantinea in Xenophon, *Hellenica* 4.5.10; 6.5.15, 20-1. For the view that such campaigns show armies relying on traditional strategies no longer effective in changed circumstances, see esp. Ober 1985, 35-8; 1996; Hanson 1998, esp. 181; 2000. For the concept of 'conspicuous destruction', see pp. 126, 240 and van Wees 1992, 61.

21. Aegina: Herodotus 5.89 (*c.* 500); Xenophon, *Hellenica* 5.1.2 (389). Thebes: see Fisher 1999, 77-80. Athenian stories about the capture of Salamis and Nisaea both featured the Megarians being lured into raiding sanctuaries (and then ambushed, see p. 132): Aeneas Tacticus 4.8-11; Plutarch, *Solon* 8. These stories (as well as the abductions of women at the start of Herodotus' *Histories*, 1.1-5) may have been the model for Aristophanes' comic story that the Peloponnesian War was started by Megarians stealing Athenian courtesans (*Acharnians* 524-9).

22. Herodotus 6.16; cf. 6.138.1 on the legendary raid for women by the Lemnians (see also p. 32).

23. E.g. Thucydides 2.25-6, 56; 3.16: Athenian fleets sail round, make landings, ravage the country, and fight some small engagements, but retreat when larger forces are assembled against them.

24. For Demosthenes, Polybius and scholars who have followed them, see pp. 115-16 with n. 1.

25. Asine: Pausanias 2.36.5; 3.7.4; 4.14.3 (see Hall 1995 for archaeological evidence confirming destruction and date).

26. Melia: see p. 10. Arisbe: Herodotus 1.151.2. Nauplia: Pausanias 4.24.4, 278, 35.2. Cirrha (*c.* 590): see p. 20. Pellene and Donoussa (*c.* 570): see p. 30. Camarina (*c.* 550): Thucydides 6.5.3, Philistus *FGrH* 556 F 5. Siris (*c.* 550): Justin 20.2.4; scholion on Lycophron 984. Sybaris (510): Herodotus 5.44-5, 6.21; Diodorus 12.9.1-10.1; Strabo 6.1.13; Athenaeus 521d. Singor 1988, 239-40, lists almost all these instances but plays down their significance.

27. Smyrna: Mimnermus F 9 West; Herodotus 1.150; Strabo 14.1.4; Pausanias 7.5.1. Leuconia and Chios: Plutarch, *Moralia* 244f-45a; cf. Herodotus 1.18; Polyaenus 8.66; Frontinus 2.5.15. Sigeum: see p. 36. Samos: Herodotus 3.54-6.

28. *The Shield of Heracles* 239-40 (sixth century); cf. Homer, *Iliad* 18.509-40.

29. 9.591-5. Destruction as normal goal of legendary wars: e.g. *Iliad* 2.286-8, 414-15; 22.62-8, 410-11; 24.732-7 (Troy); 9.529-32, 588-9 (Calydon); 5.639-42 (first sack of Troy); 11.707-13, 733 (Thyroessa); 2.691; 20.92-6 (Lyrnessos, Pedasos, Thebes). See van Wees 1992, 183-99, 210-13.

30. Archaic poets: Lesches, *Little Iliad*; Arctinus, *Sack of Troy*; Stesichorus, *Sack of Troy* (or *The Wooden Horse* = FF 196-205 Page, S88-147 Campbell). Epics were also composed on the *Sack of Oichalia*, and on the sack of Thebes (*Epigonoi*, 'the next generation'). Hesiod, *Works and Days* 246-7, and the Homeric *Hymn to Athena* 11.2-3, both list the destruction of cities as typical acts of war. Sack of Troy in archaic art: e.g. Woodford 1993, 102-16.

31. Archilochus F 98 West; Herodotus 6.126. Compare also e.g. the attacks on native towns in Sicily in Herodotus 6.23, 7.154.2 ('many' towns).

32. The main evidence for all these sieges is in Herodotus: 6.140 (Myrine, *c.* 500); 6.92, 9.75 (Aegina, 491 or 488); 6.132-5 (Paros, 489); 7.154 (Gela's captures, *c.* 490), 7.156 (Syracuse's destructions, 480s), 6.82 (Cleomenes' trial, *c.* 494).

33. Herodotus 9.86-8 (Thebes), 115-21 (Sestos); Thucydides 1.98.1 (Eion). For classical sieges, see Ducrey 1968, 107-47; Karavites 1982; and the list in Singor 1988, 334-6.

34. Lendon 2000, esp. 17-18; van Wees 1992, esp. 183-99.

35. See the authors cited in p. 115 n. 1. Note also the study of surprise attacks and ambushes by Pritchett 1974, 156-89, which concludes that open battle was the norm, despite listing numerous 'breaches' of the supposed 'rules'. Peter Krentz (1997; 2000) has convincingly argued that deception did play an important part in Greek warfare at all times. See Garlan 1989, 134-5, on Spartan hostility to walls as 'effeminate'.

36. Protection of sanctuaries and tombs: e.g. Aeschylus, *The Persians* 402-5; Aeneas Tacticus, preface; Plato, *Laws* 698e-699c; Lycurgus, *Against Leocrates* 8, 38, 150. Cf. Herodotus 4.127.2-3, with 4.46.2: even the Scythians, who do not defend their land, *will* defend their ancestors' graves.

37. Andocides F 3.1. Discomfort of evacuees: Aristophanes, *Acharnians* 32-9, 71-2; *Knights* 792-4; *Peace* 632-40; Thucydides 2.14-17; Demades 14.

38. *Odyssey* 11.262-5; cf. Thucydides 1.2, 5, 7-8; Garlan 1989, 129-33. Fortifications: see pp. 138-45.

39. Herodotus 1.18 (Miletus), 5.34 (Naxos), 6.100-1 (Eretria); see also Thucydides 3.94.2; 4.104.3, 130.1; and Garlan 1989, 104.

40. 1.170. Taking to the mountains: Herodotus 6.100 (considered by Eretrians), 8.27 (Phocians, attacked by Thessalians), 8.32 (Phocians, attacked by Persians); Xenophon, *Hellenica* 4.6.4 (Acarnanians, attacked by Spartans). Refuge in neighbouring cities: Herodotus 8.32 (Phocians). Mass migration: Herodotus 1.163-8 (Phocaeans to Corsica, Teans to Thrace); cf. Demand 1990 on the phenomenon of 'urban relocation'. See also on Athens, n. 41 below.

41. Herodotus 6.109 (debate between sitting tight and fighting in 490), 7.142-3; 8.51 (debate between evacuation of Athens and defense of Acropolis in 480), 8.62 (threat to emigrate to Southern Italy). Thucydides 2.21-22 (debate between sitting tight and fighting in 431). I see no grounds to argue (as does e.g. Ober 1985, 34-5) that before the Peloponnesian War such responses were only acceptable where the enemy was non-Greek (i.e. Persian).

42. Contra Ober 1985, 35-6; Garlan 1989, 105-14; 1974, 44-65.

43. Fourth-century evidence: Garlan 1974, 66-86; Ober 1985, 130-80, Munn 1993, 3-125; van de Maele and Fossey (ed.) 1992, 77-146. Hellenistic cities: Ma 2000, 339-43.

44. Garrisoned forts in 431: Thucydides 2.13.6 (see Appendix 1). *Peripoloi*: Thucydides 4.67.2, 8.92.2; Aristophanes, *Birds* 1177-9; Eupolis F 341 Kock; *IG* I² 99.21-4 (see pp. 94-5). Summary execution of raiders: Lysias 13.78, with Fisher 1999, 77-80. Militia reinforcements: Aristophanes, *Acharnians* 1022-3, 1073-7.

45. Herodotus 5.63 (Phaleron), 6.103.1 (Marathon, explicitly described as 'at the border' by Isocrates 4.86-7), 5.74.2 (Eleusis 506); Thucydides 1.107.3 (blocking mountain passes). Note also e.g. Argos fighting Spartans in *c.* 494 at Sepeia, near their landing place (Herodotus 6.77.1).

46. Dema wall: Munn 1993. Herodotus 6.36 (Chersonnese), 7.176, 208, 225 (Thermopylae), 8.71-2, 74; 9.8-9 (Isthmus of Corinth).

47. See pp. 233-40.

10. Ambush, battle and siege

1. The narrative is a composite of the accounts at Herodotus 8.27-28; Pausanias 10.1.3-9; Plutarch *Moralia* 244c (and cf. Polyaenus 6.18.1-2). See Ellinger 1993.

2. *Iliad* 13.276-87; *Odyssey* 11.523-32; boasting of prowess in ambushes also at 13.259-71, 14.216-21; cf. Pritchett 1974, 178; Krentz 2000, 172; contra Edwards 1985.

3. *Iliad* 18.513-40. Greeks ambushing Trojans: 1.227-8, 21.35-40, 24.778-9; *Odyssey* 14.459-502.

4. Aegina: Herodotus 5.86. Miltiades: id. 6.37 (erroneously dated to 493 by Pritchett 1974, 180, and Krentz 2000, 184: a date *c.* 550 is implied by the roles of Peisistratus and Croesus).

5. Legendary ambush of Troilus in art: *LIMC* nos 206-81 (cf. Krentz 2000, 174, fig. 2). Generic ambushes: Vos 1963, pl. VIII (see my Plate XII); Lissarrague 1990, nos A502-9 (all from 520-480 BC).

6. Esp. Thucydides 3.94.1, 4.31.1-32.2, 4.67.4; on Demosthenes: Roisman 1993; cf. id. 1998. Note also Euripides, *Phoenician Women* 724-7, cited on p. 126.

7. They were made to supplement their diet by stealing food, and thus learned the techniques of ambush and deception: Xenophon, *Spartan Constitution* 2.6-9, with Krentz 2000, 175, and Hodkinson 2000, 201-5. These skills might be especially useful in policing actions against helots (cf. Powell 1989, 186), but, as Krentz points out, they were needed in regular hoplite warfare as well.

8. Aigospotamoi: see p. 224. Other instances: Thucydides 7.39-41 (= Polyaenus 5.13.2, 5.32.1); Polyaenus 5.32.2; Xenophon, *Hellenica* 2.4.5-6; Frontinus 3.1.6 (= Polyaenus 3.9.52); Polyaenus 2.3.7. Note again Euripides, *Phoenician Women* 728-31, cited on p. 126.

9. As Krentz 2000, 177, summarises the situation; ibid., 169-70, for attitudes to deceit in war; compare Whitehead 1988 and Wheeler 1988 on 'thefts' and stratagems.

10. Main sources: Strabo 13.1.38; Plutarch, *Moralia* 858a; Diogenes Laertius 1.74; Polyaenus 1.25. For the rest, and a general discussion, see Page 1955, 152-61. These sources are late but ultimately based on the contemporary poetry of Alcaeus (T3, FF 167.7 and 428 L-P). Diogenes seems to think that this duel was meant to settle the war, but Plutarch presents it as a simple challenge to 'whoever wished', and all accounts agree that the duel did not end the war, which was later settled by arbitration by Periander of Corinth (see p. 16), before erupting again a generation later (Herodotus 5.94-5).

11. Two single combats are known from the classical period, as Ted Lendon points out to me, but at least one of these occurred in the course of battle, rather than as a staged confrontation in view of the armies. In 414, the Athenian general Lamachus was killed when he and a few of his men found themselves isolated and surrounded by enemy cavalry during pursuit (Thucydides 6.101); according to Plutarch (*Nicias* 18.2), a Syracusan cavalry officer challenged him to single combat and he accepted. In the 360s, the Elean cavalry commander Stomios, a successful pentathlete, challenged a Sicyonian general to single combat and won (Pausanias 6.3.2): we have no further details, so it is possible that this occurred under circumstances similar to Lamachus' duel. Agonistic attitudes thus continue, especially among the elite (horsemen, athletes), but they no longer have an institutional outlet. The other examples listed by Pritchett 1985, 16-21, are either

'champion combats' (not simply duels, see below), mostly mythical, or hellenistic 'duels' fought in the general mêlée of battle (nos 14, 16-17). Rome: Oakley 1985; van Wees 1984, 131-2, 140. Reasons for end of practice: see p. 240.

12. Herodotus 1.82; Thucydides 5.41.2-3, 6.95.1. The Argives asked for a chance to fight champion combat, 'as they had done *once* before' (*hôsper kai proteron* pote, Thucydides 5.41.2), i.e. the Battle of Champions of *c.* 550 had been the only such attempt in the entire history of the dispute (*contra* Hanson 2000, 206, 218, who infers that 'it had been common between the two belligerents').

13. Missiles: Strabo 10.1.12. Allies: Thucydides 1.15.3. For the other evidence, see especially Parker 1997. If the treaty recording the missile ban was genuine (and it has been argued that it was not: Wheeler 1987; cf. Donlan 1970), it cannot date much before 550 BC, the date of the earliest surviving inscribed treaties (see pp. 10-13). References in Hesiod (*Works and Days* 650-62) and Archilochus (F 3 West) show that a war was being fought already in the early seventh century.

14. One further historical example of champion combat may be the duelling of three men on each side between Tegea and Pheneos (Plutarch, *Moralia* 309d); all other stories about champion combat (as opposed to single combat for display, see above) are legendary: Menelaos and Paris at Troy (*Iliad* 3.324-80), Eteokles and Polyneikes at Thebes (e.g. Euripides, *Phoenician* Women 1227-1424), and five stories relating to the 'migration era' (listed in Pritchett 1985, 17-20, nos 2-5 and 7).

15. Herodotus 9.48-49.1; Thucydides 5.41. Hanson 1995, 341; 2000, 205-6, argues that the Spartans in 421 regard champion combat as 'idiotic' because archaic agonal rules no longer apply. Another factor is likely to have been that the Spartans accepted champion combat *c.* 550 because they were expanding in several directions and their manpower resources must have been strained, while in 421 they were solidly in control of Cynouria and had no interest in allowing a challenge of any kind.

16. As claimed by Ober 1996, 56 ('a battle is properly prefaced by a ritual challenge and acceptance of the challenge'), and Pritchett 1974, 152 ('the battle did not take place until both sides were ready'). Pritchett's survey of the evidence (esp. 149-52; incl. Herodotus 9.41.1; Thucydides 3.107.3; Diodorus 13.73.1; 15.65.4), however, highlights the tactical motivation of delays and challenges.

17. Obscured view: Thucydides 4.93-6 (Delium, 424); Xenophon, *Hellenica* 4.2.19 (Nemea, 394). Speed of advance: Thucydides 4.96.1 (Delium); 5.66.1-2 (Mantineia); cf. 5.6-11 (Amphipolis, 422). Lack of response: Thucydides 5.65.2 (Mantinea, 418); Xenophon, *Hellenica* 5.4.39ff. = Diodorus 15.32.6 (Chabrias, 378). Shame at failure to engage: Thucydides 5.60.2, 5 (Mantinea); 8.27 (sea battle, 412). Deceptions to gain advantageous position: Thucydides 6.64-5, 7.73.3-74.1 (Syracuse, 415, 413); Xenophon, *Hellenica* 7.5.21-5 (Mantinea, 362). Ambushes: Olpai, 426 (Thucydides 3.107.3); Sardis, 395 (*Hellenica Oxyrhynchia* 6.4-6); Sparta, 370 (Xenophon, *Hellenica* 6.5.30-1).

18. Xenophon, *Hellenica* 4.4.11-12; cf. Diodorus 12.10.1 (511; with Ducrey 1968, 57-9); Herodotus 6.79-80 (494); Thucydides 1.106.1-2 (460). Massacre of fleeing enemies in Homer: Willcock 1993; van Wees 1996, 46. Tactical restrictions in classical pursuit: esp. Thucydides 5.73.4 (given a moral twist by Plutarch, *Lycurgus* 22.9-10; *Moralia* 228f). Pursuit into city: Herodotus 3.55; Xenophon, *Hellenica* 4.7.6. The lack of moral restrictions on pursuit is pointed out by Krentz (2002; contra e.g. Ober 1996, 56), who also notes Thucydides 4.96.7-8; Xenophon, *Hellenica* 7.2.31.

19. Pre-battle sacrifice and the *paian*: pp. 120 and 186-7. Pritchett notes (1971,

108), that the singing of the *paian* at the Battle of Nemea alerted the Spartans to the enemy advance, which would otherwise have remained a surprise (Xenophon, *Hellenica* 4.2.19).

20. Herodotus 9.78-79; 4.202, 205; cf. Sophocles, *Antigone* 1029-30.

21. See Tritle 1997, citing esp. Xenophon, *Anabasis* 3.4.5; also van Wees 1996, 50-6.

22. See Lendon 2000, 3-11; van Wees 1996, 53-4; Vermeule 1979, 93-108. Achilles' notorious mutilation of Hector is censured in the *Iliad* only by Hector's supporters, and then only because it is too protracted. See further pp. 161-2.

23. Cf. Tritle 1997, 132. Poem: Tyrtaeus F 10.21-7 West, as explained by Tritle 2000, 40 (the alternative interpretation is that the warrior is clutching a mortal wound to the groin, but I am no longer as sceptical of Tritle's reading as I was when I reviewed his book).

24. The evidence is assembled by Pritchett 1974, 246-75 (trophy); 1985, 153-235 (retrieval of dead). On the Thebans' breach of the rule that *tropaia* should be perishable: Cicero, *De Inventione* 2.23.69-70; Diodorus 13.24.5-6; Plutarch, *Moralia* 273cd; on their use of conditional truces: Thucydides 4.97-101.1 (the episode inspired Euripides' *Suppliant Women*, which dealt with a mythical precendent; cf. Bowie 1997, 45-56); Xenophon, *Hellenica* 3.5.19-25.

25. Thucydides 1.105.5-6. The Athenians themselves made a return expedition to the scene of battle in 412, in order to set up a trophy: the enemy later destroyed this because setting up a trophy when one was not currently in control of the battlefield was not legitimate (Thucydides 8.24.1).

26. Ensuring control of bodies: Xenophon, *Hellenica* 7.1.19; cf. *Agesilaus* 2.15. Fighting to regain control: Xenophon, *Hellenica* 3.5.22-5; 4.5.8.

27. A full list of fights over the dead in Homer in van Wees 1996, 65 n. 45. For military organisation and tactics, see pp. 188-91, 195-7, 233-5.

28. Archilochus F 292 West; [Hesiod], *Shield of Heracles* 150-3. Champions: Herodotus 1.82.6.

29. Aeschylus, *Seven Against Thebes* (468/7 BC), uses *tropaion* as if it were familiar (277, 954); cf. the 'mouse-killing trophy' in the mock-epic *Battle of the Frogs and Mice* (159), attributed to roughly the same date, but possibly much later. Art: Plate XIII; Caskey and Beazley 1963, 66-7. The late development of trophy and burial truce is pointed out in an important article by Peter Krentz (2002).

30. For fifth-century military developments, see below, Chapter 13. The Persians left the body of the Greeks unburied, which may be why the Oath of Plataea included the promise 'I shall leave *no one* [of the allies] *unburied*' (see Appendix 2).

31. Herodotus 6.88-91 (attempted betrayal of Aegina, 491 or 488), 6.100 (Eretria, 490), 6.121-4 (attempted betrayal of Athens, 490).

32. See *Iliad* 12.86-7 (attack columns), 12.154-61, 287-9, 379-86, 442-71 (stones); 12.397-9, 443-4; also 16.702-4 (climbing); 12.445-62 (gates).

33. Mantinea: Xenophon, *Hellenica* 5.2.4-5; on fortification walls, see further Winter 1971; Garlan 1974, 87-103, 148-53, 183-200; Lawrence 1979; Adam 1982; 1993; Ober 1993; Gros 1993.

34. Ladders: Aeschylus, *Seven Against Thebes* 466-7 (dated to 468/7); the reference to 'ladders' in West's text of Archilochus F 98 is a modern restoration. Athenian reputation: Thucydides 1.102.2; their capture of the Persian camp at Plataea was another reason (Herodotus 9.70).

35. Siege of Samos: Plutarch, *Pericles* 27. Siege ramp, mine, flame-throwers:

Thucydides 2. 75.1-3, 76.2; 4.100.2-4, 115.2. Cf. Garlan 1974, 125-45; 1994, 682-6, 689-92; Ober 1991, 180-92.

36. Countering rams: Thucydides 2.76.4; Aeneas Tacticus 32.4-6. Detection of mines: Herodotus 4.200. Anti-arson measures: Aeneas Tacticus 32.1, 9-10; 33.3; 34. See Garlan 1974, 120-2, 145-7, 169-83; 1994, 682-6, 689-92; Ober 1991, 180-92.

37. First mention of 'catapults': Diodorus 14.42.1, 43.3; on artillery see further Marsden 1969; defensive artillery towers: Ober 1993.

38. Philip's siege tower: Diodorus 14.51.7, 74.3. See further Garlan 1974, 155-69, 201-69; Ober 1991, 180-92. Mining approach to walls: Aeneas Tacticus 32.8. Alternatively, one might obstruct the approach to the walls with large boulders: Xenophon, *Hellenica* 2.4.27.

39. See Garlan 1974, 107-20.

40. Thucydides 2.70.1; cf. Herodotus 9.118.1 (Sestos, 479); Diodorus 14.111.2 (Rhegium, 388).

41. Ritual cry and hurling rooftiles: Thucydides 2.4.2. Ritual cry also: Aeschylus, *Seven Against Thebes* 267-70; cf. Xenophon, *Hellenica* 4.3.19. Rooftiles also: Thucydides 3.74.1; Diodorus 13.56.7; Plutarch, *Pyrrhus* 34. See further Barry 1996; Powell 2003; Loman 2004, 44, and pp. 39-40.

42. Scruples expressed in the Amphictyonic Oath (Aeschines 2.115) and Oath of Plataea (Tod II.204; Fornara 57); see p. 10. 'Shame' of relying on walls and 'devices': pp. 116, 126-8.

43. Samos: Herodotus 3.56.1; Sparta in Attica: Thucydides 2.57.2.

44. Herodotus 3.55 and 5.63.

45. Spartan women who were deemed *hierai* were also granted special burials, according to Plutarch, *Lycurgus* 27.2. The abnormal usage of *hieros*, which is paralleled by the peculiar Spartan use of *theios* or *seios*, 'god-like', to designate an admirable person (Plato, *Meno* 99d; Aristotle, *Nicomachean Ethics* 1145a), has confused many scholars who have unnecessarily emended Herodotus to read *irenes* (the term for 20-year-olds in Sparta) and Plutarch to read 'women who died in childbirth'. For an excellent discussion of this problem and Spartan funerary practices in general, see Hodkinson 2000, esp. 256-62; cf. Gilula 2003, 81-5; for *seios*, see Powell 1998, 126.

46. Athenian public funeral: e.g. Thucydides 2.34; cf. Pritchett 1985, 106-24; Clairmont 1983. Casualty lists: Pritchett 1985, 139-45; Bradeen 1969.

47. Xenophon, *Hellenica* 2.4.33; for a detailed discussion of the excavated tomb, see e.g. Hodkinson 2000, 249-59.

48. Aristotle, *Politics* 1268a8-11, reports that Hippodamos of Miletos (c. 475-450) was the first (or thought that he was the first) to provide for war orphans, and that the custom exists 'now' in Athens and other cities. On Athenian war-orphans, see also esp. Thucydides 2.46.1 and Aeschines 3.154.

49. *Iliad* 11.846-7 (pain-killer); 13.598-600 (bandage); 5.663-7, 14.428-39 (friends and followers tending wounded). 'Incantations': *Odyssey* 19.457-8; cf. *Hymn to Demeter* 229-30.

50. Sparta: Xenophon, *Spartan Constitution* 13.7. Mercenaries: Xenophon, *Anabasis* 3.4.30. See further Salazar 2000, 68-74; Hanson 1989, 210-18.

51. Lucky survivor: [Hippocrates] *Epidemics* 5.46. Saved by treatment: *Epidemics* 5.96 = 7.34. Deaths: *Epidemics* 5.21, 47, 49, 60-2 (= 7.31-33), 95 (= 7.121), 98-9 (= 7.29-30).

52. Tyrtaeus F 10.29-20 West. Archaic Athens: Plutarch, *Solon* 31.3-4. Classical pensions: see especially Lysias 24; Aristotle, *Athenian Constitution* 49.4, with Rhodes 1981 ad loc.

53. Level of ransoms: p. 26. An exhaustive collection of evidence: Pritchett 1991, 245-97. For the law, see Demosthenes 53.11; Gortyn Code, col. 6.46ff. Boasts about generosity in providing ransoms: e.g. Lysias 12.20; 19.59; Demosthenes 8.70; 18.268; 19.40, 166, 169-71 (free gift), 53.8 (free of interest); Aristotle, *Rhetoric* 1400a.

54. See Pritchett 1991, 205-23 (execution), 297-312 (release), 223-45, 401-38 (enslavement, sale).

55. Troezen: Herodotus 8.41; Plutarch, *Themistocles* 10.5. For hospitality of other communities, see Pausanias 4.23.1 (Messenian War), Strabo 8.6.11; Ephorus *FGrH* 70 F 56 (Argive expansion); and pp. 12, 29 (Plataeans and Aeginetans).

56. Tyrtaeus F 10.3-12 West. The context, and specifically the reference to one's parents taking to life on the road as well, make it unlikely that the poet is thinking of a soldier exiled in punishment for cowardice or desertion, rather than a whole population on the move when their city is lost.

Part V. The Experience of Combat

1. Herodotus 7.229.1 (cf. 208.3-209.3 for Spartan composure); I owe the suggestion to Larry Tritle. That the patients went blind is evident from the fact that one of them had to be 'guided' into battle; that the problem was temporary follows from the fact that the other was able to fight heroically at Plataea a year later (9.71). The temporary nature of the affliction suggests that Herodotus used the term *ophthalmia* generically to mean 'eye problems', rather than specifically in the medical sense of *conjunctivitis* ('pink-eye'): the blindness which this disease in its most severe form, *trachoma*, can cause would not have been curable in antiquity. For Epizelos, see Tritle 2000, 63-5.

2. See also Tyrtaeus F 12.10-11 West ('No one can prove himself a good man in war unless he can *bear the sight* of bloody slaughter') and the later texts cited by Hanson 1989, 97-9.

3. The best and most detailed defence of the dominant view of hoplite battle is Hanson 1989; the most effective critiques are Krentz 1985, 1994; Goldsworthy 1997. 'The myth of the hoplite scrummage' was first challenged by Fraser 1942. See further Chapter 13.

4. Much has been made of Aristotle's brief comments on the development of 'the hoplite element' (*Politics* 1297b16-28), for which see pp. 60, 78-82.

5. See esp. Helbig 1909, 67, and 1911, 8; Lorimer 1947, 76-7, 107-11; Cartledge 1977, 20-4, and 1996; Hanson 1991, and 1995, 224-38.

6. See esp. Nilsson 1929a, 240, 244; Snodgrass 1965, 110-12, and 1993, 56-61; Salmon 1977, 91-2.

11. The deeds of heroes

1. Mead 1968, viii. In this chapter I draw (occasionally *verbatim*) on a series of earlier publications which discuss the evidence in much more detail: van Wees 1988, 1994, 1996, 1997a.

2. So e.g. Finley 1977 (1954)], 74, and recently Hellmann 2000; Singor 1995, 1991; Bowden 1993.

3. Quotations from Heider 1979, 94-6, on the Dani. Compare Meggitt 1977, 19, on the Mae Enga: 'the two lines open fire with their bows, and rapid movement up and down the field ensues as men shoot, dodge, advance, and fall back. Despite this mobility, each side tries to preserve its extended skirmishing line .... During the skirmishing, which goes on at great pace, tired men withdraw from time to time to catch their breath and replenish their arrows; in doing so they form a changing reserve force'; also Pospisil 1963, 58-60, on the Kapauku. Proportion of men active: Gardner and Heider 1968, 138 (about 100 men out of 'several hundred') and Brown 1973, 58-9 (65-75 men out of 200).

4. Heider 1979, 96; Gardner and Heider 1968, 138-9, 141.

5. See Meggitt 1977, 57, 89-90. Pride in formation: Strathern 1979, 61-2 (Melpa); warning before dropping out: Meggitt 1977, 63, 103. Similar tactics: Brown 1973, 59-9 (Chimbu).

6. *Iliad* 4.254; 11.65. All this is incompatible with the common idea that the dense crowds described before battle are organised rank-and-file formations. This idea is essentially based on the assumption that terms here translated as 'ranks' (*phalanges*) and 'lines' (*stiches*) mean single ranks and files, but in context these words appear to be used as loosely as their English equivalents are to designate groups of soldiers: see van Wees 1986, 292-5; 1994, 3-4; *contra* Franz 2002, 74-80, 94-5; Hellmann 2000, 60-2; Singor 1995, 193-9; 1991; Pritchett 1991b, 185-6; 1985, 21-5; Latacz 1977, 45-67.

7. Talking and drinking: 11.596-804 with 14.1-15; 13.208-29. Hector's commitment to fighting is illustrated by his turning down similar opportunities (6.237ff.), unlike his brother Paris, who is in no hurry to return to the battlefield (6.313-7.12). Dani chewing tobacco: Heider 1979, 94.

8. See further van Wees 1988, 12-14, and 1997a, 688-9; *contra* Latacz 1977, esp. 172, 177, who argues that the exhortations are orders to the masses to advance in a regular rank-and-file formation.

9. So especially Latacz 1977; Pritchett 1985, 7-33; Singor 1991; Hellmann 2000, 136-41; Franz 2002, 92-6, 108-9.

10. Further discussion and evidence: van Wees 1988, 5-7; 1996, 16-21; Hellmann 2000, 112-21.

11. 17.370-5; see further van Wees 1988, 7-10; 1997, 683-7.

12. See further van Wees 1988, 15-17; 1997a, 680-2. Frequent breakthroughs and rallies are incompatible with regular rank-and-file formations, which could not be reconstituted once they had fallen apart: cf. van Wees 1994, 4 with n. 12; contra Latacz 1977, 212-15 and 228 n. 9.

13. For the construction of the chariot, see Wiesner 1968; Greenhalgh 1973, 19-39. Some chariots have a third horse as a spare (8.80-7; 16.466-76), and Hector even has four horses (8.185).

14. See Anderson 1975 and 1965, contra Greenhalgh 1973, 14-17. 'Taxis': Kirk 1962, 124.

15. Importance of staying close: *Iliad* 11.339-42, 354-60; 13.384-6; 15.456-7; 17.501-2, 699.

16. Charioteers leaving dead fighters 5.9-21, 576-8; 13.384-96; 16.864-7; 20.487-9. Fighters leaving dead charioteers: 8.118-29, 312-15; 15.447-57. In three cases the survivor does attempt to protect his friend's corpse, always unsuccessfully and mostly at great cost (5.217-443; 11.91-8; 16.737-9).

17. See Singor 1991, 112-18; Kirk 1985, 360-3; Latacz 1977, 215-23; Greenhalgh 1973, 7-17; Detienne 1968, 313-18; Delebecque 1951.

18. About half of the chariots mentioned (20 of 41) are explicitly attributed to leaders: 18 men who feature as leaders of contingents in the Catalogue of Ships, plus two men elsewhere called *hêgemones*, Polydamas (12.87-9) and Deiphobos (12.87, 94). There are, however, many unnamed 'leaders' as well (12.61; 17.335), and it is likely that they are imagined as owning most of the remaining chariots.

19. For the idea that a leading warrior *ought* to bring his chariot to war, see 5.195; 11.717-21; 12.114.

20. A few passages speak of chariot-fighters as distinct from the footsoldiers (e.g. 11.150-1, 289-90; 15.352-4) but none of these need imply that the chariots form separate battalions, as is often assumed: they simply single out the chariot-fighters among the multitude. Even when Nestor stations the chariots ahead of the infantry (4.297-309), it does not follow that they fight as a unit: see van Wees 1994, 12-13 (contra e.g. Hellmann 2000, 66-7, 142; Greenhalgh 1973, 1-9; Wiesner 1968, 26-7).

21. *Iliad* 7.232, 242-3. For duelling in PNG, see esp. Meggitt 1977, 18-20: duels often end with an exchange of gifts, as in the duel between Aias and Hector (7.273-307).

22. As imagined by e.g. Parks 1990, 31, 46; Krischer 1971, 15-19; Ducrey 1985, 43; Mueller 1984, 77-80; Letoublon 1983, 27-31.

23. *Iliad* 4.306-7; 11.150-1; see further van Wees 1996, 30-4. Mae Enga: Meggitt 1977, 20.

24. The 28 'duels' out of 170 confrontations described (not including a further 130 killings merely alluded to) are listed in van Wees 1996, 73 n. 103. For screams, threats, etc., see ibid., 40-2 (and *Iliad* 16.428-30 for 'vultures'); on the recitation of genealogies, see also Adkins 1975, 241-7.

25. Rhetorical challenges: 6.143; 13.448, 809; 20.429. Genuine challenges: 3.21-32 (Paris); 13.445-8 (Idomeneus to Deiphobus, retaliating at 516-17); 13.809-10 (Aias to Hector, retaliating at 14.402).

26. No response to spear-cast which misses: 13.156-64, 502-5; 16.608-26; ditto when the spear accidentally hits another man instead: 13.183-7, 402-12; 14.459-75, 488; 15.520-4; 17.304-11. Immediate retreat after unsuccessful blow: 11.434-6; 13.561-6, 643-5; 16.806-15; 17.43-50.

27. Most men killed by shot in the back or flank as they try to retreat: Heider 1979, 94-5; men killed while busy trying to retrieve body of kinsmen or friend: Meggitt 1977, 20.

28. Single shot: for example, four out of five men killed in the opening scene of the first battle (cited p. 153) are hit by a spear thrown at them without warning. Killed while dismounting: e.g. 11.423. Killed by third party: 15.539-41; 16.319-25; cf. 11.251-2. Archers' use of surprise: 8.266-79; 11.369-79. Killed while body-snatching: e.g. 4.467-9; 15.524-9; 17.288-94. Stabbed in back during flight: e.g. 5.38-41. Killed while in shock: 13.434-44; 16.401-10, 806-21.

29. Deluded hopes: 13.374-84; 16.830-42; 21.184-99; 22.331-3. Savaging of corpse: 11.452-5; 16.836; 21.122-7; 22.335-6.

30. Hector: 22.369-94. A collective interest in humiliating the enemy explains why men other than the killer take it upon themselves to seize enemy dead (4.463-6, 491-3; 14.476-7; 16.570-8; 17.288-95), why pairs of men work together to this end (13.197-202; 15.540-5), and why massive fights develop from the attempt to seize and mutilate the bodies of Sarpedon (16.555-61) and Patroclus (18.176-7). On the revenge and mutilation, see Lendon 2000; van Wees 1996, 52-3. Among the Mae Enga, too, mutilation is motivated by revenge; collective efforts are made to kill an enemy and 'hack open his chest, planting there, as a mark of obloquy, a pandanus or casuarina seedling' (Meggitt 1977, 19).

31. *Iliad* 13.85-9, 394-6, 434-8; 16.401-3.

32. Eating, drinking, washing: e.g. *Iliad* 5.794-8; 10.572-7; 11.596-804; 19.154-72, 198-237. Fainting: e.g. 5.694-8; 11.355-9; 14.409-39; 15.10-11, 240-3.

Panicking: e.g. 16.688-90; 17.175-80. Wounded retreating: e.g. 14.62-3, 128-30; 16.509-12. See van Wees 1996, 6-9; Starr 1979.

33. So Brown 1973, 58-9; Meggitt 1977, 21; Heider 1979, 96-7.

34. See Silk 1987, 73-4; van Wees 1996, 6.

35. So e.g. Finley 1977, 116-17, and Redfield 1975, 154. The main evidence cited consists of Achilles' refusal to fight even when his comrades are dying, and Hector's decision to fight Achilles and risk death despite his father's advice to 'save the Trojans' by retreating (22.56-7). In neither case is personal glory the issue: Achilles is retaliating for a perceived slight for which he blames both his commander and his comrades, while Hector acts from a sense of shame and responsibility: he fights because he feels that this is what the Trojans expect of him, and what is in their best interests: see van Wees 1996, 23-5; Cairns 1993, 81-2; Fenik 1978, 69-90.

36. Fatherland: *Iliad* 12.243; 15.496-7; 17.156-8. Protection of women, etc.: 5.482-6; 8.55-7; 10.420-2; 15.497-9; 18.223-4; 21.586-8; cf. 9.327; 18.265. It is unreasonable to insist, as some do, that Homeric warriors are concerned only to defend their *own* families: all the above references are to the *collective* defence of *all* women, children and elderly. Hector as defender: 6.262, 403; 16.835-6; 22.433-4, 507; 24.500, 729-30; cf. 9.396 ('best men' of Greeks 'protect the towns'); 9.531, 597 (Meleager); 11.242 (Iphidamas 'helping the townsfolk'); 16.548-50 (Sarpedon 'a bulwark of the city'). On patriotism, see van Wees 1996, 14-16; Raaflaub 1993, 41-2, 57-8; Greenhalgh 1972.

37. *Iliad* 6.6; 8.182; 11.797-803; 16.39-45; 18.129, 200-1; cf. 13.47, 426; 14.391; 16.75, 362-3, 512.

38. Appeals to Achilles to help comrades: *Iliad* 9.247-51, 300-3, 515-18, 630-2; 16.31-2; cf. 11.762-3. Several heroes are criticised for (alleged) failures to help friends: 5.462-6; 16.538-40; 17.702-4.

39. Fighting as a 'favour': *Iliad* 1.152-60; 4.95-6; 5.21115.449; 9.315-27; 17.144-55, 291; also *Odyssey* 5.306-7 (cf. 3.162-4); 13.265; cf. MacLachlan 1993, 13-22. Emotional reactions: e.g. 4.153-4, 494; 5.670; 13.403; 15.436; 17.591, 694-6; 18.17, 32 (Antilochus); 18.22-15 (Achilles). On the possibility of sexual relations between Achilles and Patroclus, see also 24.130-1, with van Wees 1996, 19, 66 n. 53; Ogden 1996, 123-5; Mauritsch 1992, 111-22; Clarke 1978.

40. See *Iliad* 1.366-9, 2.689-91 for the prizes of Agamemnon and Achilles. For the rest of the evidence, and the distinction between 'prize' and regular 'share': van Wees 1992, 299-308.

41. 'Shirking': *Iliad* 1.229-32; 2.235-42; 6.326; 9.524-99; 13.107-10; 14.49-51, 131-2; cf. van Wees 1996, 19-21.

42. *Iliad* 7.124-31. 'Be men!': 5.429; 6.112; 8.174; 11.287; 15.487, 561, 661-2; 734; 16.270; 17.185. 'Women' and 'little boys': 2.235, 289, 337-8; 7.96, 235-6; 8.163; 11.389; 20.244-5, 252-5. See further van Wees 1996, 21-3; Cairns 1993, 48-146; Riedinger 1980.

43. *Iliad* 17.285-7, 321-2. For many similar passages, see van Wees 1996, 67-8 nn. 64-5.

44. Diomedes: 5.135-6, 432-44; 6.97, 100-1, 278. Achilles: 20.372; 21.542-3; 22.312-13. Hector: 8.96, 299, 355; 9.238-9, 305; 13.53-4; 15.605; 21.5; for his errors, see Redfield 1975, 146-59.

45. Blazing eyes: 12.466; 19.365-6 (also grinding teeth); 15.607-8 (also foaming); cf. 8.348-9.

46. Shivers: *Iliad* 20.261-3 (Achilles); 5.596 (Diomedes); cf. e.g. 11.254, 345; 16.119. Need for armour: 18.126-201. Modern berserkers and 'nutters', see van

Wees 1996, 47-9; Shay 1994, 77-99. 'Think and retreat': 5.440-4; cf. 16.707-11; see further Griffin 1987, 89-90.

47. Detienne 1968, 121-2, cf. 124-5; further developed by e.g. Daraki 1980.

48. For the contrast with hoplites, see also Vidal-Naquet 1986, esp. 120-2; Vernant 1980, 28-9.

12. The archaic phalanx

1. Archilochus F3; cf. *Iliad* 2.536-45. Local historian: Archemachus *FGrH* 424 F 9, cited by Strabo 10.3.6; Plutarch, *Theseus* 5.2-3.

2. For the view that the hoplite phalanx was fully developed by either 700 or 650 BC, see p. 152 with nn. 5, 6. For opposition to this view, see Wheeler 1991, 129-31; van Wees 1994, 141-3. Some of the main arguments in this chapter are developed in more detail in van Wees 2000a.

3. Dark Age armour: pp. 48-9. Hair-grabbing in sword duels: see also Ahlberg 1971, figs 47-9. Drawn swords make up 44% of weapons shown in use on Attic MG and LG vases: van Wees 1994, 144, table 1. Swords in graves: Snodgrass 1964, 180.

4. Countless warrior figures are equipped with a pair of spears, although spears actually levelled at, or hitting, someone account for only 24% of weapons shown in use That spears were mainly used as missiles is implied by (a) figures wielding spear and sword simultaneously, i.e. presumably throwing the spear first, then fighting with the sword (Ahlberg 1971, nos A1, B4 (figs 2, 31); (b) the appearance of warriors pierced by one or more spears which are not held by anyone and must thus have been thrown (Ahlberg 1971, nos A7-9, A11, B14); (c) the absence of scenes in which warriors 'duel' with spears, whereas there are many scenes of 'duelling' with swords (Lorimer 1947, 98).

5. Drawn bows account for 32% of weapons shown in use, see van Wees 1994, 144.

6. Of 23 Geometric archers featuring in Ahlberg 1971, 14 stand directly face to face with an opponent (with Dipylon shields: A4; B4; shooting opponent through head or neck: A5, A8, B5; others: B3, B4 (bis), B7, B9, B10, B11 (tris)). Another six run in a line (no. A2) and the remaining three stand behind another figure facing the same way (nos A3, A5 (bis)).

7. 'Leaning shields': *Iliad* 11.593; 13.488; 22.4; see Appendix 3 for the implications of this for Homeric warfare. 'Legs apart': Tyrtaeus F 10.31-2; 11.21-2; cf. Archilochus F 114.3-4 West.

8. The posture is clear in images from the late archaic period onwards, but it also features in earlier representations, albeit in a more stylised manner: see van Wees 2000a, 128-9.

9. Tyrtaeus F 11.23-4. There is thus no reason to take this passage to imply a shield actually reaching the feet: contra Helbig 1911, 19-21; Nilsson 1929b, 241-4; Lorimer 1947, 122-6; Lazenby 1985, 77.

10. Tyrtaeus F 11.31; 19.14-15 West. For 'pushing' see further pp. 188-91.

11. That the hoplite shield *dictated* a dense formation was posited without argument (other than a reference to Thucydides 5.71, see pp. 185-6) by Helbig 1909, 66-7, and Lorimer 1947, 76-7; it was subsequently simply taken for granted (e.g. Andrewes 1956, 32, and Forrest 1966, 90), until challenged by Snodgrass 1964, 197; 1965, 111 (also Salmon 1977, 85 n. 6; Krentz 1985, 53). In response to the challenge, Greenhalgh 1973, 73, Cartledge 1977, 20, and Hanson 1991, esp. 67-8 and n. 14, have developed and refined this view, arguing that the hoplite shield did not dictate a dense formation but *presupposed* an existing practice of close-order fighting.

12. The evidence for hoplites with javelins is discussed in detail in van Wees 2000a, 147-9.

13. Alcaeus F 140.10 L-P; Archilochus F 139.6 West; Callinus F 1.14 West; *Iliad* 11.364, 20.451.

14. Earliest illustration in art: Lechaion aryballos, *c.* 690 BC (Corinth CP-2096; Snodgrass 1964, fig. 15ab); see also an early Boeotian plaque (Johansen 1923, 139, fig. 106), and further van Wees 2000a, 152-4.

15. The phrase quoted appears at 16.773; for other passages implying a prominent presence of archers, see van Wees 1988, 11 with n. 36; 1994, 134 with n. 63.

16. Snodgrass 1964, 250; 1999 (1967), 81.

17. For detailed discussion of these vases, see van Wees 2000a, 139-46.

18. For closer analysis of this important vase, see van Wees 2000a, 134-9, and Franz 2002, 151-6, contra the common interpretation of this vase as showing two armies in tight formation, marching in step to the music of a piper, and about to engage in hand-to-hand combat (so e.g. Nilsson 1929b, 240; Lorimer 1947, 80-3; Snodgrass 1964, 138; 1967/1999, 58; Cartledge 1977, 19; Salmon 1977, 87; but note the reservations of Helbig 1911, 38-9; Krentz 1985, 52; Wheeler 1991, 130).

19. See especially the extended sequence at *Iliad* 13.330-495, and generally Chapter 11.

20. Contra Pritchett 1991b, 186-7. It is true that the hoplite shield was too heavy to be suspended by a strap and carried on one's back in retreat and flight, as lighter shields are in Homer, but the bronze cuirass protected a soldier's back at least as effectively as any light shield could, so those who could afford a cuirass at any rate took no greater risks than Homeric heroes when they turned their backs to the enemy (contra Greenhalgh 1972, 73, and Cartledge 1977, 20). The weight of the panoply should not be overestimated: the careful calculations of Franz 2002, 339-49, show that a set of Corinthian helmet, bronze cuirass and greaves would weigh about 6-8 kg (13-18 lbs), about the same as the shield, while the full range of extras, from ankle- to arm-guards, would add only about 3.5 kg (8 lbs). Franz (ibid.) points out that full hoplite arms and armour weighed less than the equipment of an Augustan Roman legionary.

21. Running hoplites are especially prominent in Athenian art from *c.* 575 BC onwards: e.g. Brijder 1983, pls 5bef, 18b, 22d, 29d, 36fij, 38ab, 41f. Race in armour: Pausanias 5.8.10.

22. See pp. 50-2 (Boeotian shield).

23. In art, this change in representation certainly occurred *after* 640, and probably after 625 BC (the date of a Corinthian 'still life' of hoplite equipment with a pair of spears: Berlin 3148; van Wees 2000a, fig. 16), which for most views of the development of the phalanx is an inconveniently late date, and thus usually glossed over (even by Snodgrass 1964, 204).

24. Tyrtaeus is conventionally dated *c.* 650, but there is no evidence for this. The *Suda*'s entry for *Tyrtaios* says that he was 'a contemporary of the so-called Seven Sages, or even older. He flourished in the 35th Olympiad' (i.e. 640-637 BC; cf. Jerome 96b Helm: 633-632). The exact date assumes that Tyrtaeus was indeed a generation older than the Seven Sages; if he was their contemporary, his date would be around 600 BC. His association with the so-called Messenian Revolt supports the latter date: the most reliable evidence for the revolt puts its end *c.* 600 BC: see Parker 1991.

25. F 11.29-34; see also FF 11.12; 12.12; 19.13 West.

26. FF 10.15; 12.19 West; cf. F 11.11-13, cited below.

27. FF 10.16-32; 11.4-27; see also 12.15-18 West.

28. Quotations: FF 11.11-13; 11.28; 23.8-11; 12.15-17 West.

29. F 14 West. Mimnermus is dated to the 37th Olympiad (632-629), or 'some say' to the time of the Seven Sages, i.e. *c.* 600 BC, just like Tyrtaeus (see n. 24 above): *Suda*, entry for *Mimnermos*.

30. Understood in this way, Tyrtaeus' exhortations do not seem at all 'confused', as has been claimed by e.g. Nilsson 1929b, 241-4; Lorimer 1947, 121-7; Cartledge 1977, 25-6; Lazenby 1985, 76-7.

31. Tyrtaeus' appeal has been explained away as epic 'pastiche' (Nilsson 1929b, 241-4; Lorimer 1947, 122-7), but that is highly unlikely in a song of exhortation addressed to real warriors fighting real wars. (In any case, Homer's language in describing the same *modus operandi* is very different from Tyrtaeus'.)

32. For the Battle of the Great Trench, see the scholion ad Aristotle, *Nicomachean Ethics* 1116a36-b1; with Tyrtaeus FF 9, 23.5; 23a.19 West; Pausanias 4.6.2, 17.2 and 7. The classical phalanx, by contrast, could not afford to retreat or flee at all and did not need such an obstacle to retreat.

33. See Tyrtaeus FF 10.1-2, 13; 12.34 (defence of land/*patris*); 10.13-14; 12.34 (protection of children); 10.16, 21, 26; 11.14-16, 19-20; 12.17 (avoidance of shame); 10.27-30; 12.1-14, 24-44 (striving for glory); cf. Meier 1998, 292-322. Cf. Callinus F 1.16-19, and Homer's *Iliad*; see pp. 162-5.

34. See e.g. Cartledge 1977, 12, 20.

35. Lissarrague 1990, 13-15; he gives references to the relevant vases in his n. 8. Cf. Ducrey 1985, 63. The vase-painting which comes closest to representing the phalanx – in some but not all respects closer than the Chigi jug – is a scene of the sack of Troy, see Fig. 21a; cf. Fig. 20.

36. See van Wees 2000a, 132-3. I fail to understand how Franz 2002, 197, can see men engaged in close combat (against an invisible enemy?) in this image. There are possible parallels for this scene in the crouching hoplite figures found in Laconian and Attic vase painting: some are clearly lying in ambush, but others may represent rear ranks, rather than troops 'digging in', as Hanson has suggested (1989, 136).

37. Around 575-550, kneeling archers appear on e.g. on a vase by the Tydeus Painter (British Museum B40; Payne 1931, no. 1373, pl. 38, 2, 4, 7) and, with a stone-thrower, on a Laconian pithos: Droop 1929, 88, 92, pls 15-16. A rare slinger appears on a Corinthian vase of *c.* 625-600: Rawlings 2000, 240, fig. 1.

38. Kneeling archer figurines: Wace 1929, 262, pl. 183, 16-17 (Lead I, *c.* 650-620); 269, pl. 191,18-19 (Lead II, 620-580); 276, pl. 97,33 (Lead III-IV, 580-500). Dates: Boardman 1963. See n. 43 below.

39. For the artistic evidence, see Vos 1963, and esp. Lissarrague 1990, who stresses the symbolism of the contrast of barbarian archer and Greek hoplite, but rejects the idea that Scythian archers might have actually fought among Athenian hoplites. See pp. 59-60, 181 for archers in the Persian Wars.

40. The evidence is assembled and discussed in Greenhalgh 1973, 84-145.

41. Other vases showing chariots horses in the thick of the action: e.g. Brijder 1983, pls 12c, 13a, 38f, 44ad.

42. Arming scenes with archers: Lissarrague 1990, 36-42 and 246-7 (22 vases of 520-500 and two of 490; one vase of 530 BC features no spears); contrast the group discussed ibid., 57-8 (12 scenes of hieroscopy dating to 520-500, featuring 14 hoplites, only three of whom have a pair of spears). For pairs of spears carried by mounted hoplites, see e.g. Greenhalgh 1973, figs 47, 53, 60, 66, 71, 73, 74 (*c.* 625-500; all on horseback) and Wrede 1916, *passim* (all on chariots).

43. For figurines of non-combatant archers, who may be hunters, see Wace 1929, 278, 98, 18-19 (Lead V, 500-425). In Lead VI (425-300) archers disappear altogether. Literary evidence: Herodotus 9.60 (Plataea); Thucydides 4.55.2 (institution of archer corps).

44. Pausanias 1.15 describes three monumental paintings in the Painted Stoa of *c.* 460 BC, featuring epiphanies of Athena, Heracles and the heroes Marathon, Theseus, and Echetlaos; the latter is mentioned again at 1.32.3-4, which also mentions the haunting of the battlefield. Cf. Herodotus 9.27 for the linking of Amazons, Troy and Marathon, and 6.105-6 for the epiphany of Pan.

45. Pausanias 1.32.3-5; 7.15.7; 10.20.2; he claims to have seen the battlefield tomb of the fallen slaves; cf. Hunt 1998, 26-8, though his assumption that the Athenians would mobilise slaves but not the free poor seems to me unlikely (for the role of the free poor in general levies, see p. 62).

46. 6.112.1. Archaic running hoplites: pp. 171-2. Normal distance: pp. 186-7.

47. For such manoeuvres, see p. 191.

48. This is true if what happened at Marathon was an accidental development, as Herodotus' account implies (and e.g. Lazenby 1993, 68-70, accepts), and even more so if one assumes, as many modern scholars do, that it was a deliberate tactic (e.g. Green 1996, 37; Santosuosso 1997, 35-6).

49. Note that Herodotus gives all credit to the 300 Spartiates, ignoring the presence of *perioikoi* and helots, see pp. 61, 83-4. The 300 Spartans at Thermopylae were not a standing unit, but they were hand-picked: Herodotus 7.205. Modern accounts of Thermopylae: e.g. Green 1996, 134-44; Lazenby 1993, 130-8, 141-8; 1985, 83-96; Hignett 1963, 141-8.

50. Plutarch, *On the Malice of Herodotus* 43 (*Moralia* 873f-74a). Herodotus' claim is evidently based on the fact that the Persians wore no helmets or greaves, but felt caps and leather trousers (5.49.3, 97.1; 7.61.1), so that, once they had lost their shields, they were left with no armour but their iron scale cuirasses (7.61.1). Once they had put down their bows, they were left only with short spears and daggers (7.61.1) to set against the longer spears and swords of the Spartans.

51. So Hunt 1997, though one should note that the hoplite and his seven helots could hardly have formed a regular eight-deep file: javelin- and stone-throwers would not have fought in an organised formation.

52. *psiloi machimoi*, 9.30, *bis*; cf. his description of the Persian army, which makes a sharp distinction between 'the combatant element' (*to machimon*) and 'the servant element' (*hê therapêiê*; 7.186, *bis*).

53. The Spartans emphatically complained about his suicidal attitude, not about leaving the ranks as such: they concluded that Aristodemus 'had wanted to die conspicuously' (9.71.3), and refused to honour him 'because he wanted to die' (71.4), whereas the men they did honour 'had not wanted to die' (71.3).

54. The final infantry battle of the Persian Wars, at Mycale, adds no further detail. In outline it almost exactly mirrors the battle of Plataea – with the Persians shooting arrows from from behind a shield barrier (9.99) until the Greeks 'push through the shields', after which there is a long battle, which ends with the Persians taking refuge behind fortifications, until the Greeks breach these as well (9.102) – with the roles of Spartans and Athenians reversed. The battle supposedly took place on the same day as the battle of Plataea (9.100-1), which makes the parallels even more suspicious.

55. See especially Boedeker 1998; 2002, 97-109.

56. Champion combat: p. 133; mounted hoplites: pp. 57-60; warrior burials: pp. 145-6.

57. Sharing out of booty: below, p. 236; and above, p. 163 for Homeric practice. A different situation is implied in one passage – and only one passage (see n. 61 below) – which refers to 'taking the *aristêion*' (8.11) for the naval battle at Artemision (see below, p. 229), as if there were a single prize for the single bravest soldier in a battle (as in classical Athens: below, p. 194). The *aristêia* given to Apollo (8.122) and to Eurybiades and Themistocles (8.124) are one-off honours, and are not awarded for personal bravery in battle, so do not imply a practice of awarding institutionalised prizes for valour.

58. It has been suggested that the Greeks in the Persian Wars did not fight in the normal hoplite manner because they faced a non-Greek enemy (e.g. Hanson 2000, 211-12). It is unlikely, however, that they completely abandoned their normal way of fighting, because (a) even in the fourth century hoplites found it very hard to adapt to fighting light-armed opponents, and (b) Herodotus' account stresses that the Spartans win by doing what they normally excel at, not by adopting radically new tactics.

59. Herodotus' statement (6.111.3) that the Athenian centre at Marathon was reduced to *taxias oligas*, often translated as 'a few ranks', literally means 'a few units' (a *taxis* in Athens was a tribal regiment) and need not imply actual ranks. His claim that at Plataea the Persian 'formation was placed in order *epi pleunas*' (9.31.2) could mean 'in greater depth' or 'over a greater space' (since it extended beyond the Spartan line to face the Tegeans also), and does not need to imply the existence of regular ranks. In any case, the lack of specific numbers is significant: contrast later battle narratives (p. 185).

60. *Tropaia*: see pp. 136-8.

61. Herodotus simply reports tradition at 7.227 and 9.73, but draws his own conclusions at 9.71.1-2 (about the Spartan performance) and 9.71.2 (about Aristodemus, as cited above). Most often, he uses the verb *aristeuein* to describe outstanding performances (e.g. 3.55; 5.112; 8.17 [bis]; 9.81, 105): this simply means 'to be the best', not 'to be awarded a/the *aristêion* (i.e. prize for bravery)', as is generally assumed (see Pritchett 1974, 276-90; Hamel 1998, 64-70): this is clear from Herodotus' arguments in deciding who was 'best', from his use of 'winning a good reputation' (*eudokimein*, 7.227; 9.73.1; cf. 8.93.1) as the equivalent of *aristeuein*, and from the fact that some who are 'best' are rewarded with special funerary honours (i.e., they are dead and not eligible for prizes).

62. See p. 157.

63. See Appendix 3 for a discussion of this point.

13. The classical phalanx

1. F 72 K-A; cf. the joke in *Lysistrata* 282 about 'sleeping seventeen shields deep in front of the gates' of the Acropolis while besieging Cleomenes in 508. See above, p. 183 n. 59, for the absence of specific depths in Herodotus. Evidence for depths is assembled in Pritchett 1971, 134-43.

2. Thucydides 4.94.1; 5.68.3 ('not all the same, but according to the decision of each *lochagos*, yet on the whole eight deep'; cf. 4.93.4: depths of Theban allies 'whatever each adopted'); 6.67.1. Depths of eight: Xenophon, *Hellenica* 2.4.34; 3.2.16; 6.2.21; *Anabasis* 7.1.23; Polyaenus 2.2.9. Note also the failed attempt to agree a standard depth at Nemea in 394 (Xenophon, *Hellenica* 4.2.18).

3. Charges against city walls: Diodorus 13.72.4, 6 (4, against Athens);

Polyaenus 2.1.24 (2, against Thebes). Display depth of four: Xenophon, *Anabasis* 1.2.15.

4. Spartans: Xenophon, *Hellenica* 6.2.12 (a depth of eight as 'weak' rather than normal), 6.4.12 (up to 12) and 6.5.19 (nine or ten); Xenophon's *Spartan Constitution* 11.4 assumes possible depths of six and 12. Thebans: Thucydides 4.93.4 (25); Xenophon, *Hellenica* 4.2.18 (much deeper than 16), 6.4.12 (50). The only other instance of such depth occurs in a battle fought in the streets of Piraeus, where a lack of space forced the army of the Thirty to stand 50 deep (*Hellenica* 2.4.11).

5. Depths of 16: Thucydides 6.67.2 (mass levy against 'picked' forces, cf. 68.2); Xenophon, *Hellenica* 4.2.18 (24,000 hoplites and 1,550 cavalry against 13,500 hoplites and 600 cavalry, 4.2.16-17); cf. the 'extreme depth' adopted by a large Peloponnesian army against an irregular force of Athenian rebels: *Hellenica* 2.4.34.

6. E.g. Pritchett 1971, 144; Hanson 1989, 119-21; Lazenby 1991, 93; Luginbill 1994, 60-1. Pritchett 1971, 144-54, assembles the evidence, but fails to consider the implications of the Polybius passage cited below (which he quotes selectively, 145, 152) and reaches his conclusions largely on the basis of hellenistic tactical manuals, which almost all refer to the Macedonian rather than hoplite phalanx.

7. Later military manuals define six feet as the 'natural' interval adopted by soldiers, and three feet as the interval of a 'dense' formation, even for the Macedonian phalanx (see n. 6 above); they also add a third interval of only 1.5 feet, feasible only for stationary defensive formations (Asclepiodotus 4.1-3; Aelian, *Tactics* 11.1-5; Arrian, *Tactics* 11).

8. So Krentz 1985, 51-5, esp. 54; 1994, 46-7; cf. Goldsworthy 1997, 15-17; Cawkwell 1989, 382-3. Thucydides' describes the phalanx as drawing closer together during the advance (n. 15 below), which implies a formation open enough to make it possible and tempting to do so. If intervals had been only three feet to begin with, there would have been no room or need for further bunching.

9. Polybius 12.21.3 and 7. The intervals in each case are not explicitly stated, but implicit in his calculations, and consistent with the intervals he assumes elsewhere (12.19.7: six feet for marching order; 18.29.2: three feet for battle order). The only classical source to use *synaspizein* is Xenophon, *Hellenica* 7.4.23 (and at 3.5.11, where it is a metaphor for 'join forces'): see Krentz 1985, 51, who points out that *synaspismos* even in Polybius does not have the technical meaning attributed to it by still later tactical manuals, as cited in n. 7 above.

10. Plato, *Apology* 28d; in 29a, Socrates' reference to *lipotaxia* makes it clear that he is indeed speaking of a station in the battle-line. The passage is all the more significant because Socrates' argument is that, as in warfare, he is obeying a higher authority and not acting on a private whim: allowing the possibility that a man might choose his own station tends to undermine his case; if he mentions it all the same it must have been common practice. In Lysias 16.15, Mantitheus boasts of having 'arranged' for himself to fight in the front rank. See Xenophon, *Memorabilia* 3.1.9 for the notion of putting the best men first and last as well as the difficulty of knowing which men are good and which are bad. For the limit of officers' authority, see pp. 109-13.

11. *Paian*: Pritchett 1971, 105-8. Trumpet signal: Krentz 1991, 115-16.

12. Length of advance: among the shortest distances recorded is Xenophon's 'less than three or four *stadia*' (= 500-700 m; *Anabasis* 1.8.17), among the longest the 20 *stadia* (3.6 km) allegedly marched by Cyrus' army before they could even see the enemy; this fictional advance was interrupted by three stops to restore order to the formation (*Education of Cyrus* 7.1.4-5). Vulnerability of phalanx and terrain: Aristotle, *Politics* 1303b12-17; Polybius 18.31.5; Pritchett 1985, 82-5.

13. Vivid images of soldiers breaking into a run: Xenophon, *Anabasis* 1.2.17, 1.8.18; *Hellenica* 4.3.17 (200 yards). See Hanson 1989, 144-6 (overestimating its duration at 'less than two minutes').

14. Diodorus 12.70.1; Plutarch, *Pelopidas* 8.1-5; and see p. 59. At Delium a front rank of 300 and a depth of 25 gives a total close to the 7,000 men cited by Thucydides 4.93.3.

15. Thucydides 5.71.1, cited p. 185 (cf. Xenophon, *Hellenica* 4.2.18). The phenomenon described by Thucydides, whereby an army's right wing which is initially stationed directly opposite the enemy's left wing will end up extending a long way to the right of the enemy, makes sense only if the formations on both sides contract towards the right during the advance because each man draws a little closer to his right-hand neighbour (so that the initial intervals between them must have been wider than the minimum three feet: see n. 8 above). Lack of formation drill: see pp. 87-8, 90, 92, 94.

16. Xenophon, *Constitution of the Spartans* 13.8, *Hellenica* 4.2.20 (Nemea); Plutarch, *Lycurgus* 22. For the blood sacrifice, see pp. 120, 135 and 192.

17. At Cunaxa, Xenophon took his place in the hoplite battle line on horseback (see pp. 57-8); Epaminondas and others had their 'boys' beside them in the battle (p. 69).

18. Cavalry and/or light armed on one or both wings, e.g. Thuc. 4.93.4, 94.1; 5.67.1-2; 6.67.2. Light-armed ahead of the phalanx: Thuc. 6.69.2. See p. 196.

19. Hanson 1989, 157, cites it as 'the most notorious evidence', but offers no other explicit evidence; he argues, however, that many battle narratives only make sense on the *assumption* 'that both sides literally collided together'. Lazenby 1991, 92, cites it as his only example of a literal collision, which he argues might 'sometimes' occur, but was not the norm. Pritchett 1985, 55-6, on the other hand, cites the passage as evidence for intense hand-to-fighting rather than a physical collision.

20. Contra Adcock 1957, 4, 6, 8; Hanson 1989, 156-7, and Luginbill 1994, 57-8, who stress the physical impact, although they also acknowledge the psychological factors. For the terrifying effect of the mere sight of the charge, see e.g. Xenophon, *Anabasis* 1.2,17-18; Hanson 1989, 161; Lazenby 1991, 91. If the physical impetus generated by the run had been important to success in battle, it is hard to understand why the most successful armies – the Spartan and the Macedonian – did *not* run.

21. Although this is a duel between heroes, it is not modelled on Homer: both the trumpet signal and the fact that both men run forward and immediately fight hand to hand, rather than throwing spears or rocks first, are non-Homeric features and correspond to the tactics of classical hoplites.

22. Ancient references to spears snapping at the outset, therefore, do not presuppose the added impetus of a running charge (contra Hanson 1989, 164, citing the sources). Pritchett notes (1985, 56 n. 167) that Homer mentions three spears which snap, and all three are *thrown* (*Iliad* 13.162, 608; 17.607).

23. For clear instances of metaphorical usage of 'push' in Homeric and naval warfare, see Krentz 1985, 55-6 (cf. Goldsworthy 1997, 17-25). Similarly, news reports on the most recent war in the Gulf were littered with references to the 'push towards Baghdad'.

24. Diodorus 15.55.4. A particularly striking example is Polybius' claim that in the Macedonian phalanx the rear ranks 'by the very weight of their bodies' forced the front ranks onwards (18.29.2-30.4): even this is a metaphor, since he also says that there were three-foot intervals between ranks, and at this distance soldiers could exert no physical pressure on one another.

25. The evidence cited by Hanson (1989, 175-6) for hoplites being trampled or crushed actually refers to armies caught in confined spaces, not in open field battles: Xenophon, *Hellenica* 4.4.12, involves an army with its back literally against a wall. (This is the only relevant evidence relating to Greek troops: Thucydides 5.72 concerns men trampled during a panicked flight; Diodorus 16.86.3, if it refers to trampling at all, concerns an advancing enemy stepping on the bodies of the fallen.) Herodotus 7.223 and Ammianus 18.8.12 refer to Persians and Romans, respectively, forcing their way through narrow passages; Lucan, *Civil War* 4.787 to Roman troops surrounded on all sides.

26. Xenophon, *Hellenica* 5.4.33 (the man in question fell and got up *three* times in the course of battle, so that one cannot argue that this could only happen 'in the very few seconds following the collison'; contra Hanson 1989, 175), 6.4.13 (king Cleombrotus carried out of battle at Leuctra); Theophrastus, *Characters* 25 (common soldier carried to camp while battle continues).

27. Classical vase-painting shows the two types of grip side by side, and both are roughly equally common, despite the fact that the spear was carried underarm during the charge: see Anderson 1970, 88; 1991, 19, 31; also Hanson 1989, 162-5; Lazenby 1991, 92-3.

28. Euripides, *Andromache* 1131-5; Herodotus 9.74.2; Homer, *Iliad* 7.237-41. For the war dance, see p. 91 with n. 4. There is no reason to think that this dance represented a more mobile 'ephebic' style of fighting.

29. The point of view expressed by Nicias in Plato, *Laches* 182a; Plato himself advocated the adoption of weapons training in his ideal city (*Laws* 833d-834a). Nicias should not be taken to say that weapons training is *slightly* useful in battle and *truly* useful only in flight and pursuit: he merely says that in the latter circumstances it is *even* more useful (because in flight and pursuit the formation breaks up, and one cannot count on the help of others but is thrown back entirely on one's own skill). For the ideology of amateurism, see pp. 89-93.

30. Euripides, *Phoenician Women* 1404-15; see also Pritchett 1985, 64; Hanson 1989, 167 ('One wonders how this was accomplished when there was pressure at his back as well': the answer must be that there was no such pressure). Armed combat no longer existed as a sport, and single combats were no longer fought before battle, so the only context in which such techniques could have been practised was battle (contra Lazenby 1991, 94).

31. Xenophon, *Hellenica* 4.3.19 (Coronea); cf. *Education of Cyrus* 7.1.33-4 (Egyptians); Thucydides 4.96.2 (Delium). See also p. 168 for the use of the shield in pushing.

32. *Education of Cyrus* 6.3.21-2, 6.4.17, 6.3.23. Strictly speaking, it is the Persian king Cyrus who orders the adoption of a two-rank phalanx, but Xenophon presents Cyrus as the ideal commander, and there is no doubt that Cyrus here serves as the author's mouthpiece.

33. So Krentz 1985; Goldsworthy 1997.

34. The limited evidence for the duration of battles is assembled by Pritchett 1985, 46-51.

35. A rare exception was the battle of Solygeia in 425 BC (Thucydides 4.43.3-44.2).

36. Xenophon, *Hellenica* 4.2.21-2; other examples include Thucydides 3.108.2

and 5.73.2-4 (stressing that 'Spartan pursuits are short and cover no great distance').

37. Xenophon, *Hellenica* 4.3.16, 21. On the introduction of the *tropaion*, see pp. 136-8.

38. Xenophon, *Hiero* 6.7-8 for pre-battle nerves; Aristophanes, *Acharnians* 241, 1172-6 for soldiers soiling themselves; cf. Hanson 1989, 101-2, who perhaps overstimates how common this would have been: the classical references are all scathing – and scatological – jokes.

39. Xenophon, *Education of Cyrus* 6.2.33; *Hellenica* 6.4.8; 7.5.20. Spartan hair: Herodotus 7.208-9.

40. For evidence end interpretations, see Pritchett 1971, 109-15; Jameson 1991; Parker 2000.

41. Short pep-talks: Xenophon, *Education of Cyrus* 7.1.14; cf. Thucydides 4.96.1 (cut short). The precise form taken by Greek battle harangues is a matter of some debate: see Hansen 1993 versus Ehrhardt 1995; Clark 1995; Pritchett 2002, 1-80.

42. e.g. Xenophon, *Anabasis* 1.8.15-16.

43. Herodotus 7.222, 227; Thucydides 4.96.3; Xenophon, *Hellenica* 4.2.20 (Thespiae). Aristotle himself (ibid.) cites another example, a battle 'at the Hermaion', in 347.

44. *Hellenica* 6.4.8 (perhaps also at 5.4.40-4): cf. Hanson 1989, 126-31, who suggests that a state of near-drunkenness helps explain how hoplites could bring themselves to crash blindly into the enemy (139, 159). Given that the few sources we have all criticise intoxication, this seems unlikely.

45. *Nicomachean Ethics* 1115a6, 1116a10; cf. Thucydides 2.40.3. Detienne 1968, 122-6, calls the ideal *sôphrosynê*, but for Aristotle this was a completely different virtue, discussed immediately afterwards in the *Nicomachean Ethics*.

46. Aristotle, *Nicomachean Ethics* 1115a6-1117b23, quotations from 1116a27-30 and 17-19; cf. Thucydides 2.42.4. On *andreia*, see also pp. 38-40.

47. Tod II. 204; Pollux 8.105; Stobaeus 43.48; cf. Burckhardt 1996, 57-63.

48. Aristophanes' first four surviving comedies composed after Delium have two jokes each about Cleonymus' cowardice: *Clouds* 353-4, 670-80 (423 BC), *Wasps* 592-3, 822-3 (422 BC), *Peace* 673-8, 1295-1304 (421 BC), *Birds* 289-90, 1473-81 (414 BC). I would suggest that this is no coincidence, but that every single play composed by Aristophanes – and conceivably by the other comic poets, too – during this period made a point of mocking a notorious coward.

49. See pp. 111-12. For shame in archaic combat, see pp. 163-4, 174.

50. For the evidence, see n. 51 below. The only earlier evidence for a *single* prize awarded to the single bravest soldier is the award to Lycomedes after the first naval engagement at Artemisium (Herodotus 8.11), which may be an anachronism, or peculiar to naval combat (see p. 229); the other passages from Herodotus adduced by Pritchett 1974, 276-90, and Hamel 1998, 64-70, do not refer to prizes at all (see pp. 182-3 with nn. 57 and 61).

51. Alcibiades: Isocrates 16.29; Plato, *Symposion* 220de; Plutarch, *Alcibiades* 7.2-3. In the first of these passages, Alcibiades' son speaks of '*the* panoply', as if it were a standard part of the award at the time. Sophocles, in *Philoctetes* 1425-31 (409 BC), assumes that *aristêia* will come from the spoils; cf. *aristêia* 'and gifts' given to outstanding fighters in Sicily in 480 and 412 (Diodorus 11.25.1; 13.34.5). The award of a crown alone is advocated by Plato, *Laws* 943c (who envisages awarding crowns for second and third best as well), and attested in Aeschines 2.169.

52. Thucydides 4.116.2 (Brasidas); Diodorus 14.53.4 (Dionysius I). Cf. the

bounty of 10,000 drachmas offered by Athens for capturing Artemisia alive (Herodotus 8.93).

53. Thucydides 2.43.3, 44.4, 45.1 and 35.2.

54. Tod II. 204; cf. Appendix 2. Limited role of officer-imposed discipline: see pp. 108-13.

55. Sacred Band: see p. 59, and Ogden 1996.

56. Aeschylus, *Persians* 402-5 (cf. Aeneas Tacticus, preface 2); Thucydides 2.43.1.

57. Aeschylus' portrayal of the two groups of champions at Thebes (Aeschylus, *Seven Against Thebes* 375-676), which Detienne (1968, 126) cites as a representation of the contrast between heroic and hoplite mentalities, actually contrasts aggressive boasters and men of action – as the *Iliad* already did.

58. Diodorus 16.3.2 is the only source which explicitly attributes to Philip II the creation of a denser and differently equipped formation; see n. 67 below. Note also that Xenophon does not mention the restructuring of the Spartan army implied by his own history (see pp. 98-9 and Appendix 2) or the reforms of Iphicrates attested elsewhere (see p. 197).

59. See pp. 95-7.

60. See pp. 58-60 (elite units), 180-3 (hoplites and light-armed during the Persian Wars). For military changes after the Persian Wars, see pp. 98-9 (Sparta); 67, 237 (cavalry and archers). For these developments in general, see further the Conclusion. The spectacular Spartan victories at Plataea and Dipaea may have encouraged the spread of classical tactics by demonstrating the advantages of closed hoplite ranks. If there is any truth in the story of hoplites-only success at Marathon, one might attribute an important influence also to this battle (so Krentz 2002, 35-7); but see pp. 179-80 for reasons to doubt the reliability of this tradition.

61. Roles of cavalry and light-armed: see pp. 61-8.

62. Ambush: Thucydides 3.107.3-108.1 (Demosthenes at Olpae); 4.96.5-6 (Pagondas at Delium). Sideways movements: Thucydides 5.71.3 (see Appendix 2). Slanted advance: Diod. 15.55.2; cf. Vidal-Naquet 1986, 61-82. On tactical advances generally, see Wheeler (forthcoming).

63. See pp. 99 (hierarchy), 185 (depth).

64. See pp. 94-5 (training), 103-4 (mobilisation).

65. Diodorus 15.44.2-4; Nepos 11 (*Iphicrates*) 1.3-4. These two sources differ slightly on details, and are wrong to suggest that (a) *all* Athenian hoplites adopted the new equipment, and (b) the new troop type was the first to be called 'peltast', but they are unlikely to have simply invented this 'reform of Iphicrates'. What we can retain from their stories is surely that Iphicrates equipped some citizen troops as a new type of 'peltast'. See Parke 1933, 79-82; contra Griffith 1981; cf. n. 66 below.

66. Best 1968, 102-10, has pointed to evidence for Thracian peltasts equipped with thrusting spears rather than the more normal javelins, but these appear to be weapons of normal length, since they are carried with one hand (cf. Best's plates 3-4, 7-8, and A). The length of the spear was surely a new feature of Iphicrates' reform.

67. Main sources are Polybius 18.29-30 (see p. 185) and Diodorus 16.3 for its invention by Philip II. See also Best 1968, 139-42 on parallels with Iphicrates' 'peltasts'.

68. Demosthenes 8.11 (standing army), Diodorus 16.3.1 and Polyaenus 4.2.10 (formation-drill and marches), Frontinus 4.1.6 (no personal servants).

69. Boeotia, *c.* 250-245 BC: the evidence for this reform and its date is epigraphi-
cal: see Feyel 1942, 187-97. Sparta: Plutarch, *Cleomenes* 11.3. Achaean League:
Plutarch, *Philopoemen* 9.2; Pausanias 8.50.1. See in general e.g. Ma 2000, 346-7,
361.

Part VI. Ruling the Waves

1. Xenophon, *Hellenica* 1.6.15: 'he said that he would stop him committing
adultery (*moichônta*) with the sea'; my free translation tries to capture the
bluntness of these words in Greek.
2. Interception of gifts: 1.70 and 3.47. Jackson 2000, 142-3, points out that the
dedication of these gifts in the temple shows that their seizure was a public act,
not a private act of piracy. The fact that they were seized in successive years (47.2)
confirms that the Samians were persistently demonstrating their naval power.
Challenge to Corinth: 3.48 (apparently dated to *c.* 600 BC). Expedition against the
Aeginetans (described as 'thalassocrats' at 5.83.2) 'when Amphicrates was king in
Samos': 3.59.4. For Herodotus' reasons for playing down earlier naval powers, see
van Wees 2002, 338-40. More on Thucydides' account of naval history on p. 207.
3. See de Souza 1999, 26-30, 38-41, for the suppression of piracy. He is rightly
sceptical of its effectiveness, but Athens did undertake small, localised campaigns
against pirates (e.g. Thucydides 2.32, 69) and this was so much a part of Athens'
self-definition as a thalassocrat that Thucydides thought that 'in all probability'
earlier thalassocracies had done the same (1.4, 1.13.5; probably a mistaken
assumption: see pp. 205-6). The suppression of piracy also featured in Athens'
so-called Congress Decree (Plutarch, *Pericles* 17), which is important even if it was
a fourth-century forgery, the Moirocles Decree (Demosthenes 58.56), and in at
least a couple of genuine late fifth-century treaties (*IG* I³ 67 and 75; see de Souza
1999, 11-12). Naval patrols: Plutarch, *Pericles* 11.
4. See the terms of the armistice of 423 (Thucydides 4.118.5) and their refusal
to allow the Persians to sail the Aegean, even when they were prepared to cede
control of Ionia and the islands (8.56.4-5).
5. Herodotus 3.46-7, 54-6. For Sparta's other possible motives, see Cartledge
1982, 245-59.
6. See Strauss 2000, 261-7: 'The traditional elites of Athens ... could not bring
themselves to look at pictures of ships or rowers', and 'Thucydides loved the ships
but not the men who rowed them'. A more positive assessment of naval imagery in
Athens is offered by Pritchard 1998, 53-5.

14. The wall of wood

1. Quotations: Homer, *Odyssey* 3.72-4 (= 9.253-5; *Hymn to Apollo* 453-5) and
14.229-34. See Ahlberg 1971 for the vases; Jackson 2000 and 1993; van Wees 1992,
207-17, for the legitimacy of private raiding in Homer. De Souza 1999, 17-21,
argues that Homer does have qualms about private raiding.
2. See p. 96. That the ships were privately owned is nowhere explicitly stated,
but seems obvious, given that there is no evidence for state-owned ships until the
late sixth century.
3. What follows is similar in outline to the views of Figueira 1986 and Vélissaropoulos 1980, 17-21; for contrary views, see n. 8 below. *Naukraros* is probably the
archaic spelling of the classical word *nauklêros*, 'ship-captain'; *nau-* at any rate
clearly refers to ships, as all ancient sources and almost all modern scholars accept.

Laws: [Aristotle] *Athenian Constitution* 8.3; Photius, *Lexicon* s.v. *naukraria*; the phrase *tous naukrarous tous kata tên naukrarian,* 'the *naukraroi* [plural] who fall under the *naukraria* [singular]', shows that each unit had several *naukraroi* (so Figueira 1986, 272).

4. Herodotus 5.71.2. The graffito is found on a potsherd voting for the ostracism of Xanthippos; it dates to between 488/7 and 485/4 (*Athenian Constitution* 22.3, 6) and reads: 'This ostrakon declares that among the offending *prytaneis* Xanthippos son of Arriphron has committed the greatest injustice' (Agora P16873; see Figueira 1986). 'The offending *prytaneis'* must be a reference to the Alcmeonid family – into which Xanthippos had married – who were known as 'the accursed' and 'the offenders against the goddess' on account of their sacrilegious role in killing Cylon's supporters (Thucydides 1.126.11), a fact which had led to the family's expulsion from Athens only 20 years before the date of the ostrakon (*contra* Figueira 1986, 263). The graffito thus shows that in the 480s the Alcmeonids were believed to have acted against Cylon in their capacity as *prytaneis* of the *naukraroi,* as Herodotus said, not as archons, as Thucydides claimed (1.126.8). Both historians were evidently puzzled by these *prytaneis,* who no longer existed in their day: both assumed that those who dealt with Cylon must have been the chief magistrates, and both drew the wrong conclusion, with Herodotus inferring that the *prytaneis* rather than the archons 'governed Athens at that time', and Thucydides concluding that the archons rather than the *prytaneis* were in charge of dealing with Cylon. The correct solution is surely that the archons and the *naukraroi* worked together in this crisis, but that the responsibility for killing Cylon's supporters lay with the *naukraroi,* among whom the Alcmeonids and their supporters would have been prominent, given that they were known as the 'coastal' faction (Herodotus 1.59.3; *Athenian Constitution* 13.4) and were therefore likely to account for a large proportion of Athens' ship-owners.

5. *Athenian Constitution* 8.3 and 21.5 (like demes); Cleidemus *FGrH* 323 F 8 (like symmories: for the existence of 100 naval symmories from the mid-fourth century onwards, see p. 218).

6. Hesychius s.v. *naukraroi* (collect war-tax in their area); Ammonius s.v. *nauklêroi, naukraroi* (collect revenue from public property); Pollux 8.108 (financial duties and 'each *naukraria* provided two horsemen and one ship'; an anonymous lexicon (*Anecdota Bekker*) describes the *naukraroi* as 'those who provided the ships and acted as trierarchs and were subordinate to the polemarch' (1.283.20) and identifies Kolias as the location of one *naukraria* (1.275.20). For the *polemarchos,* see pp. 96, 99.

7. So Androtion *FGrH* 324 F 36; cf. Jordan 1975, 160-4. The Aldine scholiast to Aristophanes, *Clouds* 37, suggests that they also organised the Panathenaic procession, which featured a ship.

8. Many scholars are sceptical about the evidence for the *naukrariai* (e.g. Gabrielsen 1994, 19-24, and 1985; Haas 1985; Amit 1965, 104), but the above seems to me to make sense of all the available material. The only problems are the slight discrepancy between Herodotus and Thucydides, which is in fact easily explained (see n. 4 above), and the question of how the locally-based *naukrariai* related to the notionally kinship-based tribes, to which the solution may be either that these tribes were in fact also territorially based or that Aristotle was wrong to say that the *naukraria* was a subdivision of a tribe. If our reconstruction of the role of *naukraroi* is correct, the transfer of most of their functions to local and other elected officials was one of the most democratic elements in Cleisthenes' reforms (see pp. 213, 234), and deserves more scholarly attention than it has received.

9. Aegina, Salamis, and war over Sigeum, south of the Hellespont, see pp. 23, 26, 28, 36. The campaigns in the Chersonese (Herodotus 6.34-39) may originally have been private ventures, but were later brought under public control: Miltiades II was 'sent out' by Athens' rulers (39.1), and subsequently occupied Lemnos from there on behalf of Athens (6.136-40).

10. Herodotus 6.108; Thucydides 3.68.5.

11. Plutarch, *Themistocles* 4.4. But Themistocles' naval programme did in other ways transform Athens: see pp. 207-8, 236-7.

12. Miletus: Plutarch, *Moralia* 298cd, who offers a fanciful etymology of the name 'permanent sailors': they took all their important decisions on board ships. Cf. Vélissaropoulos 1980, 21-6; Gorman 2001, 108-10, who also discusses the inscriptions from Chalcis (*IG* 12.909, 923) and Eretria (Petrakos 1963). Eretrian law: *IG* XII.9 1273, 1274 (*SEG* 41.725) dated to 550-500 BC; see Cairns 1991, 310-13.

13. Law: Herodotus 6.89. It has been suggested that the law implies a publicly owned navy (Scott 2000, 107; de Souza 1998, 292 n.45), but I cannot see what purpose the law would have served if the ships were public property. Borrowing ships in *Odyssey*: 2.386-7; 4.630-57.

14. The passage cannot be simply dismissed as a hostile account of outrageous tyrannical behaviour (Jackson 2000, 143): stereotypical tyrannical behaviour may be violent, but it is never nonsensical.

15. Contra e.g. de Souza 1998; Scott 2000, who argue that public navies were unknown in early Greece.

16. The Phocaeans of Alalia had 60 ships in 535: Herodotus 1.166.2. Note that fleets of precisely the same order of magnitude are envisaged in Homer's Catalogue of Ships: the largest contingent travels in 100 ships (*Iliad* 2.576) while the Athenians have 50 (2.556), which puts them in the top one-third of the 29 contingents, which on average have 41 ships (40 being the median and the mode).

17. For the trireme, see above all Morrison et al. 2000, esp. 266-7 (30% shortfall in effective power).

18. Xenophon, *Oeconomicus* 8.8; also *Anabasis* 6.4.2 for the trireme's range in a day's travel; for its speed, see further Morrison et al. 2000, 102-6.

19. For Persia and the Ionian navy, see Wallinga 1993, 118-29, who, however, suggests that Polycrates' triremes came from his former ally Amasis of Egypt (84-101, 117). The story of Polycrates' triremes is presented by Herodotus (3.42) as part of a devious plan by Polycrates to get rid of his enemies, but stripped of this hostile slant what remains is a Persian demand for military support, to which Polycrates responds by manning 40 triremes, which desert before they even get to Egypt. Given that Polycrates' power had previously rested only on *pentekontoroi*, the most likely explanation of this episode seems to me that he struck a deal: Samian manpower and naval expertise in return for Persian ships. For Ionian triremes, see Herodotus 6.8 and Hipponax F 28 West.

20. Herodotus 5.47 (Philippos) and 6.39, 41 (Militiades). Miltiades' triremes are not explicitly said to be his own, but it does seem likely since the five ships with which he returned were 'filled with all the property he had' and one was commanded by his eldest son. The five Eretrian triremes, led by another top athlete, which went to Sardis in 499 may also have been private vessels (Herodotus 5.99).

21. Thucydides does *not* date these developments. His next sentence refers to ships built by a Corinthian shipwright, Ameinocles, for the Samians, *c.* 700 BC, and it is often assumed that these are triremes (e.g. Morrison et al. 2000, 38). This sentence, however, does not expand on what goes before, but is marked by the words 'and they *also* say ...' as the beginning of a digression into Corinth's much earlier naval history, which is ultimately traced back to a time when Corinth did not yet have ships at all (1.13.3-5; cf. Wallinga 1993, 13-16). Ameinocles is said to have built 'ships', not specifically triremes, and Thucydides singled out this episode not because it marked the first time triremes were exported, but in order to make his polemic point, implicit throughout the discussion, that Herodotus was wrong to make the *Samians* the first naval power (cf. van Wees 2002a, 338-40).

22. Herodotus 8.1-2, 42-8 (catalogues of ships); 7.168 (Corcyra); 7.158 (Syracuse). Opous and a few independent islands provided only 50-oared ships; other Aegean islands, deserting from the Persian navy, did provide small numbers of triremes, which they presumably owned thanks to Persian funding.

23. Piraeus: Thucydides 1.93.3. Corinthian ships: Herodotus 6.89; Thucydides 1.41.2; these must have been triremes, since Athens surely could have mobilised more *pentekontoroi* by simply extending naukraric obligations.

24. The number initially commisioned was probably 100 (so pseudo-Aristotle, *Athenian Constitution* 22.7; Plutarch, *Themistocles* 4.1, 3; Polyaenus 1.30.6); when Herodotus speaks of 200 (7.144.1-2; echoed by Justin 2.12.12), he is surely confusing the total available in 480 with the number built in 483. Included in the figure of 200 would be the 20 Corinthian triremes acquired earlier and the remaining 80 must have been built in the annual construction of ships between 483 and 480 to which Herodotus himself vaguely alludes (ibid.; cf. Nepos, *Themistocles* 2.2, 8). For different views, see Jordan 1975, 16-20; Wallinga 1993, 148-57; Gabrielsen 1994, 27-31. For 'trireme-makers', see *Athenian Constitution* 46.1; that the final transfer to state-control was complete by 480 is implied by the Decree of Themistocles (see below), where ship-captains are appointed by the generals and allocated to ships, which would be unnecessary if they managed these ships themselves.

25. This is based on the provisions of the Themistocles Decree (ML 23), the authenticity of which has been much-disputed (see the survey of arguments and literature in ML ad loc.), but contains at least two clauses which, it seems to me, no fourth-century forger would have invented: (a) the mobilisation of captains from scratch, rather than from a pre-selected list (see p. 216), and (b) the mobilisation of only 100 citizen rowers per ship rather than a full complement. The obvious explanation for the undermanning is that 100 rowers (plus ten hoplite marines, four archers, and six 'staff' – see pp. 210-11) per ship was the maximum number of citizens of suitable age available at the time, i.e. that Athens in 480 had only about 24,000 citizens between about 20 and 40 years old (for the upper age limit, see Appendix 1). Naval service by young aristocrats: n. 44 below. Naval service by slaves: pp. 211-12.

26. Rates of pay, see p. 238. Anecdote: Plutarch, *Themistocles* 7.6. Money raised: ibid. 10.6, citing *Athenian Constitution* 23.1 and Cleidemus *FGrH* 323 F 21. Many scholars find it hard to believe that rowers were already being paid, but the archaic law from Eretria (see p. 205) and, in my view, the existence of naukraric funds, shows that they were. In any case, the numbers of poor men and slaves mobilised meant that captains would at least have had to provide *food* for their crews.

27. Herodotus 8.17; Plutarch, *Alcibiades* 1. Note also Phayllos of Croton at Salamis: Herodotus 8.47 does not say that his is a private trireme, but Plutarch, *Alexander* 34.2 does, and the fact that Phayllos' ship is the only one to come from Croton supports this.

28. See McKechnie 1984, 122-6; de Souza 1999, 26-30, 38-41; Gabrielsen (forthcoming).

29. Macedonian: McKechnie 1984, 121-2. Rhodian: Gabrielsen 1997, 101-5.

30. Demosthenes 52.5. Spartan fleet mistaken for raiders: Thucydides 6.104.3. Other Peloponnesian raiders: Thucydides 2.69.1; 4.67.3; 8.35.2; Xenophon, *Hellenica* 5.1.14-24. Theopompus: Xenophon, *Hellenica* 2.1.30. See further de Souza 1999, 31-6; McKechnie 1984, 101-15.

31. Until 340 BC 1,200 estates were deemed rich enough to be liable to produce a trireme captain (see pp. 216-17), but Demosthenes estimated that about 40% of these estates would be unable to produce an active trierarch in any given year (14.16), so that only about 720 estates were liable in practice. Trierarchs were exempt for two years after one year's service (Isaeus 7.38; see Gabrielsen 1994, 85-7), so that Athens needed three times as many potential trierarchs as it had ships: the total number of triremes was generally more than 300, but there were never more than about 250 in active use in any given year, so that 700-800 trierarchs would indeed have sufficed. After 340 BC, and the reduction of the number of potential trierarchs to 300 (Demosthenes 18.102-8; Aeschines 3.222; Dinarchus 1.42; Hyperides F 134 Kenyon; Pollux 8.100), trierarchs would have had to be liable every year, and Athens could never mobilise more than 300 ships at a time, which was realistic enough (but did not stop Aeschines' complaining about Athens being deprived of the use of 65 ships: 3.222).

32. Selection of captains: see pp. 216-17. The problems of handing over in mid-campaign are vividly illustrated by Apollodorus' speech *Against Polycles*, known as Demosthenes 50.

33. Advance payments and bonuses: Demosthenes 50.7, 12, 14; Thucydides 6.31.3. Hiring rowers: e.g. Lysias 21.10; Isocrates 18.60; Demosthenes 21.154, 45.85. Rowers hired from 'all over Greece': e.g. Thucydides 1.31.1 (by Corinth); Isocrates 8.79 (by Athens); cf. the foreigners listed among the crews in *IG* I³ 1032 (= *IG* II² 1951). Delay caused by recruiting abroad: Xenophon, *Hellenica* 6.2.11-12.

34. Demosthenes 50.7; cf. Lysias 21.10 for the use of a hired helmsman in the general levy of 405 BC.

35. Cost of trierarchy: Lysias 21.2 (average 5,142 dr.), 19.29 and 42 (average 2,666 dr.), 32.26 (4,800 dr.); cf. Gabrielsen 1994, 121-5. Replacement cost of hulls: Gabrielsen 1994, 139-45.

36. Theophrastus, *Characters* 26.6; cf. Isocrates 8.128; Xenophon, *Oeconomicus* 2.6, and the discussion of attitudes to liturgies generally in Whitehead 1983; Ober 1989, 231-3.

37. Demosthenes 51.8, 13; cf. the references to hiring out trierarchies in Demosthenes 21.80, 155, 164-6; 50.52; and the discussion in Gabrielsen 1994, 95-102.

38. Trierarchs turning from 'warriors' into 'taxpayers': Gabrielsen 1994, esp. 3, 220, and pp. 213-14, 229-30 of this volume.

39. Thucydides 3.98.4. Marines as 'volunteers': *IG* I³ 60 (see pp. 221-2 with n. 20).

40. Thucydides 6.32.1; Herodotus 8.83; Xenophon, *Hellenica* 1.1.28-30; cf. pp. 78, 82, 230-1 on their social and political status. The Sicilian expedition hired *thêtes* as marines (Thucydides 6.43.1), in 412 BC, Athens levied marines from hoplite lists (8.24.2): given that the former represents Athens spending lavishly on its fleet, whereas the latter represents Athens at a low point in manpower and resources, it seems obvious that the hiring of *thêtes* was normal practice and the levying of higher property classes an emergency measure, not vice versa (contra Strauss 1996, 323 n. 11).

41. Lysias 21.10; cf. Thucydides 7.39.2. Helmsmen were supposed to come up from the ranks of ordinary rowers, via a stint as look-outs in the bow: Aristophanes *Knights* 541-5.

42. Grudging acknowledgement: pseudo-Xenophon, *Athenian Constitution* 1.2. For the role and status of helmsmen, see pp. 213, 220, 228.

43. Higher status of *thranitai*: p. 230. The evidence for the distribution of rowers is the number of oars for each level attested in naval records.

44. Quotations: Aristophanes, *Acharnians* 162; *Wasps* 908-9. Rich excused from rowing: Thucydides 3.16.1. Cimon and his rich peers served at Salamis as marines, not rowers (Plutarch, *Cimon* 5), so presumably did the *hippeis* joining the fleet at Arginousai (Xenophon, *Hellenica* 1.6.24).

45. Inscription: *IG* I³ 1032 (= *IG* II² 1951), as explained by Graham 1992, 1998, who notes the parallel with construction workers, and points to the significance of Thucydides 7.13.2, where rowers in the Athenian fleet go in pursuit of their deserting slaves, who are also rowers (see p. 220), and pseudo-Xenophon, *Athenian Constitution* 1.19-20, which refers to 'a man and his slave' getting useful rowing practice. The mobilisation of slaves for Arginusae was only unusual insofar as it was a general mobilisation of slaves (and citizens and metics; Xenophon, *Hellenica* 1.6.24), rather than of slaves employed by professional rowers; hence the promise of freedom to slaves who joined (see especially Hunt 1998, 87-100, who points out the ideological bias against crediting slaves with a military role which is responsible for the limited attestation of slave rowers in the Athenian navy). Strauss 1996, 316, suggests that slaves served only 'occasionally', and Morrison and Williams 1968, 257-8, Casson 1971, 322-8, Rosivach 1985, and Morrison et al. 2000, 117-18, adopt the view of Sargent 1927 that the Athenian navy did not employ slaves. (Casson changed his mind in the revised edition: 1995, 466-7.)

46. Previous training of citizens who were not professional rowers was confined to what experience they might have had on private travel, as pseudo-Xenophon, *Athenian Constitution* 1.19-20, makes clear. Pericles' annual patrols may well have helped citizens acquire general rowing skills (Plutarch, *Pericles* 11) but did not create complete trained crews. Xenophon, *Hellenica* 6.2.32 notes that it was normal practice for crews to begin training 'when people expect to fight a naval battle', and that the need for such training would normally delay the departure of a fleet; Iphicrates' ability to organise training *en route* is exceptional (ibid. 27-32). Thucydides 2.86.5 has a Peloponnesian fleet train 'six or seven days' before they feel ready to sail; at 7.51.2, the Syracusans man their ships and train 'for as many days as they thought would be enough' (note that this training is still necessary although their fleet had repeatedly been in action earlier in the year). Aristophanes, *Acharnians* 554 also alludes to rowing practice in Piraeus harbour prior to launch. See Casson 1971, 278-80. The idea that captains and crews trained together before mobilisation (Morrison and Williams 1968, 124-5) has no basis.

47. Competition for places: Lysias 21.6-9; cf. Demosthenes 50.43-53. Taxiarchs in general naval levy: Xenophon *Hellenica* 1.6.29; *nauarchoi*: ibid. and 5.1.5; Demosthenes 18.18.73.

48. See Jordan 1975, 30-61, for the administration of the dockyards; see also pp. 217-18.

49. Helots: Xenophon, *Hellenica* 7.1.12. Hermon: ibid. 1.6.32; Demosthenes 23.212; Pausanias 10.9.8. Similarly, a helmsman from Corinth is regarded as the best in the Syracusan fleet: Thucydides 7.39.2.

50. Corcyraean slaves: Thucydides 1.55.1; Thessalian *penestai*: Xenophon, *Hellenica* 6.1.11; Aristotle and Heraclean Mariandynoi: *Politics* 1327b7-16. *Desposionautai*: Myron *FGrH* 106 F1.

51. 'Self-rowing' soldiers (*auteretai*): Thucydides 1.10.4; 3.18.4. Fighting role of rowers: pp. 62-4, 222-3.

15. War at Sea

1. Xenophon, *Hellenica* 2.1.31-2; Plutarch, *Lysander* 13.1, *Alcibiades* 37.4; Pausanias 9.32.9; cf. Strauss 1983. The historicity of these events has been disputed, because the actual execution of prisoners is not mentioned by Xenophon, who reports only the decision to do so (or by Diodorus 13.106.6-7): see Krentz 1989, 180. However, dwelling on the massacre did not suit Xenophon's purpose at this point in his narrative, where he presents the Spartans as agents of justice, avenging Athens' earlier acts of *hybris*.

2. Thucydides 8.42.5, as discussed by Pritchett 1974, 273.

3. Annual list of 400: Thucydides 2.24.2; pseudo-Xenophon, *Constitution of Athens* 3.4. For the subsequent selection for active service, and legal challenges, see Gabrielsen 1994, 73-8, 91-5.

4. Reforms of 358/7, list of 1,200: Demosthenes 14.17; 20.23; 21.154-5 (and scholion ad loc.); 47.21; Isocrates 15.145, Isaeus 7.38; Pollux 8.100; Harpocration, entries under *chilioi diakosioi, hegemôn symmorias, symmoria*. The nomination of 1,200 did not constitute a significant extension of the group of potential trierarchs: since there was a two-year exemption after a year of service, even before 358/7 approximately 3 x 400 households were liable: for this, and for the creation of the list of 300, see p. 209 n. 31. The organisation of the symmories has been much debated: see especially Gabrielsen 1994, 173-213; MacDowell 1986.

5. For problems with equipment, see the excellent discussion by Gabrielsen 1994, 146-69. Allocation of ships: the fact that large numbers of ships might remain unallotted throughout the year (e.g. 47 out of *c*. 100 in 378/7 BC: *IG* II² 1604) shows that triremes were allotted to trierarchs only when they were mobilised, as also indicated by the Decree of Themistocles (ML 23, lines 22-3); contra Gabrielsen 1994, 80-4, who argues that all ships were allotted to trierarchs at the start of the year, and that if any ships were left unallocated this was because of a shortage of trierarchs (which implausibly implies that Athens could muster only about 50 trierarchs in 378/7). Jordan 1975, 68-70, argues that allocation was not by lot in the fifth century, on the basis of Aristophanes *Knights* 912-18 and despite ML 23.22-3.

6. Demosthenes 47.23; 50.7, 42 (and 26-8, 33-6 for problems at hand-over); 51.5; Gabrielsen 1994, 153-5.

7. *IG* II² 1615.88-104, discussed by Gabrielsen 1994, 161-2. Symmories having trouble collecting equipment: Demosthenes 47.21-44. For the reforms, see references in n. 4 above.

8. The subdivision into 100 smaller symmories was proposed by Demosthenes in 354/3 (14.17-23) and whether or not it was adopted then, 100 symmories certainly existed by 340 BC, when Demosthenes formed The 300 from 'the leaders, seconds and thirds' from each of the symmories (18.103); cf. p. 210. Other measures: Gabrielsen 1994, 149, 157-62; ship-sheds and arsenal: Blackman 1968.

9. ML 23.27-35 and Demosthenes 50.7 (cf. p. 212).

10. See p. 212.

11. Gabrielsen 1994, 118-20; Morrison et al. 2000, 95-6 (contra Jordan 1975, 106-11). The Corinthians take three days' supplies on their triremes when they cannot rely on being able to make landings (Thucydides 1.48.1), but normally a crew prevented from making a landing would spend the night riding at anchor 'without food and without sleep' (Demosthenes 50.22). As Harrison 1999 shows, triremes would generally run up sandy beaches or anchor just off the coast; they were not normally hauled up on land.

12. Thucydides 6.22, 44.1: 30 large merchant ships and 100 other boats requisitioned to carry barley, wheat, bakers and other specialists to Sicily; many trading ships following voluntarily. Other grain transports: Thucydides 6.34.4 (two months' supplies); Xenophon *Hellenica* 3.4.3 (six months' supplies).

13. Starvation and mutiny in winter quarters: Xenophon, *Hellenica* 2.1.1-5. Drying out: ibid. 1.5.10; 5.4.66; Herodotus 7.59.2-3; Thucydides 7.12.3-5 (naval blockade at Syracuse); cf. Harrison 1999, 169-70. According to Hesiod, the only really safe sailing season lasted from late June to mid August (*Works and Days* 663-70), but it was possible, if dangerous, to sail from late April onwards (ibid. 678-88) until the start of the vintage in mid-September (674-7; cf. 609-14); other evidence is cited by West 1978, ad 610, 663ff., 678ff.; Casson 1971, 270-3.

14. The battles of Marathon and Salamis were dated to 6 and 20 Boedromion, respectively (Plutarch, *Camillus* 19.3, 6), though there is reason to think that Marathon was actually fought some ten days later, on a date corresponding to 11 September (Hammond 1968, 40-1; cf. Lazenby 1993, 118-19 on Salamis). Both battles thus took place within days of the very end of the sailing season (see n. 13 above).

15. Ionians: see p. 212; Naxos: Herodotus 5.33.2-4; Pausanias: Plutarch, *Aristides* 23.2.

16. Xenophon, *Hellenica* 1.5.11 (but cf. Diodorus 13.71); advisory role of helmsmen: Thucydides 7.39.2, 62.1. For another commander buying obedience from a trierarch, compare Plutarch, *Themistocles* 7.6.

17. Demosthenes 51.13-14, which also notes the problem of rapacious hired trierarchs (cf. Gabrielsen 1994, 100). Cattle and wood: Demosthenes 21.167; cf. 173. Themistocles: Herodotus 8.112. Public ships used in private plundering: Jackson 1973; McKechnie 1984, 115-16; de Souza 1999, 31-6.

18. Thucydides 6.32. Sacrifices: see p. 24 for Aulis and e.g. Herodotus 9.91-2, 96. Ships racing one another, see also Xenophon, *Hellenica* 6.2.28.

19. Deck room: Morrison et al. 2000, 226-7. In 494, Chian triremes carried 40 hoplites each, while in 480 the Persian fleet had 30 soldiers per ship in addition to the marines (Herodotus 6.15; 7.184.2). 'Many' soldiers served on Corinthian and Corcyraean ships in 433 (Thucydides 1.49.1); numbers given for near-contemporary Corinthian fleets average 27 hoplites per ship in 435 and 38 in 431 (ibid. 1.29, 2.33.1). In 429, a Corinthian fleet 'sailed not to battle, but more as a troop transport' (ibid. 2.83.3) and this probably applies to their earlier fleets as well, but the Chian, Persian and Corcyraean fleets were all designed to do combat, yet carried large numbers. Modification of ships: Plutarch, *Cimon* 12.2.

20. The distinction is made at Thucydides 6.31.3; 8.25.1, 62; Xenophon, *Hellenica* 1.1.36; see further Morrison et al. 2000, 150-7, 227-30. An inscription (*IG* I^3 60 = I^2 97) refers to Athenian transport ships (*tri[ê]res strat[iotidas]*, lines 12-13) carrying 40 hoplites, 10 archers and a lost number of peltasts (16-17) but also 'five volunteers per ship' (line 15), who must be the marines. In the expedition to Sicily, the 40 Athenian transport ships appear to have 100 hoplite marines (700 minus the 60 x 10 employed on the fast ships) and 100 archers (480 minus the 60 x 4 and 34 x 4 needed for the 'fast' and allied ships) to share between them, i.e. an average of five each. Assuming that the 34 allied ships each carried the normal maximum of about 40 hoplites (including marines), the 40 transport ships would have had to carry an additional 100 soldiers each to accommodate the entire force. Assuming a quite high proportion of transport ships in the Athenian fleets of 424, 423, 422, 416, 413 and 412, 100 soldiers each would just about accommodate the large forces they conveyed (Thucydides 4.53.1 and 54.1, 129.2-4; 5.2.1, 84.1; 7.33.4-5 and 35.1 and 42.1; 8.25.1; cf. Krentz, forthcoming; Morrison and Williams 1968, 246-8).

21. Expedition: Thucydides 2.56.2 (acknowledged as the largest ever, at 6.31.3; the initial Sicilian expedition had 5,100 hoplites, including the marines, so also about 4,000 extra hoplites). Fate of Corinthian fleet: ibid. 2.83-4. Fate of Athenian fleet (at Syracuse): ibid. 7.70-4.

22. Thucydides 4.11-12 (Pylos), 6.75, 7.25 (Syracuse). In legend, the Greeks had to fight to force a landing at Troy: *Iliad* 2.698-702. Night landings: e.g. Thucydides 1.115.4; 2.93-4; 4.31-32.1, 42; Xenophon, *Hellenica* 4.8.35; 5.1.10-12; Polyaenus 1.39.1; 3.11.9; 5.38 (the last five all involve ambushes set by night in preparation for the main landing by day). Disinformation: Thucydides 6.64-5 (see discussion in Krentz 2000, 167-8). Decoys: Frontinus 1.4.14; 3.2.10; 3.10.8. Disguised ship: Polyaenus 5.34.

23. Herodotus 6.114. Other examples: Thucydides 7.59; Diodorus 11.21-2; Homer, *Iliad* (esp. 15.704-46).

24. Armed rowers: see pp. 62-4.

25. Patrols: 100 ships patrolling around Attica, Salamis and Euboea: Thucydides 3.17. Blockade of Athens: Xenophon, *Hellenica* 2.2.9-11. Sphacteria: Thucydides 4.23.2, 26.5-9. Syracuse: Thucydides 7.13. Cf. Herodotus 8.79, 82, 83: three ships in a row sail through the Persian blockade of Salamis.

26. 'Bringing down' grain-ships: de Ste Croix 1972, 314; McKechnie 1984, 127-8. Tolls: Xenophon, *Hellenica* 1.1.22, 4.8.27; Diodorus 13.64.2; Polybius 4.44.4, 46.6; ML 65.35-9.

27. Demosthenes 24.11-12. Capture of a religious mission: Herodotus 6.87. Spartan fleets seizing merchant shipping: p. 215, and also Thucydides 8.35 and Xenophon, *Hellenica* 2.1.17; 5.1.21.

28. See the series of non-confrontations at Thucydides 8.25, 39, 42 (when the main fleets refuse battle, after an almost accidental skirmish), 60, 63, 79. Another example is Xenophon, *Hellenica* 1.5.1.

29. Loss of face: Xenophon, *Hellenica* 2.1.23-27. No-contest trophy: ibid. 5.4.66.

30. Wind: Thucydides 2.84; Plutarch, *Themistocles* 14.2. Syracuse: Thucydides 7.39-40.3 (= Polyaenus 5.13.2, 5.32.1; cf 5.32.2: for a Syracusan naval attack at breakfast). Eretria: Thucydides 8.95.4-5. Aigospotamoi: Xenophon, *Hellenica* 2.1.22-8; cf. a similar surprise attack by Iphicrates, ibid 6.2.33-6.

31. Xenophon, *Hellenica* 1.6.28 (Callicratidas) and 5.1.7-9 (Gorgopas).

32. Disguised ships: e.g. Plutarch, *Cimon* 13.3 (Eurymedon); cf. *Solon* 9; Diodorus 14.63.4 (cf. Polyaenus 2.11; Frontinus 1.4.12: Spartan use of Carthaginian ships in 396 BC); Polyaenus 5.34, 40, 41. Decoys: Polyaenus 1.48.5 (Conon); Frontinus 1.4.14 (Chabrias). Themistocles: Herodotus 8.75; Aeschylus *Persians* 355-83. See the catalogue of deceptions in Krentz 2000.

33. Aeschylus, *Persians* 424-8; cf. Thucydides 1.50.1 for Corinthians killing the shipwrecked, in their enthusiasm including some of their own. For the fate of captured crews, see e.g. Thucydides 2.84.4 (mostly prisoners), 2.90.5 (all killed), 2.92.2 (some killed, some captured), 7.23.4 (eight crews killed, three made prisoner – which shows that the treatment of captured crews was left up to individual captains), 7.41.4.

34. So the Spartans at Syracuse (Thucydides 7.53.1) and the Persians at Salamis (Herodotus 8.76, 95; Aeschylus, *Persians* 447-71). For the battle formation of navies, see pp. 226-8.

35. Rescue of ships: Thucydides 4.14, 2.90.6 (by infantry), 8.107.2 (by fleet). The latter passage also shows that serviceable enemy ships were brought to safety and kept, while the rest was destroyed. Towing of ships: e.g. Xenophon, *Hellenica* 6.2.33-6 (prows cut off). Dedications: e.g. Thucydides 2.84.4, 92.5

36. See Strauss 2000, who argues that citizen rowers probably were included on casualty lists. Perhaps they were included if they were part of a citizen levy, but not if professional rowers. If *all* naval casualties were included, the lists ought to feature large numbers of foreigners and slaves, which they do not.

37. Arginusae: Xenophon, *Hellenica* 1.6.35; 1.7. Sybota: Thucydides 1.54.1. That the Athenians after their final defeat at sea in Syracuse did not ask for their dead is cited as evidence of their demoralisation (Thucydides 7.72.2), but still suggests that it was a less urgent matter than in land warfare.

38. Rowing back to put up trophy, see p. 215 and e.g. Thucydides 1.50-4, where the Corinthians put up a trophy next day, and the Corcyraeans put up a counter-trophy on the day after that, when they get hold of the bodies. For a similarly contested victory and double trophy, see Thucydides 7.34.

39. As happened at Syracuse (Thucydides 7.24.2; cf. 8.43.1) and Aigospotamoi (Xenophon, *Hellenica* 2.1.29; cf. 1.1.13, 6.2.27. See Casson 1971, 235-8.

40. Single line abreast as the normal formation: Lazenby 1987, contra e.g. Morrison and Williams 1968, 313-20; Morrison et al. 2000, esp. 43, 88-93. Multiple lines for inexperienced fleets: Thucydides 2.90; Xenophon, *Hellenica* 1.6.31. Circular formation: Herodotus 8.11; Thucydides 2.83.5.

41. See e.g. Aeschylus, *Persians* 390 (*alalê*), 393 (paean), 395 (trumpet).

42. Stationary tactics were still practised during the Peloponnesian War by Corinth and Corcyra (Thucydides 1.49.1-3) and Syracuse, which, like Corinth (7.34), moved towards head-on clashes (7.36, 39, 62; cf. Morrison et al. 2000, 165-7), rather than adapt to Athenian tactics.

43. Missiles: Thucydides 1.49.1, 7.39-40, 70.5; Herodotus 8.90; cf. Aeschylus, *Persians* 456-64: marines disembark and attack infantry with stone and arrows. Triremes affected by movement on deck: Morrison et al. 2000, 226-7. Boarding-planks: Herodotus 9.98.2. Marines under 30: ML 23.24-5; the hit-and-run tactics which they practised on land also points to the 20-30 age-group, singled out for running charges against light-armed (e.g. Xenophon, *Hellenica* 2.4.32, 3.4.23, 4.5.14; or 20- to 35-year-olds: 4.5.16, 4.6.10).

44. Rawlings 2000, 236-7.

45. Thucydides 2.89.9 ('order and silence'); cf. Xenophon, *Oeconomicus* 8.8. Problem of noise: Thucydides 7.70.6; this has been amply confirmed by the sea trials of *Olympias* (Morrison et al. 2000, 248-56)

46. See Lazenby 1987 and Whitehead 1987 for *diekplous* and *periplous* as manoeuvres practised by individual ships (rather than as 'breakthrough' and 'encirclement' by entire formations, as Morrison and Williams 1968, 313-20, and Morrison et al. 2000, esp. 43, 88-93, argue). On Lazenby and Whitehead's interpretations, it is not clear how the two manoeuvres differ, as Holladay 1988 pointed out: hence my suggestion that they were stages of a single manoeuvre.

47. Chaotic combat: e.g. Herodotus 8.86-92; Thucydides 1.49.4, 7.70.4, 6. Recognising individual ships: Herodotus 8.88.2; calling by name: Thucydides 7.70.8; general's ship: Herodotus 8.92.2; national emblems: Euripides, *Iphigeneia in Aulis* 239-76; Aristophanes, *Acharnians* 547 (cited p. 216); Polyaenus 3.11.11.

48. Undecided battles: e.g. Herodotus 8.11, 16. Shouting and paeans: Thucydides 2.91.2, 7.71.5.

49. Thucydides 2.88.1 ('gathering together in groups' as sign of fear), 7.72.4 (refusal to board).

50. *Frogs* 1075, cited p. 200. For soldiers, see p. 192. Cf. Thucydides 7.71 for the emotional swings of those watching a naval battle and those aboard.

51. Hipponax has a snake emblem; Aeschylus F 134 Nauck² a horse/rooster hybrid. Boar-headed triremes are mentioned by Herodotus 3.59.3 (pace Morrison and Williams 1968, 133-4); cf. Casson 1971, 350-4; Vélissaropoulos 1980, 67-71.

52. Herodotus 8.11 (first capture at Artemision, prize), 17 (best man in second battle), 84 (first capture at Salamis, disputed), 93 (the three best captains at Salamis include the Athenian who was said to have captured the first ship; bounty on Artemisia).

53. Wreath: Demosthenes 51. For trierarchs' boasts, see also e.g. Lysias 21.1-10, and Whitehead 1983; Ober 1989, 231-3; cf. Gabrielsen 1994, 219-20.

54. See Strauss 1996; cf. pp. 78-9, 82-3.

55. Conditions on board for different tiers of rowers: Morrison et al. 2000, 237-8. Higher pay for *thranitai*: Thucydides 6.31.3; note that, if anything, it is the *thalamioi*, not the *thranitai*, who contribute more to the speed of the ship, due to the angle of their oars. Aristophanes' reference to the *thranitai* as the people who 'save the city' (*Acharnians* 162-3) suggests that they (but not the rest of the rowers) are mostly citizens. That the *thalamioi* are the only rank of rowers not made to join the fighting at Sphacteria (Thucydides 4.32.2) might suggest that they are mostly slaves, on the analogy of an episode in which a Spartan commander arms only the free men among his rowers: Xenophon, *Hellenica* 5.1.11.

56. Reciting Euripides: Plutarch, *Nicias* 29.2-3. Relations between captain and marines: pp. 210-11, 213-14. Leisure-class aspirations: pp. 35-7.

Conclusion

1. An attempt to travel further than anyone else had ever done was regarded as 'excessive' behaviour, associated with the kind of men who were inclined to acts of *hybris*: Herodotus 2.32.3, referring to Libyans crossing the Sahara, as interpreted by Fisher 1992, 98-9.

2. They did not have the 'monopoly of legitimate violence' which is widely regarded as essential to statehood: see especially Berent 2000; Hansen 2002.

3. Herodotus 5.72.1; and see p. 73 for Cleomenes' army.

4. See e.g. van Wees 1999b.

5. See pp. 96, 203-4.

6. See pp. 70-1, 97.

7. See especially Hodkinson 2000, 209-368.

8. Herodotus 7.104.4 (Law); 6.74-84 (Cleomenes); Thucydides 1.128-34 (Pausanias). On the limitation of royal power in Sparta *c.* 500 BC, see esp. Thommen 1996, 85-98.

9. See especially Morris and Raaflaub (eds) 1998; Ober 1996, 32-52; Lévêque and Vidal-Naquet 1996.

10. Xenophon, *Hellenica* 1.7.1-35. For Athenian popular control over their generals, see Hamel 1998, esp. 5-14, 32-9, 116-57; Pritchett 1974, 4-58.

11. Funding: Millett 1993. 'Mercenary' generals: Pritchett 1974, 59-116; Parke 1933, 105-32.

12. See Morris 1998, esp. 35-6, 73-9; 1994, 361-6; 1992, 128-55 for the archaeological evidence.

13. See pp. 13-15, 30-2.

14. See pp. 97-100, 103-4 for military organisation and Appendix 2 for the oaths of loyalty. That the officers of sworn bands were formally appointed seems almost certain, although it must be admitted that we have no evidence for this.

15. Speech: Herodotus 3.46; fasting: Pseudo-Aristotle, *Economics* 2.2.9. The request is surely for *food* for the rebels' fleet, but Herodotus thinks they want troops, and Aristotle thinks they want money.

16. The naval funds raised in sixth-century Athens and Eretria (see pp. 203-6) were presumably of a similarly *ad hoc* nature. Cf. Samons 2000, 54-62, for the public treasury in archaic Athens.

17. Taxable property of 36 million dr. (6,000 talents): Demosthenes 14.19. A conventional assumption is that annual income represented about 8% of the property value of farm land, which would amount to 3 million dr.; a 33% tax would have been extremely high by ancient Greek standards. *Eisphora* levies produced 200, later 300 talents, i.e. 1.2 to 1.8 million (e.g. Thucydides 2.70.2; cf. Thomsen 1977), but these were only occasional, and the same rate would not have been sustainable year-on-year. Siege of Samos: ML 55. Potideia: Thucydides 2.70.2; cf. 2.13.3.

18. Siphnos: Herodotus 3.57. Distribution of mining revenue in Athens, see p. 207; perhaps also in Thasos (Herodotus 6.46.3); cf. Samons 2000, 60-2; Humphreys 1978, 145. Borrowing from temples: Herodotus 5.36.3, and see further p. 237.

19. For later sources, raising taxes is a typical tyrant's crime, so one needs to treat their evidence with caution, but there seems no reason to doubt that Peisistratos and his sons raised regular taxes (Thucydides 6.54.5; Aristotle, *Athenian Constitution* 16.4), and anecdotes about tyrants' money-raising schemes may reflect a general preoccupation with finance (e.g. Aristotle, *Economics* 2.2.2, 4); cf. Thucydides 1.13.1. Early coinage: Kim 2001; Crawford 1986; Kraay 1976.

20. Herodotus 9.81.2; cf. 8.121, 123; Diodorus 11.33.1 (and 11.25); see above, p. 163 for Homer. Miltiades' proposal to attack Paros in 489 (p. 27) also sounds as if the expected booty will go to the participants (Herodotus 6.132). Fourth-century Homeric-style distributions: Polyaenus 3.9.31 (on Iphicrates); Xenophon, *Education of Cyrus* 8.4.29-30; cf. Pritchett 1991, 369-71, 384-9; Hamel 1998, 46-8 (both are doubtful about the existence of this form of distribution in citizen armies, but it seems to me almost self-evident that societies which distributed even mining revenues to all citizens would also distribute booty to those who fought for it, rather than keep a surplus).

21. Plutarch, *Cimon* 9.3-6 (Ion of Chios *FGrH* 392 F 13, for Sestos and Byzantium, *c.* 470: see Meiggs 1972, 72-3, 465-8), 13.5 (Eurymedon); cf. Pritchett 1971, 83; 1991, 370-1; Hamel 1998, 47 n. 20.

22. Naval pay: see below, with n. 27. Note the distribution of booty to all soldiers by Myronides after the battle of Oinophyta in 458/7 (Diodorus 11.82.5), which was probably before the introduction of hoplite pay (see n. 27 below). Note also that even when hoplites were paid for expeditions abroad, they may not have received pay during general levies mobilised to invade neighbouring territories, as in the case of Oinophyta, and on such occasions may well still have received shares of booty. On the sale of booty, see Pritchett 1991, 401-38, esp. 404-16 (*laphyropolai*).

23. Cult statue of Athena: Thucydides 2.13.5; cf. Powell 1995, 256-7. Acceptability of borrowing: Thucydides 1.121.3, 143.1. Temples as lenders: Davies 2001; Samons 2000; Migeotte 1984; Linders 1975; Bogaert 1968. Scruples: Thucydides

4.118.3; Xenophon, *Hellenica* 7.4.33-5; cf. the accusations made against the Phocians about using sacred treasure: Diodorus 16.25.1, 30.1, 36.1.

24. See Davies 2001, Samons 2000, Linders 1975.

25. See pp. 104-8 (logistics), 138-45 (sieges), 209-21 (fleet).

26. Annual tribute and surplus: Thucydides 2.13.3. The chief objective of the very first campaign of the Delian League against Eion must have been to gain access to nearby gold mines; later expeditions in the area are explicitly said to have been 'fighting for the gold mines' (Herodotus 9.75); cf. Thucydides 1.98.1, 100.3. Thasos and its revenues: Thucydides 1.100.2, 101; Herodotus 6.46.3.

27. Hoplite pay probably introduced in 450s: Thucydides 3.17.3; Aristotle, *Athenian Constitution* 27.2; scholion (Ulpian) on Demosthenes 13.11; cf. Pritchett 1971, 7-14. First siege engines built in 440: pp. 139-41. 1,600 archers and 1,000 cavalry were introduced *c*. 445-40: see Spence 1993, 15-16. Fortifications from 458 onwards: Thucydides 1.107.1. Naval pay: Thucydides 3.17.4; 6.8.1, 31.3 (1 drachma: lower pay from 412 onwards, see n. 30 below); cf. Pritchett 1971, 14-20.

28. Dionysius' fund-raising: e.g. Pseudo-Aristotle, *Economics* 2.2.20 and 41; cf. Caven 1990, 160-6. Artillery and siege engines: p. 142. Quadriremes, quiqueremes: Diodorus 14.41.3, 42.2, 44.7; cf. Pliny, *Natural History* 7.207; Clement of Alexandria, *Stromateis* 1.75.10; cf. Casson 1971, 97-8.

29. Rowers: pp. 212-13; mercenaries: pp. 45, 74-5, 83-5. Standing forces: Thucydides 4.55.2. Cf. the decision in 382 to allow Peloponnesian allies to contribute money rather than soldiers: see p. 75.

30. 'Contributions': Thucydides 3.19. Halving of pay (and attempts to raise it again): Thucydides 8.29, 45.2; Xenophon, *Hellenica* 1.5.4, 7; Plutarch, *Alcibiades* 35.4; see Pritchett 1971, 14-20.

31. Xenophon, *Hellenica* 5.4.66; 6.2.1, 37.

32. Pseudo-Aristotle, *Economics* 2.2.23; cf. other fourth-century expedients 2.2.7-8, 10-12, 16-21, 28-30. On fourth-century Athenian military finance, Millet 1993; Brun 1983.

33. Early negotiations with Persia: Thucydides 2.67; 4.50; Aristophanes, *Acharnians* 62-120. Lysander amd Cyrus: Xenophon, *Hellenica* 1.5.1-10, 20; 1.6.3, 16-18, 24; 2.1.11-14; 2.2.5, 7. Post-war Persian support: ibid. 4.8.7-13; 5.1.27-9.

34. Demosthenes' plans: p. 218. For the reforms of Euboulus, see Cawkwell 1963; for Lycurgus (and the figure of *c*. seven million drachmas (1,200 talents)), see Plutarch, *Lives of the Ten Orators* 841b-44.

35. Melting down of wreaths: Demosthenes 22.69-75; 24.176-83. Quadriremes first attested in Athenian naval records in 330; quinqueremes in 325: Gabrielsen 1994, 127. Military training: pp. 94-5.

36. 'Hoplites as dinosaurs': Hanson 1995, 327-55.

37. See pp. 29, 117, 121-6, 221-6.

38. Aristotle, *Historia Animalium* 618b9-17.

Bibliography

Adam, J.-P. (1982), *L'architecture militaire grecque* (Paris)
—— (1993), 'Approche et défense des portes dans le monde hellénisé', in S. van der Maele and J. Fossey (eds) 1993, 5-43
Adcock, F. & Mosley, D. (1975), *Diplomacy in Ancient Greece* (London)
Adkins, A. (1975), 'Art, beliefs and values in the later books of the *Iliad*', *CPh* 77, 239-54
Ager, S. (1996), *Interstate Arbitrations in the Greek World, 337-90 BC* (Berkeley)
Ahlberg, G. (1971), *Fighting on Land and Sea in Greek Geometric Art* (Stockholm)
Amit, M. (1965), *Athens and the Sea: a study in Athenian sea-power* (Brussels)
Anderson, J. (1965), 'Homeric, British and Cyrenaic chariots', *AJA* 69, 349-52
—— (1970), *Military Theory and Practice in the Age of Xenophon* (Berkeley)
—— (1975), 'Greek chariot-borne and mounted infantry', *AJA* 79, 175-87
—— (1985), *Hunting in the Ancient World* (Berkeley)
—— (1991), 'Hoplite weapons and offensive arms', in Hanson (ed.) 1991, 15-37
Andreev, J. (1988), 'Die homerische Gesellschaft', *Klio* 70, 5-85
Andrewes, A. (1956), *The Greek Tyrants* (London)
—— (1978), 'Spartan imperialism?', in P. Garnsey & C. Whittaker (eds), *Imperialism in the Ancient World* (Cambridge), 91-102
—— (1981), 'The hoplite katalogos', in G. Shrimpton & D. MacCargar (eds), *Classical Contributions: studies in honor of M.F. McGregor* (New York), 1-3
Arnould, D. (1981), *Guerre et paix dans la poésie grecque* (New York)
Asheri, D. (1966), *Distribuzioni di terre nell'antica Grecia* (Torino)
Austin, M. & Vidal-Naquet, P. (1972), *Economies et sociétés en Grèce ancienne* (Paris) (English ed. 1977)
Baker, P. (1999), 'Les mercenaires', in F. Prost (ed.) 1999, 240-55
Balot, R. (2001), *Greed and Injustice in Classical Athens* (Princeton)
Baltrusch, E. (1994), *Symmachie und Spondai: Untersuchungen zum griechischen Völkerrecht der archaischen und klassischen Zeit (8.-5. Jahrhundert v. Chr.)* (Berlin)
Barringer, J. (2001), *The Hunt in Ancient Greece* (Baltimore)
Barry, W. (1996), 'Rooftiles and urban violence in the ancient world', *GRBS* 37, 55-74
Bauslaugh, R. (1991), *The Concept of Neutrality in Classical Greece* (Berkeley)
Bellen, H. (1974), 'Der Rachegedanke in der griechische-persischen Auseinandersetzung', *Chiron* 4, 43-67
Bennett, M.J. (1997), *Belted Heroes and Bound Women* (Lanham, MD)
Berent, M. (2000), 'Anthropology and the classics: war, violence, and the stateless polis', *CQ* 50, 257-89
Best, G. (1982), *War and Society in Revolutionary Europe 1770-1870* (no place, 1982)

Bibliography

Best, J. (1968), *Thracian Peltasts and their Influence on Greek Warfare* (Groningen)

Bettali, M. (1995), *I mercenari nel mondo greco*, vol. 1 (Pisa)

Billows, R. (1995), *Kings and Colonists: aspects of Macedonian imperialism* (Leiden)

Black, J. (1994), *European Warfare 1660-1815* (London)

Blythe, P. (1977), *The Effectiveness of Greek Armour against Arrows in the Persian War* (unpublished dissertation, Reading)

Boardman, J. (1963), 'Artemis Orthia and chronology', *BSA* 58, 1-7

———— (1983), 'Symbol and story in Greek Geometric art', in W.G. Moon (ed.), *Ancient Greek Art and Iconography* (Madison, WI), 15-36

Boedeker, D. (1998), 'The new Simonides and heroization at Plataia', in N. Fisher & H. van Wees (eds), *Archaic Greece: new approaches and new evidence* (London/Swansea), 231-49

Boedeker, D. (2002), 'Epic heritage and mythical patterns in Herodotus', in E. Bakker et al. (eds), *Brill's Companion to Herodotus* (Leiden), 97-116

Bogaert, R. (1968), *Banques et banquiers dans les cités grecques* (Leiden)

Bowden, H. (1993), 'Hoplites and Homer: warfare, hero cult and the ideology of the polis', in J. Rich & G. Shipley (eds) 1993, 45-63

Bowie, A. (1997), 'Tragic filters for history: Euripides' *Supplices* and Sophocles' *Philoctetes*', in C. Pelling (ed.), *Greek Tragedy and the Historian* (Oxford), 39-62

Bradeen, D. (1969), 'The Athenian casualty lists', *CQ* 19 (1969), 145-59

Bravo, B. (1980), '*Sulân*. Répresailles et justice privée contre des étrangers dans les cités grecques', *ASNP* 10, 675-987

Bremmer, J. (1982), 'The *suodales* of Poplios Valesios', *ZPE* 47, 133-47

Brijder, H. (1983), *Siana Cups and Komast Cups I*, Amsterdam

Brown, P. (1973), *The Chimbu* (London)

Brun, P. (1983), *Eisphora-syntaxis-stratiotika: recherches sur les finances militaires d'Athènes au IVe siècle av. J.-C.* (Paris)

Bugh, G. (1988), *The Horsemen of Athens* (Princeton)

Bull, H. (1977), *The Anarchical Society* (New York)

Burckhardt, L. (1996), *Bürger und Soldaten: Aspekte der politischen und militärischen Rolle athenischer Bürger im Kriegswesen des 4. Jahrhunderts. v. Chr.* Historia Einzelschriften 101 (Stuttgart)

Burford, A. (1993), *Land and Labor in the Greek World* (Baltimore)

Cairns, D. (1993), *Aidos: the psychology and ethics of honour and shame in ancient Greek literature* (Oxford)

Cairns, F. (1991), 'The "Laws of Eretria" (*IG* XII.9 1273 and 1274): epigraphic, historical and political aspects', *Phoenix* 45, 291-313

Cargill, J. (1981), *The Second Athenian League* (Berkeley)

Cartledge, P. (1977), 'Hoplites and heroes: Sparta's contribution to the technique of ancient warfare', *JHS* 97, 11-27

———— (1978), 'The new fifth-century Spartan treaty again', *LCM* 3, 189-90

———— (1982), 'Sparta and Samos: a special relationship?', *CQ* 32, 243-65

———— (1987), *Agesilaos and the Crisis of Sparta* (London)

———— (1996), 'La nascita degli opliti e l'organizzazione militare', in S. Settis (ed.), *I Greci: storia, cultura, arte, società*, vol. 2 (Turin), 681-714

———— (2002), *Sparta and Lakonia* (London) (1st ed. 1979)

Caskey, L. and Beazley, J. (1963), *Attic Vase Painting in the Museum of Fine Arts, Boston* (Boston)

Casson, L. (1971), *Ships and Seamanship in the Ancient World* (Princeton) (rev. ed. 1995)

Caven, B. (1990), *Dionyius I. War-lord of Sicily* (New Haven)

Cawkwell, G. (1963), 'Eubulus', *JHS* 83, 47-67

————— (1989), 'Orthodoxy and hoplites', *CQ* 39, 375-89

Ceccarelli, P. (1993), 'Sans thalassocratie, pas de démocratie? Le rapport entre thalassocratie et démocratie à Athènes dans la discussion du Ve et IVe siècle av. J.C.', *Historia* 42, 444-70

————— (1998), *La pirrica nell-antichità greco romana* (Pisa)

Chaniotis, A. (1996), *Die Verträge zwischen kretischen Poleis in der hellenistische Zeit* (Stuttgart)

Chase, G. (1902), *The Shield Devices of the Greeks* (Cambridge, MA)

Christ, M. (2001), 'Conscription of hoplites in classical Athens', *CQ* 51, 398-422

Ciccotti, E. (1901), *La guerra e la pace nel mondo antico* (Turin)

Clairmont, C. (1983), *Patrios Nomos: public burial in Athens during the fifth and fourth centuries BC* (Oxford)

Clark, M. (1995), 'Did Thucydides invent the battle exhortation?', *Historia* 44, 375-6

Clarke, W. (1978), 'Achilles and Patroclus in love', *Hermes* 106, 381-96

Connor, W. (1988), 'Early Greek land warfare as symbolic expression', *Past & Present* 119, 3-29

Constantineau, P. (1998), *La doctrine classique de la politique étrangère* (Paris)

Crane, G. (1992), 'Power, prestige and the Corcyrean affair', *Classical Antiquity* 11, 1-17

————— (1998), *Thucydides and the Ancient Simplicity* (Berkeley)

Crawford, M. (1986), *La moneta in Grecia e a Roma* (Bari)

Dalby, A. (1992), 'Greeks abroad: social organisation and food among the Ten Thousand', *JHS* 112, 16-30

Daraki, M. (1980), 'Le héros a *menos* et le héros *daimoni isos*: une polarité homérique', *ASNP* 10, 1-24

Davies, J. (1994), 'The tradition about the First Sacred War', in S. Hornblower (ed.), *Greek Historiography* (Oxford), 193-212

————— (2001), 'Temples, credit and the circulation of money', in A. Meadows & K. Shipton (eds), *Money and its Uses in the Ancient Greek World* (Oxford), 117-28

de Romilly, J. (1968), 'Guerre et paix dans la poésie grecque', in Vernant (ed.) 1968, 207-20

————— (1971), 'La vengeance comme explication historique dans l'oeuvre d'Hérodote', *REG* 84, 314-37

de Souza, P. (1998), 'Towards thalassocracy? Archaic Greek naval developments', in N. Fisher & H. van Wees (eds) 1998, 271-93

————— (1999), *Piracy in the Graeco-Roman World* (Cambridge)

de Ste Croix, G. (1972), *The Origins of the Peloponnesian War* (London)

Delebecque, E. (1951), *Le cheval dans l'Iliade* (Paris)

Demand, N. (1990), *Urban Relocation in Archaic and Classical Greece* (Bristol)

Detienne, M. (1968), 'La phalange: problèmes et controverses', in J.-P. Vernant (ed.), *Problèmes de la guerre en Grèce ancienne* (Paris), 119-42

DeVoto, J. (1992), 'The Sacred Band', *Ancient World* 23, 3-19

Dillery, J. (1995), *Xenophon and the History of his Times* (London)

Donlan, W. (1970), 'Archilochus, Strabo and the Lelantine War', *TAPA* 101, 131-42

————— (1979), 'The structure of authority in the *Iliad*', *Arethusa* 12, 51-70

————— (1981), 'Reciprocities in Homer', *Classical World* 75, 137-75

319

Bibliography

——— (1994), 'Chiefs and followers in pre-state Greece', in C. Duncan & D. Tandy (eds), *From Political Economy to Anthropology* (Montreal), 34-51

Dover, K. (1974), *Greek Popular Morality in the Time of Plato and Aristotle* (Oxford)

Droop, J. (1929), 'The Laconian pottery', in R. Dawkins (ed.), *Artemis Orthia*, 52-116

Ducat, J. (1999), 'La société spartiate et la guerre', in F. Prost (ed.) 1999, 35-50

Ducrey, P. (1968), *Le traitement de prisonniers de guerre dans la Grèce antique* (Paris)

——— (1986), *Warfare in Ancient Greece* (New York)

Edwards, A. (1985), *Achilles in the Odyssey: ideologies of heroism in the Homeric epic (Beiträge zur klassische Philologie* 171).

Ehrhardt, C. (1995), 'Speeches before battle?', *Historia* 44, 120-1

Ellinger, P. (1993), *La légende nationale phocidienne: Artémis, les situations extrêmes et les récits de guerre d'anéantissement* (Paris)

Engels, D. (1978), *Alexander the Great and the Logistics of the Macedonian Army* (Berkeley)

Fenik, B. (ed.) (1978), *Homer: Tradition and Invention* (Leiden)

Feyel, M. (1942), *Polybe et l'histoire de la Béotie* (Paris)

Fields, N. (2001), 'Et ex Arcadia ego', *AHB* 15, 102-30

Figueira, T. (1986), 'Xanthippos, father of Pericles, and the *prytaneis* of the *naukraroi*', *Historia* 35, 257-79

Finley, M. (1963), *The Ancient Greeks* (London)

——— (1973), *The Ancient Economy* (London; rev. ed. 1985)

——— (1977), *The World of Odysseus*, 2nd rev. ed. (London; 1st ed. 1954)

——— (1981), *Economy and Society in Ancient Greece* (Harmondsworth)

——— (1985), *Ancient History: evidence and models* (London)

Fisher, N. (1992), *Hybris: a study in the values of guilt and shame in ancient Greece* (Warminster)

——— (1993), *Slavery in Classical Greece* (London)

——— (1998), 'Gymnasia and the democratic values of leisure', in P. Cartledge et al. (eds), *Kosmos: essays in order, conflict and community in classical Athens* (Cambridge), 84-104

——— (1999), ' "Workshops of villains" Was there much organised crime in classical Athens?', in K. Hopwood (ed.), *Organised Crime in Antiquity* (London/Swansea), 53-96

——— (2000), '*Hybris*, revenge and *stasis* in the Greek city-states', in H. van Wees (ed.) 2000, 83-123

——— & van Wees, H. (eds) (1998), *Archaic Greece: new approaches and new evidence* (London/Swansea)

Fornara, C. (1971), *The Athenian Board of Generals from 501-404*. Historia Einzelschriften 16 (Wiesbaden)

——— (1983), *The Nature of History in Ancient Greece and Rome* (Berkeley)

Forrest, W. (1966), *The Emergence of Greek Democracy* (London)

——— (1968), *A History of Sparta* (London)

——— (2000), 'The pre-polis polis', in R. Brock & S. Hodkinson (eds), *Alternatives to Athens: varieties of political organisation and community in ancient Greece* (Oxford), 280-92

Foxhall, L. (1993), 'Farming and fighting in ancient Greece', in J. Rich & G. Shipley (eds) 1993, 134-45

——— (1997), 'A view from the top: evaluating the Solonian property classes', in L. Mitchell & P. Rhodes (eds), 1997, 113-36

——— & Forbes, H. (1982), '*Sitometreia*: the role of grain as a staple food in classical antiquity', *Chiron* 12, 41-90

Franz, J. (2002), *Krieger, Bauern, Bürger: Untersuchungen zu den Hopliten der archaischen und klassischen Zeit.* Europäische Hochschulschriften, Reihe III, Bd. 925 (Frankfurt)

Fraser, A. (1942), 'The myth of the phalanx-scrimmage', *Classical Weekly* 36, 15-16

Fröhlich, P. (1999), 'Les magistrats de la guerre', in F. Prost (ed.) 1999, 108-36

Frost, F. (1984), 'The Athenian military before Cleisthenes', *Historia* 33, 283-94

Gabrielsen, V. (1985), 'The *naukrariai* and the Athenian navy', *C&M* 36, 21-51

——— (1994), *Financing the Athenian Fleet* (Baltimore)

——— (1997), *The Naval Aristocracy of Hellenistic Rhodes* (Aarhus)

——— (2002), 'The impact of armed forces on government and politics in archaic and classical Greek poleis: a response to Hans van Wees', in A. Chaniotis & P. Ducrey (eds), *Army and Power in the Ancient World* (Stuttgart), 83-98

——— (forthcoming), 'Warfare and the state' in P. Sabin et al. (eds), *The Cambridge History of Greek and Roman Warfare* (Cambridge)

Gallant, T. (1991), *Risk and Survival in Ancient Greece* (Stanford)

Gardner, R. and Heider, K. (1968), *Gardens of War: life and death in the New Guinea Stone Age* (Harmondsworth)

Garlan, Y. (1974), *Récherches de poliorcétique grecque* (Paris)

——— (1975), *War in the Ancient World* (London; French original 1972)

——— (1989), *Guerre et économie en Grèce ancienne* (Paris)

——— (1994), 'Warfare', in *Cambridge Ancient History*, vol. 6. 2nd ed. (Cambridge), 678-92

Gauthier, P. (1972), *Symbola* (Nancy)

Gehrke, H,-J. (1987), 'Die Griechen und die Rache', *Saeculum* 38, 121-49

Gilula, D. (2003), 'Who was actually buried in the first of the three Spartan graves (Hdt. 9.85.1)?' in P. Derow & R. Parker (eds), *Herodotus and his World* (Oxford), 73-87

Golden, M. (1998), *Sport and Society in Ancient Greece* (Cambridge)

Goldsworthy, A. (1997), 'The *othismos*, myths and heresies: the nature of hoplite battle', *War in History* 4, 1-26

Goodman, M. and Holladay, A. (1986), 'Religious scruples in ancient warfare', *CQ* 36, 151-71

Gorman, V. (2001), *Miletus, the Ornament of Ionia* (Michigan)

Graham, A. (1964), *Colony and Mother City in Ancient Greece* (Manchester)

——— (1992), 'Thucydides 7.13.2 and the crews of Athenian triremes', *TAPA* 122, 257-70

——— (1998), 'Thucydides 7.13.2 and the crews of Athenian triremes: an addendum', *TAPA* 128, 89-114

——— (2001), *Collected Papers on Greek Colonization* (Leiden)

Green, P. (1996), *The Greco-Persian Wars* (Berkeley)

Greenhalgh, P. (1972), 'Patriotism in the Homeric world', *Historia* 21, 528-37

——— (1973), *Early Greek Warfare* (Cambridge)

Griffin, J. (1987), 'Homer and excess', in J.M. Bremer et al. (eds), *Homer: beyond oral poetry* (Amsterdam), 85-104

Griffith, G. (1935), *The Mercenaries of the Hellenistic World* (London)

——— (1981), 'Peltasts and the origins of the Macedonian phalanx', in H. Dell (ed.), *Ancient Macedonian Studies in Honor of Charles F. Edson* (Thessaloniki), 161-7

Gros, P. (1993), '*Moenia*: aspects défensifs et aspects représentatif des fortifications', in S. van der Maele & J. Fossey (eds) 1993, 211-25

Gröschel, S.-G. (1989), *Waffenbesitz und Waffeneinsatz bei den Griechen* Europäische Hochschulschriften, Reihe 38, Band 23 (Frankfurt)

Haas, C. (1985), 'Athenian naval power before Themistocles', *Historia* 34, 29-46

Hainsworth, J. (1993), *The Iliad: a commentary*, vol. III: Books 9-12 (Cambridge)

Hall, J. (1995), 'How Argive was the Argive Heraion?', *AJA* 99, 577-613

—— (1997), *Ethnicity in Greek Antiquity* (Cambridge)

—— (2002), *Hellenicity: between ethnicity and culture* (Chicago)

Hamel, D. (1998), *Athenian Generals: military authority in the classical period* (Leiden)

Hamilton, C. (1987), 'Social tensions in classical Sparta', *Ktema* 12, 31-41

Hammer, D. (forthcoming), 'Ideology, the symposion and archaic poltitcs', *AJPh*

Hammond, N. (1968), 'The campaign and battle of Marathon', *JHS* 88, 13-57

—— (1983), 'Army transport in the fifth and fourth centuries', *GRBS* 24, 27-31

Hansen, M. (1981), 'The number of Athenian hoplites in 431 BC', *SO* 56, 19-32

—— (1988), *Three Studies in Athenian Demography* (Copenhagen)

—— (1993), 'The battle exhortation in ancient historiography. Fact or fiction?', *Historia* 42, 161-80

—— (1995), 'The "autonomous city-state". Ancient fact or modern fiction?', in M. Hansen & K. Raaflaub (eds), *Studies in the Ancient Greek Polis*. Historia Einzelschriften 95 (Stuttgart), 21-43

—— (2002), 'Was the polis a state or a stateless society?', in T.H. Nielsen (ed.), *Even More Studies in the Ancient Greek Polis*. Historia Einzelschriften 162 (Stuttgart), 17-47

Hanson, V. (1989) *The Western Way of War* (London)

—— (1991), 'Hoplite technology in phalanx battle', in Hanson (ed.) 1991, 63-84

—— (1995) *The Other Greeks* (New York)

—— (1998), *Warfare and Agriculture in Classical Greece*, rev. ed. (Berkeley)

—— (1999), *The Wars of the Ancient Greeks and their Invention of Western Military Culture* (London)

—— (ed.) (1991), *Hoplites: the classical Greek battle experience* (London)

Harrison, C. (1999), 'Triremes at rest: on the beach or in the water?', *JHS* 119, 168-71

Hartmann, A. & Heuser, B. (eds) (2001), *War, Peace and World Orders in European History* (London)

Heider, K. (1979), *Grand Valley Dani: peaceful warriors* (New York)

Helbig, W. (1909), 'Ein homerischer Rundschild mit einem Bügel', *Jahreshefte des Österreichischen Archäologischen Instituts in Wien* 12, 1-70

——— (1911), 'Über die Einführungszeit der geschlossenen Phalanx', *Sitzungsberichte der Königlichen Bayerischen Akademie der Wissenschaften. Philosophisch-philologische und historische Klasse*, Munich, 3-41

Hellmann, O. (2000), *Die Schlachtszenen der Ilias*. Hermes Einzelschriften 83 (Stuttgart)

Herman, G. (1987), *Ritualised Friendship in the Greek City* (Cambridge)

Hignett, C. (1963), *Xerxes' Invasion of Greece* (Oxford)

Hodkinson, S. (1993), 'Warfare, wealth, and the crisis of Spartiate society', in J. Rich & G. Shipley (eds) 1993, 146-76

—— (1997), 'The development of Spartan society and institutions in the archaic period', in L. Mitchell & P. Rhodes (eds) 1997, 83-102

—— (2000), *Property and Wealth in Classical Sparta* (London/Swansea)

Holladay, A. (1988), 'Further thoughts on trireme tactics', *G&R* 35, 149-51

Hornblower, S. (1991), *A Commentary on Thucydides*, vol. I: Books I-III (Oxford)

—— (1996), *A Commentary on Thucydides*, vol. II: Books IV-V.24 (Oxford)

—— (2000a), 'Sticks, stones and Spartans. The sociology of Spartan violence', in H. van Wees (ed.) 2000, 57-82

—— (2000b), 'The *Old Oligarch* (pseudo-Xenophon's *Athenaion Politeia*) and Thucydides. A fourth-century date for the *Old Oligarch*?', in P. Flensted-Jensen et al. (eds), *Polis and Politics: studies in ancient Greek history* (Copenhagen), 363-84

—— & Greenstock, M. (1983), *The Athenian Empire*. Lactor 1 (London)

Howard, M. (1983), *The Causes of Wars and Other Essays* (London)

Humphreys, S. (1978), *Anthropology and the Greeks* (London)

Hunt, P. (1997), 'Helots at the battle of Plataea', *Historia* 46, 129-44

—— (1998), *Slavery, Warfare and Ideology in the Greek Historians* (Cambridge)

Jackson, A. (1969), 'The original purpose of the Delian League', *Historia* 18, 12-16

—— (1973), 'Privateers in the ancient Greek world', in M. Foot (ed.), *War and Society: historical studies in honour and memory of J.R. Western* (London), 241-53

—— (1993), 'War and raids for booty in the world of Odysseus', in J. Rich & G. Shipley (eds) 1993, 64-76

—— (2000), 'Sea-raiding in archaic Greece with special attention to Samos', in G. Oliver et al. (eds), *The Sea in Antiquity* (Oxford), 133-49

Jameson, M. (1978), 'Agriculture and slavery in classical Athens', *CJ* 73, 122-45

—— (1991), 'Sacrifice before battle', in V. Hanson (ed.) 1991, 197-227

Jarva, E. (1995), *Archaiologia on Archaic Greek Body Armour* (Rovaniemi)

Jeanmaire, H. (1939), *Couroi et courètes* (Lille)

Jehne, M. (1994), *Koine Eirene: Untersuchungen zu den Befreihungs- und Stabilisierungs-bemühungen in den griechischen Poliswelt des 4. Jhdt. v. Chr.* (Stuttgart)

Johansen, K. (1923), *Les vases sicyoniens* (Paris/Copenhagen)

Jones, A. (1957), *Athenian Democracy* (Oxford)

Jones, C. (1999), *Kinship Diplomacy in the Ancient World* (Cambridge, MA)

Jordan, B. (1975), *The Athenian Navy in the Classical Period* (Berkeley)

Karavites, P. (1982), *Capitulations and Greek Interstate Relations: the reflection of humanistic ideals in political events* (Hypomnemata 71) (Göttingen)

Keil, B. (1916), '*Eirene*', in *Berichte über die Verhandlungen des königlichen sächsischen Gesellschaft der Wissenschaften* 58

Kelly, T. (1970), 'The traditional enmity between Sparta and Argos', *American Historical Review* 75, 971-1003

Kennell, N. (1995), *The Gymnasium of Virtue: education and culture in ancient Sparta* (Chapel Hill)

Kim, H. (2001), 'Archaic coinage as evidence for the use of money', in A. Meadows & K. Shipton (eds), *Money and its Uses in the Ancient Greek World* (Oxford), 7-21

Kirk, G. (1962), *The Songs of Homer* (Cambridge)

—— (1985), *The Iliad: A Commentary*, vol. I: Books I-IV (Cambridge)

Knorringa, H. (1926), *Emporos* (Amsterdam)

Kraay, C. (1976), *Archaic and Classical Greek Coins* (London)

Bibliography

Krentz, P. (1985), 'The nature of hoplite battle', *ClAnt* 4, 50-61

—— (1989), *Xenophon, Hellenica I-11.3.10* (Warminster)

—— (1991), 'The *salpinx* in Greek battle', in Hanson (ed.) 1991, 110-20

—— (1994), 'Continuing the *othismos* on *othismos*', *AHB* 8, 45-9

—— (1997), 'The strategic culture of Periclean Athens', in C. Hamilton & P. Krentz (eds), *Polis and Polemos* (Claremont), 55-72

—— (2000), 'Deception in archaic and classical Greek warfare', in H. van Wees (ed.) 2000, 167-200

—— (2002), 'Fighting by the rules: the invention of the hoplite *agôn*', *Hesperia* 71, 23-39

—— (forthcoming), 'Archaic and classical Greek war', in P. Sabin et al. (eds), *The Cambridge History of Greek and Roman Warfare* (Cambridge)

Krischer, T. (1971), *Formale Konventionen der homerischen Epik* Zetemata 56 (Munich)

Kunze, E. (1991), *Beinschienen. Olympische Forschungen* XXI (Berlin)

Larsen, J. (1937), 'Perioikoi', *Real-Enzyklopädie* XIX.1 (Stuttgart), col. 816-33

Latacz, J. (1977), *Kampfparänese, Kampfdarstellung und Kampfwirklichkeit in der Ilias, bei Kallinos und Tyrtaios* (Munich)

Lavelle, B. (1997), '*Epikouros* and *epikouroi* in early Greek literature and history', *GRBS* 38, 229-62

Lawrence, A. (1979), *Greek Aims in Fortification* (Oxford)

Lazenby, J. (1985), *The Spartan Army* (Warminster)

—— (1987), 'The *diekplous*', *G&R* 34, 169-77

—— (1991), 'The killing zone', in Hanson (ed.) 1991, 87-109

—— (1993), *The Defence of Greece* (Warminster)

—— & Whitehead, I. (1996), 'The myth of the hoplite's *hoplon*', *CQ* 46, 27-33

Lendon, J. (2000), 'Homeric vengeance and the outbreak of Greek war', in H. van Wees (ed.) 2000, 1-30

Letoublon, F. (1983), 'Défi et combat dans l'*Iliade*', *REG* 96, 27-48

Lévêque, P. & Vidal-Naquet, P. (1996), *Cleisthenes the Athenian* (Atlantic Highlands) (French original 1964)

Lévy, E. (1988), 'La kryptie et ses contradictions', *Ktema* 13, 245-52

Linders, T. (1975), *The Treasurers of the Other Gods in Athens* (Meisenheim am Glan)

Link, S. (1994), *Das griechische Kreta: Untersuchungen zu seiner staatlichen und gesellschaftlichen Entwicklung vom 6. bis zum 4. Jhdt. v. Chr.* (Stuttgart)

Lintott, A. (1992), 'Aristotle and democracy', *CQ* 42, 114-28

—— (1982), *Violence, Civil Strife and Revolution in the Classical City* (London)

Lissarrague, F. (1990), *L'autre guerrier: archers, peltastes, cavaliers dans l'imagerie attique* (Paris/Rome)

Lloyd, A (ed.) (1996), *Battle in Antiquity* (London/Swansea)

Loenen, D. (1953), *Polemos. Een studie over oorlog in de Griekse oudheid* (Amsterdam)

Loman, P. (2004), 'No woman no war: women's participation in ancient Greek warfare', *G&R* 51, 34-54

Lonis, R. (1969), *Les usages de la guerre entre grecs et barbares* (Paris)

Loomis, W. (1992), *The Spartan War Fund, IG V.1.1 and a New Fragment* (Stuttgart)

Loraux, N. (1986), *The Invention of Athens: the funeral oration and the classical city* (Cambridge, MA)

Lorimer, H. (1947), 'The hoplite phalanx', *BSA* 42, 76-138

———— (1950), *Homer and the Monuments* (London)

Luginbill, R. (1994), '*Othismos*: the importance of the mass-shove in hoplite warfare', *Phoenix* 48, 51-61

Luraghi, N. (1994), *Tyrannidi arcaiche in Sicilia e Magna Grecia* (Florence)

Ma, J. (1994), 'Black Hunter Variations (I)', *PCPhS* 220, 49-57

———— (2000), 'Fighting poleis of the hellenistic world', in H. van Wees (ed.) 2000, 337-76

MacDowell, D. (1986), 'The law of Periandros about symmories', *CQ* 36, 438-49

MacLachlan, B. (1993), *The Age of Grace: charis in early Greek poetry* (Princeton)

Mann, C. (1998), 'Krieg, Sport und Adelskultur. Zur Enstehung des griechischen Gymnasions', *Klio* 80, 7-21

———— (2002), *Athlet und Polis im archaischen und frühklassischen Griechenland.* Hypomnemata 138 (Göttingen)

Marek, C. (1984), *Die Proxenie* (Frankfurt)

Marinovic, L. (1988), *Le mercenariat grec au quatrième siècle* (Paris)

Marsden, E. (1969), *Greek and Roman Artillery: Historical Development* (Oxford)

Martin, V. (1940), *La vie internationale dans la Grèce des cités* (Paris)

Mauritsch, P. (1992), *Sexualität im frühen Griechenland* (Vienna)

McKechnie, P. (1989), *Outsiders in Fourth-Century Greece* (London)

Mead, M. (1968), 'Introduction' to R. Gardner & K. Heider 1968, vii-x

Meggitt, M. (1977), *Blood is their Argument: warfare among the Mae Enga tribesmen of the New Guinea Highlands* (Palo Alto)

Meier, M. (1998), *Aristokraten und Damoden* (Stuttgart)

Meiggs, R. (1972), *The Athenian Empire* (Oxford)

Mertens, N. (2002), '*Ouk homoioi, agathoi de*: the *perioikoi* in the classical Lakedaimonian polis', in A. Powell & S. Hodkinson (eds), *Sparta: beyond the mirage* (London/Swansea), 285-303

Migeotte, L. (1984), *L'emprunt public dans les cités grecques* (Quebec)

Miller, H. (1984), 'The practical and economic background to the Greek mercenary explosion', *G&R* 31, 153-60

Millett, P. (1989), 'Patronage and its avoidance in classical Athens', in A. Wallace-Hadrill (ed.), *Patronage in Ancient Society* (London), 15-47

———— (1993), 'Warfare, economy and democracy in classical Athens', in J. Rich & G. Shipley (eds) 1993, 177-96

Mills, S. (1997), *Theseus, Tragedy and the Athenian Empire* (Oxford)

Missiou, A. (1998), 'Reciprocal generosity in the foreign affairs of fifth-century Athens and Sparta', in C. Gill et al. (eds), *Reciprocity in Ancient Greece* (Oxford 1998), 181-97

Mitchell, L. (1997), *Greeks Bearing Gifts: the public use of private relationships in the Greek world, 435-323 BC* (Cambridge)

———— & Rhodes, P. (eds) (1997), *The Development of the Polis in Archaic Greece* (London)

Mitchell, S. (1996), 'Hoplite warfare in ancient Greece', in A. Lloyd (ed.) 1996, 87-105

Momigliano, A. (1966), 'Some observations on the causes of war in ancient historiography', *Studies in Historiography* (London), 112-26

Morris, I. (1992), *Death-Ritual and Social Structure in Classical Antiquity* (Cambridge)

———— (1994), 'The ancient economy twenty years after *The Ancient Economy*', *CPh* 89, 351-66

—— (1998), 'Archaeology and archaic Greek history', in N. Fisher & H. van Wees (eds) 1998, 1-91

—— & Raaflaub, K. (eds) (1998), *Democracy 2500? Questions and challenges* (Dubuque)

Morrison, J. et al. (2000), *The Athenian Trireme*, 2nd ed. (Cambridge)

Morrison, J. & Williams, R. (1968), *Greek Oared Ships 900-322 BC* (Cambridge)

Mueller, M. (1984), *The Iliad* (London)

Munn, M. (1993), *The Defense of Attica: the Dema Wall and the Boiotian War of 378-375 BC* (Berkeley)

Murray, O. (1983a), 'The symposion as social organisation', in R. Hägg (ed.), *The Greek Renaissance of the Eighth Century BC: tradition and innovation* (Stockholm), 195-9

—— (1983b), 'The Greek symposion in history', in E. Gabba (ed.), *Tria Corda: scritti in onore di Arnaldo Momigliano* (Como), 257-72

—— (1993), *Early Greece*, 2nd ed. (no place; 1st ed. 1980)

Nafissi, M. (1991), *La nascita del kosmos: studi sulla storia e la società di Sparta* (Perugia)

Nestle, W. (1938), *Der Friedensgedanke in der Antiken Welt*. Philologus Supplement Band 31, Heft 1 (Leipzig)

Nilsson, M. (1929a), 'The introduction of hoplite tactics at Rome', *JRS* 19, 1-11

—— (1929b), 'Die Hoplitentaktik und das Staatswesen', *Klio* 22, 240-9

Nussbaum, G. (1967), *The Ten Thousand* (Leiden)

Oakley, S. (1985), 'Single combat in the Roman republic', *CQ* 35, 392-410

Ober, J. (1985), *Fortress Attica: defense of the Athenian land frontier* (Leiden)

—— (1989), *Mass and Elite in Democratic Athens* (Princeton)

—— (1991), 'Hoplites and obstacles', in V. Hanson (ed.) 1991, 173-96

—— (1993), 'Towards a typology of Greek artillery towers: the first and second generations (*c.* 375-275 BC)', in S. van der Maele and J. Fossey (eds) 1993, 147-69

—— (1996), 'The rules of war in classical Greece', in J. Ober, *The Athenian Revolution: essays on ancient Greek democracy and political theory* (Princeton), 53-71

Ogden, D. (1996), 'Homosexuality and warfare in ancient Greece', in A. Lloyd (ed.), *Battle in Antiquity* (London/Swansea), 107-68

Olshausen, E. and Biller, H. (eds) (1979), *Antike Diplomatie* (Wege der Forschung 462) (Darmstadt)

Olson, S.D (1998), *Aristophanes: Peace* (Oxford)

Osborne, R. (1985), *Demos: the discovery of classical Attika* (Cambridge)

—— (1987), *Classical Landscape with Figures: the ancient Greek city and its countryside* (London)

—— (1998), 'Early Greek colonization? The nature of Greek settlement in the West', in N. Fisher & H. van Wees (eds) 1998, 251-69

Ostwald, M. (1982), *Autonomia: its genesis and early history* (New York)

Page, D. (1955), *Sappho and Alcaeus* (Oxford)

Parke, H. (1933), *Greek Mercenary Soldiers* (Oxford)

Parker, R. (2000), 'Sacrifice and battle', in H. van Wees (ed.) 2000, 299-314

Parker, V. (1991), 'The dates of the Messenian Wars', *Chiron* 21, 25-47

—— (1997), *Untersuchungen zum Lelantischen Krieg und verwandten Problemen der frühgriechischen Geschichte*, Stuttgart

Parks, W. (1990), *Verbal Duelling in Heroic Narrative: the Homeric and Old English traditions* (Princeton)

Bibliography

Payne, H. (1931), *Necrocorinthia: a study of Corinthian art in the archaic period* (Oxford)

Peek, W. (1974), 'Ein neuer spartanischer Staatsvertrag', *ASAW* 65, 3-15

Petrakos, B. (1963), 'Dédicace des AEINAYTAI d' Erétrie', *BCH* 87, 545-7

Piccirilli, L. (1973), *Gli arbitrati interstatali greci*, vol. 1 (Pisa)

Pleket, H. (1998), 'Sport and ideology in the Graeco-Roman world', *Klio* 80, 315-24

Poliakoff, M. (1987), *Combat Sports in the Ancient World* (New Haven)

Powell, A. (1989), 'Mendacity and Sparta's use of the visual', in A. Powell (ed.), *Classical Sparta: techniques behind its success* (London), 173-92

—— (1995), 'Athens' pretty face: anti-feminine rhetoric and fifth-century controversy over the Parthenon', in A. Powell (ed.), *The Greek World* (London), 245-70

—— (1998), 'Sixth-century Laconian vase-painting: continuities and disconti-nuities with the "Lykourgan' ethos" ', in N. Fisher & H. van Wees (eds), *Archaic Greece: new approaches and new evidence* (London), 119-46

—— (2003), 'Les femmes de Sparte (et d'autres cités) en temps de guerre', in J.-M. Bertrand et al. (eds), *La violence dans le monde grec* (Paris)

Pritchard, D. (1998), ' "The fractured imaginary": popular thinking on military matters in fifth-century Athens', *Ancient History* 28, 38-61

Pritchett, W. (1956), 'The Attic Stelai, Part II', *Hesperia* 25, 178-315

—— (1971), *The Greek State at War*, vol. I (Berkeley)

—— (1974), *The Greek State at War*, vol. II (Berkeley)

—— (1985), *The Greek State at War*, vol. IV (Princeton)

—— (1991a), *The Greek State at War*, vol. V (Princeton)

—— (1991b), *Studies in Ancient Greek Topography*, vol. VII (Amsterdam)

—— (2002), *Ancient Greek Battle Speeches and a Palfrey* (Amsterdam)

Prost, F. (1999), 'Les combattants de Marathon: idéologie et société hoplitiques à Athènes au Ve s.', in F. Prost (ed.) 1999, 69-88

—— (ed.) (1999), *Armées et sociétés de la Grèce antique* (Paris)

Qviller, B. (1981), 'The dynamics of the Homeric society', *SO* 56, 109-55

—— (1995), 'The world of Odysseus revisited', *SO* 70, 241-61

Raaflaub, K. (1991), 'Homer und die Geschichte des 8. Jh.s v. Chr.', in J. Latacz (ed.), *Zweihundert Jahre Homer-forschung* (Stuttgart), 205-56

—— (1993), 'Homer to Solon. The rise of the polis. The written sources', in M. Hansen, *The Ancient Greek City-State* (Copenhagen), 41-105

—— (1996), 'Equalities and inequalities in Athenian democracy', in J. Ober and C. Hedrick (eds), *Demokratia* (Princeton), 139-74

—— (1997), 'Politics and interstate relations in the world of early Greek poleis', *Antichthon* 31, 1-27

—— (1999), 'Archaic and classical Greece', in K. Raaflaub & N. Rosenstein (eds), *War and Society in the Ancient and Medieval Worlds* (Cambridge, MA), 129-61

Rawlings, L. (2000), 'Alternative agonies. Hoplite martial and combat experiences beyond the phalanx', in H. van Wees (ed.) 2000, 233-59

Redfield, J. (1975), *Nature and Culture in the Iliad: the tragedy of Hector* (Chicago)

Rhodes, P. (1981), *A Commentary on the Aristotelian Athenaion Politeia* (Oxford) (new ed. with addenda 1992)

Rice, E. (1993), 'The glorious dead: commemoration of the fallen and portrayal of victory in the late classical and hellenistic world', in J. Rich & G. Shipley (eds) 1993, 224-57

Rich, J. & Shipley, G. (eds) (1993), *War and Society in the Greek World* (London)

Riedinger, J.-C. (1976), 'Remarques sur la *timè* chez Homère', *REG* 89, 244-64

—— (1980), 'Les deux *aidos* chez Homère', *Revue de Philologie* 54, 62-79

Rihll, T. (1993), 'War, slavery and settlement in early Greece', in J. Rich & G. Shipley (eds) 1993, 77-107

Roisman, J. (1993), *The General Demosthenes and His Use of Military Surprise.* Historia Einzelschriften 78 (Stuttgart)

—— (1998), 'General Demosthenes goes to Lebanon', *Classical Bulletin* 74, 55-63

—— (2003), 'The rhetoric of courage in the Athenian orators', in R. Rosen & I. Sluiter (eds) 2003, 127-43

Rollins, R. (1994), *Black Southerners in Gray: essays on Afro-Americans in Confederate Armies.* Journal of Confederate History Series, vol. XI (Murfreesboro)

Rosen, R. & Sluiter, I (eds) (2003), *Andreia: studies in manliness and courage in classical antiquity* Mnemosyne Supplement 238 (Leiden)

Rosivach, V. (1985), 'Manning the Athenian fleet, 433-426 BC', *AJAH* 10, 41-66

—— (2002), *'Zeugitai* and hoplites', *AHB* 16, 33-43

Roy, J. (1967), 'The mercenaries of Cyrus', *Historia* 16, 287-323

—— (1998), 'Thucydides 5.49.1-50.4: the quarrel between Elis and Sparta in 420 BC', *Klio* 80, 360-8

—— (1999), 'The economies of Arcadia', in T. Nielsen & J. Roy (eds), *Defining Ancient Arcadia.* Acts of the Copenhagen Polis Centre 6 (Copenhagen),

Runciman, W. (1998), 'Greek hoplites, warrior culture, and indirect bias', *Journal of the Royal Anthropological Institute* 4, 731-51

Ryder, T. (1965), *Koine Eirene* (Oxford)

Sage, M. (1996), *Warfare in Ancient Greece: a sourcebook* (London)

Salazar, C. (2000), *The Treatment of War Wounds in Graeco-Roman Antiquity* (Leiden)

Salmon, J. (1977), 'Political hoplites?', *JHS* 97, 84-101

Samons, L. (2000), *Empire of the Owl: Athenian imperial finance.* Historia Einzelschriften 142 (Stuttgart)

Sanchez, P. (2001), *L'amphictionie des Pyles et de Delphes.* Historia Einzelschriften 148 (Stuttgart)

Santosuosso, A. (1997), *Soldiers, Citizens and the Symbols of War* (Boulder)

Sargent, R. (1927), 'The use of slaves by the Athenians in warfare', *CPh* 22, 201-12, 264-79

Sartre, M. (1979), 'Aspects économiques et aspects religieux de la frontière dans les cités grecques', *Ktema* 4, 213-24

Schefold, K. (1966), *Myth and Legend in Early Greek Art* (London)

Scott, L. (2000), 'Were there polis navies in archaic Greece?', in G. Oliver et al. (eds), *The Sea in Antiquity* (Oxford), 93-115

Sealey, R. (1957), 'Thucydides, Herodotus and the causes of war', *CQ* 51, 1-12

Seibert, J. (1979), *Die politische Flüchtlinge und Verbannten in der griechischen Geschichte* (Darmstadt)

Shay, J. (1994), *Achilles in Vietnam: combat trauma and the undoing of character* (New York)

Shipley, G. (1993), 'Introduction: the limits of war', in J. Rich & G. Shipley (eds) 1993, 1-24

Silk, M. (1987), *Homer: The Iliad* (Cambridge)

Singor, H. (1988), *Oorsprong en betekenis van de hoplietenphalanx in het archaïsche Griekenland* (unpublished dissertation, Leiden)

—— (1991), 'Nine against Troy. On epic *phalanges, promachoi,* and an old structure in the story of the *Iliad'*, *Mnemosyne* 44, 17-62

—— (1995), *'Eni protoisi machesthai*: some remarks on the Iliadic image of the battlefield', in J.-P. Crielaard (ed.), *Homeric Questions* (Amsterdam), 183-200

Bibliography

——— (1999), 'Admission to the *syssitia* in fifth-century Sparta', in S. Hodkinson & A. Powell (eds), *Sparta: new perspectives* (London/Swansea), 67-89

——— (2002), 'The Spartan army at Mantinea and its organisation in the fifth century BC', in W. Jongman & M. Kleijwegt (eds), *After the Past: essays in honour of H.W. Pleket* (Leiden), 235-84

Snodgrass, A. (1964) *Early Greek Armour and Weapons* (Edinburgh)

——— (1965), 'The hoplite reform and history', *JHS* 85, 110-22

——— (1993), 'The "hoplite reform" revisited', *DHA* 19, 47-61

——— (1999), *Arms and Armour of the Greeks* (Baltimore; 1st ed. 1967)

Spence, I. (1990), 'Perikles and the defence of Attika during the Peloponnesian War', *JHS* 110, 91-109

——— (1993), *The Cavalry of Classical Greece: a social and military history* (Oxford)

Spiegel, N. (1990), *War and Peace in Classical Greek Literature* (Jerusalem)

Stahl, M. (1987), *Aristokraten und Tyrannen im archaischen Athen* (Stuttgart)

Starr, C. (1979), 'Homeric cowards and heroes', in id. *Essays on Ancient History: a selection of articles and reviews* (Leiden), 97-102

Storch, R. (1998), 'The archaic phalanx, 750-650 BC', *AHB* 12, 1-7

Strathern, A. (1979), *Ongka: a self-account by a New Guinea Big Man* (London)

Strauss, B. (1983), 'Aegospotami reexamined', *AJPh* 104, 32-4

——— (1993), *Fathers and Sons in Athens: ideology and society in the era of the Peloponnesian War* (Princeton)

——— (1996), 'The Athenian trireme, school of democracy', in J. Ober & C. Hedrick (eds), *Demokratia* (Princeton), 313-25

——— (1997), 'The art of alliance and the Peloponnesian War', in C. Hamilton & P. Krentz (eds), *Polis and Polemos: essays on politics, war and history in ancient Greece in honor of Donald Kagan* (Claremont), 127-40

——— (2000a), 'Perspectives on the death of fifth-century Athenian seamen', in H. van Wees (ed.) 2000, 261-83

——— (2000b), 'Democracy, Kimon and the evolution of Athenian naval tactics in the fifth century BC', in P. Flensted-Jensen et al. (eds), *Polis and Politics: studies in ancient Greek history* (Copenhagen), 315-26

Taplin, O. (1992), *Homeric Soundings: the shaping of the Iliad* (Oxford)

Thommen, L. (1996), *Lakedaimonion Politeia: Die Entstehung der spartanischen Verfassung*. Historia Einzelschriften 103 (Stuttgart)

Thomsen, R. (1977), 'War taxes in classical Athens', in *Armées et fiscalité dans le monde antique*. Colloques nationaux du CNRS, no. 936 (Paris), 135-47

Thorne, J. (2001), 'Warfare and agriculture: the economic impact of devastation in classical Greece', *GRBS* 42, 225-53

Townshend, C. (ed.) (1997), *The Oxford Illustrated History of Modern War* (Oxford)

Tritle, L. (1989), '*Epilektoi* at Athens', *AHB* 4, 54-9

——— (1997), 'Hector's body: mutilation of the dead in ancient Greece and Vietnam', *AHB* 11, 123-36

——— (2000), *From Melos to My Lai: war and survival* (London)

Trundle, M. (1999), 'Community and identity among Greek mercenaries in the classical world', *AHB* 13, 28-38

——— (2001), 'The Spartan revolution: hoplite warfare in the late archaic period', *War & Society* 19, 1-17

Ulf, C. (1990), *Die homerische Gesellschaft* (Munich)

Usher, S. (1993), *Demosthenes: On the Crown (De Corona)* (Warminster)

van de Maele, S. & J. Fossey (eds), (1994) *Fortificationes Antiquae* (Amsterdam)

329

Bibliography

van Effenterre, H. (1976), 'Clisthène et les mesures de mobilisation', *REG* 89, 1-17

van Wees, H. (1984), 'Overwinnaar onder overwinnaars. De krijgshaftige civilisatie van de Romeinse aristocratie, 300-100 v.C.', *Sociologisch Tijdschrift* 11, 120-62

—— (1986), 'Leaders of men? Military organisation in the *Iliad*', *CQ* 36, 285-303

—— (1988), 'Kings in combat. Battles and heroes in the *Iliad*', *CQ* 38, 1-24

—— (1992), *Status Warriors: war, violence and society in Homer and history* (Amsterdam)

—— (1994), 'The Homeric way of war: the *Iliad* and the hoplite phalanx (I) and (II)', *G&R* 41, 1-18 and 131-55

—— (1995a), 'Princes at dinner: social event and social structure in Homer', in J.-P. Crielaard (ed.), *Homeric Questions* (Amsterdam), 147-82

—— (1995b), 'Politics and the battlefield: ideology in Greek warfare', in A. Powell (ed.), *The Greek World* (London), 153-78

—— (1996), 'Heroes, knights and nutters', in A. Lloyd (ed.), 1996, 1-86

—— (1997a), 'Homeric warfare', in I. Morris & B. Powell (eds), *A New Companion to Homer* (Leiden & New York), 668-93

—— (1997b), 'Growing up in early Greece: heroic and aristocratic educations', in A. Sommerstein & C. Atherton (eds), *Education in Greek Fiction*. Nottingham Classical Literature Studies, vol. 4, 1996 (Bari), 1-20

—— (1998a), 'The law of gratitude: reciprocity in anthropological theory', in C. Gill et al. (eds), *Reciprocity in Ancient Greece* (Oxford), 13-49

—— (1998b), 'Greeks bearing arms', in N. Fisher & H. van Wees (eds), *Archaic Greece: new approaches and new evidence* (London), 33-78

—— (1999a), 'Tyrtaeus' *Eunomia*: nothing to do with the Great Rhetra', in S. Hodkinson & A. Powell (eds), *Sparta: new perspectives* (London), 1-41

—— (1999b), 'The mafia of early Greece', in K. Hopwood (ed.), *Organised Crime in Antiquity* (London), 1-51

—— (2000a), 'The development of the hoplite phalanx. Iconography and reality in the seventh century', in H. van Wees (ed.) 2000, 125-66

—— (2000b), 'Megara's mafiosi: timocracy and violence in Theognis' in R. Brock & S. Hodkinson (eds), *Alternatives to Athens: varieties of political organisation and community in ancient Greece* (Oxford), 52-67

—— (2001), 'The myth of the middle-class army: military and social status in ancient Athens', in T. Bekker-Nielsen & L. Hannestad (eds), *War as a Cultural and Social Force: essays on warfare in antiquity* (Copenhagen 2001), 45-71

—— (2002a), 'Herodotus and the past', in E. Bakker et al. (eds), *Brill's Companion to Herodotus* (Leiden), 321-49

—— (2002b), 'Tyrants, oligarchs and citizen militias', in A. Chaniotis & P. Ducrey (eds), *Army and Power in the Ancient World* (Stuttgart), 61-82

—— (2002c), 'Homer and early Greece', *Colby Quarterly* 38, 94-117 (corrected reprint from: I. de Jong (ed.), *Homer: critical assessments* (London 1999), 1-32)

—— (2003), 'Conquerors and serfs. Wars of conquest and forced labour in archaic Greece', in N. Luraghi & S. Alcock (eds), *Helots and their Masters* (Washington), 33-80

—— (ed.) (2000), *War and Violence in Ancient Greece* (London/Swansea)

Vélissaropoulos, J. (1980), *Les nauclères grecques* (Geneva)

Vermeule, E. (1979), *Aspects of Death in Early Greek Art and Poetry* (Berkeley)

Vernant, J.-P. (1980), *Myth and Society in Ancient Greece* (London) (French original 1974)

Vidal-Naquet, P. (1986), *The Black Hunter: forms of thought and forms of society in the Greek world* (Baltimore; original French ed. 1982)

Vos, M. (1963), *Scythian Archers in Archaic Attic Vase-Painting* (Groningen)

Wace, A. (1929), 'The lead figurines', in R. Dawkins (ed.), *Artemis Orthia*, 249-84

Walcot, P. (1978), *Envy and the Greeks* (Warminster)

Wallinga, H. (1993), *Ships and Sea-Power before the Great Persian War* (Leiden)

Welwei, K.-W. (1974), *Unfreie im antiken Griechenland*, vol. I: *Athen und Sparta* (Wiesbaden)

Wéry, L.M. (1979), 'Die arbeitsweise der Diplomatie in Homerischer Zeit', in E. Olshausen and H. Biller (eds), *Antike Diplomatie* (Wege der Forschung 462) (Darmstadt), 13-53

West, M. (1978), *Hesiod: Works & Days* (Oxford)

———— (1995), 'The date of the *Iliad*', *Museum Helveticum* 52, 203-19

Wheeler, E. (1982), '*Hoplomachia* and Greek dances in arms', *GRBS* 23, 223-33

———— (1983), 'The *hoplomachoi* and Vegetius' Spartan drill-masters', *Chiron* 13, 1-20

———— (1987), 'Ephorus and the prohibition of missiles', *TAPA* 117, 157-82

———— (1988), *Stratagem and the Vocabulary of Military Trickery*. Mnemosyne Supplement 108 (Leiden)

———— (1991), 'The general as hoplite', in Hanson (ed.) 1991, 121-70

Whitehead, D. (1977), *The Ideology of the Athenian Metic*. Cambridge Philological Society, Supplement 4 (Cambridge)

———— (1983), 'Competitive outlay and community profit: *philotimia* in classical Athens', *C&M* 34, 55-74

———— (1986), *The Demes of Attica 508/7 – c. 250 BC* (Princeton)

———— (1988), 'KLOPE POLEMOU: "Theft" in ancient Greek warfare', *Classica et Medievalia* 39, 43-53

Whitehead, I. (1987), 'The *periplous*', *G&R* 34, 178-85

Whitley, J. (1991), 'Social diversity in Dark Age Greece', *BSA* 86, 341-65

Wickersham, J. (1994), *Hegemony and Greek Historians* (London)

Wiesner, J. (1968), *Fahren und Reiten: Archaeologia Homerica F* (Göttingen)

Willcock, M. (1993), 'The fighting in the Iliad', in *Spondes ston Omirou: proceedings of the sixth conference on the Odyssey, 1990* (Ithaki), 141-7

Wilson, D. (2002), *Ransom, Revenge and Heroic Identity in the Iliad* (Cambridge)

Winter, F. (1971), *Greek Fortifications* (Toronto)

Woodford, S. (1993), *The Trojan War in Ancient Art* (London)

Wrede, W. (1928), 'Kriegers Ausfahrt in der archaisch-griechischen Kunst', *AM* 41, 222-374

Select Index of Passages

References to the pages of this book are in bold type.

General Index

339

women in war 32, 39-40, 123, 144,
    229-30
working class 47, 55-7, 68, 81, 95,
    200-1, 211, 213
wounded 146-8, 154
wreaths 194, 230, 239

xeinoi 16
xenos 6

zeugitai 56
zygioi 211

CPSIA information can be obtained
at www.ICGtesting.com
Printed in the USA
LVHW041732150120
643722LV00006B/129

9 780715 629673